Diamond Dreams

20 YEARS OF BLUE JAYS BASEBALL

◆

STEPHEN BRUNT

VIKING

VIKING

Published by the Penguin Group

Penguin Books Canada Ltd, 10 Alcorn Avenue, Toronto, Ontario,
Canada M4V 3B2
Penguin Books Ltd, 27 Wrights Lane, London W8 5TZ, England
Viking Penguin, a division of Penguin Books USA Inc., 375 Hudson Street,
New York, New York 10014, U.S.A.
Penguin Books Australia Ltd, Ringwood, Victoria, Australia
Penguin Books (NZ) Ltd, 182–190 Wairau Road, Auckland 10, New Zealand

Penguin Books Ltd, Registered Offices: Harmondsworth,
Middlesex, England

First published 1996
1 3 5 7 9 10 8 6 4 2

Printed and bound in Canada on acid free paper ∞

Canadian Cataloguing in Publication Data

Brunt, Stephen
Diamond dreams: 20 years of Blue Jays baseball

ISBN 0-670-85703-3

1. Toronto Blue Jays (Baseball team) - History. I. Title.

GV875.T67B78 1995   796.357'64'09713541   C95-930037-6

For Holly, Jake, Nat and Jeanie

Acknowledgments

A LONG, COMPLICATED project like this one could not have been completed without the help and cooperation of many people. Virtually all the key characters involved in the twenty-year history of the Toronto Blue Jays were generous with their time and memories. I would especially like to thank Gord Ash, Peter Bavasi, Paul Beeston, Lou Cauz, Bobby Cox, Milt Dunnell, Trent Frayne, Cito Gaston, Pat Gillick, Paul Godfrey, Peter Hardy, Roy Hartsfield, Gord Kirke, Al LaMacchia, Bobby Mattick, Don McDougall, Bill Singer, Herb Solway, Howie Starkman and Peter Widdrington for sitting down with me—in some cases, sitting down several times—so that I could write a complete and balanced history of the franchise.

A second round of thanks to Lou Cauz, who also fact-checked the book, and saved me time and time again with his extensive knowledge of the sport of baseball and its history. Wendy Thomas edited the manuscript with a sure hand and a delicate touch. Working with her was a pure pleasure. At Penguin, thanks once again to Cynthia Good, publisher and baseball fan extraordinaire, who was the first to suggest this book, to Lori Ledingham and to Scott Sellers, my boon companion.

Also, I should acknowledge my primary employers, the *Globe and Mail,* and especially sports editor David Langford, for encouraging and supporting outside projects.

Several books were consulted on the early history of baseball in Canada and the Blue Jays, and proved invaluable: *Ballpark Figures: The Blue Jays and the Business of Baseball* by Larry Millson, McClelland and Stewart, 1987; *Baseball's Back in Town* by Lou Cauz, Controlled Media Corporation, 1977; *Diamonds of the North: A Concise History of Baseball in Canada* by William Humber, Oxford University Press, 1995; *Let's Play Ball* by William Humber, Lester and Orpen Dennys, 1989; and *Road to Glory: An Insider's Look at 16 Years of Blue Jay Baseball* by Tom Cheek with Howard Berger, Warwick Publishing, 1993.

Finally, thanks to my wife and first reader, Jeanie MacFarlane,

Acknowledgments

and my children, Nat, Jake and Holly, who, already having put up with the long absences of a sports writer/father/husband, also watched me disappear into the attic for long stretches of 1995 and 1996 to get this book finished. Time to get back to real life.

Stephen Brunt

Introduction

VIEWED FROM ABOVE, from the Gardiner Expressway, the decaying remains of Maple Leaf Stadium were hard to relate to a living game. I had the experience of looking at a skeleton and trying to imagine the flesh and muscle, the colour and movement that would make the beast real.

My father tried to explain what the place had been like, what the team there had been like, the same way he would pull out old black and white snapshots, captured with a box camera, of Bob Feller pitching in Detroit's Briggs Stadium. The man they called Rapid Robert was just a little grey speck among other grey specks, and baseball was something you played. If you watched, it was local boys against other local boys at a fairgrounds diamond or it was on television. The major leagues seemed impossibly far away.

Baseball in Canada enjoys a long, rich history, dating back to the very beginnings of the game. Canadians played at all levels, including the big leagues, and through radio and television broadcasts, the same contests that held Americans' rapt attention crossed the great unguarded border.

Still, when the Expos came to Montreal in 1969, they were exotica, someone else's national pastime imported here and stuck in funny, three-coloured hats. And in southern Ontario, where the Maple Leafs of the International League went under in 1967, with hardly a whimper of public protest, baseball was far from the sporting forefront. Toronto was a hockey town, first and foremost. In the summer, it was a football town, where in the mid-1970's the Argonauts routinely drew the largest crowds in the Canadian Football League. In the years immediately before major league baseball came to the city, fans might have followed the building of the Oakland A's dynasty, the travails of fellow Ontarian Ferguson Jenkins, and of course, the gradual rise to respectability of the team at the other end of the Macdonald–Cartier Freeway. But the big leagues were, by definition, viewed only from a distance.

It is tempting to look back now to 1976 and 1977 and think of the arrival of the Toronto Blue Jays as something long anticipated and long desired. But even though people had been talking about bringing major league baseball to the city since A.G. Spalding, the sports equipment manufacturer, passed through town in 1886 and suggested Toronto apply to join the National League, it was not nearly so automatic. There was certainly a baseball audience in Toronto, a hard core who had maintained the faith through the dry years, but far more prevalent were those who knew who Reggie Jackson was and who paid attention at World Series time but not much before or after. There were others, also, who had no natural cultural connection to the sport, who were part of the massive immigrant wave that had so changed the face of the city. There were still others, 51 percent of the population, who by gender had been regarded as pretty much irrelevant to the business of professional sports. Women might go to Maple Leaf hockey games or Toronto Argonaut football games, but they weren't the ones buying the tickets.

The story of the franchise appears seamless now. Peter Bavasi selling the sizzle in the early years, when the visiting teams were the attraction, and bus tours from Buffalo helped fill the stands after the Jays had fallen miles out of contention for the pennant. Meanwhile, Pat Gillick began building the foundations of the contender to come. When Bavasi departed, Paul Beeston took over the business side of the operation, while Gillick continued to hoodwink his rivals, plucking from the draft pearls who would become the stars of tomorrow. Just when things appeared darkest during the strike season of 1981, and as the fans began to tire of the long building process, the team started to show signs that it was coming of age.

Out went the good organization man, Bobby Mattick, and in came the man, Bobby Cox, who would take the team to a championship. In 1985, his Jays would come within a hair of a berth in the World Series. And though difficult times would follow, there was never an opportunity for the fans to lose faith. Every year brought renewed hope, nearly every year brought a trip to the playoffs, and finally, in 1992 and then again in 1993, the Toronto Blue Jays were World Series champions. The SkyDome was full for virtually every game; attendance records were shattered. Toronto had become the best baseball town in North America.

Of course it wasn't really so simple. Several times during franchise history, if different decisions had been made, if different people had stayed and different people had left, the team would have followed a different course, possibly the one the Expos were doomed to travel after Rick Monday's terrible blast. But the combination of genius, of dumb luck, of the right things happening at the right time, came together to produce something far greater than a successful professional sports franchise.

The modern world defies consensus. There is no common faith, no common interest, but instead millions and millions of self-interests, some of which occasionally coincide. How remarkable it is, then, that in a city with as diverse a population as Toronto's, and with a myriad of entertainment options, a total of four million people would attend eighty-one games a year, and that millions and millions more would tune in through radio and television? The Blue Jays weren't just another team. They became a social phenomenon, a fundamental part of the local identity that crossed the lines of gender, ethnicity and class. To be of the place meant in some way identifying with what was taking place down on Front Street. Looking at a Blue Jay crowd, the economic barriers to entering the stadium aside, was the closest thing to looking at a genuine cross-section of the city.

My father, and all the others who loved the game from afar for so many years, could never have imagined it. He lived to see the Blue Jays through their first seasons of existence, he sat on the cold aluminum seats at Exhibition Stadium, saw the first playoff in 1985, saw at least a couple of the players who would be part of the World Series champions. Maybe, like some of those who kept the faith when few others did, he'd have resented the bandwagon-jumpers who came on board in the good times, resented the followers of fashion who filled out the crowd.

I'd like to think not, though. I'd like to think that he would have enjoyed the moment, enjoyed sharing his passion. And I'd like to thank him for taking me along.

Stephen Brunt

Diamond Dreams

◆

Chapter 1

I T ONCE WAS a baseball town, a place where the game took root soon after it took form, where the Maple Leafs of the diamond long preceded the Maple Leafs of the ice, where Babe Ruth hit his only minor league home run at a stadium on Hanlan's Point in front of a crowd of men in bowler hats and women in long dresses. That Toronto and this Toronto, two very different places, shared a passion in common.

A form of baseball, a recreation of common folk that evolved from the English game rounders, which in turn had its roots in bat-and-ball games dating back to the Middle Ages, was played even before the Revolutionary War in what became the United States, long before Abner Doubleday was wrongly given credit for its invention.

The game was played in Canada at least thirty years before there was a country called Canada, with a set of rules distinct from those followed south of the border. Thanks to a letter written to the *Sporting Life* in 1886 that contains one of the earliest descriptions of a sport identifiably baseball, and the work of Canadian sports historians (most notably Bob Barney of the University of Western Ontario), we know of one particular game, played in Beachville, Ontario, on June 4, 1838. In this game, played under distinctly Canadian rules, the teams competed with between seven and twelve men a side and threw the ball overhand, rather than underhand, as was then the practice in the United States. Only during the years of the U.S. Civil War did American rules take hold in Canada and the Canadian variant disappear.

Cricket was still popular at that time, especially with those who had direct ties to England, and field lacrosse was considered the national game. (Without indoor rinks or artificial ice, hockey's popularity was limited by the weather.) But still, more than a hundred years before Joe Carter hit the blast heard across the Dominion, it was suggested that baseball was really Canada's national pastime—which grated on those Canadians who saw this as an unfortunate sign of American cultural imperialism—they felt that Canadians were becoming Americanized by adopting their game.

Hamilton, Ontario, claims the first organized baseball team in Canada—the Maple Leafs of 1854—and London and Guelph were the first two great hotbeds of the sport, but Toronto's baseball history stretches back nearly as far. Contemporary newspapers mention a team being organized in the late 1850s, and in 1876, a club called the Toronto Clippers was part of the Canadian Professional Baseball League, along with clubs in London, Guelph, Markham, Port Hope and Kingston. The league folded after a single season, though, and the London and Guelph franchises went on to join the International Association, generally regarded as the first minor league. Guelph won the championship in 1877.

In 1885, baseball returned to Toronto, when a team joined the new Canadian League, playing at the Jarvis Street Lacrosse Grounds, then located at the corner of Jarvis and Wellesley streets. This was the beginning of the Maple Leaf franchise, which operated almost continuously until 1967. A year later, the sports equipment manufacturer A.G. Spalding passed through town promoting the game and said for the first time what would be said many times over the next ninety years.

"Spalding was always going around hustling his equipment and his company," says Louis Cauz, journalist, historian and author of the book *Baseball's Back in Town*, a history of baseball in Toronto. "He said in 1886 that this would be an ideal place to put a major league franchise. It went on like that every ten years or so—there would be more talk about Toronto getting a major league franchise."

Toronto didn't secure a National League franchise, as Spalding had suggested it should, but it did forsake the Canadian League the year of his visit, along with the Hamilton team, to join the International League. (Thus began another recurring theme—that Toronto was just too big and too sophisticated to limit itself to competing against other Canadian towns.) With interruptions when the league struggled or reconfigured, that's where the Maple Leafs stayed. At about the same time, construction began on the first stadium in the city built specifically for baseball. It was located off Queen Street, just east of the Don River (and until the 1980s commemorated by a short, one-way street in south Riverdale known as Baseball Place). It seated two thousand spectators and was usually referred to as Sunlight Park, because of its proximity to the

Sunlight Soap Works, whose sign dominated the skyline. Seats in the 550-seat reserved section had backs, arms and cushions and were located in a grandstand that was shaped like a half-octagon. On May 22, 1886, Sunlight Park was officially opened, as the local lads beat the Rochester Hop Bitters 10–3.

Between 1890 and 1894, the turbulence in the major leagues brought about by the formation of the breakaway Players' (Brotherhood) League, in which Toronto was not involved, left the city without professional baseball. The Maple Leafs returned in 1895 and two seasons later moved to a wooden stadium at Hanlan's Point on Toronto Island; it was built by the great entrepreneur Lol Solman, certainly the key figure in the early history of the game in Toronto. He owned the Royal Alexandra Theatre, amusement parks at Sunnyside and Hanlan's Point, as well as a restaurant on the island. Then he purchased the Toronto Ferry Company, which shuttled passengers across the harbour. With the acquisition of the baseball team, Solman created a bit of perfect business synergy: get the fans to the island, feed them, entertain them, bring them back, and make money every step along the way.

The team returned to the mainland in 1901 and stayed until 1907, when a group of businessmen led by Ed Mack bought the Maple Leafs from Solman and moved its games to Diamond Park, south of King Street and east of Dufferin Street. The club won pennants in 1902 and 1907—the former under manager Ed Barrow, the man who went on to build the New York Yankees' dynasty. When the ownership group faltered, the Maple Leafs wound up back on the island and back with Solman in 1908. After the old stadium burned to the ground in 1909, construction began on a new facility, a state-of-the-art concrete stadium seating eighteen thousand dubbed Maple Leaf Park.

Thus began the first golden age of baseball in Toronto. Wee Willie Keeler and Nap Lajoie played their final seasons of professional baseball in Toronto in 1911 and 1917 respectively. A nineteen-year-old pitcher named Babe Ruth, while in the process of throwing a one-hitter for the Providence Grays, hit his only minor league home run in the stadium on September 5, 1914. Toronto won pennants in 1912, 1917 and 1918.

Meanwhile, another doomed competitor for the major leagues,

the Federal League, was formed in 1914. Other International League cities such as Baltimore, Buffalo and Newark were invited to join. Toronto, though, was left out in the cold.

By 1920, crowds attending the island games had begun to dwindle, and it was widely suggested that the city needed a new, more easily accessible stadium on the mainland. In 1926, Solman sold off some of his assets to finance construction of a twenty-thousand-seat stadium located on reclaimed Toronto Harbour Commission land at the foot of Bathurst Street. It cost $750,000 and took five months to build. When it was completed, Maple Leaf Stadium was the equal of some stadiums in the major leagues and, with plans to add a second deck, could have been better than many—as baseball commissioner Kenesaw Mountain Landis acknowledged when he visited the park. Again, talk began of Toronto securing a big league franchise.

"It was a terrific park," says sports writer Trent Frayne. "Great betting went on behind third base in all the boxes there. The guys all yelling: 'He won't hit! The next pitch is a strike! A hundred he doesn't hit!' and so forth. A covered stand went from left field to right field. The outfield fence was a covered deck of billboards. It was cosy. Just the one stand with the roof over it. I remember the home runs that used to fly out of there."

The 1920s were boom years for baseball, and for everything else in Toronto. Future hall-of-famers such as Charlie Gehringer and Carl Hubbell played for the team. In 1926, the Maple Leafs won 109 games, the International League pennant, and then swept Louisville 5–0 to win the Junior World Series, emblematic of minor league supremacy. Until the World Series champions of nearly seven decades later, it may have been the best baseball team ever to represent the city.

Following the stock market crash of 1929, baseball went into decline. After drawing a high of 221,846 for the great 1926 team (a record that would stand until 1948), attendance fell as low as 49,963 for all of 1932. Throughout the 1930s and into the war years, the team struggled both on and off the field. "The truth of the matter is that in that period, the Toronto Maple Leafs were kind of a joke," says Milt Dunnell, long-time columnist and sports editor with the *Toronto Star*, who started coming to games in 1925 while he was sports editor of the *Stratford Beacon-Herald*. "But then in 1943, they had Burleigh Grimes as manager, and they won that year by ten-and-a-half games." It wasn't until the post-war boom, though, that fans again started flocking through the turnstiles, including a team record 353,247 in 1949 to watch a fourth-place club.

"I started going to the stadium in 1948, coming over from Hamilton," Louis Cauz remembers. "Their infield was considered the finest in the International League. It had great grass, so well taken care of. It was a cold place. They used to advertise when it was ninety degrees out, 'Come down to Maple Leaf Stadium where it's ten degrees cooler—cool off here.' Of course in September or April, it was just cold. Opening Day would always draw eighteen or twenty thousand. They used to rope off the outfield to get more people in."

"You'd get a ground rule double if you hit the people leaning up against the fence," Frayne says. Any player who could hit the hole in the "O" of the Stoney's sign won two thousand dollars, cash. Other signs along the outfield fence advertised cigarettes, tires and Shopsy's deli.

Entering the 1950s, minor league baseball in Toronto was doing just fine, third in the hearts of locals behind the Maple Leafs hockey team and the Argonauts football team, but nonetheless a solid if unremarkable part of the local sports landscape. Attendance was slowly but steadily on the rise. And then came Jack Kent Cooke.

A quarter of a century before Peter Bavasi arrived to "sell the sizzle," Cooke was a sports huckster unlike anything Toronto had ever seen before, the heir to Lol Solman and then some, a little bit Branch Rickey, a lot P.T. Barnum. A native of Hamilton, Ontario, the owner of radio station CKEY and the Casino Theatre, Cooke bought 84 percent of the Maple Leafs in 1951 for $200,000 and immediately combined sports and his own brand of showbiz. He hired excellent baseball men to run the team, first bringing back Joe Becker and Burleigh Grimes, and then Luke Sewell and Dixie Walker. But what he did, mostly, was lure people into the park with a huge variety of promotions and stunts that were only remotely related to the game being played. Anyone who first saw the Blue Jays on Hat Day or Bat Day or Seat Cushion Day got just a taste of what attending a Maple Leaf game in the 1950s was like.

"Cooke did it all with his radio station and the Casino Theatre,"

Frayne says. "The Hollywood second bananas would come to town—women especially—and Cooke would bring them down to the ball park. He'd instruct the guy who was on the PA, who was also a CKEY announcer, to play tunes from the radio station. Then he'd put the arm on merchandisers, telling them that if they'd donate so much to the people who were coming into the ball game, such as silk stockings just after the war, they'd get a big plug on CKEY."

"Cooke always did the spectacular thing in the way of promotions," says Dunnell, who first met Cooke back when he was running a radio station for Roy Thomson in Stratford, Ontario. "It wasn't long before there was a flagpole sitter in front of the Maple Leaf Stadium. He was going to stay up there until the Leafs got into first place or won the pennant—something like that. Havana was in the league at that time, and after the revolution Fidel Castro was regarded as a saviour. So Cooke had a Fidel Castro night and presented him with a tractor."

At the height of the Cooke era, the Maple Leafs were outdrawing two or three teams in the major leagues. For six years in a row, between 1952 and 1957, the Leafs drew over 300,000 fans, including a remarkable 446,040 in 1952, to watch a fourth-place team that finished just two games over .500. At a time when drawing a million fans in the major leagues was the mark of enormous success, those were terrific numbers for minor league ball. And so naturally, talk turned often to Toronto's prospects of attracting a big league team of its own. In 1954, the *Sporting News* did a survey of cities that might one day house major league teams. Toronto came out on top.

No one talked about bringing big league baseball to the city more than did Cooke himself.

"He talked incessantly about how this was a big league city that deserved a big league club," Frayne says. "Here he owns the Maple Leafs, and he's talking endlessly about how we've got to get a major league team in the city. He made a speech of that nature before one of the Opening Day banquets. The fans would read it and hear it in broadcasts on his station."

Baseball boosterism also showed up in some unlikely places. On August 21, 1954, even the *Globe and Mail* jumped on the bandwagon. "Metropolitan Toronto is the largest municipality in Canada, and the seventh largest on the continent," read the lead editorial of the day. "Toronto has the brains and the money and the other necessary resources to invite the possibility of the World Series being played here. That opinion is shared by a group of Toronto businessmen who are prepared to obtain a major league franchise, provided a stadium is constructed large enough for major league baseball, and is shared by the Board of Control, which is prepared to underwrite the cost of constructing such a stadium.

"The project is worthy of Toronto and it is hoped that both parties will combine their best efforts to make it a reality.

"Whether or not private interests here will be able to acquire the franchise of the Philadelphia Athletics—the only one available—remains to be seen but it is certain that any negotiations to bring major league baseball here will be useless if they are not backed with guaranteed plans to build a suitable stadium."

Philadelphia was just one of the teams rumoured to be headed for Toronto. At the winter meeting following the 1954 season, the Athletics were on the block, and Cooke appeared to be the most likely purchaser. He had plenty of friends among the powerful men of baseball, including Branch Rickey and Frank Lane, and had been named the minor league operator of the year after his first season with the Maple Leafs. "There's no doubt about it," Dunnell says. "Toronto would have been in major league baseball when the Philadelphia Athletics moved to Kansas City if there had been a ball park in Toronto."

That was, and remained, the big "if." Despite endless studies and committees, and plans to add a second deck to Maple Leaf Stadium, nothing came to fruition. "At the baseball meetings, everybody was saying, 'Where's Cooke? We thought Cooke was going to be here,'" Dunnell remembers. "When I got back to Toronto, I asked Cooke, 'Hey, what the hell, they were pleading for you and Toronto. Where were you?' Cooke told me that he had approached a number of people, and they had agreed that if they could get assurances immediately that a start would be made on a stadium, they would take over the old Philadelphia Athletics. But he couldn't get any assurance from the city and decided there was no purpose in going to the meeting. So Toronto wasn't even represented. The team was there begging for them and the league was there begging for them."

In the 1950s, any major league team that wasn't drawing—or any team that was trying to get a better deal from its landlord—was automatically a candidate for relocation. "Every time a team was in trouble in the majors with attendance, and any time an owner of a major league team was trying to get extra goodies as far as tax reductions, they'd always say, 'Well, if we don't get it, we're going to go to Toronto,'" Cauz says. "Detroit used this. Detroit was a prime candidate for Toronto, as well as the weak franchises like Washington, the St. Louis Browns and Philadelphia. When Toronto was outdrawing these three teams, the people would say, 'Geez, why can't we have major league baseball here? We put more people into our small ball park than go to watch major league baseball in those ball parks. We have major league hockey. Why can't we have the same in baseball?'"

In 1956, when Walter Briggs put the Detroit Tigers up for sale, Cooke bid $5.6 million, the second highest offer. But Briggs—and the American League—wanted the team to stay in Detroit, and so it went to a local buyer who offered less.

It is no small irony that Cooke's efforts to bring major league baseball to Toronto—and especially, his persistent suggestions that Toronto was a city that was all but owed a big league team—almost certainly helped hasten the demise of his own Maple Leafs. It was a situation not unlike the one that faced the Canadian Football League's Toronto Argonauts in the 1980s and beyond, when talk centred on whether the National Football League would one day expand to town. Toronto had come to think of itself as a "major league city," a place that, although not quite the cosmopolitan equal of New York or Los Angeles, was at least gaining rapidly on Montreal, host to a World's Fair, the Olympic Games and, since 1969, a major league baseball team. That self-image, especially for those of the television generation, simply didn't connect with supporting minor league baseball or, later, a provincial football league.

Throughout the 1950s and into the early 1960s, people in Toronto supported the Maple Leafs baseball team better than just about any minor league team in North America. But lurking, always, was the notion that this city on the move, this town growing out of its backwater past, didn't just desire major league ball—it deserved major league ball.

While Cooke kept talking about the big leagues, nothing materialized. No major league team moved to Canada, there was no hint of expansion, and so Cooke eventually turned his attentions to the Continental League, a proposed professional circuit that was the brainchild of Branch Rickey and that was to compete with the major leagues. After the Giants and Dodgers left New York for California, Rickey figured he could get a new league off to a flying start by locating a Continental franchise in New York. Toronto and Cooke would have been a big part of the plan, but the major leagues outmanoeuvred Rickey by granting New York a National League expansion team that became the amazing Mets. "As soon as New York got a National League team, they had no interest in the Continental League," Dunnell says. "So the Continental League went out of existence almost overnight."

For Cooke, that was nearly the end. There was one final blow, though, that sent him off in pursuit of more friendly, manageable business ventures—like selling professional hockey to southern Californians. For big league baseball to come to Toronto, there would have to be a stadium, either the increasingly unlikely prospect of renovating and expanding Maple Leaf Stadium, the building of a new park, or the conversion of Exhibition Stadium into a facility that might house both a baseball team and the Argonauts of the CFL—much as actually happened fifteen years later. Cooke was outsmarted, though, by John Bassett, then the owner of the Argos and someone who had the ear of local politicians. While Cooke was out of town on a business trip, Toronto council decided that CNE Stadium would be renovated for use as a football facility only.

"That's what really pissed Cooke off," Frayne says. "He was this far from getting a major league franchise, and the city finally turned down the park idea. They weren't going to spend the money. When Cooke came home and found out he was going to have a football field down there and not a baseball park, that was about the final straw for him leaping off to California."

The lack of a new stadium and Cooke's departure for California weren't the only things that conspired to kill minor league ball in Toronto. Television, and more specifically American television, had become the dominant medium in the city. Every Saturday afternoon during the baseball season, fans in Toronto could sit at home and watch two of the best teams in major league baseball play the game of the week. Just as the National Football League's television presence helped make the CFL look minor league by comparison, seeing the greatest baseball stars of the day in the comfort of your living room could only diminish what was happening at the foot of Bathurst Street. One year, the Maple Leafs tried to strike back, televising twenty games of their own, but the experiment was deemed a failure.

"Immediately the interest in the Maple Leafs started to fade," Dunnell says. "Cooke started to concentrate his promotions on Sunday afternoons. Well, then they started Sunday-afternoon major league telecasts. The televising of big league games kept increasing and the interest in minor league baseball just started dropping. The bigger the city, the less interest. Montreal was the first to go. Newark was an early departee. Toronto eventually. The bigger they were, the less interest they had in minor league sport."

The other problem was Maple Leaf Stadium itself. It was, after all, nearly forty years old, and in the final years of the franchise there wasn't any money to maintain it properly. "In its later years, there were chunks of cement falling, pieces of plaster falling off down there," Cauz says. "People started saying to themselves, 'This isn't such a great place to visit after all.'"

Cooke finally sold the Maple Leafs in 1964 for $50,000 to Bob Hunter and Sam Starr. (For their purchase price, they received six players, including Sparky Anderson, and a selection of used equipment.) Their plan was to operate a community-based team and to give the local fans a real stake in the organization. To that end, they offered shares for sale, 208,149 of them, at a dollar apiece. Hunter and Starr between them held 42,000 shares. They sold only 50,000 more.

On the field, the Maple Leafs of the early 1960s were a roaring success, winning the International League regular season pennant in 1960 under Mel McGaha and the Governor's Cup—awarded to the playoff champion—in 1960, 1965 and 1966, the latter two under manager Dick Williams.

But one of the surest signs that a franchise is in terminal decline is the fact that winning no longer matters. In 1965–66, the hockey Maple Leafs drew 494,634 for thirty-five home games. The Argonauts, in 1965, drew 173,461 for seven home games. The baseball Maple Leafs, en route to a championship, drew only 118,310 for fifty-six dates, down from 144,785 the year before. (The club's break-even point was 285,000.)

"You can only bang your head against a wall for so long," Hunter said at the end of the 1965 season.

The Leafs were dying, and no heroic measures were going to save them. Attendance fell again in 1966, despite a championship team featuring future major league star Reggie Smith. At the beginning of the 1967 season, the club owed the Harbour Commission $37,000 in back rent and had to cut a deal just to get permission to open the doors. "Now all we need is the support of the people," Hunter said. The support never came.

On September 4, 1967, the final game was played at Maple Leaf Stadium. The Leafs lost to Syracuse 7–2, in front of a crowd announced at 802. There was talk that Harold Ballard, owner of the hockey Maple Leafs, might buy the club, but it was idle chatter. The team declared bankruptcy and was sold to Walter Dilbeck, a real estate developer from Evansville, Indiana, who moved the franchise to Louisville, Kentucky. For his money, Dilbeck received three players, equipment and a pile of debts.

"It went out," Cauz says, "with a whimper."

"There was scarcely a sigh," Dunnell says. "There were a few people voicing regrets when the Leafs folded. But it was mostly old people crying from nostalgia."

An auction was held to divide up the contents of Maple Leaf Stadium before it faced the wrecker's ball. Paul Rimstead, the newspaper columnist, bought home plate. In later years, there was all kinds of nostalgic talk about what a great place the stadium had been, about how baseball in the good old days was in some ways preferable to what came later at Exhibition Stadium or SkyDome.

But the fact is, the day Toronto lost baseball, hardly anyone in Toronto cared. And two years later, when the major leagues finally arrived in Canada, albeit four hundred miles to the east, it was as if it had come into a vacuum, as though it were all brand new.

Chapter 2

LABATT HAD A problem. A beer problem. The brewery, based in London, Ontario, was doing good business in Quebec, Western Canada and rural Ontario. But in the urban areas of its home province in the mid-1970s, and especially in Toronto, Labatt was struggling against the competition. Molson had a brand new building at the foot of Bathurst Street—just across the street from where Maple Leaf Stadium had stood—a very visible presence to go with a healthy market share. Carling O'Keefe, the final member of the big three breweries that enjoyed a virtual monopoly on the Canadian beer business, was successfully making inroads in the ethnic community, taking advantage of the huge immigration waves of the time.

On the other hand, market research showed that Ontarians didn't even seem to know that Labatt was an Ontario brewery and that in Toronto, the demographics for its consumers didn't match up very well with its brands. In what may have been the most competitive business in Canada, where pitched battles were—and continue to be—fought over tiny fragments of market share worth millions of dollars, that hardly bode well for the future.

"We hadn't done anything exciting in Toronto in quite a while," says Peter Widdrington, then CEO of John Labatt Ltd. "And Toronto was a somewhat more sophisticated market, a more fickle market, a younger market, a triers' market. We wanted to do something in Toronto that would give us a lot of attention."

The link between sport and beer—between sport and beer and whisky and cigarettes, for that matter—had by 1974 already been very well established. The consumers of those products shared a demographic slice with the audience that would pay to watch sporting events and that spent its idle hours in front of the television watching even more. Young men—the eighteen-to-thirty-five group in particular—tended to be serious beer drinkers and serious sports fans, a fact that didn't go unnoticed by the breweries. Molson, of course, through its ownership of the Montreal Canadiens and sponsorship of "Hockey Night In Canada," was already the beer of hockey. Carling O'Keefe had a hand in several sports, including the

Canadian Football League, then thriving in Toronto.

"We thought, gee whiz, hockey is kind of shut out—Molson's have got that locked up. Football doesn't have very many games. It's not really going to do it. Auto racing, maybe, but it hasn't really taken off yet. Maybe baseball would be a good thing to try to pursue." In 1974, Don McDougall, who at age thirty-six was president of Labatt Breweries, was the wunderkind of the Canadian brewing industry. In fact, all the men who would eventually bring big league baseball to Toronto were in their thirties. McDougall, Paul Godfrey, Herb Solway—they were part of a time when there seemed to be no limits to growth, when being young and smart and ambitious could put you at the vanguard of a city just beginning to come into its own.

In many ways, though, McDougall was an unlikely member of the group, a small-town boy from Prince Edward Island blessed with a native charm, a quick mind and absolutely no interest in baseball. He had studied at what was then St. Dunstan's University—now the University of Prince Edward Island—and had earned his teacher's certificate. While at university, McDougall also first became involved with politics, specifically those of the Progressive Conservative Party. It was Brian Mulroney, then a student at St. Francis Xavier University, who persuaded McDougall to form a Young P. C. club at St. Dunstan's. In later years, McDougall would be one of those behind Mulroney's first unsuccessful run for the Tory leadership in 1976. He himself would make a single, failed run for a federal parliamentary seat in 1972 in the riding of Vancouver South. (In 1983, when Mulroney finally got the leader's job, McDougall had switched horses, playing the good party loyalist by backing Joe Clark. That decision effectively cut him out of the mainstream during Mulroney's years in power.)

After graduation, McDougall taught school for a year on the island and then headed east, to London, Ontario, where he enrolled in the highly regarded Master of Business Administration Program at the University of Western Ontario. During the summer of 1960, he gained his first experience with the beer business other than as a consumer. John Labatt Ltd., based in London, offered him a summer job that any red-blooded young Canadian male would envy. It was his task to sit in bars and watch people drink, to determine beer-buying habits, maybe to buy them a pint or two along the way. The brewery was in the process of deciding which of two brands—IPA or 50 Ale—to push in the marketplace, and it was McDougall's job, through observation and conversation, to see which the buying public preferred. An amiable conversationalist and an amiable drinker, he excelled at the task.

That job led to McDougall's first post-graduate employment, as an assistant to Labatt's general manager of marketing, earning $525 a month. Eight months later, at age twenty-four, he was transferred to Prince George to work as a salesman. Two years later, he was named Toronto sales manager—before then, he'd spent hardly a night in the big city. A year later, he was named Ontario sales manager. Two years after that, in 1968, he became vice-president and general manager of Labatt's Alberta operations. Two years later, he was given the same job in British Columbia. Finally, in 1973, at age thirty-five, Don McDougall was named president of Labatt Breweries of Canada, the largest subsidiary of John Labatt Ltd.

Beer, he knew, obviously. Sales, he knew as well. Baseball, though, was something in which he had no interest at all. To illustrate the point, his friends all tell the same story. During his early pursuit of a baseball franchise, McDougall attended games in the 1974 World Series between the Oakland Athletics and Los Angeles Dodgers, the first major league baseball games he had ever seen in person. "McDougall knows not a fucking thing about baseball," says Herb Solway, the lawyer who became his friend and partner in pursuit of the Blue Jays franchise. "He goes to the '74 World Series, and now it's August or September of the next year, 1975. He says to his secretary, 'I want to go to the World Series again. I need some hotel reservations in Los Angeles.' His secretary says, 'Mr. McDougall, Los Angeles is in fourth place.' He thought the World Series was in Los Angeles every year."

In 1974, as president of the brewery, McDougall was asked to look into baseball by the Labatt head office. An early feasibility study prepared by the company laid out all the perceived advantages of associating with the sport:

• Satisfies need for strong marketing tool to reinforce and stimulate current Ontario market penetration

- Reconfirms aggressive marketing leadership
- Positive association with new major sports vehicle
- Activity prior to and during high volume periods (that is, the summer beer drinking and baseball seasons happened to coincide)
- Strong Toronto-based marketing thrust
- Compatible with other (sports) involvements
- Hedge against advertising restrictions (should the government decide to clamp down on beer advertising as it had on liquor and cigarettes)
- Precludes competitive involvement in baseball (by another brewery)
- Positive reinforcement of employee morale and motivation

The idea of Labatt owning a sports franchise had come up some years before, when the company—and particularly its planning head, Jack Mennie—was part of an effort to buy the Oakland Seals of the National Hockey League and move them to Vancouver. The fallout from that failed venture was positive—B.C. beer drinkers apparently appreciated the effort—so those at Labatt were open to other sports possibilities. There had been a couple of overtures from the baseball world already, one about the opportunity to buy the Cleveland Indians, another about buying the Baltimore Orioles and moving them to Toronto. By then, though, others had already begun to lay the groundwork for securing a major league franchise. Others still were angling to own a team.

◆ JUST A YEAR after the Maple Leafs had gone to their great reward, Paul Godfrey had a bright idea. He was thirty years old, freshly elected to North York council—the only publicly elected post he would ever hold during a political career that made him the single most powerful figure in Metropolitan Toronto. That said, his first job was hardly a position of influence. North York was a suburban borough, a backwater, and as alderman, Godfrey didn't even merit a place on Metro Council.

He was determined to change that, though, to find his own trademark issue, something to set him apart from the pothole-fillers and ticket-fixers who made up the municipal scene. It came to him, he says, in 1968. "I woke up one day and heard that Jean Drapeau had landed a baseball team for Montreal. For a guy who loved politics and who loved sports—and who grew up in a household that had a very active political mother and a father who weaned you on sports—it really irritated me to find out that here Montreal had pulled off a coup. Not only did they get the 1967 World's Fair, but here they were going to pull off a major league baseball team. And there wasn't one public official in Toronto who had even said, 'Hey, what about us?' That really irritated me. I occupied a very minor position—an alderman not even in the main municipality. But I figured there hadn't been a politician since Allan Lamport who did anything public in the area of sports. [It was Lamport who, among other things, pushed to legalize Sunday sports in Toronto.] I thought this over very carefully. I figured that there was no political downside for me. Only a political upside in any event. So I started this campaign to try to bring major league baseball to Toronto. I was going to be the guy who brought major league baseball. I thought maybe it would take a couple of meetings."

That was a wildly naïve notion, which Godfrey realized almost immediately. He remembers his first encounter with the world of baseball, at the 1969 winter meetings, held at the Americana Hotel in Bal Harbor, Florida. He had paid his own way south and, arriving at the hotel, immediately headed for the bar, since that's where he figured he might encounter the movers and shakers of the sport. Just one problem, though—he didn't know who the movers and shakers were, or at least what they looked like. "I walked in and the only guy I recognized was Frank Lane, who was the general manager of the White Sox and later of Cleveland."

Godfrey sidled up beside Lane, introduced himself as a "representative of Toronto" and started buying him drinks. He talked about the city, about baseball, about what a great thing it would be if Toronto had baseball. It took him a couple of hours before he got up the nerve to pop the question.

"Do you have anything to do with it?" he asked Lane.

"Hell, me?" Lane laughed. "I deal with the player end of it."

"Here I was feeding this guy booze, and it turns out I'm wasting my time," Godfrey remembers.

Lane was kind enough to offer a bit of friendly advice, though.

The owners are meeting upstairs, he told Godfrey. Eventually, they'll have to come down those stairs just outside the bar.

"Do you know who Bowie Kuhn is?" he asked. Godfrey said, sure, he's the commissioner of baseball.

"He's a big tall guy," Lane said. "You'll have no trouble recognizing him. I suggest you wait for him."

So Godfrey set up shop at the foot of the stairs. Finally, the meeting broke and the imposing figure of Kuhn, all six feet four inches of him, made its way down. Before he reached the bottom, Godfrey was in front of him.

"Mr. Kuhn, I'm Paul Godfrey, I represent Toronto, I'd like you to give us a major league baseball team…" his spiel began.

Kuhn looked down at him and cut him off before he could get any further.

"Son," he said, emphasizing that first word to make sure it carried the intended effect, "where are you going to play?"

"Well," said Godfrey, not missing a beat, "you give us a team and we'll build it a stadium."

Kuhn put his hand on Godfrey's shoulder. "Let me tell you the way we do it in major league baseball," the commissioner said. "First you build a stadium. And then we consider if we want to give you a baseball team."

"After hearing that," Godfrey remembers, "I kind of slipped away into the night."

In 1973, Godfrey was elected by his fellow politicians as chairman of Metropolitan Toronto. That day, he audaciously promised to deliver the city a major league baseball team, a domed stadium and a convention centre. First, though, he had to come up with a ball park—any kind of ball park—so that the rest might be possible.

There was no support at any level of government—municipal, provincial or federal—to fund the building of a new stadium. The best Godfrey could hope for was to somehow retrofit Exhibition Stadium so that it might accommodate both football and baseball. It wouldn't really work. The layout, the location, everything was wrong. But without the money to build from scratch, there was no alternative. Get the team, Godfrey figured, and someday, down the road, a real baseball stadium would follow.

In November of that year, standing on the stadium field at the

Canadian National Exhibition grounds waiting for the Governor
General to arrive for the ceremonial kick-off of the Grey Cup game,
Godfrey and Ontario premier Bill Davis had what has come to be
regarded as one of the most significant conversations in the history
of Canadian sports.

Here's how we can do it, Godfrey told Davis: build a new south
stand, put home plate there, stretch a temporary outfield fence
here, use the far end of the covered north stands as the left field
bleachers, and as for the rest of the seats, which would extend off
beyond centre field, a world away from any baseball action—well,
they wouldn't need them that often anyway. He figured he could
get $7.5 million out of Metro. He needed another $7.5 million out
of the province. A grant.

"I can't give you a grant," Davis said. "But I can get you an inter-
est-free loan. Don't worry. You won't ever have to pay it back."

From that conversation came the worst stadium in major league
baseball. Godfrey knew that it wouldn't be an easy sell getting the
money out of Metro. The left wing of council was opposed on principle, and any sniping about the makeshift park could sway those
sitting on the fence. Godfrey pulled in all of his political favours,
while at the same time trying to mould public opinion to suit his
needs. "This one I knew I couldn't lose, because personally, I didn't
want to lose, and I knew if I did I'd be fried by everybody," he says.
"I knew I was going out on a limb a bit. But I was really convinced
that baseball would not ultimately say no to Toronto."

In January 1974, Godfrey summoned the local sports media to
the Sheraton Hotel for an off-the-record meeting. Virtually all the
leading lights attended with the exception of *Globe and Mail* columnist Dick Beddoes, who wanted no part of it—and ripped into
Godfrey the next day in the newspaper for attempting to manipulate public opinion by manipulating the media. "When a politician
or anybody else demands silence as the price of information,"
Beddoes wrote, "this department always beats them with the hat
trick. That is, I grab my hat and run." (In fact, Beddoes supported
the plan to renovate Exhibition Stadium, arguing that that was what
the city could afford—and not a new domed stadium.)

Those who did see fit to cross the threshold heard an interesting
pitch. "If you hammer me in the media—and you have every right

to do that—I can't deliver what I'm about to tell you," Godfrey said. "I'm going to build you a rebuilt ball park at Exhibition Place. It's in the wrong location. It's got terrible sight lines. There's going to be a terrible traffic mess. But I want to tell you something. It's the only thing I can do. So if you crap on it from great height, this thing will die. But I think with this temporary facility, I can convince the barons of baseball to at least consider Toronto."

The reporters, all of whom had more than a passing interest in baseball coming to Toronto, may not have totally complied with Godfrey's wishes. But the truth is the stadium project proceeded with hardly a discouraging word—at least from the sports press.

Because Godfrey's involvement with attempts to get major league baseball predated the successful partnership of Labatt, Howard Webster and the Canadian Imperial Bank of Commerce, and because he would be extremely visible later on, especially during the negotiations to purchase the San Francisco Giants, the idea evolved that he was exactly what he had hoped to be—"the man who brought baseball to Toronto"—a notion that Godfrey didn't actively discourage. Some of those more directly involved with bringing the team to town—and especially with paying the bills—came to resent that image, though the friction never became public.

"People at Labatt were pissed off at Godfrey because of the idea that Godfrey brought baseball to Toronto, but he didn't write the cheque," says one high-level Blue Jay official, who asked to remain anonymous. "But if they hadn't built the stadium, there's no way there would have been a team. They took a bad football stadium and they made it a worse baseball stadium. But Paul had the guts to spend the $15 million, put it through Metro Council, and built the stadium that allowed the franchise to come here. He was young and he was enthusiastic, he had guts and he could speak and he could do all these things."

Another whose connections with the Blue Jays stretch back to the franchise's beginnings tells much the same story (and from the same position of anonymity). Godfrey was resented by some at the brewery (though not by McDougall) for his high public profile, he says.

"Godfrey was very helpful from a general point of view as far as getting the stadium and baseball going, and getting baseball people to appreciate the desirability of Toronto....But he didn't play any role in getting the team. The guys at Labatt resent Godfrey being credited with bringing baseball to Toronto, because he didn't put up the money. I think Godfrey deserves a reasonable amount of credit for bringing baseball to Toronto, but I think calling him 'the man who brought baseball to Toronto' is a bit of an overstatement. Still, Godfrey hasn't postured to get more credit than he deserves. And I think the Labatt resentment was an over-reaction."

◆Now there was a ball park, or at least the real possibility of a ball park. And it seemed as though there was also a prospective owner. Sydney Cooper was president of C.A. Pitts Engineering Construction Ltd. In the 1930s and 1940s, he had been a promising shortstop, playing in and around Toronto; not long after Montreal got the Expos, he put together a group to try to secure a National League team for Toronto. The Toronto Baseball Company included Cooper, his three Toronto partners—Robert Hilborn, Ray Wolfe and Harold McNamara—and two Americans—Roy C. Jackson, a former executive with the Philadelphia Phillies, and Joseph Buzas, the president and general manager of three Boston Red Sox farm teams, who had enjoyed a very brief major league playing career.

The Cooper group had helped Godfrey persuade Metro Council to go ahead with the renovation of Exhibition Stadium, putting up the money for a study that demonstrated the benefits of a new facility at the CNE. They had begun courting the National League owners. And they had targeted the franchises most likely to be on the block. During the 1973 season, seven major league teams drew under a million fans, and three—Cleveland, Texas and San Diego—drew under 700,000 paying customers. Surely one of those would be available on the open market. As well, there was talk of expansion, suggestions that baseball would add as many as four teams in 1976, with New Orleans, Jacksonville, Washington, D.C., and Toronto considered the leading candidates.

In an interview in 1974, Cooper was optimistic about the chances of landing a team, one way or another. But he was also letting it be known that this was no potential gold mine. "There are no prospects of making any money," Cooper said, adding that he didn't expect the team to make a profit for at least the first ten years.

Cooper was the first person Don McDougall sought out when he began his mission to get Labatt involved with baseball. Labatt actually owning the baseball team wasn't seen as a necessity. If the brewery could lock up marketing rights, be seen to be involved with bringing the team to Toronto, and then be involved through advertising and television in the future, that would make the necessary connections in the beer-drinking public's mind.

The two men, along with McDougall's friend, lawyer Alan Eagleson, met for lunch in the fall of 1974. "[Cooper] told me that he had talked to his partners," McDougall remembers. "They thought that being associated with a brewery would be a bad idea, because it would adversely affect their chances of getting a franchise. I can remember coming out from lunch. Al Eagleson was with me. He was just a friend but he was also very big in sports in those days. We got out on the street and Al, of course, is very quick. He said, 'That's bullshit.' I thought it was kind of strange, but I wasn't quite that strong about it."

McDougall got in touch with Kuhn, who said that personally, he had no problem with brewery involvement—after all, breweries owned the teams in Baltimore, St. Louis and Milwaukee, and beer and baseball seemed a natural fit. Kuhn encouraged McDougall to attend the World Series and talk to the owners, who would be responsible for any decision. He met the league presidents, Chub Feeney and Lee MacPhail Jr., and was very warmly received. We're not saying you'll get a franchise, they told him, but if Toronto is in our plans, we certainly don't have any problem having a brewery associated with it.

"We realized fairly quickly that we had a better chance than any other group in Toronto at that point," McDougall says. "There were only two other groups. One was tied in with Ballard, and we really didn't think that was serious. And the other was Cooper's group, which was serious. They had some money and they had some status in the community and they were well-connected. We were prepared to compete with them." (The Harold Ballard–bankrolled group, headed by Lorne Duguid, a vice-president of Hiram Walker and Sons distillers, would lurk around the edges almost until the day the Blue Jay franchise was awarded. "We're already involved in the operation of a sports franchise, and we feel we have the right people," Duguid said in March 1974, referring to Ballard and his Toronto Maple Leafs.)

It was at that point that Labatt decided to pursue a franchise on its own, in competition with Cooper. McDougall took the proposal to the company board of directors, who gave him the go-ahead—but on one condition. The brewery wouldn't have more than a 50 percent stake in the team. They needed a partner. A high-level executive at Labatt was friends with the chairman of the Canadian Imperial Bank of Commerce, Page Wadsworth. Wadsworth in turn had a friend named Webster—Howard Webster—who had expressed an interest in baseball in the past. Perhaps they ought to meet.

HOWARD WEBSTER WAS born into privilege, the son of Senator Lorne Webster, the scion of a wealthy Montreal establishment clan. But while he could have spent his life watching the family money grow, Webster instead chose to mark his own path. He graduated, not unexpectedly, from McGill University, but then rejected his father's choice, Harvard Business School, for the rather less prestigious Babson (where you could get a degree in a year). In his twenties, backed by Imperial Trust, the business his father had built, Webster, through savvy investments in real estate and the bond and securities markets, began to amass a substantial fortune of his own. Soon he gained a reputation for shrewdness, for his willingness to gamble when an opportunity presented itself, for usually making the right call. At one time or another, he owned part of the Schick razor company, artichoke groves in California, a ski resort in Colorado, part of Eaton's College Street store in Toronto, the Lord Simcoe Hotel in Toronto and the Windsor Hotel in Montreal, the CIBC building, the Penobscot Building in Detroit, large amounts of real estate on the west island in Montreal and in Orange County, California, and the *Globe and Mail* newspaper. "He was a very smart businessman," says his long-time associate Bill Ferguson, "very astute." One of his best friends was the former heavyweight boxing champion of the world, Gene Tunney, who served on several of Webster's boards. Together, they would travel from New York to California.

"He was always interested in baseball as such," Ferguson says. "He looked at Toronto as being an ideal spot to have it. We were involved with the Expos—we had an equity ownership through [his nephew] Lorne Webster as part of the original group. We helped finance parts of the whole thing. [Mr. Webster] was more enthused about the business end of it. We watched baseball games here in Montreal, and later we went to Toronto a number of times to watch. He thought that Toronto would be a better market. After seeing what happened in Montreal, he thought that Toronto was a better deal—a much better deal."

By the time Labatt approached him, Webster had already put out feelers about buying the San Diego Padres and moving them to Toronto. He had been represented at baseball meetings by Montreal businessman Gerry Snyder, and he had had discussions with both of the other players in the Toronto baseball sweepstakes, Syd Cooper and Lorne Duguid. "Cooper was going to go into it with him and then Cooper ran into some problems. And consequently it didn't happen," Ferguson says. "Then this opportunity presented itself." Among Webster's business interests was Burns Foods, and he thought that they might handle the concessions at Exhibition Stadium, that maybe visiting teams could stay at the Lord Simcoe.

What McDougall didn't know was that Webster, very low profile despite his wealth, was also something of an unconventional personality. "A Howard Hughes enigma," Paul Beeston calls him, a man who on first encounter seemed like anything but a multi-millionaire. A loner (he was married, briefly, during the 1960s), a big man who was also extremely shy, Webster would sit quietly drinking at the bar of one of his hotels, making the acquaintance of whoever happened to occupy the next stool, rarely letting on that he owned the joint—and being treated with scepticism if he did.

Tony Tracy, the father of race-car driver Paul Tracy, tells a typical Howard Webster story. One night, he was relieving himself in the washroom attached to the bar of the Lord Simcoe Hotel, when an older gent at the next urinal struck up a conversation. "The wolves are howling tonight," he said, cryptically. "You'd better stick with me." Tracy decided the fellow was an oddball, but still followed Webster back to the bar where, being a teetotaller, he turned down the offer of a drink, settling instead for a cup of coffee. The conversation eventually turned to what each did for a living. Tracy explained that he was a house painter, working for a contractor. "I own this hotel," Webster said. "It needs painting. I want you to paint it." Webster scrawled a name and address on a piece of paper, handed it to Tracy, and told him to report there first thing on Monday morning.

Tracy was suspicious but curious, though his boss was dismissive of the whole idea. He kept the appointment, representing no one but himself. Arriving at a downtown office tower, Tracy was greeted by a secretary who knew his name and immediately led him to one of the executive suites. The man there was equally cordial and explained that he was to paint all of the hotel rooms and hallways, to begin at the top floor and to work his way down, and to start right away. Tracy, still battling disbelief, explained that he wasn't equipped for a job of that scale, that he'd need to hire men and buy supplies. An accountant was summoned, who immediately wrote him a cheque. Just bill us every week for what you need, he was told. It was the beginning of the business that Tracy still operates today.

Beeston tells his own story about Webster, and about how it took a while to understand the owner's idiosyncratic personal habits. "He'd call me up at the office and say, 'Paul, I've got to meet you over at the Lord Simcoe.' I'd say, 'What the fuck am I going to go to the Lord Simcoe for?' He'd say, 'I'm just having a few drinks with our old buddy.' It was always 'our.' He never used 'my' and he never used 'you.' He always said our old buddy—Jack Dominico [the proprietor of the Toronto Maple Leaf baseball team, which plays in the Ontario-based Intercounty League, and a character in his own right]. It's three o'clock in the afternoon. I don't know what to do. I'm a little accountant from London, Ontario. I don't know whether he's testing me to find out whether I'm supposed to go over there in the middle of the day and drink or not go over there. But what I'd say is, 'Mr. Webster, I'll come over at five o'clock. I've got a couple of meetings I've got to go to.' He'd say, 'Oh, okay, we'll still be here.' I'd never go at three o'clock. As it turned out, as I got to know Howard and as I had seen him when he was in his drinking stages, I realized he wasn't worried—he was just looking for someone to drink with. And he was a good guy. He loved baseball."

Knowing how important the meeting with Howard Webster was to the future of their endeavour, McDougall and his associates from Labatt were determined to come prepared. "We figured we were going to get a grilling," McDougall says. "If we were going to bring in a partner, the partner is obviously going to have a lot of questions." The parties got together in Wadsworth's office.

"How much do you think it's going to cost?" Wadsworth asked.

McDougall explained that the going rate for an existing franchise was between ten and twelve million dollars.

"How much is Labatt prepared to buy?" Wadsworth asked.

No more than half, McDougall said.

"Would you be upset if the bank came along as a partner, maybe 45–45–10?" Wadsworth wondered. "Does that sound like something you guys could live with?"

McDougall said that sounded fine.

Turning finally to Webster, who hadn't said a word, Wadsworth asked, "What do you think, Howard?"

"That sounds pretty good to me," Webster said.

"Well," said Wadsworth, "thank you very much, gentlemen."

And that was that.

"We were gone," McDougall remembers. "We were outside. We had all of these hours of preparation. And we weren't there more than a half hour, and that was with all of the niceties and coffee."

Webster was adamant about bringing the bank in as a buffer between himself and the brewery. (Ten percent was the limit that the CIBC could own under the Bank Act, though just the idea of its vast resources would prove useful in impressing the powerbrokers of baseball.) But the truth of the matter is that from the beginning, until Webster's share of the team was sold to Labatt for $67.5 million in 1991, a little over a year after his death at age eighty, there was little friction between the parties. The balance of powers, the balance of egos, the balance of wealth, never seemed to get out of kilter, which was significant in securing the franchise and even more significant later, as the decisions were taken that made the Toronto Blue Jays the model of a successful expansion franchise.

And as unlikely as it might have seemed at the beginning, a strong relationship grew between Webster and McDougall.

"You could say that Webster liked his style," Beeston says.

"Whether he saw himself and said, 'I wish I could be like Don McDougall but I've got too much money,' or 'I wish I could be like Don McDougall because Don can meet people as well as anybody.' McDougall's got this charm about him that's infectious. But he's also tough, and he made decisions. He's got guts. And that's how Howard made his money. Howard made all of his money with guts. He took chances."

With that group, with those combined resources, McDougall was ready to compete with anyone for the right to bring baseball to Toronto. What he didn't know at the time was that the competition was about to thin out considerably, because of those "problems" of Syd Cooper's. On March 12, 1975, Cooper was one of five men charged with defrauding the public of $4.2 million by rigging bids on seven dredging contracts between 1969 and 1975. He went on trial in February of 1978, and on May 5, 1979, was convicted on three counts. The Crown asked for a sentence of nine to twelve years, but largely because of his age—Cooper was fifty-seven years old—he was sentenced in June 1979 to three years in jail. When his appeal of the conviction was denied in April 1981, he surrendered to police and began his term. That September, he was released on parole, just in time to catch the first glimmer of the pennant contender to come at Exhibition Stadium.

Chapter 3

A POLITICIAN, A brewery, a bank and an eccentric businessman set out to buy a baseball team for Toronto. Not one of them really knew for sure how to do it.

Today, the process seems relatively straightforward, no matter what the sport. A league suggests that it is about to expand. Cities and potential owners bid for expansion franchises, offering sweetheart deals of one sort or another: free stadiums, free rent, the concession rights and parking thrown in, no taxes until the end of time. The league governors sit, they ponder, they listen to proposals, paying rapt attention to the details. And then they invariably give the team to the people willing to pay the largest amount of money in the quickest, least complicated fashion.

There are variations on the theme—the National Hockey League granted instant franchises to the people behind the Disney Studios and Blockbuster Video without bothering with the preliminaries; the National Basketball Association didn't have firm plans to expand until pigeons from Toronto convinced them that it was too hot a market to turn down; and there is very occasionally the opposite scenario, when a struggling organization like the Canadian Football League all but begs people to take teams off its hands. Generally, though, it is the case that those willing to pay an exorbitant price without asking too many questions step to the front of the line.

Buying a major league baseball team in 1975 was another matter. It was more like a one-way flirtation, a desperate attempt first to be noticed, then to be acknowledged, then to be taken seriously, and finally, perhaps, to do business. The baseball owners didn't really like adding teams—even though, since they didn't do much revenue sharing among themselves, it was pretty much a case of getting money for nothing. There was an essential conservatism about the sport and the business, Charlie Finley and his orange baseballs aside, the notion that a game so steeped in tradition shouldn't be in too much hurry to change. If a team were in desperate trouble, it could move, as had happened many times in baseball history. But actual expansion was a relative rarity; the last one had taken place in 1969, when the National League added the Montreal Expos and San Diego Padres, and the American League brought in the Kansas City Royals and the ill-fated Seattle Pilots.

In 1975, there was no strong evidence that further expansion was on the horizon, though there was certainly talk, especially in the American League, which tended to be a little bit more aggressive than the staid, self-satisfied senior circuit. The American League was also facing some legal unpleasantry, a $20-million class-action suit launched in Seattle after the Pilots packed up and headed for Milwaukee in 1970, where they became the Brewers. There was plenty of precedent in baseball for solving problems by handing out teams: the Senators arrived in Washington in 1961 to head off a lawsuit after the original Senators fled for Minnesota the same year. And the Mets came to New York in 1962 in no small part to keep the upstart Continental League from setting up shop there.

But initially, the Seattle situation didn't matter to Toronto, because it was the National League in which Toronto was destined to land. There was an understanding in baseball that Toronto was National League territory, by virtue of the city's natural rivalry with Montreal, and Charles Bronfman, the Expos' owner, was more excited than anyone about putting a second team in Canada.

By the time Labatt added Howard Webster and the Bank of Commerce as partners, the dance had already begun. Paul Godfrey had continued his forays to the annual baseball meetings, with ever-increasing degrees of sophistication and ever-increasing legitimacy, as he rose from no-name alderman to Chairman of Metropolitan Toronto. His role, by definition, was limited to civic boosterism, to selling the virtues of the city as though he were trying to convince the Shriners to hold their annual convention there. When plans moved ahead to expand Exhibition Stadium for baseball, he could talk about that as well, since there obviously wouldn't be a team if there weren't a ball park (although given what the stadium was going to look like, it might not have been a great idea to get into the details).

The most important factor, though, remained ownership. If the baseball fraternity decided to grant an expansion team or to allow a team to move, and if they decided that Toronto was a more desirable site than the other cities angling for a team, and if they could live with a makeshift stadium by the lake, it would still be up to the money people to make their case. Part of it was simply having the necessary financial resources. Another part, of nearly equal importance, was convincing this very exclusive club that you were acceptable for membership. The people who owned major league baseball teams were an extremely diverse lot, of varying wealth and varying moral character. What they had in common, though, and what they valued, was that they were in, they were the custodians of the National Pastime. Anyone who cared to join them would have to court them and flatter them and show that they, too, belonged.

First and foremost, that was Don McDougall's job, and he was a natural when it came to the art of the schmooze. A major part of the process involved standing around bars or around the 21 Club in New York, a favourite owners' hangout, buying drinks, chatting, staying up late, making friends. All of that fell very much within his comfort zone.

But McDougall needed a counterbalance, a detail man, someone to plot strategy, to wonder about all the what-ifs, to play devil's advocate when things seemed to be proceeding a little too smoothly. That role would fall to Herb Solway. Solway was a lawyer, a backroom boy at City Hall who represented numerous developers and who could bridge the public and private sectors. He was known for his quick mind, his ability to assess character and his dry sense of humour. He also had extensive experience in the world of professional sports, serving as a director of the Toronto Argonauts of the Canadian Football League, bringing the Rifles of the Continental Football League to Toronto, and working with John Bassett Jr. to bring a World Football League team—the ill-fated Northmen—to the city. Solway was the Northmen's chairman of the board and was in the room the day Bassett signed Larry Csonka, Jim Kiick and Paul Warfield to contracts. But the federal government stepped in and prevented the WFL from setting up shop in Canada as a way of protecting the CFL, and so the Toronto Northmen became the Memphis Southmen. (Both Bassett and McDougall's friend Alan Eagleson would serve as unofficial advisers to the Labatt group. "He and Eagleson were the people that I thought of as being knowledgeable about professional sport in Toronto," McDougall says.

"And they were my age. They were kind of kindred souls.")

Labatt retained Solway early in the process, around the time John Alevisos, a former executive with the Boston Red Sox, approached the brewery about the possibility of buying and moving the Cleveland Indians to Toronto. (Any thoughts of a deal fell apart because of complications with the Indians' ownership structure, which included a large number of limited partners.) He was part of the team before Howard Webster came on board, and by the time the final drive to secure a franchise began, he and McDougall had already become the brewery's one-two punch. "They knew that I had been involved in professional sports, and my partner was a director of Labatt," Solway says. "So they retained me to help get the franchise. My job was to plan the strategy. [McDougall] had the final decision, he said yes or no. It was his money.... I had not known McDougall until that point in time. I liked McDougall a lot. I thought he was bright. I thought he had a lot of energy. And people liked him."

"You had the perfect combination," Paul Beeston says. "You had a rounder like McDougall, who was the guy that hired me and was my friend. If it wasn't for McDougall, I'd probably be finishing off tax returns in London, Ontario, right now. McDougall was a guy who could drink, go to the bar, people would like him. Then you had Herbie, who was a little more cerebral, the designated fretter. He was always worried about something. If we were to get the top five closers in the game, we wouldn't have enough. Herbie's never, ever happy enough."

After Alevisos came and went, the Labatt group turned its attentions to buying the Baltimore Orioles. It was rumoured that the Orioles' owner, Jerry Hoffberger, had put the team on the block, as well as his primary business, National Breweries. "We actually got very close," McDougall says of the negotiations, which took place from November 1974 through January 1975. But then Hoffberger sold his brewery to Carling's, one of Labatt's chief rivals, and that ended any talk of the ball club being sold. (Hoffberger, though, became an important player later, when the focus shifted to securing an expansion team.)

What followed then for McDougall and Solway were months of frustration, wondering whether expansion might be in the cards, looking for owners who might be willing to sell their team, looking over their shoulders at the Cooper group or any other potential competitors in Toronto and elsewhere, and all the while attempting to curry favour with the people who controlled the game. Even getting a chance to make your pitch, to extol the virtues of your ownership group and your city, was no sure thing.

"You'd wait in the lobby, they'd tell you they might let you in at the end of the meeting to make your presentation," Solway remembers. "And then at the end of the meeting you'd wait in the lobby, wait in the lobby, wait in the lobby, and then suddenly they'd all come out carrying suitcases in their hand, saying we've got to catch a plane, we'll get you in the next meeting. You'd never get called in. The only productive time you'd spend would be in the bar the night before when you'd meet some of these guys. You'd get some guys who'd promise you their support, they were all for you, and then you'd find out they were talking out of both sides of their mouth. They were for somebody else, or they were against you."

There was a bunch of teams allegedly available for purchase: Minnesota, Baltimore (still), Atlanta, the Chicago White Sox, Cleveland. But when you looked a bit closer, the owners weren't really that interested in making a deal, at least on any kind of reasonable terms. Dave Cashen, then Labatt's Ontario sales manager, attended one of the baseball meetings during the All-Star break in 1975. "I don't think anything is going to happen here," he said at the time. "It seems that every team is for sale—until you contact them. Then nothing is for sale. We're here not because our presence can do anything positive, but because our absence might have a negative effect. We haven't heard the same story from anyone we've talked to. Everyone has a different statement. If you listened to all of them, you'd go bonkers."

Still, it was becoming clear that something was cooking, that the American League's need to solve its Seattle problem was going to lead to some type of restructuring in baseball, involving expansion and/or relocation of franchises. A month before the Webster/Labatt/CIBC partnership was announced, sports writer Neil MacCarl reported in the *Toronto Star* that baseball's interleague committee was prepared to recommend adding Toronto to the National League and Seattle to the American League for the 1976 season—Seattle as an expansion team, Toronto as the new home of the San Francisco Giants. (There were rumours, also, that it would be Japanese interests who would purchase the Giants and move them to Toronto.)

The Giants had been owned by the Stoneham family for the past fifty-three years and had at times enjoyed tremendous success. But by the mid-1970s, the people of San Francisco seemed to have lost interest in baseball, and all indications were that the team was dying a quick death. Horace Stoneham, the principal owner, desperately wanted out. In 1974, the team had drawn just 519,987 to Candlestick Park, the worst attendance in the majors, and followed that up by drawing just 3,000 more in 1975. (The Oakland Athletics, coming off their third consecutive World Series, had drawn only 845,693 the same season, but perhaps with only one team in the Bay Area they might have a better chance to survive. "If they keep the Giants in San Francisco," said the ever-charitable Charlie Finley, owner of the A's, "I'll run so many promotions for our ball club they'll be lucky to draw 300,000 fans.") The cash crunch was such that to save money the Giants had fired their manager and coaches immediately after the season ended, forced their front office staff to take a 33 percent pay cut, and had borrowed $500,000 from the National League to try to partially offset a $1.4-million loss for the year. Because of that loan, the league would have even more control than normal over the terms under which the club might be sold.

The questions, then, weren't so much whether the Giants would change ownership, but who would get them, where would they be located, and would baseball approve any move. In addition to the Labatt group, Syd Cooper was still hanging in to some degree. "I now think that Syd Cooper was being counselled by the Expos," McDougall says. "He thought that one way or another, Mr. Bronfman could make it happen." The Harold Ballard-backed group, fronted by Lorne Duguid, was making regular appearances at the baseball meetings. And there were interests, as well, who wanted to move the team to Washington, D.C., as well as two groups who hoped to keep the team in San Francisco, one headed by businessman Bob Lurie, the other backed by the American Fund Inc. of Beverly Hills.

In September of 1975, McDougall and Solway met with Charles Rupert, the Giants' executive vice-president, to discuss a possible sale. McDougall arrived fresh from his mother's funeral, and the meeting was "disastrous," he said. Not disastrous enough, though, to kill the negotiations. Little happened for the next two months. In November, in the days leading up to baseball's winter meetings, McDougall and Solway met with Walter O'Malley, the owner of the Los Angeles Dodgers. Because the Dodgers–Giants rivalry was one of the hottest in baseball, it was widely believed that O'Malley would use his considerable power and influence within the sport to try to block any move. "O'Malley said that he wasn't in favour of losing San Francisco," McDougall remembers, "but his loyalty to Horace Stoneham meant he wouldn't oppose it.

"We really thought that the owners would not be that unhappy to get the team out of San Francisco," McDougall says. "It was unsuccessful there, and we had better financing and a better ownership structure. I don't mean that arrogantly. We just had deeper pockets."

By the time of the winter meetings in Florida in December 1975, the action had begun to heat up, though it remained unclear whether the baseball owners actually wanted the Giants to leave San Francisco. Godfrey (necessarily impartial as far as the competing Toronto groups were concerned) was there with four city officials in tow, boasting that the renovations to Exhibition Stadium were on time and on budget. Duguid was also there, accompanied by Maple Leaf Gardens' treasurer Donald Crump, who many years later briefly served as commissioner of the Canadian Football League. The Giants were worth about $8 million, Duguid said, but the bidding was competitive enough to push the price far beyond that. A group in Washington, where the second Senators had left for Texas, was offering $10 million, the Labatt group was offering $12.5 million. Ballard, Duguid said, was willing to go as high as $15 million.

But it was Solway and McDougall who were doing most of the real bargaining. They met with Rupert and Don Crist, Stoneham's lawyer, from midnight to four in the morning and then talked to each other until 5:30 before finally falling asleep. There was a complication—the Giants had nineteen years remaining on their lease at Candlestick Park at $125,000 a season. If they broke the lease, there was sure to be a lawsuit, and any potential purchaser was going to have to help shield Stoneham from the damages.

It was all possible, but when the meetings broke up on December 9, the Toronto group left discouraged. The owners voted to give the Giants until December 30 to find a buyer who would keep the team in San Francisco. "Our intelligence sources tell us most of the owners want to keep the team in San Francisco if at all possible," McDougall said.

Though it was barely reported in Toronto, there was one other important matter of business that came out at those meetings. The owners of the American League had voted 11–1 to go ahead with expansion.

On December 28, after hearing nothing, Solway called Jim Hunt, the Giants' lawyer. He was told that their offer was the best on the table, and that what was apparently the last local bidder—the American Fund—wouldn't be able to come up with the money. Crist would fly to Toronto and work out the final details of the deal. Some restructuring took place—the original offer, which was $10 million for the team and $2.5 million to cover the legal liabilities, became $8 million and $5.25 million. That appeared to be acceptable to both sides, pending approval by the Giants' board, and of course by the league.

The owners extended San Francisco's deadline to January 13, 1976. On January 5, Solway was summoned to New York to work out the legal fine points of the sales agreement. That took three days to complete. Finally, everything looked to be in place, pending the approval of the Giants' board of directors, who would meet on Friday, January 9.

Because the Giants were a publicly traded company, the sale would have to be announced immediately after the board took its vote. The timing would be delicate—the would-be Toronto owners couldn't alert the press until they knew the board had actually begun its meeting. That was at 11 A.M. San Francisco time, 2 P.M. in Toronto. The press was told to be at City Hall at four o'clock for a major announcement regarding major league baseball in Toronto. (Co-owner Howard Webster was in Toronto the night of the announcement but didn't want anything to do with a press conference. "If you want me," he told Godfrey, "I'll be at my usual spot in the Lord Simcoe Hotel.")

Four o'clock came and went without word from San Francisco. McDougall, Solway and Godfrey waited in Godfrey's office for the phone to ring. McDougall called Eagleson and invited him down for the announcement. While he was talking to him, Godfrey's private line rang and Solway picked it up. A few seconds into his conversation, he signalled the others with a thumbs-up. "I told you guys I'd be around for the start and at the end," Eagleson told McDougall. "I left all that crap in between for you guys to straighten out."

At 4:52 P.M., Paul Godfrey stepped to the microphone and announced to the world that the San Francisco Giants had been sold to the Labatt/Webster/CIBC group and would be moving to Toronto. They would be called the Toronto Giants. The purchase price: $12 million, with an additional million placed in trust to cover any legal costs Stoneham might incur for walking out on his lease at Candlestick Park. The National League owners would meet on January 14 in Phoenix to vote on the deal, with the Giants excluded from the voting. Nine of eleven votes would result in approval, but that now was seen as a mere formality. Toronto was in. A member of the fraternity, of the senior circuit to boot—just as A.G. Spalding had predicted it would be a mere ninety years before. The Giants were scheduled to open the season at home, April 9, against the Los Angeles Dodgers.

Meanwhile, in San Francisco that same day, a new mayor, George Moscone, was taking office just as the news came that the baseball team was leaving town. "The first day in office is always the easiest," Moscone joked.

FOR GODFREY, McDOUGALL, Solway and the rest, snaring the Giants was a huge personal triumph. For the baseball fans of Toronto, who were greeted the next day with front-page headlines announcing the deal in the city's three newspapers, it was the end of a long wait for the big leagues to finally arrive. The sports pages were filled with stories about the Giants' starting line-up, about how the team might be a contender that very season, about how there would surely be some arrangement to move the Giants to the National League East, to encourage the Toronto–Montreal rivalry to flourish. Officials with the Expos said they were thrilled with the developments.

There were some, however, who weren't so thrilled at the news. Duguid, whose group had lost out in the bidding, said he was "shocked" at the announcement, especially since he claimed that Harold Ballard had been willing to put up $2 million more than the Labatt group had offered. "I guess we can draw some satisfaction that the Toronto Baseball Company did all the spadework," he said. "However, it's kind of ironic that the people who came in at the last moment got to pick up all the marbles. That's competition. If I were a drinking man, I'd get loaded tonight. But I wish them every success." (Later, Godfrey was to catch some of the fallout. Bill Ballard, Harold's son, called him to complain that Godfrey had soured their chances of getting a team by telling the baseball owners that Ballard senior was a "jailbird." Ballard, of course, did do time for income tax evasion, but Godfrey tried to assure Bill Ballard that it wasn't he who spilled the beans and that besides, the owners certainly could have come up with that information on their own. He tried to speak to Harold, whom he could hear cursing in the background, but Ballard refused to come to the phone.)

Equally unimpressed was Colin Vaughan, then a city alderman who would later find greater fame as a local television reporter.

"My worst fears have been realized," he said. "Now we've got the team, which will be a bigger drain on the treasury than before. Up to now, without a baseball team, Metro has been subsidizing an empty stadium. A team will only add to the cost of the stadium as far as the taxpayers are concerned."

And there certainly wasn't universal rejoicing among citizenry, either. A *Toronto Sun* street poll of ten Torontonians found seven people saying they weren't baseball fans. Three of them, without prompting, mentioned hockey. Even though the ticket prices for baseball would be the lowest for any sport in the city—one to six dollars versus four to twelve dollars for the Maple Leafs and three to eight dollars for the Argonauts—it seemed no sure thing that the stadium would ever be filled. A letter to the editor of the *Toronto Star*, dated January 20, 1976, voiced the opinion of what was at very least a significant minority.

"I would further venture to guess that, should Toronto be unfortunate enough to get a team, it will fold or be transferred out of Toronto within five years at the most, whereupon it would be proven beyond a doubt that baseball is indeed dead (in Canada at least).

"Baseball is part of Canadian culture only so far as Canada is part of the United States."

Ian D. Cappon
Toronto

It was typical of the tone of the sceptics, those who thought Toronto was too provincial, too hockey mad, too staid, too conservative, too Canadian to take to major league baseball. The memory of rotting Maple Leaf Stadium wasn't so distant, and baseball madness wasn't in the air.

As it turned out, Vaughan, Cappon and all the other naysayers wouldn't have to worry—at least not quite yet.

"We certainly knew it was coming apart," McDougall remembers. "And there was nothing we could do about it."

"It was stolen away from us," Solway says.

Chapter 4

IT ALL CAME apart quickly, decisively, and there was nothing any one in Toronto could do about it. American civic politics, baseball politics, American law—all of them worked against those who wanted to bring baseball to Exhibition Stadium. As it played out, as it became clear that the move would never happen, they could complain, they could suggest that baseball had once again betrayed the city. But mostly, they could just sit back and watch it happen.

Newly elected San Francisco mayor George Moscone understood what many civic leaders have come to understand since—that the gaining and losing of professional sports franchises is something voters tend to remember at election time. So he acted swiftly to keep the Giants at Candlestick Park, or at least to block the move to Toronto while he came up with some sort of acceptable option. Three days after the announcement that the Giants were moving, the city attorney for San Francisco obtained a temporary restraining order, shutting down the transfer process. With that order in hand, Moscone would head for Phoenix, where the owners were meeting on January 14, 1976, to persuade and threaten and make his point. He promised that by then, he would have an alternative offer, better than the one from Toronto, which would keep the team in San Francisco and include a substantial number of local investors.

Godfrey, McDougall and Solway flew to Phoenix as well, to try to protect Toronto's interests, but really, what could they do? It wasn't an issue of the city's merits, or the stadium, or the amount of money available to the potential owners. What mattered was the threat of a lawsuit, and the fact that it wouldn't be just Horace Stoneham or the Labatt/Webster/CIBC partnership that might wind up liable for damages, but rather the National League itself. The Giants might be a problem in San Francisco, but not enough of a problem to make it worth millions of dollars to the league to move them.

Moscone told the owners that he had received by telegram an offer to purchase the club and keep it in San Francisco. The prospective owners were Bob Short, who had been involved with the Washington Senators, the team that later became the Texas Rangers, as well as the Los Angeles Lakers basketball team, and Bob Lurie, a San Francisco businessman. And he pointed out that if they had any intention of being part of a move to walk out on the lease at Candlestick Park, they were asking for one heck of a legal battle. The owners, not surprisingly, decided to postpone their vote until the courts had had their say.

Meanwhile, at the same meeting in Phoenix, the American League owners voted eleven to one in favour of solving their problems in Seattle by expanding. "Though no deal has been worked out, our interest is in expanding to Seattle," American League president Lee MacPhail said. "The desire of Seattle is to have a baseball club. I don't think they want the suit any more than we do." The owners endorsed a report from baseball's expansion committee, which recommended that each league add one team in 1977. MacPhail said he hoped that the National League would go along, "but if they don't, it is possible we would expand on our own."

On February 3, the city of San Francisco went to court seeking a permanent injunction, which would prevent the Giants from leaving. A lawyer for the city told State Supreme Court Judge John Benson about the new ownership group that would keep the team in California and asked for a three-week grace period to finalize the deal. Richard Murray, the lawyer for the team, argued strongly against any delay. "The Giants are broke. They have no cash. They are living on handouts from the National League. The season is about to start. The Giants must have an answer, or they'll be destroyed." Benson reserved judgment for a week. A day before he was to rule, Moscone filed an affidavit with the court, saying that the prospective owners wanted salary information from the Giants before they could proceed. With the National League owners in New York, ready to meet and vote on the sale—either to Toronto or to the San Francisco group—and with McDougall and Solway holed up in a Manhattan hotel room waiting for a call, the ruling was delayed until noon on February 11.

Word came that day. The injunction had been granted. Lurie and Short would each put up $4 million to match the Toronto offer. The Giants were staying in San Francisco.

"Let us say, Bobby Thomson lives again!" Moscone shouted on

hearing the announcement, hearkening back to the shot heard round the world. (There later were complications with the San Francisco ownership group, forcing Short to drop out. But in the end, Lurie managed to come up with enough money on his own to win the approval of the other National League owners.)

The baseball analogies were flying in Toronto as well, but the mood was understandably different. "Somewhere the sun is shining but...Toronto Has Struck Out," read the front-page headline in the *Toronto Sun* the next day.

"There have been lots of ups and downs," Godfrey told the press. "We're going to have a ball team in Toronto, and it's going to be sooner rather than later. It may be the Giants. It may not be. I am disappointed. But you have to give their mayor credit. He said he would do it, and he apparently did."

Privately, he wasn't feeling quite so sanguine about the situation and understood that just as surely as Moscone's political stock had risen, his had taken a tumble. "When the Giants were swiped away from us, I remember the empty feeling I had," Godfrey says. "It was just awful. It was one of the worst feelings, because I thought now I'm really in political trouble. Anybody who really wants to take a shot can—because there's an empty stadium sitting there."

McDougall, as downcast as at any time during the process, could only express his admiration for what Moscone had managed to accomplish. "This guy sounds like he might become president of the United States some day," he said.

There are two postscripts to the saga of the Toronto Giants.

In August of 1976, after the American League had voted to expand to Toronto, August Busch, the owner of the St. Louis Cardinals, called for Chub Feeney's resignation as president of the National League. Feeney had withheld information to stall the move of the Giants to Toronto, he charged, and had helped his personal friend, Lurie. "San Francisco should be in Toronto today as a National League team," Busch said. "Is there anyone in this room who honestly believes that our president did not purposely and deliberately deceive and manipulate us regarding the San Francisco matter?" (Feeney was a lifelong resident of the San Francisco area—he was, in fact, the nephew of the Giants' owner, Horace Stoneham.)

On November 27, 1978, Moscone, along with city councillor Harvey Milk, was murdered by former supervisor Dan White.

DON McDOUGALL AND Herb Solway headed for Florida in the middle of February. They had found their baseball team, they had bought their baseball team, and now they were left with nothing. It was time to sit back, relax, and come up with a new strategy, though the course they would follow was anything but clear. Back to looking for a team on the block, back to courting the owners, fending off competitors and making an offer that might be accepted. After the San Francisco débâcle, none of it seemed very appealing. But they were determined enough, or naïve enough, to be willing to continue.

"In the whole process [of bringing major league baseball to Toronto], there were two key decisions that were made—one at my initiation and one at his," Solway says. "But the one he made I didn't see as clearly as I should have. And if he hadn't made that decision at that time, we would have lost the franchise."

Solway's moment of glory came on that Florida beach. He was with McDougall, soaking up the sun, reading the *New York Times* on a Friday morning, when a story in the sports pages caught his eye. "Look," he said to McDougall. "The owners are meeting in New York tomorrow. They're going to talk about Seattle."

"We had been away a while, and we felt like getting home," Solway remembers. "He said, 'Well, we won't go.'"

"We weren't invited," McDougall says. "We had no reason to be invited."

"I said, 'We've been to every other meeting, Don. I think it's a mistake for us not to go.' I urged him to go, and we went."

They flew to New York that afternoon, as it happened on the same plane as San Diego owner Ray Kroc. On landing, they immediately headed for the 21 Club to have dinner, knowing that many of the owners would be there, as always. They ate, they renewed old acquaintances, and then Solway went to bed, leaving McDougall at the bar.

"Herb was the early-to-bed guy. I tend not to be," McDougall says.

After a long evening of socializing, McDougall found himself walking back to his hotel with National League president Chub

Feeney. "I think it would be a good idea if you came to our meeting tomorrow [March 20]," Feeney said. Expansion was on the agenda, he explained. Some of the owners were worried that if they didn't move quickly, the American League was going to beat them to the punch, even in Toronto, which had long been considered National League territory. And the talk was that Bowie Kuhn, the commissioner of baseball, wanted Toronto and Washington to join the National League, the latter to satisfy political pressure to bring a franchise back to the country's capital.

The next morning over breakfast, McDougall told Solway they were going to make a presentation to the National League owners that afternoon. There would be a subtle change in strategy. With the spectre of American League expansion lurking in the background, McDougall decided to turn up the heat. If you're going to expand to Toronto, expand now, he told the owners, and we'll be happy to be a part of it. But if the American League decides to go into Toronto, the Labatt/Webster/CIBC partnership wasn't going to sit back and watch someone else bring baseball to the city. They'd change horses, approach the American League, and take their chances with them.

The owners decided to vote on expansion—a vote that in the National League required unanimous approval. The first time the roll was taken, it was eight to four in favour, with Cincinnati, Philadelphia, St. Louis and Los Angeles objecting. The meeting was adjourned for fifteen minutes—fifteen minutes of arm-twisting— and then another vote was taken. This time the result was nine to three, with Cincinnati, Philadelphia and St. Louis still resisting.

"I was dispatched to talk to [St. Louis owner August] Busch," McDougall says. The Busch family also owned the Anheuser Busch brewing company. "I hit him with the beer arguments and all the rest of it. He said, 'I don't favour expansion. I don't think we should be expanding.' The National League didn't have the Seattle problem, and it didn't really want to water down the product." As well, they were generally a more conservative lot than the American League owners. They resisted—and continue to resist—the designated hitter, and at that time there was still very much a sense of the junior and senior circuits, reflected in the substantial difference in price between an American League and National League team. "I think basically they were purists," Solway says. "The National League, until fairly recently, looked down on the American League. They thought they were better owners, that they had better stadiums, that they had better teams. They thought that the American League was really the junior circuit. The feeling among the National League owners was that they had wealthier guys, while the American League had Charlie Finley, George Steinbrenner, people they wouldn't allow into their group. They were really an old boys' club, and very snobbish."

One last vote was taken. Finally, Busch came on side, but Cincinnati and Philadelphia weren't about to change their minds. It was ten to two.

That wasn't quite the end of it, though. One of the owners moved to adjourn the meeting, which was normally a routine procedure, but Atlanta owner William Bartholomay demanded a vote be taken, a gesture of protest at what had (and hadn't) taken place. It came out eight to four against adjourning. "Here are all of these powerful people in a room in New York City in the Plaza Hotel, and they can't get an agreement, and they can't get a motion to adjourn," McDougall says. Faced with being stuck in limbo, the owners had no choice but to postpone the meeting, which they did for two weeks. In the meantime, Montreal Expos' owner Charles Bronfman assured the Toronto group he'd be able to secure the necessary votes to get them a team.

At the same time in the same hotel, just down the hall, the American League owners had voted to add a second expansion team to go with Seattle, avoiding the scheduling problems of operating a thirteen-team league. "We saw people in the hall," McDougall remembers. "We knew they were going to vote and expected they were going to vote to expand. We thought the odds were that they would choose Toronto over the other possible cities, like Washington." They couldn't go into Toronto if the National League decided to go into Toronto, since the city was still deemed to belong to the National League. But if the National League chose not to expand, as seemed a reasonable possibility, then it also seemed likely that the American League would move quickly to claim the city for itself.

"After the meetings, we didn't get into the National League. But it looked like we might be getting close to getting into the National

League, and Bronfman extracted from us a promise that we'd hang in there," Solway says. "I had a bit of a commitment to Bronfman, and I was in favour of going that route. And then people from the American League spoke to us and said that they were going to do something. Bronfman said, 'Hold on, I'll get Bowie Kuhn to veto anything, don't worry.'" Bronfman told Solway that within a week, he'd have met with the Philadelphia and Cincinnati owners and would be able to deliver a team for Toronto. "Bronfman thought that it was very important for him to have Toronto in the National League, that the rivalry would be very good for him," Solway says.

Solway and McDougall flew back to Toronto from New York that Saturday night. It was on the plane, high over New York State, that the other key decision that brought baseball to Toronto was made. This time, it was McDougall's turn.

"I said to Herb, 'I think this is dangerous ground. We've put a lot into this. We're betting on Bronfman, but if he really wanted to do this, he could have done it anytime over the last two years.'"

Solway remembers, "On the plane going home, McDougall said, 'Listen, we're going to switch horses. We're going with the American League.' And he was absolutely right."

The next morning, McDougall, back home in London, Ontario, met with others from Labatt, and it was decided that they would immediately pursue an American League team. He phoned American League president Lee MacPhail to tell him that his group was interested in the proposed expansion. "I'm delighted to hear that you've decided to pursue an American League franchise," MacPhail said. "As a matter of fact, I'm coming to Toronto tomorrow."

What followed wasn't quite so encouraging. The American League was new territory for McDougall and Solway, a new group of owners whom they hadn't bothered trying to charm either during the attempts to buy the Giants or while pursuing a National League franchise. Someone else, though, had already anticipated that courting the American League was the quickest route to a team. MacPhail was going to meet with a group headed by Phil Granovsky, the chairman of Atlantic Packaging. Also on board were Jimmy Kay, the president of Dylex; David Dennis, president of the Sutton Place and Bristol Place hotels; and Fred McCutcheon, vice president of Loewen, Ondaatje, McCutcheon and Co. Ltd.—heavy hitters all. Lawyer Trevor Eyton would be the spokesman. Jerry Hoffberger, the owner of the Orioles, was a friend of Granovsky's and a supporter of the group, and for McDougall that had particularly ominous overtones. Hoffberger had sold his National Breweries to Carling O'Keefe, becoming president of Carling's U.S. operations in the process. If Hoffberger was involved, then Carling O'Keefe was involved on some level. All that effort, all that money spent, and now one of Labatt's two great rivals might slip in the back door and grab the team for itself.

McDougall did some quick manoeuvring. He sent a driver to pick up MacPhail at the airport and deliver him to his meeting with Granovsky. He knew that the new group planned to hold a press conference the next afternoon at two o'clock, announcing that they were going to pursue an American League team—apparently with MacPhail's blessing. McDougall hastily scheduled a press conference for eight o'clock that night at the Harbour Castle hotel. There, the Labatt/Webster/CIBC partnership announced that it was switching leagues. By the time Granovsky and company made their announcement the next day, it looked like they were following in McDougall's wake.

"It appeared that MacPhail was coming to meet him, and that the Carling O'Keefe group was jumping in on our action," Solway says. "McDougall really handled the whole thing well. And [MacPhail] was favourably inclined to us anyway."

MacPhail also toured the renovated Exhibition Stadium while he was in Toronto and gave it his conditional blessing—one that now might not ring particularly true for anyone who actually had the pleasure of watching a baseball game there. "I was not impressed with the plans," he said, "but I'm impressed with the way the stadium turned out. I think it should be a fun place to watch a ball game. The fans will be extremely close to the players. There are a limited number of good seats, but the good seats are very good."

There would be a meeting of the American League owners on March 29 in Tampa, Florida, where they would hear presentations from any groups interested in an expansion franchise, including the two from Toronto, and then make a decision. Only nine of twelve votes were needed for approval. But these were different owners, with different personalities, not the people McDougall and Solway had been working with in the National League. They divided the owners between themselves—McDougall took the lion's share, since he'd met a few during his late-night lobbying of the National League, while Solway took some, like Nick Mileti, one of the general partners who owned the Cleveland Indians and whom he had met in other places (in Mileti's case, through John Bassett Jr. in the World Football League days).

Every owner they contacted pledged his support. It all seemed too easy, too simple. There was no sign of opposition, of resistance. That stoked Solway's paranoia. In his role as the "designated fretter" of the group, he came up with a conspiracy theory to explain what was going on.

"You needed nine out of twelve votes," he says. "It occurred to me that Hoffberger clearly had one vote of his own. And Hoffberger would get three other guys to vote with him—and so we'd get eight votes, to four for the other group. And then Hoffberger would say, 'You guys don't have nine votes, you can't expand to Toronto, if you want to expand to Toronto, I've got four votes in my pocket. You either take my group or you don't expand to Toronto.' And they had to expand to Toronto because they had Seattle. So these guys would say, 'We'd rather have Labatt, but when push comes to shove we'll take the other group.'"

"We'd better make sure we've got a commitment from at least nine teams," he told McDougall. "Because it's not seven teams we need. It's nine teams we need."

In Florida, a day before the meetings, Godfrey was staying at a condominium. "Hoffberger was the one owner I tried to get to see for two years. He wouldn't even take my phone calls. I'm in my condo in Florida and someone knocks on the door—it's eight-thirty in the morning. I go to the door, and there's Hoffberger." He asked Godfrey to support Granovsky's group at the meetings. "I told him, 'One group has been with us for three years, and the other one has been around for two weeks.'"

By the time the meeting was convened, the Labatt group believed it had ten teams on side. Yankee owner George Steinbrenner was the last to come around, committing to them that morning. Of course, there remained the possibility that they were being double-crossed, that in a secret ballot, those who had pledged their support one way would vote another. So, confident but not overly confident, McDougall and Solway made their presentation one more time, the same old slide show, the same stuff about facilities and financing and the wealth of the owners. "Our argument was basically our ability to put together and manage a franchise—that we had more resources dedicated to the thing than anyone else," McDougall says. "I think our work over the past two years held us in good stead. We had made a good impression on the Bowie Kuhns and MacPhails of the world. They felt comfortable with us. MacPhail was a major influence. We always got along, we always played by the rules, and we always did what we were supposed to do. We weren't trying to change baseball. We never bitched and lamented. And the others were too new, and too quick."

"When we came out of our presentation, Milt Richman, who was the head baseball writer for UPI, asked, 'How did it go?'" Solway remembers. "I said, 'You never know, I think it went okay but you can't be sure.' Richman said, 'Listen. I was speaking to Charlie Finley [Finley wasn't there, he'd sent his cousin]. I asked him what was going to happen. He said you'll see a cop outside the room. The reason that cop is there is that they've got Labatt, they've got the bank and they've got Webster. They've got the cop there to make sure those guys don't get out of there without giving them the money.' Milt told me, 'You've got it.'"

The vote was eleven to one. Only Hoffberger dissented. The partnership of Labatt Breweries, Howard Webster and the Canadian Imperial Bank of Commerce had been granted an expansion team in the American League. The price: $7 million.

"The other guys were angry," Solway says. "They were clearly angry and upset. I couldn't understand why they were so angry and upset. They haven't lobbied, they came in at the last minute. McDougall told me later that he'd met Hoffberger subsequently at a brewing meeting. Hoffberger told him that indeed I had been right. That he had four votes in his pocket. But it was a secret ballot and these guys all stiffed him. And they stiffed him because they knew his strategy, and they figured what's the difference—the vote will be nine to three, Labatt will get it and I'll say I voted for you because it was a secret ballot. But none of them voted for him."

◆Major league baseball would come to Toronto in 1977. That part
was now certain. So was the ownership group. But there remained
one small hitch. The National League hadn't officially signed off on
expansion, and baseball commissioner Bowie Kuhn had his own
agenda—to put a team back in Washington, D.C. There had been
considerable pressure on baseball from politicians, including
President Gerald Ford, to do something for the capital after the
Senators fled for Texas in 1972. With so much of its business success
contingent on the anti-trust exemption the sport had been granted
by Congress—and that, presumably, could be revoked by Congress—
baseball tended to listen when Washington powerbrokers spoke.

Kuhn decided to use the Toronto situation to force one league
or the other to solve that problem for him. No one was particularly
enthusiastic about the prospects for a team in Washington—especially since two incarnations of the Senators had packed up and left
within a decade. But maybe they would do it to keep their hands on
what looked like a very attractive market north of the border. Find
a way to play some games in Washington—in all probability by the
Baltimore Orioles—within seven days or lose the right to expand to
Toronto, Kuhn told the American League owners, invoking his
power to act "in the best interests of baseball." If the American
League didn't satisfy that demand the National League would be
given another chance to move into the city. The National League
owners had already asked Kuhn to block the American League, and
lobbying efforts were continuing to bring the two dissident owners
on side so that the expansion vote might pass.

"Any attempt by the commissioner to intervene is neither just
nor fair," MacPhail responded, saying that the American League
intended to proceed with expansion to Toronto no matter what.
"What I have to say about Bowie Kuhn's reactions wouldn't be
printable," Charlie Finley said. "The only thing I can tell you is that
the American League is going to Toronto. Period. Bowie Kuhn or
no Bowie Kuhn. If the National League doesn't like it, that's just
too bad."

Eventually, MacPhail and the American League owners did come
up with a plan under which the Orioles would play thirteen games
in Washington, with each of the other thirteen teams also playing
one "home" game there, for a total of twenty-six. Kuhn rejected

that, demanding that at least forty games be played in Washington. When the American League owners refused to budge, he gave the National League two weeks to come up with an expansion plan for Toronto and Washington.

The backroom lobbying, especially by Bronfman, continued. On April 26, the National League owners voted seven to five in favour of expanding to those two cities for the 1977 season—a vote that still required unanimity. (As it turned out, some of the owners who had voted for expansion in the previous meetings never really supported the notion. They voted in favour simply as a courtesy to Bronfman, knowing that the Reds and Phillies would object in any case, and the vote would be lost.) Kuhn was humiliated and weakened as commissioner, some of the factors that would eventually lead to his ouster. He was left with no choice but to grudgingly approve Toronto's entry into the American League.

Finally it was official: a Toronto team, in the same division as the storied Yankees and Red Sox. Real major league baseball. For all the fans, for all the dreamers, the long wait was over.

The naysayers were still out there, of course, those who thought that the franchise was doomed to failure, that this alien game—albeit an alien game with roots stretching back more than a century—couldn't possibly flourish.

McDougall knew better, though, or at least he thought he knew better. In 1976, in a profile written by Earl McRae for *Canadian Magazine,* he went far out on a limb with a vision that not even all those involved directly in bringing baseball to town would have shared. It wasn't just going to be successful. It wasn't just going to hold its own with football and hockey. The times were about to change, McDougall figured, and they were going to change in a way that made baseball the perfect entertainment.

"Baseball is going to be bigger than ever," McDougall said. "It has to do with the social climate these days. People are looking for gentler, more relaxed diversions. All of the violence, it's turning people off. I see the 1980s in Canada as being beer, baseball and the Conservative Party."

Nostradamus couldn't have predicted better.

Chapter 5

I N THE FALL of 1981, a gathering was held by Toronto Blue Jay
employees and ex-employees, a chance to drown their sorrows
and share a few laughs. None knew that the source of so many of
their troubles, the despotic boss, would choose to call it quits that
very same day. The tenor of the get-together changed when the
news of his departure spread through the room, from wake to giddy
celebration. For several years after that, they got together annually
on the anniversary of the day Peter Bavasi said goodbye to Toronto.
People who worked for the Blue Jays—and given the low turnover
in the organization, there are to this day a large number of current
employees who actually experienced directly the franchise's first,
flawed, charismatic leader—gathered to celebrate his passing. He
has become a bogeyman, made larger over time, but always with
qualifications. Bavasi had his good points, they'll tell you. He was
brilliant, he was charming, he could light up a room. He wrote fab-
ulous letters. He could choreograph a meeting down to the gestures and the chit-chat. He could sell baseball the way the Music
Man sold marching bands, taking a bad team in a worse stadium
and peddling it to those who wouldn't know an infield fly if it flew
in their window and bit them. Without him, the Toronto Blue Jays
would not ever have been what they are.

And with him, they could not ever have been what they became.
For with his arrival and with his exit, Peter Bavasi was the central
player in two of the key events in the history of the team—not turning points, for the course never really varied, not epiphanies, for
the way was already clear. It was more the case that his greatest
assets couldn't really be duplicated, and his greatest liabilities
couldn't really be overcome. A personality operatic in its highs and
lows had its career alpha and omega built in. It was his nature then
and it has remained his nature since, as Bavasi has followed a mean-
dering path in and out of the world of professional sport. It is also
true that in Toronto, there has never been, and probably never will
be, anyone quite like him.

Bavasi was in fact not the first employee hired by Don McDougall, though all agreed that the franchise's first general manager would be the single key to the building of the team, the person to structure the organization, to set the tone on and off the field. But before that could take place, the Blue Jays needed the bare framework of a business, a secretary to answer the phone, and someone to begin the process of setting up the franchise's financial skeleton. They needed an accountant, a number cruncher, a guy to keep the balance sheets straight, to make sure everything added up, to work with the money men at Labatt, at the bank and in the Webster organization.

"You needed to get control of the administrative side. We didn't want it to be done by the brewery and we didn't want it done by the bank. It was important to have a little centre of activity. Early on, we knew that we needed somebody who was interested in sports and a good reliable administration accountant type," McDougall says. "The bank and Labatt were both public companies, and Mr. Webster was interested in being protected. So it was extremely important to have somebody you could trust in that job who was able to gain the confidence of the owners. I suppose there might have been a hundred people. But my next-door neighbour in London is Dr. Peter Fowler, an orthopaedic surgeon. He suggested Paul Beeston, who was with Coopers & Lybrand. There was a committee—one guy from the bank, one guy from Labatt—to screen the applicants. They interviewed him and they liked him. He was young. That was considered an attribute. He was a professional accountant, a CA. And he had public relations skills and personnel skills. He had all the essential credentials, plus he was kind of one of us."

"One of us": twenty-nine years old, a guy from Welland, Ontario, via London, someone who could understand the corporate culture of the brewery, who knew his role, who would grow with the business. Beeston became something far more than that as time passed, but at the beginning, that possibility wasn't even remotely in anyone's mind.

"With a guy like Beeston, you've got to be lucky," Herb Solway says. "When he was hired at twenty-nine, he showed no signs of being able to do what he's done. Believe me, if you had said to me in the first five or six years that he was there that he would develop into a chief executive officer, I would have laughed at you."

Beeston was officially hired on June 9, 1976, given temporary quarters in the offices of Goodman and Goodman—Solway's law firm—and set about his actuarial duties while the excitement of putting the team together took place elsewhere. There is no manual setting out the right way to build a professional sports franchise, no hard and fast rules for success. The only certainty is that the other owners, immediately after welcoming you into the fold and cashing your cheque, will do their damnedest to make sure you won't be providing real competition for them any time soon. They will offer up only the dregs of their rosters in an expansion draft. They won't hand out high draft choices until it's absolutely necessary. And as for marketing, in major league baseball in 1976, there was really no such thing on a league-wide level. The game was supposed to sell itself, and if players could turn themselves into commodities along the way—as a few, like the charismatic Reggie Jackson had done—then that was just a happy by-product. Happy, that is, so long as they never considered themselves bigger than baseball.

What Toronto needed, then, was a baseball man with marketing sense, someone who could put together the kind of scouting and development team that could build a contender quickly, and who in the meantime could sell the game to the city. The novelty factor would help, and so would some of those visiting stars wearing famous uniforms. But to a large degree, this would have to be a grassroots process. The hard-core baseball fans, however many there really were in southern Ontario, would come out no matter what. The challenge was to attract the rest, those with an interest—or none at all—in other professional sports, who might come to take a look or who might be dragged to the park by their kids. The head man would have to understand that dynamic, he'd have to be able to put a contemporary face on the game, and he would have to be able to explain away the bad teams that were sure to take the field in the early years, with the promise of World Series to come.

Many names were kicked around in the first weeks after Toronto was granted an expansion franchise, not surprising since the opportunity to build a team from scratch was something any baseball man trying to make his reputation would covet. It was clear that a decision would have to be made quickly, since Opening Day was just a few months away. The team's original board of directors, which included McDougall, former Ontario premier John Robarts, David

Lewis from the Bank of Commerce, and Howard Webster, would make the final selection.

In the end, of all the names brought forward, only three candidates were interviewed. One was Frank Cashen, the former general manager of the Baltimore Orioles, then enjoying his first summer away from baseball in twenty-five years. He had also worked for Jerry Hoffberger's National Breweries and had public relations and writing experience, all of which seemed like a good fit for the job of taking over a brand new brewery-backed baseball team. Another was Bill Giles, who would go on to become president of the Philadelphia Phillies and who was the first to fall out of the Toronto sweepstakes.

The third was Peter Bavasi, a man with a perfect baseball pedigree. He had been born in Bronxville, New York, in 1942, when his father, Buzzie, was working for the Brooklyn Dodgers organization (he later became general manager of the team in Los Angeles). The family had moved to Montreal in 1947 and lived there until 1949, during which time Buzzie was general manager of the Montreal Royals, and so Peter even had some experience with the foreign land to the north. "In our home, there was an ever-present sense of the business of baseball," Bavasi told the *Boston Globe* in 1976. "I grew up in a baseball household, so I wasn't quite as awestruck [as other kids]. I had a friend whose father operated a supermarket, and I thought that was the most fascinating thing going. The checkers and the back room and all of that were very exciting for me." That said, from a very early age there was little doubt that Bavasi would follow in his father's footsteps—and spend much of his life trying to get out of his father's shadow. "I was lucky enough to grow up in a household with a man who learned from [Branch Rickey, Larry MacPhail and Walter O'Malley] and then took his own abilities and put them to work. So I really had the opportunity to learn from four very distinct operators and personalities, which, to my mind, is an education I could not have secured elsewhere."

Bavasi took that education and applied it to the part of the sport he most enjoyed—not the game on the field, but the game of the front office. After graduating from St. Mary's College in California in 1964 with a B.A. in philosophy, he immediately took a job as business manager of the Albuquerque team in the Texas League, part of the Dodger organization run by his father. Two years later, he was named general manager of Santa Barbara of the California League. A year after that, he was back in Albuquerque as general manager. Then, in 1969, at age twenty-seven, he was named director of minor league operations for the expansion San Diego Padres, after Buzzie was named president of the new team. Four years later, he had become the Padres' vice-president and general manager.

Obviously, his last name didn't hurt him along the way. But Bavasi was also something very different from his father. He was one of the first of a new generation of baseball men who understood the game as product. He would become famous later for talking about "selling the sizzle" of major league baseball in Toronto, when the on-field production left a lot to be desired. But really it was more than that, the now-popular notion that selling professional sports requires something far beyond printing tickets, opening gates and wondering who will wander in.

"I look upon professional baseball as truly an entertainment experience," Bavasi once said. "What we are are the sights, sounds, smells, touches and tastes of baseball in the park. The smell of popcorn. The crack of the bat. The sight of the ball going over the fence. All the sensory things that go together to make the experience that is baseball, and make the fan favourably disposed to come back again...and again."

It was left to McDougall and Gerry Snyder, representing Webster, to interview the three candidates. One of Beeston's duties was to make sure the candidates arrived as scheduled. ("I picked [Cashen] up at the airport in a borrowed Corvette," Beeston remembers. "I had long hair then, and I was smoking a cigar. I'm sure that when I picked him up, Cashen said to himself, 'Who the fuck is this guy?'") Immediately after that interview, McDougall met Beeston for a drink at Toronto's Harbour Castle hotel. "If I owned the team 100 percent, I would hire Peter Bavasi," McDougall told Beeston. "But I think the right guy for the team, considering everybody else, is Frank Cashen."

What he meant was that he felt Webster and the people at the bank, older and more conservative, would feel more comfortable with someone like Cashen, then forty-seven years old, an established, no-risk choice who could undoubtedly do the job. But McDougall saw in Bavasi the possibility for something more. And he saw in him as well something of himself. Here was another thirtysomething ready to change the world, someone with charm, with presence. When he entered a room, every head turned his way. "Pete's the most charming guy I ever met," Beeston says, no small concession given how sour their relationship became. "I mean, Pete can sell. First of all, he's brilliant. He's a very, very smart guy. Tremendous energy. One of the very few guys you'll ever meet in your life who has a hundred ideas a day. Maybe only one of them is any good, but I can find guys who won't have a hundred ideas in their lifetime and who won't have one good idea in a year. This guy had one good idea a day."

But however sexy Bavasi might have been, the job was Cashen's for the taking. Beeston delivered him to Winston's restaurant, then the favourite watering hole of the Toronto establishment, where Howard Webster had his own table. McDougall formally offered him the position and they cut a deal on the spot. Gordon Kirke, the lawyer for the club, was dispatched to draw up the contract. Cashen said he'd look at it over the weekend, send it back signed, and they'd close the deal the next week. That was Friday. The next Monday, Cashen phoned and said he was having second thoughts. On Tuesday, he withdrew.

"He was our first choice," McDougall says. "Then things fell apart over the issue of an evergreen contract. He wanted a five-year contract that was always five years—after year one, you add on a year. The board wouldn't go for that."

At the time, McDougall took the rejection very hard. "I've seen McDougall crushed once or twice—once when he eventually got fired from Labatt," Beeston says. "But that day it was unbelievable. It was like McDougall, the quintessential salesman, Mr. Smooth, the man who when he wants something is going to get it—you want a baseball team, I'll get you a baseball team. He was on a high. He was going gangbusters. He was unbelievable. And he'd been fucked. He had an agreement. The agreement was broken."

But there was an upside as well. "Now McDougall had to regroup," Beeston says. "And when he regrouped, the next obvious candidate was Pete, because Pete was his choice in the first place."

"Of the rookies' list, Peter Bavasi seemed to have the best potential," McDougall says. "His strength was around the marketing side of it. He knew the game really well, he knew the business side of the game really well. He wasn't thought of as being a great baseball strategist and his heart wasn't really there, either. But he obviously had all the connections. He knew people and he knew how to talk to people. Plus, he came at a completely different price and under completely different terms. That I think appealed to the board. We felt really good about Peter from the brewery perspective. We thought he gave a good, kind of modern image to the ball club. He was a good speaker and he had some life and some charisma."

As far as Bavasi knew, the job was his from the beginning, Cashen or no Cashen. McDougall had phoned his father, Buzzie, and asked for permission to speak to him about the position. When they met at a Los Angeles hotel, Bavasi said he made it clear he wasn't interested in competing for the job, that he already had a position he enjoyed, working for a franchise that then seemed on the way up. "I wasn't playing coy," Bavasi says. "But I felt it was kind of unseemly. I already had a good job. And leaving Buzzie...."

But McDougall was persuasive. "He set it out. He said these were the job descriptions—he gave me a copy of what they were looking for. Frankly, I don't know to this day whether he wrote it, but it looked like it might have been written for me—youthful, with experience as a farm director, and experience as a general manager. They probably had one for Frank as well—not quite so youthful and far more experienced, etc."

During the interview, McDougall asked Bavasi about potential managers, and he answered with a name that surely came as a surprise. "I think for a team like this you need a guy like Roy Hartsfield," Bavasi said. McDougall, quite understandably, asked, "Who's Roy Hartsfield?" Bavasi explained that he was the manager of Hawaii in the Triple A Pacific Coast League, that he was good with the press, great with young players. "And the other thing that's really important when you're hiring a manager in this situation," Bavasi said, "is you've got to hire somebody who you can fire in three years, and who will be happy that they were hired—because they were never going to get hired by anybody else, and this is the ultimate in their career."

"I was thinking, we're hiring the guy and we're already firing him," McDougall remembers. "This coming out of an organization like Labatt, where we hire people for the rest of their lives." (The irony of that last sentiment was surely not lost on him, considering that his own career with the brewery was abruptly terminated.)

Even before they parted at the airport later that day, Bavasi was left with the impression that the job was his. "Don said this is a done deal, he'd call. He gave me every indication that I was their guy, but he had to go back and bullet-proof it with the board." A few days later, a phone call came that confirmed the decision. "I've got bad news for you," McDougall said, pausing for effect. "You've got the job."

On June 18, 1976, Bavasi, just thirty-three years old, was introduced at a press conference at the Lord Simcoe Hotel as the new vice-president and general manager of Toronto's American League baseball team, signing a five-year contract with an annual base salary of $65,000—a hefty raise from the $42,500 he had been making in San Diego. "I didn't seek the job," he said. "Mr. McDougall called my father for permission to talk to me and I was flattered. I was at San Diego when the team started and I know the problems of expansion. But there is a great sense of satisfaction when the team turns out to be a success as the Padres are now. My father did it there and I'm looking forward to the challenge here."

His father: armchair psychologists could have loads of fun with that recurring theme. "It's an opportunity that came along that I wanted to make the best of for its own sake," Peter once said. "But it's also—and I say this most sincerely—I would like to think that several years down the line, Buzzie can look back at the type of job that I've done in Toronto and say, 'I'm proud of my boy.'"

"He in his own mind had to prove to his dad that he could make it on his own," Pat Gillick says of Bavasi. "I really think that was what was in the back of his mind all along."

Once Bavasi was in place, attention turned to other matters: finding a name for the team, and especially finding a field manager to guide it. Other news about the organization was given very little notice. There were a few newspaper stories noting that Howie Starkman, who for six-and-a-half years had worked in public relations for the Toronto Maple Leafs, had been signed on to run that aspect of the operation for the ball club. The hiring in August of Elliot Wahle as the team's director of player personnel caused a bit more of a stir—especially since Wahle, a veteran of two years as assistant director of minor league operations for the Yankee organization, was just twenty-five years old. Lost in the shuffle almost completely, though, was the arrival of another ex-Yankee employee. Pat Gillick, then thirty-two, had been hired as vice-president of player personnel. He was on the road scouting when his appointment was announced—in fact, he would spend virtually his first year on the job somewhere other than Toronto, checking out the players who might be available to the Blue Jays in the upcoming expansion draft.

"McDougall didn't know who Gillick was until Steinbrenner called him and complained that I should be fired for hiring away Pat Gillick," Bavasi says. "McDougall says to him, 'Who's Pat Gillick?' He says, 'Pat Gillick is the finest young baseball operator in the business. He's my scouting man and Bavasi is trying to hire him away, and so you should fire Bavasi.' 'Fire him?' McDougall said. 'I'm going to give him a raise. If you had told me that this Gillick guy was the worst operator in baseball, then I would have fired him.'"

The real story, though, was the field manager, the man whose job it would be to introduce Toronto to major league baseball, presumably to introduce most of his team to major league baseball, to suffer through the inevitable bad times, to tutor whatever young talent the organization possessed, and then to be dismissed—for all managers of expansion teams, famous or obscure, get fired—after two or three years. It was the opportunity of a lifetime and a thankless task all at once. Speculation in Toronto naturally centred on the big names in the business who might be available to the club—Joe Altobelli, Elston Howard, Preston Gomez, Billy DeMars, even Warren Spahn. Bavasi told the press he had a list of twenty potential candidates.

What Bavasi didn't bother to tell anyone was that the Toronto Blue Jays' managerial job had actually been filled eleven years earlier. He was working in Albuquerque then, business manager of the minor league Dukes, when he came across Roy Hartsfield, a fringe player who had begun his professional career with the Atlanta Crackers in 1943, spent parts of three seasons with the Boston Braves in the early 1950s, and then turned to coaching and managing, at which he found considerable success. He spent twenty years in the Dodger organization, fifteen years managing in the minors, and hadn't finished below second in any of the past ten seasons. But when Walter Alston finally decided to retire, the Dodgers gave the major league job to Tommy Lasorda, and Hartsfield knew that he'd likely never make it to the bigs as a manager—except for the remote possibility that an almost forgotten promise might be kept.

"He was a wonderful teacher," Bavasi says. "I would rush down in between my chores of closing the ticket windows and opening the concession stands, rushing down to the dugout of old Tingley Field to listen as Roy would describe the difference between a run-and-hit and a hit-and-run to his players as the game was in progress. He coached third base. Then he'd come in and explain what had occurred. I would take these notes down on index cards which I had in my pocket. By the end of the year I had about 150 index cards on parts of the game, inside baseball, strategy. It wasn't stuff I hadn't heard. It was just the way it was explained. And part of his descriptions were lyrical.

"I called my father, who was the general manager of the Los Angeles ball club then, which owned the Albuquerque ball club. 'Dad,' I said, 'Roy Hartsfield is the greatest manager in the world.' He said, 'What would you know? He's your first manager'—which of course was right. Judy and I had a tiny little apartment. We'd just gotten married the year before. I remember it was an off day and Judy invited Roy over for dinner. His wife, Alice, had gone back to Atlanta. Roy came over, we had a nice dinner and a chat. I said, 'Hey skip, if I ever become a major league general manager and have a team of my very own, you're my manager.' He said, 'You're just saying that. I'll never hold you to that.' I said, 'It's true. I'm so grateful for what you taught me and the way you went about your business.'"

A couple of days after the press conference announcing his appointment in Toronto, Peter Bavasi made a phone call.

"Skip?" he said.

"Yeah," said the voice at the other end.

"It's Peter."

"I was expecting your call," Hartsfield said, in the thick Georgia drawl that would be the first voice of major league baseball for Toronto fans. He had seen the news of Bavasi's appointment in the newspaper, and he remembered.

"Pete said, 'I've got a job, you've got a job,'" Hartsfield remembers. "He said, 'This is what I'm going to pay you. You can't say anything about it because I'm going to let the media play with it. You're going to hear names like Yogi Berra, Elston Howard, Dick Williams. But you can't say anything. Just go about your business.'"

When Hartsfield was introduced to the Toronto press on September 21, he could hardly contain his emotions. "To say that I am very happy and excited to be here would be the understatement of the year. I've waited a long, long time to manage at the major league level."

But as with all lovely, sentimental stories, even those that are apparently true, there is another aspect as well—the bottom line.

"Hartsfield was the type of guy who knew the game, who could spin a story, who could teach, who would be fired," Beeston says. "He knew that, but more important was the relationship between Pete and Roy. Pete didn't have to worry about what his manager would do. Pete said this is the curfew, this is the way the guys are going to dress, this is what we're going to do. Roy would never, ever question it. Plus he didn't have a drinking problem. He might have chewed a bit. And he was cheap. There's no question. He wasn't being paid the big dollars."

THERE REMAINED THE business of just what to call this enterprise. A team's nickname is forever, after all. It outlasts any player, any manager, any president or owner. It was decided that the club would hold a contest to name the team, an easy, risk-free way of building community interest in a franchise; the method has become the norm in succeeding years. More than thirty thousand entries poured in containing four thousand names, covering just about everything under the sun. The top vote getter, by far, was Maple Leafs, for obvious historical and cultural reasons, but it was obviously unworkable, as well, unless Harold Ballard was somehow moved to share. Another favourite was Towers, after the city's great landmark, the CN Tower, but somehow that seemed too sterile. Despite the phallic symbolism, it lacked sex appeal.

The name Blue Jays was in there somewhere, although some who worked on the committee appointed to sort the wheat from the chaff claim they never even knew it was in the running. There was certainly a precedent for naming baseball teams after relatively innocuous birds (cardinals, orioles), and as McDougall liked to point out, it was the official bird of his home province, Prince Edward Island. But the real champion of the name, and the person who did the most to sell it within the organization, was Art Lennox, then the national director of advertising for Labatt. At McDougall's request, he put his pitch into words for the board: "The blue jay is a typically North American bird, bright blue in colour with white undercoverings and a black necklace. It's strong, aggressive and inquisitive, it dares to take on all comers. It's down to earth, gutsy, and good looking. We feel the blue jay is a true representative of major league baseball in Toronto."

It also just happened to have a word in common with the popular name of Labatt's most important brand of beer: Labatt Pilsener, known far and wide as Labatt's Blue. Long afterwards, it was assumed that the naming was just a cheap advertising ploy, a way of subliminally making people think of a cold Labatt product when they thought about the baseball team. Fans might even call them the Blues for short, rather than the Jays. "It wasn't lost on us but it wasn't decided because of that," McDougall insists. "It probably was a 10 percent factor."

Other names were discussed, but Blue Jays was the only one recommended to the board. During the debate, no one was more on side than Robarts. He had seen a blue jay frolicking on his lawn that morning and took it as an omen. ("It's a good thing he didn't see a pigeon," Webster's associate Gerry Snyder joked later.)

The name was approved, but when it was announced that the city's major league baseball team would thereafter be known as the Toronto Blue Jays, it was hard to find much enthusiasm for the moniker among the general public.

"To be honest," Paul Godfrey said, "I'm not impressed."

Neither was anyone else, judging by the endless vox populi features that filled the local papers. A typical sentiment was expressed in a letter to the editor of the *Toronto Star* from the Reverend James G. McDonald of Don Mills.

"I am looking forward to the time I can greet one of the ballplayers of Toronto's upcoming major league baseball club and call him what is to me the most inconceivable name that could have been picked.

"No thought could be more completely hilarious than the thought of saying to him, 'So, you're one of the Blue Jays.'"

Chapter 6

THE FIRST DAY Peter Bavasi arrived for work, he had a secretary in his employ, he had an accountant at his disposal—Paul Beeston—he had a box of files, and he had a desk containing two paper clips and nothing more. Nine months later—an appropriate gestation period, Bavasi likes to point out—the Toronto Blue Jays played their first game in the snowy confines of Exhibition Stadium. An entire organization had been built from scratch, and most of the people who would go on to make the team the most successful expansion franchise in professional sports history to that time had been hired.

It was a remarkable period, even more remarkable when you consider that the two most recent additions to baseball, in Tampa Bay and Arizona, had three years of lead time before they began play. To do it so quickly, and to get it right, required skill, luck, good judgment and a force of personality. Bavasi certainly had the latter, working hundred-hour weeks, micro-managing every aspect of the organization, making everyone's job his as well. He was the engine that drove the team towards Opening Day, even if at times it seemed others didn't share his sense of urgency. He recalls one board meeting early in the process, when the sheer volume of what had to be done appeared nearly impossible to complete. "If you don't get everything done," one of the board members said to Bavasi, "we have a great relationship with [American League president] Lee MacPhail—they'll just delay Opening Day."

A baseball man, of course, knew that was heresy, that Opening Day wasn't put off for war or pestilence or famine (labour disputes proved to be another matter), and that it certainly wouldn't be put off just because a new member of the fraternity couldn't get its act together. But then that was Bavasi's job, to explain this new culture to the foreigners, the outsiders, with their different sensibility.

It wasn't the first time the two solitudes would clash. There is some irony in the fact that though the Toronto Blue Jays would eventually thrive in the business of baseball, it wasn't because they learned to do everything the baseball way. The philosophies of those who in the beginning didn't know that Opening Day was sacrosanct eventually influenced the franchise more than the philosophies of the sport. These were two distinct business cultures meeting, two irreconcilable methods of personnel management.

Labatt, the dominant partner in the ownership triumvirate, was an old-style, paternalistic company with its roots in another era. The brewery, and that which had grown out of the brewery, was in many ways a profit-driven enterprise like any other. But there was also a rationale that went with the drive to make money, a combination of the moral and the pragmatic that eventually also came to characterize the way the Blue Jays were run.

When someone was hired by Labatt, it was implied that this was a job for life. The company would invest in its people, develop them—the way the bright young Don McDougall had been developed—expose them to different aspects of the business, and when the time came, allow them to play out their careers in dignified fashion. The employees in turn would be able to live with a measure of security, to voice opinions contrary to their bosses' if they thought something wasn't being done right, to add to the overall value of the organization. "We always tried to be very conscious of the individual," Peter Widdrington says. "We always tried to be very fair with the individual, and be a damned good employer. Not just a good employer but a damned good employer."

And in return, the theory goes, the good people you hire work their tails off, they remain loyal to the company, and they rise to their level of competence. It's a utopian vision, it didn't always work then (as McDougall would find out), and it worked less and less as the seventies turned into the very different eighties and nineties. But for most of those years, the soul of the old London brewery remained with the company, and as far as the Toronto Blue Jays were concerned, it was personified by Peter Hardy, who had run John Labatt Ltd. and who would become vice-chairman of the board for the baseball team.

All of that ran directly in the face of the prevailing baseball orthodoxy, which like Labatt had its roots in the nineteenth century but which grew out of a very different tradition. "Baseball over the years had a master–servant relationship—the idea that you do or you're gone," Hardy says. "It would be abusive. Scare tactics kept people in line. That was fine, I guess, when the twentieth century started out, but baseball was still living with that tradition. That's the way it's done, that's the way we'll continue to do it, and that was their method of operation."

In some ways, the development of the baseball business culture is entirely understandable, the natural end product of traditional capitalist principles. From the early part of the century, the owners of major league baseball franchises enjoyed a legal monopoly, exempt even from anti-trust laws. Their labour force was also their product—the players—and so the athletes obviously had value within the system. But by the same token, those players couldn't sell their services anywhere else. They were bound by contract and, more specifically, by the reserve clause in their contracts, to the team that signed them, usually as teenagers. From the day they committed to an organization until the day they retired from the game, they had virtually no leverage. They could be traded or sold without their permission. They could withhold services in return for a raise, but realistically that was an option open only to the game's greatest stars, and even they risked being blackballed for challenging the lords of the game.

Managers, coaches, scouts and everyone else employed by a baseball team were in the same position. And even as players won greater freedoms through the labour battles of the 1960s, 1970s, 1980s and 1990s, for many of those in the lower echelons of the organization, the situation remained much the same as it had half a century before. Managers were hired to be fired. They hired their coaches, who it was understood would lose their jobs when the manager lost his. Scouts and others employed to spot and develop talent could similarly gain or lose jobs at someone's pleasure.

What developed from that kind of insecure environment was a system based on personal loyalties and allegiances, a system of cronyism. Friends hired friends, rising young talents hired former mentors, favours were returned with jobs down the line, old debts were repaid. And with so many people beholden to those who controlled their paycheques, there was little place for dissent. Disagree with the guy at the top, and you'd have to move along or risk being fired without warning.

Bavasi was very much of that baseball tradition, schooled by his father, immersed in the management side of the game. His goal was to put bottoms in the seats, to produce an attractive balance sheet (appropriate, since even if Labatt's concerns were mainly selling beer, there was still Webster and his 45 percent stake to consider, as well as the bank), and if by chance he won a championship along the way, so be it. The ownership deferred to him because of his baseball background, and he in turn tried to present his ideas in a way that they would understand. In the end, the board would come to realize that there was a discrepancy between concept and reality, or at least that the way Bavasi tried to implement his ideas ran against their grain. But on paper, and in meetings, what he proposed to do with the club seemed logical, in tune with the accepted wisdom of the sport yet modern as well, traditional and innovative all at once.

"I wanted to have that club and that organization resemble something that I was designing inside my head," Bavasi says. "This was a chance to build from absolute scratch, a completely empty canvas. It was a wonderful experience."

Bavasi's best attempt to explain what was in his head to those who paid the bills were the Operating Plans, presented annually to the board in the middle of September, in anticipation of the end of the team's fiscal year, October 31. He began working on the first one in July 1977, halfway through the team's first season, and crammed like a college kid preparing for exams to get it done on time. It was a masterwork, everyone connected with the team agrees, a document explaining the vagaries of baseball in terms that would be familiar in any corporate environment. For the Blue Jays' directors, it was exactly what they desired. And for those who worked for the team and worked for Bavasi, well, it was something else altogether.

"These guys [the owners] wanted an operating plan," Beeston says. "Pete had us all mobilized to develop an operating plan—management by objectives—it was brilliant, an absolutely brilliant piece of work. It would have been a one-hundred-percenter or more in a university course. He did it by himself, he was working on three hours or four hours of sleep, everybody was feeding him information and he would write it. I remember it very well, because as soon as it was done, it was put on the shelf. He never intended to use it.

It was intended to get through the meeting. And here you had what amounted to a bible about how a sports franchise should work and what the Toronto Blue Jays should be doing. The fact of the matter was that it was never referred to again."

That said, the introduction to the original plan perfectly describes the baseball business environment in Toronto that first season, just as the subsequent plans show the team's evolution, the changes in the baseball world as a whole, and Bavasi's own attempts to remain one step ahead of the board.

The financial success of the Toronto Blue Jays during fiscal 1977 was not entirely expected and should not be misread as an indicator of the same results flowing in fiscal 1978. The most important element in the Blue Jays marketing mix last season—novelty—will be absent in 1978.

However the foundation for a financially successful franchise remains strong and the elements are:

    population density

    high personal disposable income of the trade area

    relative financial success of local major league teams

    baseball perceived by public as inexpensive "family
      entertainment"

    credibility and strength of ownership

    present good public and press relations

During 1977, because the Blue Jays did not have a sufficient pool of talented players from which to draw, the club's marketing concept was to "sell the sizzle and not the steak." With the assistance of extremely generous media coverage the club sold the novel experience of Major League Baseball at prices which everyone could afford. With an eye on the family entertainment market, the club merchandised the positive image of Major League Baseball in general, the visiting star players in particular, and (until some of them became established) the Blue Jay players hardly at all. A strong media advertising campaign coupled with the widespread distribution and sale of Blue Jays merchandise aimed at the youth market helped establish the Club's name and logo throughout the marketplace. Fans coming to Exhibition Stadium were treated to many giveaway promotions and in-park happenings in addition to the baseball games. This strategy was conceived in order to reduce the attention which might have otherwise been given to the bad field performance of the Club.

However, beginning in the 1978 season, the quality of the product on the field will come under closer scrutiny by the media and public, and while continuing to sell the sizzle and offering the in-park fan something more than just the baseball game, management recognizes that winning ballgames is the key to immediate and long-term attendance success.

Therefore, the financial commitment of the Club to player acquisition and development must be primary in budgeting considerations at all times. If the ballclub is competitive on the field, and a solid marketing and merchandising plan is continued, consistently high attendance and good profitability should follow. Fan interest will not be sustained if the Club does not show signs of gradual improvement in 1978 and significant improvement in seasons thereafter. A total commitment, financial and philosophical, to player acquisition and development by ownership and management is essential to the immediate and long-term financial success of the Blue Jays.

Operating Philosophy
- win ballgames
- provide ownership with a reasonable return on investment
- operate in such a manner as to be consistent with the standards and high public image of the ownership entities.

BUT THERE IS another paper trail as well. Everybody who worked in the Blue Jays' front office in those early days under Bavasi has a story to tell, of his mercurial personality, of his good days and bad days, his sudden furies and generous gestures, of his need to be at the centre of everything: *l'équipe, c'est moi.* Whether it was selecting a spring training site (Bavasi cut the deal to play in sleepy Dunedin, Florida, with mayor Cecil Englebert, sketching out the details on a paper napkin) or the colour of the typewriter ribbons in the office, it was a Peter Bavasi Production. "The problem was that Pete was not a delegator," Beeston says. "The job was not too big for him but it was too big for his style. He could have come in and not delegated to a mature operation. Because everything was there. But there were so many decisions that had to be made here that you had to delegate. Whether it was what type of furniture we were going to have in the office or what our letterhead was going to look like. The little things, it was ridiculous." The evidence bears that out. From the beginning, the memos—some of them directly from Bavasi, some of them sent with the imprimatur of intermediaries like Beeston, or the team's first director of operations, Terry Barthelmas—which became enshrined as team policy, suggest a rather difficult place to work, and a one-man show.

Jan 10/77
To Paul Beeston
From Peter Bavasi

I would like to see all invoices and billings of every nature before they are paid

Jan 13/77
To Paul Beeston
From Peter Bavasi

Please put out a memo to every employee indicating that our office will open at precisely 9 AM every morning. This goes for EVERYBODY

Jan 17/77
To Paul Beeston
From Peter Bavasi

Please post a notice on both the xerox machine and the postage meter that they are not to be used for personal mail or copying under any circumstances
Thank you

Jan 18/77
To Howie Starkman
From Peter Bavasi

In Dunedin prior to the beginning of the exhibition season you will have a number of requests from people who are watching our workouts. Please see that the girl in the spring training offices is supplied with a number of press radio and television guides which you will sell for two dollars per copy. Please do not print up a special roster for free distribution to anyone. Sell the press guide instead.

Jan 24/77
To Terry Barthelmas
From Peter Bavasi
Subject: Typewriter Ribbon

We should probably begin phasing out the black typewriter ribbon now being used by all departments and replace it with blue ribbon for use on all typewriters. Perhaps Millie can arrange for the return of any black ribbon now in stock and order blue typewriter ribbon from now on.
cc Paul Beeston

Jan 27/77
To Paul Beeston
From Peter Bavasi
Subject: Invoice routing

In addition to all outside invoices and statements which you have been sending my way prior to payment, I would like to see all internal requests for payment such as expense accounts, player bonus requests from the player personnel dept, and all other internal requests for payment made to you from various dept heads

Feb 1/77
To Terry Barthelmas
From Peter Bavasi
Subject: Long distance

At your convenience, perhaps you could lay out a plan whereby we have some strict controls on accounting for long distance phone calls

Feb 14/77
To All Staff

From Terry Barthelmas
Subject: Coffee

For your information we have calculated that we are spending approximately $200 per month for coffee for all staff personnel. If you look at this cost on an annual basis you will find that we will spend in the neighbourhood of $3000 which is shocking to say the least. This is for coffee only, and does not include sugar, cups, or any other necessary items. This is a benefit that the company is providing at this time. However, as you can imagine, we may have to look into the costs of this benefit to determine whether the company can provide the coffee for all staff personnel.

In order for us to continue with this benefit it is necessary for all staff personnel to try to make sure that the coffee is not wasted in any manner.

It may come to a situation where it will be necessary for us to ask all staff members to help share the cost of the coffee.

We appreciate your cooperation concerning this matter. Thank you.

Feb 28/77
To All Staff
From Terry Barthelmas

Now that we're basically set up in our administrative offices, I would like everyone to turn their office lights off when leaving the offices at night. If by chance you are the last person leaving please turn out all the hall lights.

Apr 6/77
To All Staff
From Peter Bavasi
Subject: Cocktails At Lunch

I am not a teetotaller, but effective immediately anyone on the staff of the Blue Jays should not be consuming any alcoholic beverages—even if it is only a beer—at any time during the working day (including lunch and those hours that the game is in progress).

There are common sense rules for this policy, most importantly the adverse effect upon our customers should they smell the aroma of alcohol on anyone connected with the Blue Jays.

This policy will be one of the most strictly enforced of any that we have.

Thank you for your cooperation in this matter

Peter Bavasi

P.S. Of course the co will continue to supply complimentary beer in the lounge area when all of the work is done each evening.

April 13/77
To Ken Carson
From Peter Bavasi
Re Team Physicians

My experience has been that when team physicians are too available to the players artificial injuries and illnesses crop up—especially among those players who may not be playing well at the time. Therefore our doctors may want to consider visiting the clubhouse and training room only upon your request or the request of the visiting trainer....

Apr 13/77
From Terry Barthelmas
To All Staff

Effective with the next homestand Apr 22, all staff members who are required to work the day of the game will be required to wear their staff blazer.

Jan 6/78
To All Staff
From Paul Beeston

We are now a mere three months away from opening day and halfway through what could be termed the off season. I believe it is imperative that we return to our former policy of commencing work promptly at 9 AM and observe the one hour lunch rule.

◆ MEANWHILE, AS BAVASI tended to the administration, the baseball side of the organization, operating with a degree of autonomy, began to take shape under Gillick. On October 16, 1976, Hartsfield began filling out his coaching staff, hiring Don Leppert and Harry

Warner. Bobby Prentice was also brought on board to scout out of Toronto. Next came hitting instructor Bobby Doerr, out of baseball since 1969, once a coach with Dick Williams with the old Toronto Maple Leafs, and pitching coach Bob Miller, who had worked with Hartsfield in Hawaii.

Three days later, the Jays announced the signing of four more scouts: Duane Larson, from the San Diego organization, John McLaren from Houston, and a couple of real veterans, Al LaMacchia, who had worked for the Milwaukee organization, and Bobby Mattick, a player with the Cubs and Cincinnati in the 1930s and 1940s, a scout for Cincinnati, Milwaukee, Seattle and Montreal, among others. Mattick and LaMacchia had actually been hired by Gillick before Hartsfield's appointment. Hartsfield was obviously Bavasi's, and not Gillick's, choice for the job. But it would be Gillick who would have a free hand to build the baseball operation, who would have to come up with the talent to fill out the 1977 roster and, more importantly, who would come up with the talent that might win a pennant long after Roy Hartsfield was gone.

Their primary building block was the expansion draft, the sole method of stocking the Toronto and Seattle teams with something approximating major league talent, since the new teams were prohibited from entering the newly active free agent market that first year. Each of the twelve American League teams could protect fifteen players of their forty-man roster. Each time they lost a player, they could add three more to the protected list. Only players who had signed their first professional contract before December 1, 1974, were eligible, and those who had played ten years in the big leagues, five with the same team, were excluded—as were those with no-trade clauses in their contracts.

That still left some interesting players potentially available: Lou Piniella, Sparky Lyle, Oscar Gamble, Boog Powell, Ray Fosse, Alex Johnson, Rico Petrocelli, Paul Blair, Bernie Carbo, Brooks Robinson—stars with big contracts near the end of the road. (In addition, there were just two Canadians eligible to be drafted: Dave Pagan, a pitcher with the Orioles, and Dave McKay, an infielder with Minnesota.) But while the team might gamble on one or two of those for the sake of name recognition—Bavasi figuring that someone with marquee value would help sell a few seats—what they really wanted were players not with a past, but with a future. Gillick said that it was imperative that the first six or seven players chosen would be able to start for the Toronto Blue Jays in 1977. After that, they could take some chances.

"We felt that we had a three- or four-year honeymoon here," Gillick says. "Our goal was just to try to accumulate as many young players as we could over that period of time and try to develop those players. We felt that there was going to be a day of reckoning four years down the line. That's kind of been the history. All of a sudden people want results."

The draft took place on November 4. In the first round, with their first pick, Toronto selected Bob Bailor, a twenty-five-year-old shortstop and seven-year minor-leaguer who had hit well at Triple A, but hadn't made much of an impression during two brief stints with the Baltimore Orioles.

Bailor was out turkey hunting when the news arrived. "My dad was standing on the porch and was hollering before I got there," he said. "I'm thrilled. I've been to Niagara Falls a couple of times, but that's it.... It's been quite a day. We got three turkeys for Thanksgiving and I get home to find out I'm the first pick in Toronto."

The other picks followed: in the first round Jerry Garvin, Jim Clancy and Butch Edge, twenty-year-old pitchers from the Minnesota, Texas and Milwaukee organizations respectively, along with outfielder Gary Woods from Oakland, and thirty-seven-year-old Rico Carty, in the twilight of a great career, serving as a designated hitter for the Cleveland Indians.

The second round brought Al Fitzmorris, a thirty-year-old pitcher from the Royals; Alvis Woods, a twenty-three-year-old outfielder from Minnesota; pitchers Michael Darr (Baltimore), Pete Vuckovich (Chicago) and Jeff Byrd (Texas); and outfielder Steve Bowling from the Brewers. Fitzmorris was traded immediately to Cleveland for catcher Alan Ashby and infielder Doug Howard.

The big names in round three were veteran pitcher Bill Singer, who had split the 1976 season between Texas and Minnesota, and shortstop Jim Mason, who had just finished playing in the World Series with the New York Yankees. "That was Peter's idea," Gillick says. "He said we had to have some recognizable names." Also selected in this round were pitcher Dennis DeBarr, first baseman Doug Ault, catcher Ernie Whitt and infielder Steve Weathers.

Subsequent rounds brought (in order of selection) infielder Steve Staggs, pitcher Steve Hargan, infielder Garth Iorg, pitcher Dave Lemanczyk, pitcher Larry Anderson, pitcher Jesse Jefferson, infielder Dave McKay, pitcher Tom Bruno, outfielder Otto Velez, pitcher Mike Willis, outfielder Sam Ewing and pitcher Leon Hooten.

All in all, it wasn't the greatest collection of talent. "We didn't get too much out of it," Gillick says. "Though we got a few guys who ended up hanging around for a while." But for those selected, expansion team or no expansion team, foreign country or no foreign country, it was a dream fulfilled, an opportunity that most felt they'd never get.

"The whole thing is so surprising to me," Ashby said. "I don't know what to say. Only time I was in Canada was to Windsor."

"I think getting a chance to bat regularly will help restore my confidence," said Mason, who had hit a home run for the Yankees in the 1976 World Series.

"Heck, a few years ago, no one wanted to buy me," said the thirty-four-year-old journeyman Hargan. "Now Toronto thinks I'm worth $175,000. That's progress. I must be improving."

"This could be the opportunity of a lifetime for me," said Vuckovich, who had already earned a reputation in the game as a flake, a non-conformist.

"Maybe with the Blue Jays I'll make the majors quicker than I would have with the Rangers," Clancy said.

"I think Roy is a great man," said Ault, "and I'm happy to be playing for him in Toronto."

"How close is hunting and fishing to Toronto?" wondered Bruno.

"I'm so excited I can hardly talk," Weathers said. "It's wonderful to have somebody believe in your ability to play ball.... All I hope is that I'm good enough to make the Blue Jays."

"Say," wondered DeBarr, "how cold does it get there anyhow?"

"What a week," said Whitt. "My wife had our first child—a little girl—and now I've been drafted."

Chapter 7

S NOW DID NOT flatter Exhibition Stadium even as it fell gently on Opening Day. The makeshift ball yard, cobbled together from the old CNE grandstand and a new, formed concrete section that hugged the baseball baselines, wasn't warm and inviting at the best of times. But turn down the temperature, turn up the wind, and it seemed all the more desolate—never mind the fact that the seats in the new grandstand were made of aluminum, which perfectly transferred cold right up the spines of the spectators. Except for those located between first and third base, they didn't face the field at the right angle, either, leaving fans to crane their necks left or right to see that action. And what passed for the bleachers, the huge covered grandstand, extended on from the left-field foul pole to a point more than fifty yards from the furthest reaches of the centre field fence. Wrigley Field it wasn't.

Many beyond the 44,649 in attendance on the Opening Day of opening days would later claim to have been there, to have been a part of history, and to have enjoyed every crazy minute of it. But on April 7, 1977, welcoming the Blue Jays and major league baseball to Toronto for the first time, how many would just as soon come back a day later, when it might seem a bit more like spring had arrived? To add insult to injury, hundreds of those with tickets wound up missing the first pitch, courtesy of a hellish traffic jam, a taste of things to come.

These nascent Blue Jays had first come together in Dunedin, Florida, a sleepy retirement town on the Gulf Coast just across the causeway from Tampa. The local burghers there had travelled to Toronto and sold Bavasi on the place, sold him on its charms and its potential. "They sold him a bill of goods," Gillick says. The stadium and clubhouse were a mess that first year, but the deal held fast and eventually things got better.

"For the only time in the history of the Blue Jays," Hartsfield said to his charges in his camp-opening address, "there are 25 jobs on the team and they're all open. No one is assured of a job. So if you want a job, you want to be one of those 25, all you have to do is go out and be better than somebody else. It's that simple. No one is going to force you. No one is going to beg you. No one is going to kick you. If you don't want it, you aren't going to get it."

That spring, the media attention was unprecedented by Toronto standards, with the team issuing more than two hundred press credentials. So intense was the coverage that Harold Ballard, owner of the hockey Maple Leafs and lover of headlines, along with his frequent companion King Clancy, travelled to Florida just to see what all the excitement was about. The Jays beat the New York Mets in their first exhibition game. They beat the Montreal Expos the first two times the Canadian rivals played. And they beat a reasonable facsimile of the world champion Cincinnati Reds, with only one regular starter missing from their Grapefruit League starting line-up.

BY THE TIME the Jays reached Toronto to open the season against the Chicago White Sox, a twenty-five-man roster had been culled from draft picks and castoffs left available to the expansion team. Of those, there was only one marquee name, Bill Singer, Bavasi's choice in the expansion draft, and one other familiar veteran, Ron Fairly, who had played for the Expos. Even Singer might not have made the trip if Gillick had had his way. His former employers, the Yankees, were looking for some veteran pitching help, and offered a promising kid in return for Singer. "I knew Billy Martin wanted some veteran players and I knew he didn't like [Ron] Guidry—because I came from over there," Gillick says. But Bavasi would have none of it. "He's the only recognizable guy we've got, the only guy we can market," he said, exercising absolute veto power on the baseball side for the only time during his tenure. It was not Bavasi's finest moment.

Singer, naturally, was given the Opening Day start, though until they removed the tarp from the infield—providing a nice contrasting touch of AstroTurf green amidst all the white—it seemed unlikely he'd get his chance. The umpiring crew, wearing the burgundy jackets that were then the official American League uniform, awaited word from Bavasi to go ahead or to call it a day. Once given the okay, the game would be in the hands of crew chief Nestor Chylak, beginning his twenty-fourth season in big league ball. Umpiring with him that day were Ed Brinkman, with two great balls of fuzzy black hair squeezing out from under either side of his cap; Rich Garcia (who later became Cito Gaston's chief tormentor), seeing the cold white stuff for the first time in a life lived entirely in warmer climes; and Steve Palermo, umpiring his first major league game and looking perhaps sixteen years old (he was actually twenty-seven).

"You've got some beautiful people out here to watch the ball game, and I'm not saying that we're going to go under any adverse conditions," Chylak said. "But if we get started, we're sure going to try and finish it."

"I'm looking for a lot of snow," Garcia said. "I want to make a snowball and throw it at somebody."

Finally came the word from Bavasi to play ball, the kind of decision that would become a franchise trademark until they moved under the Dome. Not giving in to the elements—and not giving out rainchecks—became the Blue Jay way.

Quickly, attempts were made to squeeze in the pre-game festivities, lest anyone—especially the weather gods—change their mind. While they squeegee-ed the last snow off the infield, the 48th Highlanders marched to the outfield and played "The Star-Spangled Banner." Next, Anne Murray came out wearing a red parka, to sing "O Canada." She did it quickly, which everyone appreciated.

And all the while, the fans chanted, "We want beer." For this was not only the worst stadium in major league baseball, but the only dry stadium in major league baseball—Toronto still being Toronto the Good.

Bob McCown, the public address announcer, called out the unfamiliar names as the Jays took the field: Doug Ault at first, Pedro Garcia at second, Dave McKay, the only Canadian on the roster, at third, Hector Torres at shortstop, Steve Bowling in right field, Gary Woods in centre, John Scott—who played for Roy Hartsfield in Hawaii—in left field, Rick Cerone behind the plate, and Singer on the mound. The designated hitter, formerly of the New York Yankees, was Otto Velez.

Things started badly for Singer, who was especially bothered by the cold. Facing lead-off hitter Ralph Garr, he threw the first pitch in Blue Jay history, a high fastball for a called strike. But from an 0–2 count, Garr battled back to 3–2, finally drawing a walk. Shortstop Alan Bannister followed. He hit a harmless flyball out, but not before Garr stole second, then advanced to third when catcher Rick Cerone's throw skipped into centre field. Jorge Orta, a future Jay, hitting third, lofted a sacrifice fly to centre, which allowed Garr to score easily with the first run in stadium history. Richie Zisk followed close behind with the second, smashing a high fastball over the wall in straight-away centre field: the stadium's first homer, and a 2–0 Chicago lead.

A single and a walk brought the first grumbles from the crowd and the first visit to the mound from Roy Hartsfield. Jerry Johnson got up in the bullpen. But then Singer convinced Eric Soderholm to hit into a fielder's choice, shortstop to second, and a huge cheer erupted as the half inning ended.

How new was baseball to Toronto? As the next inning began, Don Chevrier—working with colour man Whitey Ford, who was subbing for the otherwise engaged Tony Kubek—informed his CBC audience that Cerone had been charged with an error. Not for the errant throw to second, but for letting a pitch skip by him with no one on base. Perhaps someone called to correct him, but it's unlikely. (That first season, the Jays appeared on television just sixteen times.)

Scott, earning his place in history, took a called strike on the first pitch to a Blue Jay, and eventually swung through strike three from Chicago starter Ken Brett. Torres followed and struck out as well. Then Doug Ault stepped to the plate. A twenty-seven-year-old career minor leaguer with only nine games of major league experience, the tall Texan had been the Jays' sixteenth pick in the expansion draft.

On a 1–1 pitch, he lined an inside slider from Brett deep to left, over the outfield fence, into the football stands masquerading as bleachers. The first hit, the first run, the real beginning. Two–one Chicago. It was 4–1 by the time the Jays came to bat again in the bottom of the second, Singer still having trouble getting anyone out. The Jays scraped out another run—Gary Woods bunted for a single, stole second, and scored on a single by Garcia.

In the crowd were familiar faces: Paul Godfrey, with his son sitting on his lap; Foster Hewitt, who called the Leafs' playoff game with the Pittsburgh Penguins later that night; David Crombie, Toronto's tiny perfect mayor; and Murray, who looked frozen but happy: "We're gonna take this game," she said.

In the Toronto third, Hector Torres led off with a single, bringing

Ault to bat. With the count 1–1, he again drove the pitch, this time a fastball outside, this time to the opposite way, down the right field line and over the temporary fence, where the ball bounced on the artificial turf. It was an alley that would become the favourite of every power hitter in the American League. "These fans are making heroes, batter by batter and pitch by pitch," Chevrier said, spinning a nice phrase to make up for his earlier gaffe. "Right now, Doug Ault heads that list." The game was tied at four. An inning later, the franchise enjoyed its first lead, McKay singling Garcia home from second.

Singer needed only to complete the next half inning to have a shot at the victory. But after striking out Chet Lemon, Brian Downing singled, Ralph Garr singled and Hartsfield headed for the mound. That day, the CBC had secured permission to mike the Blue Jays' skipper, though the only time it really worked was in capturing this one conversation between manager and pitcher.

"You've already overextended yourself," Hartsfield said. "I'd like you to get this win, but this win's important to all of us. You've done a good job."

Singer mumbled something about being able to continue.

"I know you can. But I'm going to get someone else. You've done a helluva job.... You'll have another start, pal."

With that, Singer handed over the ball and headed for the dugout, offering a tip of the cap and a sheepish grin in response to a standing ovation. His place in team history was secure, but in fact that game was the beginning and end of it for him. In July, he underwent back surgery that effectively ended his career. Singer was on the disabled list for Opening Day 1978 and back in California selling real estate by Opening Day 1979.

Reliever Jerry Johnson took over and recorded Chicago's final two outs in the fifth. In the bottom of the inning, Alvis Woods, pinch-hitting for Steve Bowling, homered to right, bringing Otto Velez in ahead of him. It was 7–4 Toronto, and the Jays had scored in every inning of their existence. The White Sox came back with a run in the sixth to narrow the score to 7–5, while overhead, a plane flew, dragging a banner: "Good Luck Jays! Now Give Us Beer, Bill," referring to Bill Davis, the premier of Ontario.

The score remained that way until the eighth. Pete Vuckovich made his Blue Jay debut to start the inning and struck out the first two batters he faced before giving up a walk and a single, then getting a ground ball to slip out of trouble. Ault, the mighty, singled in a run in the bottom of the inning, to make it 8–5, then another run was scored on a double play to make it 9–5. The crowd began to thin—another Toronto tradition born. The game had begun in three-degree temperatures, and it sure wasn't getting any warmer.

Three outs to go. Vuckovich retired Jorge Orta on a grounder back to the box. He struck out Zisk, Chicago's star of the day with four hits in five at-bats. Jim Spencer hit a line drive to left, which seemed like the finisher, except that Scott dropped the ball for a two-base error, one of the few hints of what expansion baseball would really be like. Then Oscar Gamble grounded out to short, and the celebration began. The undefeated Toronto Blue Jays.

Johnson was the winner of record. The next year, he was released during spring training and wound up working as a Hollywood stuntman. Vuckovich got the save. He was traded to St. Louis at the winter meetings in return for Tom Underwood, wound up in Milwaukee, and won the Cy Young Award in 1982 as a starter.

Still they were the bit players. That night the city had a new celebrity, the equal instantly of any Maple Leaf or Argonaut.

"Everybody was really up for this game," Ault said. "They really wanted to win. It was kind of a silent, quiet atmosphere. Everybody was really getting ready in their own way. There are a lot of people on this team that other major league teams didn't protect. I think everybody has a feeling that they want to show somebody something, and they want to win for Toronto.

"We're going to go out and play every game just like this. We have a lot of enthusiasm and everybody really wants to win. All we've been hearing all through spring training is how we're going to lose two-thirds of our games. Then they ask us how many of the other third we're going to win. We don't feel that way. We feel that we can win every day we go out, no matter what team we're playing."

Relegated to a back-up by the beginning of the 1978 season, Ault was back in the minors for good by 1979.

The skipper's story was in so many ways the same as his players'. He too was a career minor leaguer finally getting his taste of the bigs, his opportunity to show everyone who had passed him over, who had considered him unworthy, that he had the stuff. Roy Hartsfield would have enjoyed that first win immensely that day even if he had known his team would win only fifty-three more the entire season.

"I've been around this ball game for a long, long time," Hartsfield said. "Since I was named manager, I've been thinking about Opening Day.

"I'm a very happy man right now. We'll try our best every day."

In the distance, behind him, the few fans who hadn't yet walked off into the grey twilight could be heard chanting, "We're number one!"

THAT WAS THE show, that was putting a face with the name and the uniform. That was Pete Bavasi's sizzle. But what happened on the field that April afternoon was also a thing apart from the long-term business of building a contending baseball team. Those first Blue Jays, nearly all of them, including the manager and coaches, were caretakers, time-fillers, temporary heroes. When the tide turned, when the fans became demanding and sceptical and sophisticated, they would be distant memories, trivia answers.

While they were doing their best to entertain the new faithful at Exhibition Stadium, the franchise's three wise men were already laying the groundwork for what was to come. Pat Gillick, Bobby Mattick, Al LaMacchia—three distinct personalities, two different generations—were bound together by the game. Gillick is bright, so shy that he sometimes seems aloof, cryptic and straightforward all at once, sensitive to the point that he's easily moved to tears. Mattick, crusty, difficult, slow to trust, has mellowed only slightly in old age. LaMacchia, a natural charmer, a storyteller, is warm, open, always willing to believe the best of people. They shaped the franchise on the field, put together an all but unprecedented string of successes, turned a hastily assembled expansion team into a consistent winner and finally into a back-to-back World Series champion.

Pat Gillick grew up in southern California, his father a former pitcher in the Pacific Coast League who later served as sheriff of Butte County, his mother a former silent-movie actress. His parents split up when he was less than a year old, and Gillick grew up in a home with his mother, his maternal grandparents and a great-aunt. When Gillick was nine years old, his mother remarried and moved out; he stayed with his grandparents, attending military school, from grades four to eleven. His grandfather died when he was fourteen years old, leaving him in the care of his grandmother and great-aunt.

Gillick was both cerebral—graduating from Notre Dame High School in Sherman Oaks at the age of sixteen—and a gifted athlete, lettering in three sports, including football, where he played centre in front of quarterback Bobby Beathard, who later became well-known as an NFL general manager. He played on an NCAA championship baseball team at the University of Southern California and graduated from there at the age of twenty. Then he set out to become a major league pitcher, giving himself five years in the minors to make it. One season, in Class B ball, he went 11–2 with a 1.92 ERA. But as with so many other pitchers, an arm injury put an end to any hopes he had of playing in the major leagues. "I really wanted to be a player," Gillick says. "But it didn't happen. And so you've got to readjust your goals."

He had readjusted them quite completely, deciding to head back to USC and do a master's degree in business, covering his tuition costs by helping to coach the varsity team. But then, in 1963, an offer came to join the Houston Astros as assistant farm director under Eddie Robinson. "I kind of decided that if I was going to do it, I might as well do it now," Gillick says. "And if I didn't like it, I could always come back. So I ended up going there in '63. And I liked it."

Gillick spent ten years in the Astros' organization, working his way up to director of scouting. "They gave me responsibilities right off the bat," Gillick says. "It was kind of like on-the-job training. I kind of felt my way along. You kept an eye on what they wanted done and how they wanted you to do it." He became part of the scouting fraternity, knit together by life on the road, by nights spent sitting in small-town ball parks trying to see something others can't. It remains the part of the business closest to his heart.

"He was a guy that was always asking questions," LaMacchia remembers. "As a young man he came out into the field and he would always get near the older people and sit and ask questions.

Bits and pieces here and there. A lot of people kind of sloughed him off. I kind of took an interest in him. I knew he was aggressive. I befriended him early. And I think he never forgot it. He knew that I was sincere in how I treated him and how we talked. That's basically where our friendship started." Some of the other scouts, LaMacchia says, weren't quite so welcoming of the bright newcomer. "Some of them were insecure in what they were doing. They didn't want to share whatever they had with him for whatever reason. Didn't want him to know that they weren't that knowledgeable. I, on the other hand, would tell him, 'Don't push yourself on people. Sit there. Never use the word "I" around them because it's touchy with older scouts. Always say what do you think and go from there. You've got a better chance of getting the bees with some honey.' Around me that's just the way that he acted.

"His personality was basically the same as it is now. It's really tough to get to know Pat. Pat's not an easy guy to go and make friends with people.... Pat's basically a shy individual. But when you get to know Pat, you know what his reasons were for being as he is. Pat was unfortunate that he never had a father. He had his mother and grandparents.

"Still, there was something about Pat—he had an air as he walked that people didn't like maybe. I, on the other hand, saw it as a guy that was sure of himself. I said to myself, this guy's going somewhere. He's bright."

"He's very sensitive—extremely sensitive—towards the people he works with and who work for him," Bavasi says. "And he hates conflict. But he'll be very tough on a position he takes if he thinks he's right. When he's made up his mind on something, it's very tough to move him off that position. But that's the sign of a top-flight scout."

In 1974, Gillick was hired by the New York Yankees as co-ordinator of player development and scouting under general manager Gabe Paul. It was widely assumed that Gillick was the heir apparent, though in the George Steinbrenner era, orderly succession had never been a strong suit. "They told me I was going to be the next general manager of the club," Gillick says. "I said that's fine, put that in writing. They wouldn't put it in writing. I had worked for Gabe, and I knew he wasn't the kind of guy who would ever want to get out. They'd have to carry him out."

"That's what Steinbrenner would have you believe many years afterwards," says Bavasi. "Who knows who would have been the GM in New York? Ten years later, in retrospect, in hindsight—which is so clear—Steinbrenner would have you believe that he knew how great Pat was. But he didn't. Pat was just a jewel stashed somewhere within the Yankees' organization."

Bavasi had met Gillick only in passing before he hired him but, based on a recommendation from the Yankees' Tal Smith, who had worked with Gillick both in Houston and New York, he decided he was the right person to get the baseball franchise off the ground. He wasn't thinking of the long term—who knew what would transpire two or three seasons down the road, never mind eighteen—but only of the few short months available to put together something resembling a major league baseball organization.

"You needed somebody who was totally fearless, and who had a lot of determination and confidence—complete confidence—in his own abilities," Bavasi says.

"It's probably an easier situation than trying to renovate an organization that's already in place," Gillick says. "You don't have to clear out before you can start. You can start from scratch and hire the people that you want."

It was more than a year before Gillick moved permanently to Toronto. That first season, he kept his home in Georgia but rarely saw it, spending by his own account 270 days out of 365 on the road scouting talent. At first, the job was simply finding enough players to fill out the system, but later drafting and signing prospects became more important.

"That's his strength," Blue Jays' president Paul Beeston says. "Whether it be signing a John Olerud or working on Shawn Green and Shawn Green's family. It's what he can do better than anyone in baseball. No one is close to him. Forget the evaluation. It's about bringing his personality into play with the family so that they can understand that their kid is going to a good place. Dollars are part of it, but sometimes dollars don't mean anything if you've already got money. For instance, John Olerud had no intention of signing with us. He had none, zero. He was going back to Washington State. Pat worked on him and worked on him. He got to know John and John's father, John, and John's mother, Linda. They became disciples of Gillick's. And he still talks to them. He's got this uncanny memory. He remembers all the names."

GILLICK MET BOBBY Mattick for the first time in 1956. "He probably didn't remember," Gillick says. Of course Gillick does remember. He remembers names, places, phone numbers. "He was in Los Angeles, scouting for Cincinnati at the time. They had a team in a winter league in L.A. and I was playing for Baltimore's winter league team. I was around him and met him as a kid, when I was eighteen or nineteen years old."

Mattick had spent his entire life in and around baseball. His father, Chick, had played briefly in the majors with the White Sox and the Cardinals and then went on to own and operate minor league teams. Mattick himself signed his first professional contract in 1933. But three years later, he suffered a fractured skull when he was hit by a foul ball. He made it to the major leagues, but the injury left him with double vision, which needless to say seriously hampered his career.

"My last year was in Cincinnati in '42—when I had about six operations on my eye," Mattick says. "I talked to an old scout who played for the old Baltimore Orioles and scouted for years for the Cubs, Jack Doyle. He asked me, 'What do you want to do?' I said I wanted to manage. He advised me against managing. He said the thing to do is get in the front office or scout—you'll last longer. So I took his advice and went into scouting."

Mattick was out of the game altogether for a year, in 1943 when he was declared unfit to serve in the army because of his vision problems and wound up spending the year working in the shipyards. It would be the only year in the sixty-three since then that he wasn't employed in baseball. In 1944, Mattick ignored the old scout's advice and took a job managing in the Southern League. "Of course I was too ambitious," he says. "I expected a lot out of the ball players. At that level they didn't give it to you. But we did accomplish something. But I was a crazy guy at the time, I guess. I couldn't put up with imperfection. I didn't have any desire to manage after that season." By 1946, he had embarked on his true calling, searching for, discovering and evaluating baseball talent.

Among those he signed were Frank Robinson, Curt Flood, Vada Pinson, Tommy Harper, Mel Queen, Bobby Grich, Don Baylor, Dave Giusti, Rusty Staub, Darrell Porter and Sixto Lezcano. He accomplished that while bouncing from one organization to another, New York, Cincinnati, Chicago, back to Cincinnati, Houston, Cleveland, Baltimore, Seattle, Milwaukee and Montreal. "I don't know why guys did it, but I know why I did it," Mattick says of his career path. "I was kind of a rebel. I'd get fed up. My wife used to say, 'You'll never be happy until you own a club yourself.' Unfortunately, or fortunately, however you want to put it, I could always get a job. I guess I was a little cocky or something. I wouldn't put up with anything. When I got tired of something, I just moved on."

"He would move a lot because his personality was that if he didn't like somebody he would speak out, and then he was out of a job," says Al LaMacchia.

"He was one of those guys who sooner or later, he'd piss somebody off and get bounced, or tell somebody something that was the truth—but they didn't particularly like it," says Gillick. "At that time he had spurts where he'd be drinking, and when he got drinking he'd be a little bit nasty. So he bounced around quite a bit."

When the time came for Gillick to start building a scouting staff, Mattick just happened to be at one of those career crossroads with which he had become so familiar. "I bumped into him in the summer of 1976 and talked to him about the possibility of coming over when his contract was finished," Gillick says. "He decided to leave the Expos and come with us."

Al LaMacchia was and is a very different sort—outgoing, automatically friendly, a storyteller by nature. He and Gillick first crossed paths when Gillick was working for the Astros, and he was scouting for the Braves out of his home in San Antonio; they continued that association when Gillick moved to the Yankees.

There is a story LaMacchia tells to explain their close, father–son relationship. It speaks volumes as well about the art of hard sell/soft sell, which is nearly as important an ability for the scout as being able to recognize talent in the raw. LaMacchia, and later Gillick, excelled in taking a kid who might otherwise go to college to play football or basketball, and getting his name on a baseball contract.

On one of Gillick's visits to Texas while he was working for the Yankees, he overheard LaMacchia talking about a prospect named Willie Upshaw and asked if he might tag along to watch him work out. While Upshaw went through his paces, Gillick told LaMacchia that the Yankee scouts didn't think much of the player. But he kept watching. On draft day, LaMacchia figured the Braves could safely wait until the eighth or tenth round to select Upshaw. In the fifth, Gillick snapped him up for the Yankees.

Three weeks later, LaMacchia and his wife came home from church to find a note on their door, written on the back of a blank contract: "I forgot something at the motel. Will be right back. Pat."

"I said to my wife, put another pound of pasta on," LaMacchia says. "It looks like we're going to have Pat eat with us."

Gillick turned up for dinner and explained to LaMacchia that he was in town trying to sign Upshaw, who had seemed reluctant to commit to baseball. He was going to Upshaw's house that afternoon and wondered if LaMacchia might come along for moral support.

"On the way up I asked him had he discussed the fellow at the bowling alley. Willie was working for this guy who was an alumnus of Texas Lutheran and who was trying to get Willie to go to Texas Lutheran as a middle linebacker in football and a baseball scholarship," LaMacchia remembers. "I said, 'I've got to believe your trouble is the guy at the bowling alley where Willie works. But to make sure, we'll go to the coach's house.'"

They visited the high school coach, who confirmed LaMacchia's suspicions. Then they headed for the Upshaw residence.

"Mr. Upshaw sees me walk in and says I'm a little confused. He works for the Yankees and you work for the Braves. What are you doing here?

"I said, 'Mr. Upshaw, we in baseball try to help each other once in awhile. Because we'd hate to see a boy like Willie go into football at Texas Lutheran. Football is a very competitive game. I can see an offensive lineman or somebody really hurting him. I'd hate to see his baseball career go out the window.'

"He kind of understood that. So they begin to talk. And as he was talking, Willie was very shy. He kept his head down. He very rarely looked Pat in the eyes. So after about ten minutes of this I said,

'Willie, it bothers me a little bit that you don't look Mr. Gillick in the eye when he's talking to you. I know that your mom and dad have done a tremendous job raising you. They've brought you this far and they've done a great job with you. I don't think they'd like it much that you don't look Mr. Gillick in the eye when he's talking to you.'

"Then the father spoke up, and he said, 'That's right, Willie. We taught you better than that. When that man talks to you, you look him in the eye.' I said, 'And furthermore, you're so fortunate to be drafted by the Yankees and not the Braves. Because if you had been drafted by the Braves, I would not have offered you what he's offering you. And number two, he is the scouting and farm director of the Yankees, so he's the one who says release the boy if he gets to the point where he's not a prospect any more. I don't have that privilege with the Braves. You're very, very fortunate.'

"Mrs. Upshaw spoke up and said, 'Willie, sign the contract.'"

He did, and of course he would later become a member of the Toronto Blue Jays. LaMacchia signed on with Toronto just after Mattick in the late summer of 1976. Gillick had long before made one of those promises people make, that if he were ever in a position to do the hiring, perhaps the two of them could work together.

Soon after Gillick got the Toronto job, he headed for Texas. "All of a sudden Pat shows up in San Antonio," LaMacchia says. "He calls me and comes up to the house. He was in town to see a player and the player was Jim Clancy."

LaMacchia told Gillick that he didn't think the Rangers were going to protect Clancy in the expansion draft, and that he'd probably be a good prospect. Then Gillick asked him how things were with the Braves. He had been with the organization for sixteen years, but there were changes taking place. There was a new general manager, and he and LaMacchia weren't seeing eye to eye. Gillick offered to check things out. He came back with the news that LaMacchia's future with Atlanta was anything but secure.

"The next day we talked and the first thing you know, I said, 'I'll come with you,'" LaMacchia says. "I didn't know that he was going to have Mattick come too. After I said I was going to come he said, 'By the way, keep this under your hat, Bobby's coming.'"

Mattick was five years older than LaMacchia, and LaMacchia was fifteen years older than Gillick. Their personalities were distinct, and yet in many ways they were really three facets of the same character: the baseball man. "My wife one time said to me when the three of us first got together, 'You three guys are like three peas in a pod,'" LaMacchia says. "The only difference was our ages." All were go-getters, willing to put in long hours on the job. One's weaknesses were the others' strengths. The synergy there—like the synergy that developed later between Gillick and Paul Beeston—would lie at the heart of a successful baseball organization. It wasn't just the savvy, but the continuity: for two decades, the three men worked as one.

WHILE THEY BEGAN the process of building the Toronto Blue Jays of the 1980s, the Blue Jays of 1977 were struggling through their first season in major league baseball. Understandably, it wasn't pretty. But it was also no certainty that the owners of the team, neophytes in the game, would fully understand the nuances of building an expansion team from scratch.

To put the proper spin on things for the Blue Jays' board, Bavasi again used the operating plan. Gillick was given the task of translating the baseball part, a task he approached with very little enthusiasm. In a world where decisions are often based on seat-of-the-pants instinct, where one guy's dud is another guy's prospect, how to explain it like the selling of popcorn? And especially, how to put numbers with it, how to project wins in future years, how to say with certainty when the team would be competitive?

The first year was the simplest of the lot, with expectations low, with the talent base minimal, with the future uncertain. But still Gillick's information, as written by Bavasi, managed to make it sound like science:

"While the management of the Company is committed to building a strong farm system, it may not be until 1981 before the first minor league players are ready to perform capably for the major league Blue Jays. In fact, the progress being made by the farm system will not be readily apparent to the Toronto media and fans until these young players assemble together on the Toronto club and historically with expansion clubs the best minor league players arrive at the major league level at the same time.

"With regard to the 1978 forecast for artistic success by the Blue Jays, expectations should not be raised. It must be remembered that the established American League clubs in 1978 will be recovering from the expansion dilution of their rosters by means of their own fully-developed minor league players. Consequently, the won/loss record of the Blue Jays in 1978 may be comparable to what it was last season...."

The team would expand its farm system, look for minor and major league free agents, seek talent in unexpected places like Korea, Cuba and China, "where baseball is played extensively." By the end of 1978, it would have ninety-eight players under contract in the minor leagues.

"By trading, drafting and development, coupled with the added experience of players presently under contract at the major league level, the artistic performance objective for the Blue Jays in 1980 would be to play close to .500 baseball."

And what of the 1977 Blue Jays, currently carrying the hopes and aspirations of their wide-eyed fans?

"The consensus is that the following eight current Blue Jay players are major league prospects:

Bailor

Clancy

Howell

Cerone

Garvin

Byrd

Ashby

Darr

"The remaining players on the Blue Jays' roster will be disposed of or replaced if better players can be secured through trades, draft or waiver claims. Veterans Fairly, Torres and Rader are considered good major league stabilizers and will remain with the club unless trading them becomes more advantageous."

All the Blue Jays' major league coaches were polled as to which players on the roster they thought might be successful. Only one of them (not pitching coach Bob Miller) even mentioned Vuckovich, the future Cy Young Award winner, putting him seventh on his list.

So much for sure things. And so much for today's heroes.

Chapter 8

T HE 1978 SEASON was in many ways like the 1977 season, with a few more bells and whistles. There was Calendar Day, Jacket Day, Helmet Weekend, Italian Heritage Night, T-shirt Night, Autograph Night, Poster Night, Camera Day, Cap Day, a players vs. players' wives game, German Heritage Night, Country and Western Day, Halter Top Day, Back to School Day, Tuque Night, and Fan Appreciation Day. The Blue Jays were selling, and selling hard. Ominously, though, attendance dropped significantly—from 1,701,052 the year before to 1,562,585. Drawing more than a million-and-a-half fans was still more than a respectable number by baseball standards of the time, and it was especially respectable for a team of the Jays' modest abilities. For the owners, that amount of turnstile spinning represented a healthy operating profit on their investment. But the decrease also suggested that after a single season, the novelty of major league baseball in Toronto was already beginning to wear just a bit thin.

Anticipating such an occurrence before the season began, Bavasi had made an entirely characteristic move to restore his beloved sizzle. With Singer gone, the team again lacked a marquee player, a name the fans would likely pay to see, no matter how bad the rest of the club might be. John Mayberry, the power-hitting first baseman acquired in the spring, would partially do the trick, but they needed someone else as well. Not a Reggie Jackson, not anyone who cost a whole lot of money: what Bavasi required was bargain-basement celebrity.

Rico Carty seemed to fit the bill. Originally selected by the Jays in the expansion draft, the "Beeg Mon" had been greatly relieved to be dealt away from a bad team in a bad climate long before that first Opening Day. Now he was available again, clearly near the end of his career and without very many options. Because of those circumstances, the Jays could realistically make a bid to sign him. With Gillick handling the negotiations, the deal came together rather easily. A press conference was called at the Hotel Toronto, where Carty would put his signature on the dotted line. In the ballroom, a huge sign was erected that read "Welcome Back Rico." (That was a Bavasi touch.) The sign was then covered with brown butcher paper, to be dramatically pulled away when the star arrived. (Another Bavasi touch.) But fifteen minutes before his scheduled appearance, with the city's sports press assembled in giddy anticipation, Carty balked. Something had put him off, some little detail, and he wasn't going to budge—which sent Bavasi into a frenzy.

"Hold the butcher paper!" he hollered through the phone to one of his minions on the main floor. "The son of a bitch won't sign."

Understanding Carty's psyche, Gillick came up with a last-minute concession, a bonus of $10,000 that would kick in if Carty hit fifty home runs that season—which of course he wouldn't. "It was kind of an appeal to his pride," Gillick says. Carty signed. The butcher paper came down. And the team had a new poster boy. With Carty hitting twenty home runs, Mayberry hitting twenty-two and Jim Clancy winning ten games, the Jays as a team still won just five more games than they had in 1977, finishing at 59–102, a mere forty games off the pace.

"I was not accustomed to finishing last," Hartsfield says. "In the minor leagues, we won a few times. I'm human like everyone else. I like to win. I want to be on top. But you have to accept reality. When I took this job, I knew we were going to lose a lot more than we were going to win."

◆THE TRULY SIGNIFICANT baseball action was still happening elsewhere, in those far-flung locales where the Jays' scouting and development staff would discover and nurture the stars of a better future. Sometimes they were obvious: in their first crack at the June free agent draft in 1978, the Jays selected second and picked Lloyd Moseby, an outfielder from Oakland, California, whose prodigious athletic gifts were known to everyone in baseball. And sometimes they would turn up in unexpected places. That same year, one of the Jays' scouts, Don Welke, had spotted a centre fielder from California named David Stieb attending Southern Illinois University, and thought he might be a prospect. Gillick dispatched Mattick and LaMacchia to check him out. Two games were to be played that day on the SIU campus. Stieb played the outfield in the first.

"Stieb was a pretty good centre fielder," LaMacchia says. "He could run, throw. Go get the ball. But we didn't particularly like the way he hit." A freshman had started the game for SIU and had begun to falter in the fifth inning. To the surprise of LaMacchia and Mattick, the team's coach didn't go to the bullpen but instead summoned Stieb in from centre to pitch. "We thought, this is going to be a farce now," LaMacchia says. "We were totally relaxed. He starts to warm up. And finally he starts. Jesus man, you immediately saw that he had a feel for the mound—like he'd been pitching his whole life. And he was pitching pretty good. The next inning he went back out and, boy, we thought, this guy is something."

"They brought him in to pitch and he had this hellacious slider," Mattick remembers. "A hard slider plus a good arm. That's why he came on so quickly."

A scout from the Giants was in the park that day as well, equipped with a radar gun to clock the pitches. Just in case he got the right idea, LaMacchia said loudly enough so that everyone could hear: "That's just like an outfielder. Come back and see him tomorrow and he'll look atrocious."

The first game over, the scouts took a break, including Mattick, who went off in search of a Coke. LaMacchia passed up the invitation and instead went searching for Stieb, who was in the process of changing his uniform.

"Young man, have you ever pitched before?" he asked him.

"Nah. I've been piddling around. But they have some tired arms and they asked me to help. I'm a centre fielder. I'm going to be selected as an All American centre fielder in the NCAA."

"I have no doubt in my mind. You're a pretty good outfielder. But let's assume that you didn't hit."

"Don't worry about that. I'll hit."

("He wouldn't give me a chance to finish what I was going to say," LaMacchia remembers. "That's Stieb.")

"Now I'm going to ask you a question," LaMacchia said, pressing on. "Just relax a little bit. Don't answer me until you think about it a little bit. Let's assume that you're selected by a baseball club and they give you the opportunity to play the outfield. And you fail as a hitter. Would you then give it the maximum effort as a pitcher? Now think about it before you answer."

"I would have to be the one to say that I couldn't hit," Stieb replied.

"Fine. Now forget that you and I ever discussed this about pitching. If your coach sees us talking here now, don't mention to him what we discussed."

"Yeah, I won't tell anybody."

In the second game, while Stieb did absolutely nothing at the plate, LaMacchia talked to Mattick about his conversation. "To get him, we have to give him a chance to play centre. But I think he'll fail. There's not any doubt in my mind that he'll fail. And then we will make a pitcher out of him."

Stieb was signed and was sent to the Dunedin team of the Florida State League, where Denis Menke was the manager. Menke was given specific instructions as to how to handle him. Use him as a designated hitter, then as a pitcher, then as a designated hitter, then let him play centre for a day or two, DH him again, and then back to pitching. LaMacchia remembers, "After about twenty-five or thirty ball games, Stieb says to Denis Menke, 'Well, maybe that old guy knows what he's talking about. I guess maybe I'm a pitcher.'"

He went to the Instructional League that year to hone his craft. With Bavasi, Mattick and Gillick in the stands to watch one particular start, Stieb pitched five strong innings, only to get roughed up in the sixth. "I waited and then I followed him inside," LaMacchia remembers. "When he left I could see him, and you know how he'd get. He was sitting in the trainer's room and I could see that his eyes were kind of bloodshot." Stieb the cocky, strutting golden boy brimming with confidence was also Stieb, the self-critical competitor who was torn up inside every time he failed.

"Goddammit, give me five, man," LaMacchia said. "You were outstanding."

"What do you mean?" Stieb asked.

"That's part of baseball," LaMacchia told him. "For that five innings they didn't touch you. They didn't come close to touching you. They maybe left you out an inning too long. You're going to make a lot of money in this game—no doubt in my mind. I'm proud of you."

"Then I left him," LaMacchia remembers. "He never forgot that. Never did he ever forget that."

A year later, Dave Stieb would make the jump all the way from Class A ball to Triple A to the big leagues, faster than anyone could have imagined.

MEANWHILE, BACK IN Toronto, Bavasi continued to alternately charm people and drive them crazy, though with the exception of a few skirmishes with the fourth estate, most of the tensions remained pretty much confined within the Blue Jay headquarters at Exhibition Stadium.

Some in the press, though, did have a bead on Bavasi, especially Christie Blatchford, then a young columnist from the *Globe and Mail*; she was the first to report on the dissent in the Jays' front office even before the beginning of the first season. The organization had been embarrassed by several trivial but telling stories, all of them examples of Bavasi's obsessive micro-management. He insisted that all ushers stand with their hands over their hearts, American-style, during the national anthems. He sent a memo to employees suggesting they phone in, anonymously, as part of a poll conducted by the *Toronto Sun* on whether the team's policy on facial hair (it was *verboten*) was appropriate. They were to stack the results in the team's favour. When a fan in the stands was hit by a foul ball, Bavasi verbally assaulted the reporter (the *Sun*'s Paul Palango) who dared go to the stadium's medical clinic to see if the fan was all right. Within the office, Bavasi referred to Toronto reporters, derisively, as "the expansion press."

Once, the local chapter chairman of the Baseball Writers Association of America, Neil MacCarl of the *Toronto Star*, formally complained to Bavasi because the CBC was using a reporter in the dugout and in the bullpen during games. If the TV guys could be there, MacCarl said, the newspaper guys should be represented as well.

Bavasi fired off one of his internal memos, which showed exactly how he felt about the complainants and the complaint.

Enclosed is a letter I received from the chairman of the Toronto chapter of the BBWA. It is self explanatory. The answer to this request is of course, no. The reasons are many, not least of which is that the CBC pays us handsomely for the exclusive right to telecast our games and we have encouraged them to use interesting and creative techniques. I have told MacCarl that I will look into this matter. My intention is to do absolutely nothing—except to continue to cooperate with the CBC, which I urge you to do also.

It is possible that the issue will ultimately wind up in the hands of the commissioner. If it does we will let him fight it out with the CBC. He is sure to be a loser, since the last thing a Canadian crown corporation wants to do is bend to some arbitrary decision made by an interfering outsider.

Please destroy this memo after you've read it.

ASIDE FROM THOSE isolated stories, fans didn't notice the turmoil. All they saw of Bavasi was the big, young, handsome, outgoing guy. They noticed the razzmatazz at the stadium, the very modern look of the club—at least compared to its competition in the city, the tradition-bound Maple Leafs of the NHL and the Argonauts of the CFL. If Hartsfield could play the role of baseball incarnate in the traditional sense, all sun-made wrinkles and country wisdom, Bavasi was both of the sport and of the moment.

In the board room, the club's directors continued to defer to the man whom they had named the team's president in November 1977—a move that made official what was already the case and that also made it clear that Gillick was the club's real general manager, in charge of the baseball part of the operation. Every once in a while, one of the people from Labatt might hear stories about some Bavasi sin or another, or they might read newspaper reports of his indiscretions. But for the first years, the board remained onside, deferring to Bavasi because he knew baseball, and they didn't. (Bavasi says that, in fact, the board only once turned down one of his ideas—when he wanted to buy a motel near the club's spring training site in Dunedin, use it to house players during the Grapefruit League season, and the rest of the year operate it for profit as the Blue Jay Motel.)

"I really almost never saw the downside of Bavasi," says Herb Solway, who sat with the board from the beginning. "All that I know about the downside of Bavasi is second-hand. The pluses were that he had tremendous energy, he was smart, he knew what to do to build an organization. Remember he hired Pat Gillick and he put some pretty good people in place. He knew for a while how to handle people. He was great the way he dealt with the board. He had a different gift for the board at every board meeting. A sweater with the Blue Jay crest. An autographed ball. He'd always have something. They'd come to me right at the start of the meeting and they'd have this gift. [A guy] could be worth $400 million but he's got this autographed baseball or this sweater with the Blue Jays' crest, and he was eating out of Bavasi's hand. They wouldn't ask him the tough questions. But Bavasi had this ability, which I think in the long run was a mistake, that he had an answer for everything. And there was never a problem at the board meetings. You might sit there knowing there was a problem and you'd hear Bavasi talk about it and there was no problem. He was very articulate. He never had a problem at a board level, ever. Every meeting just went swimmingly. And so on the surface of it, when there were all sorts of problems in the office, the board never heard of them. They never got to the board. I found in business that if you're dealing with somebody where nothing is a problem, you know that there's more to it than that. Because there are problems with any situation."

In hindsight, at least, Peter Widdrington, who became the club's chairman, puts a slightly different spin on those times. "He didn't charm us. There wasn't anybody on the board who didn't see through Peter pretty well. But they did respect the fact that he had good baseball credentials. And he had good contacts. He knew the game well. So the decision was, do we let this guy go, and leave the thing in the hands of three people—Peter Hardy, Beeston and Gillick? There was no problem with Gillick. But Beeston didn't have much of a background at that point, and Peter had none. And remember, we didn't still have a helluva lot to lose. It's not like we had a dynasty that was going to collapse overnight."

Only within the Blue Jays' office was the dark side of the boss on full display. "Pete's one of those Jekyll and Hyde type of guys," Gillick says. "A very smart guy, very quick, an ideas type of guy, good marketer. Down deep a pretty good person. But he was one of those guys where you never know what to expect out of him. You'd leave one night, everything was great. You'd come in the next morning and all hell was breaking loose. You never knew what to expect from this guy. He tried to deal with people with compassion. But I don't know if he really knew how to do it. He in his own mind had to prove to his dad that he could make it on his own. I really think that's what was in the back of his mind. I think Peter wanted to prove to himself and to his parents that he could make it on his own."

"He committed himself to the ball club," Beeston says of Bavasi. "The problem was he didn't trust anybody. It was his way or no way. That was it. But on the other hand, he didn't like people to dislike him. As much as he did and created it, he didn't like people to dislike him. He wanted to be liked, he wanted to be loved. He wanted to be respected. He wanted all of those things. I don't think in his own mind he knew who he was reporting to in life. Forget about business. Was he reporting to his father, was he reporting to his mother, was he reporting to his family, [his wife] Judy and the kids, was he reporting to God? I'm not so sure he ever had that straight. Until he had that straight, he couldn't do it."

It was as though Bavasi couldn't help himself, as though he was going a hundred miles an hour in ten different directions at once, while the rest of the world was cruising along comfortably at fifty. Both Gillick and Gord Kirke remember walking into Bavasi's office to find him sitting on the floor, cross-legged, in a corner, meditating, trying to focus himself, to calm himself down.

Beeston was one of the first to reach his limit. He had had his fill of working for Bavasi, wasn't wed to baseball in any case, and was looking for a change. McDougall, by then a good friend, offered him a position with the Labatt brewery, overseeing its operations in Saskatchewan. The understanding was that it would be a start, the beginning of a career path that would eventually lead Beeston back to Toronto or the head office in London and the security of what could be a lifelong employer. He was just thirty-four years old, young enough to change directions. And with McDougall still apparently on the ascendancy within the organization, he would have a protector in a high place who wouldn't forget that he was out selling beer on the prairies.

"I was getting out of here," Beeston says. "I was going out west to Saskatchewan to work for the brewery. I'd had enough of it. I had to get out of here. There was no question."

It was a done deal, approved by the Labatt board. Beeston had talked to his family about the decision, and they had decided to make the move. He told Bavasi that he was leaving and then went to Howard Webster to explain why he was quitting the ball club. "I lied all the way through," Beeston says. "I talked about how this is a great organization, all that stuff, about how I wanted to spend more time with my family and all that."

But while he was preparing for his departure, two events took place that caused him to have a change of heart. The first was the sale of Brascan, the company that controlled Labatt, to Edper, the corporate arm of the Bronfman family. The second was the firing of Don McDougall as the president of the brewery.

"McDougall was out in PEI," Beeston remembers. "He thought he was coming back to get a promotion. Instead he got fired." Beeston, Bavasi and Gillick climbed into a car with a couple of cases of beer—Heineken, for the symbolic value—and headed for McDougall's house in London to commiserate.

"Some of us were more sincere than others," Beeston says. "But give Pete credit. He didn't have to go and he did."

Whether or not that was the case, the truth was that McDougall was gone, and suddenly Beeston's escape wasn't quite so simple. "The Edper thing I could live with. I can deal with ownership problems. And I can deal with management problems. But I ain't going with both. What if I get out there and I get buried? My idea wasn't to be out there forever. You could get forgotten out there. And who was going to run the brewery?"

So Beeston beat a hasty retreat. He went to Peter Hardy, told him that he wouldn't be able to take the job, and then went to Bavasi, who offered him his old job back immediately.

Around the same time, Gillick also flirted with leaving the organization. "Peter was the kind of guy that you had to sell on stuff," he says of the frustrations of working with Bavasi. "You knew if you pounded on him enough that he would come around and see your way. I think he played it sort of as a game. It would be no, no, no, and then maybe, and finally, that's the greatest deal I ever heard. He in his own mind would throw up all these barriers to see how hard you'd fight to get the guy. Well, that stuff gets old after a while."

Bill Lucas, the general manager of the Atlanta Braves, had died, and the team's owner, Ted Turner, tried to talk Gillick into becoming his replacement. There were all kinds of financial inducements, including stock options, that with the phenomenal growth of Turner's media empire might have eventually made Gillick a wealthy man. "I told Turner to let me think it over," Gillick says. "So I thought it over and came back—it was a Friday night. I called him. He has kind of a plantation over in South Carolina. I said, 'I think I'm going to stay here.' He said, 'Why would you do that?' I said, 'They gave me a break over here, I think we're starting to see some light. I'm going to stick it out.' He said, 'I could see that if it was an American club. But you being an American and that's a Canadian club, I can't understand that.' I said, 'I don't really agree with that. It's just baseball.'"

◆ AND SO BLUE Jay business continued, albeit with plenty of tension in the air. "Everything that we did, there's a reason for it," Bavasi says. "Don't be distracted by the style, the harsh, rigid, overbearing, arrogant, ruthless style that I employed to advance these policies. That's a separate issue. That's a style issue. From a substance point of view, every single thing that was done, and that Pat did, had a purpose that would advance the growth of the company. Everything."

Bavasi's marketing theories were based on the notion that baseball was familiar and foreign all at once. "It was not as if we were putting roller hockey in the middle of Saudi Arabia. But there was also the attraction of owning something uniquely American, a piece of the rock. That's why we put the maple leaf in the logo." (There remains a continuing debate about whether the maple leaf was Bavasi's idea, and about whether he wanted to keep it or discard it after the first season.)

"You had to try to understand the cultural aspects and then you approached decisions, and that's what I tried to do on every front," Bavasi says. He encouraged his staff to listen to alternative radio stations, to read alternative magazines, in an attempt to tap into the wants and needs of the youth market. He encouraged them to attempt to sell to the city's large, and largely untapped by professional sports, ethnic communities. At one point, he even suggested a marketing campaign targeted at the gay community. That didn't come to anything, but an ad blitz aimed at single working women did soon appear in TTC subways and streetcars: two women wearing business suits, carrying briefcases, discussing the game. "Today that sort of campaign would be found terribly offensive and politically incorrect," Bavasi says. "But it was our way of trying to get to those markets."

The other half of the equation was image, presentation, the product—not just the team, not just what happened on the field, but every employee. "We tried to be very vigilant not only about creating customers but customer attention," Bavasi says. That meant blazers and ties for all staff, no jeans, ever (Bavasi once got caught out wearing "designer" jeans and was forced into some fast double-talk), Blue Jay emblems on every chest. "We wanted to make a presentation as an organization everywhere that we went, because the players and the staff members inside those blue blazers, grey slacks, ties with the Blue Jay emblems—the bodies in those uniforms would change, but we wanted to make a presentation."

And of course, being Bavasi, he tended to take that credo to the extreme, whether it was the "no drinking at lunch lest our breath offend" edict, or this memo—which Gillick keeps stashed in a desk drawer, purely for amusement's sake—sent to the manager of a no-hope team, complaining not about all those losses, but about the players' deportment.

To Roy Hartsfield
From Peter Bavasi
I would like to meet with the players this evening and go over the following two items in no uncertain terms.
1/ Attached is a copy of the story which appeared in this morning's edition of the *Globe and Mail*. I do not mind our players knocking the writers. But the business of criticizing our fans for not cheering our meagre efforts is getting to be ridiculous and is starting to affect our otherwise good public relations format. You must tell our players not to bite the hand that feeds them. In spite of our miserable record for the last two seasons, the Blue Jays' attendance is still in the upper third of the American League. But any more public outbursts like the ones from Roy

Howell and from Ashby will only turn our fans away from the ticket windows. The players must understand that the sports fan of Toronto is a fairly quiet sort, as is evidenced at Argo or Maple Leaf games. And furthermore some of the things that our club does on the field are worthy of boos. We have worked our ass off to build a strong image in this community and will not tolerate any of our players even suggesting that our fans are not among the best in baseball. We work all winter to reinstill the spirit in our fans after the players have left a mess behind after the season. I am getting very sick of having to explain to our subscribers why some of these players are saying the things that are published. I expect that you will convince them to knock this off. What are our players looking forward to? The day that we start drawing as poorly as Cleveland?

2/ I have been advised by a number of subscribers that a disgusting and revolting habit is taking place during and after some of our games. Wads of chewing tobacco are being tossed onto the roof of the Blue Jays dugout. I assume that this is being done by a few of our rabbit-eared players as a protest against the comments of the fans. For whatever reason, I want it stopped immediately. Let's get these players to understand that we are in the entertainment business. The games are not being played for their own benefit. These customers are paying a pretty penny to watch, in many cases, sub-standard major league baseball. The last thing we want to do is insult them and drive them away from the stadium.

Finally, the players should be urged to tip their caps and wave to acknowledge our fans when they cheer their efforts.

Many thanks for your cooperation on these matters

Peter

ANOTHER STORY BAVASI tells himself. In those early years, one of the Blue Jays' first stars was outfielder Rick Bosetti, a player blessed with more charisma and chutzpah than talent. But on a very bad team that was more than enough to make him stand out. It was Bosetti who became the first Blue Jay to publish a book under his name, which only in retrospect seems like an act of colossal hubris.

But Bosetti did have an attitude, which occasionally left him on the wrong side of his public—and of his employers. In the first Grapefruit League game during spring training in 1980, Bosetti became upset by what fans at the Clearwater Stadium were hollering at him. So he flipped them the finger. A few days later, he yelled at some fans. That earned him a reprimand from Bavasi and a pledge that if he did it again, the fine would be $250.

During the Jays' first road trip of the season in Milwaukee, Brewers' general manager Harry Daulton called Bavasi to file a complaint. It seemed that Bosetti had been asked by a young boy for his autograph and that he told the young boy to fuck off. It also seemed that the young boy was the son of one of the Brewers' top advertisers.

Bavasi immediately rushed down to the team's clubhouse, summoned the union rep and the manager, and then called Bosetti into Hartsfield's office and informed him that he was being fined (the procedure mandated by the players' association). Bosetti said that he'd bring in the money the next day.

A day later, there was no money and no Bosetti. Bavasi called the clubhouse and asked trainer Ken Carson to summon Bosetti to the phone.

"Hey, Ricky, what about the $250?" Bavasi asked.

"Peter, I talked to my agent who talked to the union," Bosetti replied. "And we're not going to pay."

The prospect of filing a grievance and bringing in a lawyer didn't sit well with Bavasi so he decided to try an alternative strategy. The next day he phoned the Toronto clubhouse and had Carson send Bosetti to his office. Bosetti arrived, still wearing his shower shoes.

"Sit down," Bavasi said. "We're going to have a chat."

"I don't have representation," Bosetti protested.

"You don't need representation," Bavasi said. "Remember? You're going to go to arbitration." Bavasi then got up, closed the door and began to dial a number on his speaker phone.

"What are you doing?" Bosetti asked. But Bavasi just continued with his call.

"Hello? Mrs. Bosetti? This is Pete Bavasi."

"You sound like you're in a barrel," Bosetti's mother replied.

"I'm here with Rick," Bavasi continued.

"Is anything the matter?"

"No. I just wanted to call and have a little chat."

By this point, Bosetti was getting agitated and actually tried to turn off the phone. "Mrs. Bosetti, hang on a second," Bavasi said. "We have a bad connection." He put her on hold.

"Now," he said, turning to Bosetti, "I'm going to tell her exactly what you did on those three occasions, what you did to that little kid, if you don't rush back to that clubhouse and get 250 in bills—no cheques."

"What are you going to tell her?"

"Don't worry. You come back with the 250, you're going to be in good shape."

While Bosetti ran off to get the money, Bavasi returned to his call.

"I just wanted to call you and thank you for getting Rick on that diet, Mrs. Bosetti. We talked about it in the spring when we saw you in Florida. Whatever you did, you got fifteen pounds off him. As you can see by the box scores, he's getting some hits and that's terrific.

"You'll hear from him after the game tonight, I'm sure. He went back because of this bad connection."

Bavasi hung up just before Bosetti returned. "He comes back, he's got tens and twenties. I scoop it up. He gave me $260—I never told him he gave me an extra ten. 'What about my mother?' he asked. I said, 'You call her after the game, everything will be fine. I didn't tell her anything.'

"Now you're going to make a phone call. You're going to call that bleeping agent of yours and drop this arbitration."

And that was that. "In every player's life there is a dominant woman," Bavasi says. "And rarely is it his wife."

BY THE END of the 1979 season, the Blue Jays were at a minor crossroads. The first real talent from the minor league system had begun to crack the major league roster, and the few blue-chippers from the expansion draft were just beginning to come into their own. The year had seen the major league debuts of Stieb and third baseman Danny Ainge. There would be more to come after that.

But selling dreams wasn't easy, considering that in its third season of existence, the team had actually posted a worse record than in its first, a woeful 53–109, fifty-and-a-half games off the division lead. Attendance dropped again, to 1,431,651. Said the operating plan heading into the 1980s: "The honeymoon concluded with the end of the 1979 season.... In year four, 1980, the magic of 'Big League Fun,' 'the sights and sounds...,' and 'more than a game' will not be enough to sustain peak level media and public interest in the Blue Jays. More attention will be directed toward the performance of the Blue Jays on the field; in effect, the baseball side of the operation will be dragged onto centre stage. This reality cannot be avoided. It must be planned for and dealt with."

And the easiest way of dealing with it, as in all professional sports, is to offer a ritual sacrifice. You can't fire all the players, so the saying goes. So you might as well fire the manager.

"I've never really been through this before," Gillick said to Bavasi, when the subject of Hartsfield's imminent departure came up. "When do you think we should make a change?"

"When the press calls for his head on a platter," Bavasi said, "we'll give it to them."

"Roy was worn out," Bavasi says. "So we were going to tell him, Pat and I, the last day of the season. We were closing in New York. Roy took it very, very badly, even though we had a spot for him doing colour commentary [apparently along with the club's radio colour man, Early Wynn]. He didn't want to do that. He left in a huff, big time, which surprised me. I said to myself, see this is what happens, they get infected with this stuff. I told him when I hired him: I said, Roy, this is a three-year gig. We did the actuarial studies of all prior expansion clubs. Three years. That's it. You're dead."

"Roy did an all-right job," Gillick says. "He didn't have much. We had terrible teams and he did a pretty good job. By the end of 1979, I thought that we'd assembled some pretty good players. We needed someone to bring those guys along at the major league level."

"The decision had clearly been made in August," Beeston says. "It had probably been made in August of 1978. This wasn't one where you were firing a guy who was expected to win. We weren't expected to win. But it was a time to move on. And he wasn't Pat's guy and Pat was clearly in charge at this point. In Pat's mind, a change had to be made. It wasn't that he disliked Roy—because he didn't, I didn't, Pete didn't—nobody disliked Roy. But he wasn't the right guy. Roy got a year more than probably even he expected."

"It depends on how you look at it," Hartsfield says. "A lot of people say I was fired. But I fulfilled my contract and they fulfilled theirs. They just decided not to renew it—whatever their reasons were."

As Bavasi says, they did the deed on the final road trip of the season in New York, the whole scene planned and scripted in classic Bavasi style. Whether or not Hartsfield knew it was coming, the news hit him hard. It was as though he was the only person who didn't understand the arrangement, the only one who didn't realize that the managers of expansion franchises are necessarily doomed to an inglorious exit. Any gratitude towards Bavasi, any pleasure he took from three years at the helm, dissipated immediately when he got the boot. One of the things the Toronto organization prided itself on in later years was the fact that employees, past and present, would very rarely criticize their bosses. Even players released or traded away invariably heaped praise on the franchise as they were walking out the door. In many ways, that was an extension of the old Labatt philosophy, the patriarchal employer that didn't treat workers as though they were disposable.

But the team was never really able to mend fences with Hartsfield. In future years, when there was some nostalgic need to bring back the first manager, he generally wanted no part of it. After Toronto, his career petered out with a couple of short stints as a minor league manager. He would never get a look at the big leagues again.

"I really don't want to get into that," Hartsfield says today. "It's all water over the dam. It happened a long time ago. Let's just say I was a little disappointed, and leave it at that."

It later turned out that Hartsfield wasn't the only one who was disturbed by his dismissal. Bavasi had sold the change to the team's board of directors and in doing so had encountered no real resistance. But Peter Hardy, the club's chairman, found the action ethically wrong. He was still learning about the business of the game, though. It had been only three years.

"I became aware more about baseball then," Hardy says. "The field manager only deals with what is supplied to him, with what he's got to work with. That he's hired to be fired is a philosophy I can't agree to. I find that rather distasteful. I like to think that people who come here come to work for us for a lifetime, in one job or another."

◆ WHILE HARTSFIELD'S DISMISSAL may have been no surprise to those who had been carefully charting the progress of the team, the man named as his replacement certainly was. Long ago, Bobby Mattick had been advised to stick to scouting, that a career as a manager meant a career of insecurity. Except for one short stint in the minor leagues, he had followed that advice. While Hartsfield had been Bavasi's choice, offering Mattick the job was Gillick's idea. The team, at that point in its history, needed a teacher, he felt. And no one knew more about young ball players and what made them tick than the elder statesman of the organization.

"Pat and Bavasi just about knocked me off my feet when they asked me to be a manager," Mattick says. "I hadn't been on a field in thirty-eight years. They had lost over a hundred games each year, so they wanted to make a change. And I think Pat's philosophy was that we've got a young club, we want somebody to come along and try to develop them while they're playing. I turned him down about three times and they kept asking me. So I said, well, all right. And I enjoyed it. We had some good young players—we had Stieb and Clancy, Leal, Upshaw, Moseby, Barfield, and Damaso Garcia. The potential was there."

"He was the oldest manager in the major leagues," Gillick says. "Pete thought it was a really good idea, an excellent idea."

"Mattick was a company guy," Bavasi says. "He's like Gillick's daddy. So we put him in, and he was going to be there for two years tops."

There was one minor sticking point. Before he finally accepted the job, Mattick had to be convinced that he would have to wear a uniform. It just didn't seem right, he said. Why couldn't he just wear street clothes in the dugout, the way Burt Shotton did, the way Connie Mack did? Who would notice? Who would object?

"But Bavasi said that the league wouldn't allow it," Mattick says, "so in the end, I put it on."

Chapter 9

CAME THE DAWN of a new decade, and Peter Bavasi was bored, which was very bad news for those who served at his pleasure. The team had long been on the field, the baseball side of the organization, under Pat Gillick, was running along smoothly, even if the fans in Toronto couldn't see the progress. Eventually, the prospects from the farm system would come along, the draft picks would mature and the deals would come to fruition. Nothing to do there, except occasionally meddle in Gillick's business, throw up a few roadblocks just to get a rise out of him. On the business side, things were similarly uneventful. Selling tickets remained a challenge, but once the ball club turned around, attendance would surely start to rise. The bottom line wasn't a problem, since a roster made up of kids and fringe major leaguers didn't cost a lot—any more than it does today. It was hard to get cranked up about one more Hat Day, one more Fan Appreciation Day, one more wrinkle to make the worst ball park on the planet a slightly more hospitable place.

And Bavasi, as everyone knew, was a restless soul, one incapable of sitting back, relaxing and enjoying his baseball team. In the early days, that energy—directed and otherwise—had been his strength, even if it made other people's lives miserable. But as the franchise settled into automatic pilot, there was no real outlet for the ideas and schemes and temporary passions. He could flirt with things like pay-per-view television (which he did, fourteen years before it became a reality in Canada) or the home video market (at a time when no one outside of the entertainment industry could have conceived of the revolution to come), but those were just time-fillers. He was a man without a cause.

Then, in January 1981, it appeared that he had found one—the salvation of his sport, or at least the salvation of the business of his sport. Baseball was on the verge of its greatest labour crisis, a strike that would abbreviate and divide the regular season. Owners had yet to adjust to the still relatively new realities of free agency, unable to balance spending and revenues.

That, of course, was the side of sport that interested Bavasi the most. For someone steeped in baseball tradition, raised in a base-ball family, and in the rarefied environment of the Dodgers' organization, the strange truth was that Peter Bavasi didn't really much care about the game—that is, the game on the field, the winning and losing part that is codified every day in the box score and that is what draws the fan to the park in the first place. What Bavasi loved was the business of the game, what to do with the money those fans spent at the park, how to entice them back to the park, and how to spin this hundred-year-old pastime into new commercial areas. A beautiful balance sheet was far more likely to move him to tears than a World Series trophy.

The deteriorating state of baseball economics was therefore something he found particularly troubling and particularly fascinating. A pure baseball guy, whose business was on the field, would have assumed that somehow the game would stumble along as it always had, through Black Sox banned and colour bars broken and a couple of world wars. But Bavasi saw threatening clouds on the horizon and felt moved to issue a storm warning to those who paid the bills—whether they chose to fully absorb the information or not. His address to the Toronto Blue Jays board of directors on January 5, 1981, was a masterpiece. Whatever anyone thought of the man, of his abilities as an administrator, of his mercurial personality, this was without question a visionary piece of work, one that rang as true during baseball's darkest hours in 1994 as it did thirteen years before.

The Blue Jays have tried to march to a different drummer who beats a rhythm of fiscal responsibility and common sense management. But we are one of the few clubs left in a very short line.

Our dual objective has always been to make a profit and win ball games by developing our own players and trading for others. Now it appears that if we are to develop our roster sufficiently to become competitive in the long term, we will need to spend more lavishly, not only to recruit better veteran players through trades, but to bind over our own young players so that they are unable to escape to free agency.

If we are forced to spend in this manner, the achievement of our profit objective—given our present ticket pricing policy and income pattern—is very questionable.

Being confronted with these economic realities, and with a desire to preserve the dual corporate objective, it appears that major price adjustments will have to be made in the near future, or a commitment made to suffering substantial cash losses until the club can perform well enough to attract consistently high attendance....

CURRENT AND PROJECTED FINANCIAL STATE OF BASE-BALL AND BLUE JAYS OPERATING OPTIONS FOR 1982 AND THEREAFTER

The continuing trend among many major league clubs to spend wildly on free agents and bind over present roster players at unnecessarily high salaries has resulted in a spiral where the average player payroll has escalated at the rate of nearly 30 per cent in each of the last four years, with no end in sight.

Because ticket prices and other operating revenue has not kept pace to counterbalance excessive spending, the long-term profit prospects for the industry are bleak.

Blue Jays management recognizes a need to set out for its ownership the current and projected financial state of Baseball, and the various operating options available to the Toronto club for possible implementation in 1982 and thereafter, in the hope of achieving the long-term financial and artistic objectives of the club.

Since it is clear that the majority of the clubs has no real intention of restraining itself from free spending, and because self-help programs most likely will be effectively introduced only when a number of clubs converge at once on the brink of financial disaster, it is now every club for itself.

The Blue Jays had been treading water in dealing with the developing financial vagaries of Baseball, but we are now fighting a tidal wave of salary escalation. If not carefully monitored, planned for and dealt with, it will surely engulf us by forcing player wages so high without offsetting operating revenue as to cause our players to flee to free agency, leaving the Blue Jays financially incapable of replacing them from the market, given our current fiscal cash basis operating policy.

It is within this unfortunate context that the following observations, comments, and options are offered.

BACKGROUND

When the American League granted Toronto a franchise in 1976 each major league club held perpetual renewal rights to the contracts of all its major and minor league players and each club established its own player salary structure in accordance with that club's financial condition and ability to pay. No market existed for a player to sell his services to the highest bidder, nor could a player opt to be traded or otherwise escape from his original signing club.

It was based upon this rigid player reserve system that the early pro-forma budgets and forecasts were developed for Metro Baseball Ltd. Until 1976, baseball had operated in a controlled economic environment. Player wages and ticket prices escalated moderately, but in tandem, and operating earnings fluctuated with attendance as a function of team performance and weather.

Beginning in 1976, the balance of power shifted to the players. An arbitration decision and subsequent new union contract effectively created a virtual open player market. Now even the most financially distressed club must pay what the new market bears or risk losing its most talented players to free agency.

To further fuel the escalation of baseball salaries, the re-entry draft permits many players to become instant millionaires while ostensibly permitting the less competitive clubs to bolster their rosters in the most expensive manner in professional sports history.

With exorbitant free agent signings has come a dramatic escalation of average player salaries; blind bidding to retain current roster players; and excessive salary arbitration awards. Prior to 1976, if the Yankees wished to pay a player $100,000 for hitting .250 there was no obligation for the Giants to do likewise, even for a .300 hitter.

Now, salary comparability and the market are key to all

negotiations and are often mutually exclusive of length of service and player performance.

For the Blue Jays this condition has meant playing "catch up", as salary comparability and market pressures have forced our 25-man payroll to increase from $850,000 in 1977 to $2-million in 1980.

Bavasi then went on to discuss the various options open to the Toronto franchise, which boiled down to a straight money-in, money-out proposition. If you're going to pay higher salaries, you have to charge higher ticket prices. No one knew what the market would bear, and you risked alienating consumers. But if you held salaries down to keep ticket prices where they were, that was bound to have an effect on the field. Fan confidence could crumble if the ticket buyers didn't believe management was really trying to build a winner. All of this was uncharted territory. No one really knew what would work best.

No recommendation was offered at the time, though Bavasi would return to the topic at a later date, when the baseball situation—and his personal situation—had become more precarious. For the time being, he left the board on an upbeat note, since the last thing any manager wants to tell his masters is that a problem has arisen that he can't solve.

This paper should not be read as a portent of doom nor as an expression of despair on the part of Blue Jays management. Indeed, Baseball has some severe financial problems, mostly self-inflicted. But, it has survived worse and it will likely survive this, if imaginative and creative energy, albeit at the local club level, is not spared.

BOBBY MATTICK'S TWO seasons at the helm of the Toronto Blue Jays were more difficult than even a veteran of forty years in the game would have imagined. His role coming in was clearly defined: to play the kids developed in the Blue Jay system; to teach them about the game as it is played on the major league level; to try to explain to the press and (through them) the fans why watching a worse team than they had ever watched before in Toronto was actually a harbinger of better days ahead; to take his lumps, and eventually be replaced by the man designated to lead the Jays into contention. That was a tall order for anyone, let alone a man who had done his best to shun the spotlight, who was most at home sitting quietly in the stands of some minor league ball park swapping tall tales with kindred spirits. But it was Mattick's two greatest skills—evaluating talent and teaching—that got him the job in the first place. Even if the paying public were getting restless, those at the top of the organization understood the plan.

"There's a problem with managers," Paul Beeston says. "All of them. There are twenty-eight of them, and all of them think they're really beyond instructing. They all know the game, but they don't want to get out there at three in the afternoon. They say they do. But there's not a manager in baseball that doesn't think he works hard. Not one. There ain't one. But I'll tell you what, they don't know what hours are. They knew what hours were when they were in the minor leagues. When they were throwing batting practice and all that stuff. Mattick, on the other hand, is a compulsive worker. He wants to teach kids and bring kids up. And so when Mattick was named, he came as a manager-teacher, not as a manager-strategist.

"He took Bosetti out of centre field. He would work in Barfield. He had the guts to put Stieb in there. He didn't have a lot of choice, but he did those things to bring those guys along. The only guy he ever complained about having to play was Danny Ainge, because he didn't think Danny Ainge could ever do it.... You could see the team somewhat coming together. Bobby made the game challenging and fun, and he would not tolerate anybody who would not give the best of themselves. He considered Moseby special. He considered Barfield special. He considered Stieb special. He considered George Bell special, but he felt George was over his head at the major league level. George always resented that. George hates him. But he's always resented Bobby for not playing him back in 1981. But the fact was the only reason we carried him was because he was a Rule Five draft guy and we had to carry him. Otherwise he would have been back in Syracuse, which is where he was the next year."

Mattick also brought with him coaches who would become integral parts of the organization: Denis Menke, John Felske and Jimy Williams. In his first season at the helm, there was a sense of renewal and optimism. Gradually, the expansion heroes began to disappear from the roster, replaced by players who would come into their prime two or three seasons in the future. Dave Stieb and Jim Clancy won twelve and thirteen games respectively, with earned run averages under four. Second baseman Damaso Garcia, acquired in a deal with the Yankees, showed signs of being an offensive force and, with shortstop Alfredo Griffin, the 1979 rookie of the year, gave the Jays their first bona fide double-play combination. There was Ainge, the two-sport wonder, looking more and more like a one-sport wonder (not baseball), and Moseby, the blue-chipper, still struggling at the plate. The 1980 Jays still won sixty-seven games, a fourteen-game improvement on the year before—still last, still thirty-six games out of first when the season ended, but a real sign the program was beginning to bear fruit.

But in 1981, all that optimism seemed misplaced, as the Jays struggled through the first half of the season even as baseball fell into the worst labour–management crisis in its history. The season was interrupted by a players' strike and was split into two forty-eight-game segments. The first of those may have been the low point in franchise history. In came even more kids—Barfield and Bell, who had been acquired from Philadelphia in the Rule Five draft, which meant the Jays had to keep them on their major league roster for the season. Eventually, people would talk about Barfield, Bell and Moseby making up the best young outfield in baseball. In 1981, they hit .232, .233 and .233 respectively, albeit in very limited action for Barfield and Bell. Stieb continued to progress, in the end becoming the first Jays starter to win more games than he'd lost in a season. But Clancy took a step backwards, falling to 6–12. Willie Upshaw, pegged as John Mayberry's successor at first base, hit only .171. When the strike mercifully halted proceedings, the Jays were sitting at 16–42—a .276 winning percentage, the worst in the short history of the franchise. Just as significantly, attendance fell precipitously. Had the Blue Jays played a full season in 1981, they would have drawn fewer than a million fans, which is when alarms sound, signalling a franchise in trouble. "We were going shit," Beeston says.

"Everyone thinks this is a fucking goldmine that we've got here. You know the year of the strike in '81, we wouldn't have drawn a million people. We had one crowd over twenty thousand people. We won. That's why we've drawn here. We won. In '82, we started winning."

It was during those desperate times that Bavasi first started making noises about firing Mattick. That kind of public sacrifice might at least satisfy the fans and the press, and of course the club didn't really have much invested in the interim skipper. That Mattick would go eventually wasn't an issue. Everyone knew that he was a temporary solution, a time-filler, and that sooner rather than later, he would be replaced.

But there are two ways of handling that kind of transition, particularly when it involves a loyal company man whose talents might come in handy later on. There is the way an old-style, patriarchal company like Labatt would do the deed. And then there was the baseball method. In the end, Bavasi's inability or unwillingness to understand the difference would be one of the final straws that cost him his job.

"I went to watch a game in California," Peter Widdrington remembers. "Mattick was the manager. And I went upstairs to talk to Bavasi and his father, Buzzie [who was then running the Angels]. I forget who the California manager was, but Bavasi's father was gonna fire the manager that night. And Mattick of course wasn't doing too well with the club. Bavasi got this great idea that his father would fire one manager one night and he'd fire his manager the same night, and it would make headlines. I was following a sort of approach where I didn't step in at that juncture. I went back to Hardy. I phoned Peter and said, 'You'd better jump on this goddamned thing right away. That asshole has got some bright idea that he's going to fire this guy. You'd better jump on it right away.' And Hardy phoned right away and said, 'Don't even try.' But it was those sorts of things that were just alien to us. While we recognized that that wasn't completely out of line in the baseball world, it was sure as shit out of line as far as we were concerned."

Thwarted in his efforts to make a spectacle out of the firing, Bavasi tried to persuade Mattick to do the honourable thing. "Bavasi wanted me to resign after our bad start and I wouldn't do it," Mattick says. "I said, 'You have to fire me.' I wasn't going to let him come out smelling like a rose and the fault was all mine. I thought the guys were trying, and we were only hitting 211. You can't win too many ball games when your team is hitting 211. I think baseball players try to get a base hit when they go up there. That's one thing they want to do. So I couldn't get on them. I think they were trying.

"I wasn't going to make managing my career. That's a cinch. The only thing I thought is that when we were going bad, I just didn't feel I should resign. If they wanted to get rid of me, they could."

In the meantime, the strike was settled—another victory for the players—and the game resumed. And then something completely unexpected happened. The same sad-sack Blue Jays who had been such an embarrassment before the work stoppage suddenly had learned to win. A godawful team was a .500 team. If you squinted a bit, it could even look like a contender for what had become half a division title. During one particularly successful streak, Bavasi was heard to muse aloud about the necessity of printing World Series tickets. They couldn't keep it up, of course, finishing at 21–27, seven-and-a-half games off the lead and still mired in seventh place. But the breakthrough was at hand.

Mattick wouldn't be around to enjoy it, at least from the manager's chair. He was told in July 1981 that he wouldn't start another season at the helm, and he wasn't happy about it. In the old days, the young, fiery, to-hell-with-you Bobby Mattick would probably have hit the road. But he was past sixty, he was still working for Pat Gillick, and another job in another organization seemed unlikely. "He still would like to have managed another year or two," Beeston says. "He says, I never knew if I was a major league manager because I never had a major league club."

Mattick wasn't the only one who was unhappy with the turn of events. When he was informed of Mattick's dismissal, Peter Hardy immediately went to talk to him. He had disagreed with the way Roy Hartsfield had been fired, but at the time wasn't confident enough in his knowledge of the baseball business to make it an issue. By 1981, Hardy had a pretty good idea of how a baseball team was run. And he had developed a close personal relationship with Mattick—among other things, the two were about the same age.

Hardy met with Mattick, intending to give him every chance to hold onto the job if he wanted to, ready to overrule Bavasi and Gillick and anyone else who got in the way.

"He gave it up voluntarily," Hardy says. "He didn't have to give that job up. I don't care what Mattick says. Because I recall very clearly going down to the clubhouse and seeing Mattick and saying this is what they tell me. Is that what you want to do? Because if you don't, say so. He obviously didn't have enough faith in me. If he wanted it, the job was there. He said no, he'd rather do this other job."

Later, Hardy found out that that wasn't quite the case, that Mattick was just being a loyal organization man when he said that he was leaving voluntarily, that in fact he had been shunted aside. And he found out that he had been sold a bill of goods by the man who ran the team. "I found that they did lie. They weren't above trying to snow you," Hardy says. That was something he would remember very well.

IN THE SUMMER of 1981, Bavasi began preparing his annual state of the union address, to be delivered to the board of directors that fall. This one would be different from all the rest. Baseball was going through a period of turmoil. And the franchise, which he had once told the board would be a .500 team by 1980, was struggling at the box office, and for the first half of the season struggling dreadfully on the field. The pressure was building, externally and internally, and Bavasi must have sensed his own job was on the line. Long ago, he had told Don McDougall that in five years, he'd be fired, that any executive starting a new franchise had half a decade in him before he burned out, or before those who paid his salary got tired of him. He could read the calendar. He could sense the discontent. And so he turned to what he did best, laying out the big picture for those who might not be quite as receptive to his song and dance as they once were. This time, they would get something special, a blueprint not just for the year to come, but for the full future of the franchise. As usual, the document was an impressive piece of work.

As a preface to this proposal and a reminder to ownership and management of Baseball's economic realities, the following items of concern are set out to serve as warning beacons for us.

1. The new owners coming into Baseball (5 in the past 18 months) have not shown the hoped-for self-restraint in player spending. The new White Sox ownership (having spent heavily on Fisk, Luzinski, Essian and LeFlore with reasonably good results) will be challenged in 1982 by the Chicago Cubs' new ownership, the Chicago Tribune Company. It is reported that the new Seattle ownership is ready to spend heavily and it is not anticipated that too many of the former big spenders will be drawing in their horns. Result—the Blue Jays will be pressed even harder by the media and the public to demonstrate a willingness to splurge in the player market.

2. It should be acknowledged where the Blue Jays stand in the order of Major League 25-man payrolls. Had the 1981 season been completed uninterrupted, the Blue Jays 25-man payroll would have totalled approximately $2.5-million. The average 1981 Major League payroll is estimated at $4.9-million. The Blue Jays had projected an operating profit of $1.7-million (if all games had been completed and attendance reached expectations). THEREFORE, if the Blue Jays had been operating in 1981 with an average Major League payroll, the Blue Jays would have lost $700,000.

3. The foreign exchange rate which impacts upon the Blue Jays and Expos is an ever-present burden acting against the financial viability of the club.

4. Given the quality of Exhibition Stadium and the obvious limitations in seating areas and ticket pricing options, no beer sales, and local Government interference in obtaining an advantageous concession contract, the Blue Jays operate under one of the worst stadium lease agreements in Major League Baseball. Our share of concessions (16.2%) is too small and for the facility we receive, the rental is too high. Opportunities to correct these problems are not presently available to the Blue Jays.

In light of the above economic realities, ownership is cautioned that if we embark upon a plan of acquiring veteran high-profile players, the club may enjoy higher attendance than expected (if the new players perform up to expectations and weather permitting) but, in spite of higher attendance and an extraordinarily high-income local television contract, it is an absolute certainty that by 1983 the Blue Jays will be in a substantial loss position.

Whatever loss position might result from spending on high-priced talent is correctable, of course, by trading away the offending salaries, thereby bringing the club's financial position into better balance. As a consequence, attendance would probably decline and the "public confidence" problem could reappear.

In this contest, it might be well to heed the adage, "once you open a can of worms, the only way to recan them is to use a larger can."

Bavasi presented the board with four dramatically different budget plans, each of which would send the team in a particular direction, both fiscally and on the field.

BUDGET #1
Contemplating No Material Alteration of Major League Roster and Reducing Farm Team System From Six Teams to Five

Bavasi projected that even without adding any new player contracts other than through minor trades, Rule Five or waiver claims, the Jays' payroll would increase to $3,483,500 in 1982 from $2,500,000 in 1981, when the team had the lowest average player salary in the major league.

That, in addition to continuing foreign exchange problems, would eat away at any profit, which would drop from slightly more than $1 million to slightly more than $600,000. Attendance under the plan was estimated at 1.4 million.

BUDGET #2
Contemplating No Material Alteration of Major League Roster and Leaving Farm System at Six Minor League Teams

Under this plan, the team would have to continue paying the

cost of a sixth minor league club, which would cut profits to $429,584. There would of course be a payoff in the future from the money invested in the farm system.

BUDGET #3
Contemplating Alteration of Major League Roster
Through Acquisition of Two or Three Veteran Stabilizers and
Leaving Farm System at Six Minor League Teams

Those "stabilizers" would be added not through free agency, but through trades, purchases or waiver claims. Add two of them at a total cost of $500,000, and the team's profit would drop to just $5,000, even though revenues would increase by $168,000 (presuming that the team played better) from increased attendance to 1,450,000.

Bavasi offered a list of some of the players who might be available, most of them at the tail end of their career: Tony Perez, Don Money, Bobby Murcer, Lou Piniella, Oscar Gamble, Jay Johnstone, Del Unser.

BUDGET #4
Contemplating Material Alteration of Major League Roster
Through Acquisition of Two or Three Veteran Stabilizers
and Re-entry Draft Players and Leaving Farm System
at Six Minor League Teams

This was the Cadillac option. Add two veterans through trade, as well as two first-rate free agents. That increases the projected payroll to $5,895,000, which Bavasi projected as the average major league payroll in 1982.

The team would in all likelihood play better and draw better, attracting something close to the more than 1.7 million spectators the Jays had drawn in 1977. But that increase in revenue notwithstanding, it was projected that the Toronto team would lose $1,275,000.

Bavasi provided the board with a list of possible free agents and made note of those who might be of particular interest to the Jays: Bobby Grich, Reggie Jackson, Dave Collins, Dave Concepcion, Ken Griffey, Bill Madlock.

Finally came the all-important endorsement.

Management is recommending Budget #3 (The Break Even) which, of all of the budgets submitted, comes nearest to fulfilling the following requirements when these items are regarded as inter-related club objectives for 1982…. The need to be both artistically and financially successful in 1982…. The need to fulfill the expectations of the public, media, subscribers, sponsors, rightsholders and rightsholders/owners as to Blue Jays field performance in 1982…. The need to preserve or restore public confidence in the Blue Jays, depending upon our performance in the Second Season, 1981…. The need to preserve the large farm system/player development program and philosophy in order to ensure an uninterrupted flow of quality players to the major league club in all future years.

The only untouchables on the roster: Dave Stieb, Luis Leal, Joey McLaughlin, Tony Fernandez, Damaso Garcia and Lloyd Moseby.

By following that plan, the Blue Jays could aspire to being a good baseball team, maybe even a very good baseball team. And from a bottom-line point of view, that's exactly where Bavasi wanted them—good, but not great. In the era of free agency, the same dictum applies in all professional sports: the most lucrative course is to contend, year after year, to play at a .500 clip or better, but never to win it all. Championships cost money. Players with a championship ring on their finger automatically are showcased in the marketplace and automatically demand more than those who have fallen short. Instead, keep turning over the roster. Stay in the hunt enough to whet the fans' appetites. If two or three teams break down ahead of you, you might stumble into a pennant, and in the post-season anything can happen. But don't blow your brains out to win, since that short-term glory, and the short-term satisfaction, will soon enough be replaced by all kinds of red ink. It is a strategy that in the National Hockey League has been followed successfully by the Boston Bruins. In baseball, it has been followed somewhat less successfully by the Montreal Expos. Had Peter Bavasi had his way, the owner of the Toronto Blue Jays would have enjoyed not just enormous increases in the value of their franchise, not just the spin-off benefits by association that might have sold them more beer, but also an operating profit on the team itself, year in and year out.

And the history of the team would have been a very different one.

There was also an addendum to the operating plan that turned again to Bavasi's interest in the overall economic state of the game. The other owners and the commissioner had come to share his concerns after the strike and had decided to do something about them.

We trust that each of the directors has received and has had a chance to review the roster improvement play which was sent along about ten days ago.

Paul [Beeston] has developed some financial information, which we will pass out today, that will pinpoint our profit position at various levels of player payroll expense and corresponding attendance levels.

But before discussing the roster improvement plan as submitted, we wish to report on some action taken at a recent special joint meeting of the major league clubs which was held in conjunction with the general manager meeting in Phoenix, Arizona, and concluded this past Sunday.

With your permission, Mr. Chairman, I would ask that we go off the record for this report with no notes being kept on the subject matter. Mr. Solway has been advised of the nature of the pending report.

The two major leagues met jointly in Phoenix at a special meeting convened for the sole purpose of adopting a new league broadcasting and telecasting agreement, which will better define local territories in keeping with past practice and will better protect each club against broadcast signal penetration by any other club into the designated home territory of the former club.

While it was not on the agenda, the commissioner, at the urging of the general managers who had been meeting the day before, began an earnest discussion of the dire need for financial safeguards and controls within baseball with particular attention on initiatives which could be implemented in time for the upcoming re-entry free agent draft.

This discussion evolved to a point where the commissioner formulated a specific suggestion for consideration by each club.

The suggestion, which was subsequently adopted as a separate independent business decision by each of the 26 clubs (none in concert with the other), is as follows:

If a club has a free agent player, and if that club has made a fair offer (based upon salary guidelines as established in the market and tabulated by the PRC [Player Relations Committee]), and if that club wants to keep that free agent player, then all other clubs would be contacted and would refrain from offering that free agent a contract in competition with the offer of the former club. Any club could draft that free agent, but would sign the free agent only if his former club claimed no interest in him, and then to a contract where the terms were no better than those last offered by his former club. Further, each club made an independent business decision to limit the length of any future guaranteed contract to no more than three years.

Recognizing the practical, and perhaps legal, concerns attendant to this decision by each of the 26 clubs, it is nonetheless a positive sign that the industry may be self-correcting. We will have to wait and see.

In other words, collusion, a word that would soon enough become part of the sporting vocabulary.

But as it turned out, Peter Bavasi wouldn't have the chance to see that, or any of his grand plans, executed.

Chapter 10

WHEN BOBBY MATTICK returned to the scouting and development side in the organization, it gave Pat Gillick an opportunity to put his final stamp on his team. The players who were discovered by his scouting staff and were trained by his minor league managers and coaches were just beginning to make their presence felt in the major leagues. Other players whom he had traded for or who had come over as Rule Five claims were proving themselves to be potential stars. Danny Ainge was headed back to basketball, where he clearly belonged, but otherwise there had been no false steps.

Now the Gillick team needed a Gillick manager. Roy Hartsfield had been Peter Bavasi's choice, and while Mattick was a Gillick man, he was by definition temporary. The next field boss would be for the future, in for the long haul. The next manager would be expected to do something no other Blue Jay manager had been asked to do: win.

Gillick chose Bobby Cox, a bright young baseball talent, someone who had managed in the big leagues and had worked for both Ted Turner and George Steinbrenner, circumstances under which Job would have found it tough to do his job. For a new organization on the rise, for a team filling up with talented but inexperienced players, he seemed the perfect fit.

"Pat had Cox when he was with the Yankees," Beeston says. "Cox had managed Syracuse [then the Yankees' Triple A farm club]. After that he had been fired in '81 by Turner—I'll never forget watching television and seeing the press conference. Turner was sitting there as only Turner can do and said, 'The best guy for managing this team'—there's Turner sitting there and Cox sitting right beside him—'the best guy for managing this team is Bobby Cox. But we can't have Cox because I just fired him.' It was a gas and a half."

"I was let go by the Braves," Cox says. "Within days, Pat had contacted me through somebody, and so had the Mets. I remember flying to Tampa to meet Frank Cashen from the Mets, and he was going to get back to me. The Blue Jays wanted to know if I wanted to manage and I accepted right away. I knew Pat. I knew it would be a first-class organization and a great work ethic within the organization with him. I knew Pat real well. I spent a lot of time with him. He's just a first-class baseball person that you like to be around. You know how you like to be around certain people? He's one of them. Pat told me he thought we had a pretty good team that should win eighty, eighty-five games. I didn't know—only from what I had read about their team. Pat suggested I keep some of the coaches. If he liked them, that was fine with me. I respected his judgment. Jimy Williams and Al Widmar. Then we hired Cito Gaston. I knew him from the Braves' organization and winter ball. I knew him real well."

Of course, as usual when decisions were made anywhere but the president's office, there would be one small problem. Bavasi didn't want to hire Cox. Or at least he didn't want to make it easy for Gillick to hire Cox, just for the sake of being difficult.

"He didn't like Cox. I got mad. He had somebody—I can't remember who it was. He didn't want Cox coming. I think I said something like 'Whose decision is it to make?' So we got into it on Cox. Again a battle and then we won out. But that's Peter," Gillick says.

That battle, which would be the last one between Gillick and Bavasi, became fuel for the events to follow. Others in the organization were thrilled with the hiring—especially Beeston, who was slowly coming to think of himself as a baseball guy as well as a number cruncher. He and Cox eventually built a strong friendship based on mutual respect, and it was through people like Cox and Bobby Mattick that Beeston really came to understand the game.

"Cox's biggest strength was the players loved to play for him," Beeston says. "They loved him. He was the quintessential players' manager. I have met no one in this world other than Cox who doesn't have an ego. I have met no one. Zero. He doesn't want to talk to the press. He doesn't want to be seen. He doesn't want his picture in the paper.

"Those guys never knew whether he liked them or didn't like them. But they all thought he liked them. And you know he was just mean enough and tough enough that you weren't going to take a chance. Bobby had the ability—he was a man's man. It's a politically incorrect thing to say now, but that's what he is.

"The thing that he was perceived to be was fair. Players know which players need a kick in the ass. Players know which guys you can't kick in the ass. You can't kick Tony Fernandez in the ass. You couldn't do it. Because he'd quit, he'd sulk. Coxie knew that. But on the other hand, he knew he had to kick Lloyd in the ass, he knew he had to kick George in the ass. You let Doyle Alexander do his own thing. And you had to keep Jimmy Key away from what Doyle was teaching. Because pitchers typically become pitching coaches. Especially when they become elder statesman—Doyle was an example, Mike Flanagan was an example. They end up having disciples. And you've got to watch it. And you've got to get the most out of your coaches too. Bobby was good at that, he was very good at delegating. He was very supportive, very loyal. He would fight for anybody on that team. He was just a helluva guy and he continues to be a helluva guy."

BASEBALL JOBS DON'T last forever, and no one knew that better than Peter Bavasi. He had been born and raised in the Dodger organization, the most stable in all the sport, but he understood the business of the game well enough to know that virtually everyone is hired to be fired. Whether he understood his own failings then the way he appears to understand them now is another matter. All the big highs and big lows, all the petty battles fought with employees, all the fast dancing to make the board happy. Eventually there would be a bend that Bavasi couldn't negotiate, that his charm couldn't guide him through, or his bullying couldn't straighten. Eventually, like all other owners in all other sports, those nice Canadian beer people who had deferred to him, to his American-ness, to his baseball-ness, would start to believe that this wasn't rocket science, that they could run the show as well as anyone. (The only difference between franchises is the length of the learning curve and the degree of chutzpah. Not every owner is like Ted Turner, who from the minute he signed the cheque knew it all, to the point where he once appointed himself field manager.) At that moment, they would decide, surely, that someone like Bavasi was far more trouble than he was worth.

From nearly the day that he was hired, Bavasi actually said as much. "I maintain that he predicted his own demise," Don McDougall says. "He always said the same thing. 'You'll want to get rid of me too. People in these jobs, they don't last. [For] the guy that starts a franchise, five years is a long time. You'll be firing me in five years.' He believed it. He really did believe it. And he could cite examples. I maintain it was kind of like a death wish he had. So when the world started to fall apart around him, instead of doing logical things, he did nothing. You'd think he would have phoned the chairman—he never phoned the chairman. He never phoned Webster. He never phoned any of the people who might have been able to help him. Because I think he had a death wish, almost subconsciously. And if you followed through what happened, he acted like that. And when he left, he was kind of relieved. He had done his thing. He had his five years. The only thing that I think is unfortunate is that I don't think there was anything terrible about him leaving, or the way he left, it's just that I don't think he ever got the credit for what he did. I think he did play a very significant role in positioning the Blue Jay organization."

"He said that to me a hundred times," Herb Solway says. "He would say to me, 'Just tell me when they're tired of me, because they'll be tired of me sooner or later.' I don't know whether he was really referring to himself as [much as] he was referring to his position—that that's what happens in his position. I don't think he saw himself that way, necessarily. I think he saw that anybody in that position would find himself like that. I never got the feeling that he was talking about himself or any personality quirks of his own."

It's tempting in hindsight to leave it there, to see the firing as inevitable and to see Bavasi as some sort of strange ego-monster who had to be stopped before it was too late. "He would just lose control of himself," Solway says. "There were two things he could do. He could either lose control of himself completely or he would go into an act where he would try to embarrass somebody in front of somebody else. It was just awful behaviour. He would never do it with anyone who could give him some difficulties. He would never do it to anyone who was in a position to do something about it." But to the end, there remained another side to his personality that loomed nearly as large. In public and at times in private, he could charm and delight to the same degree that he could make his employees' lives miserable. Even his enemies acknowledge that. "Back then he weighed about two hundred pounds, an immaculate dresser," Beeston says. "He'd walk into any room and people would say, 'Who is that guy?' Because he had the Pepsodent smile on, he could do it, he could turn on the charm. Everything he did was to extremes. When he went on a diet, he didn't eat. It wasn't like he had fruit. He just didn't eat for three or four days. When he went out to eat, he could order as well as anybody. He went through the whole table and he made sure that everybody had something that they liked. And he could eat like crazy. When he wanted to do something, he could do it well. But when he didn't want to do something, he could do it equally bad. If he really wanted to do something bad, it would be bad."

Or consider this. Bavasi was an amateur musician—he liked to play the drums. In the early days of the franchise, finding out that some of his players also dabbled in rock and roll, he set up a room beside the Jays' clubhouse, filled it with instruments and invited players from the home team and the visiting sides to jam whenever they felt the urge. Jim Clancy played the guitar. Alfredo Griffin liked to bang on the bongos. And Tommy Hutton, during his brief stint with the team, was the vocalist. When Hutton was dealt to the Expos, Clancy told Bavasi: "You're the dumbest GM I ever played for. You traded Hutton to the Expos and you didn't even get a bass player in return." They called it the Blue Jays Blues Band. Peter Bavasi, the man of a thousand faces, was that kind of guy, as well.

In the spring of 1976, it was his time. But by the fall of 1981, it was time for him to go. "I would say that those were the turning points," Solway says. "The key decisions, really, in the history of the Toronto Blue Jays were the hiring of Peter Bavasi and the firing of Peter Bavasi."

"I don't know if anyone else could have done it," Beeston says. "I'll give him that. As a matter of fact, I'd like to like Pete. In fact, I do now. We just don't see each other any more. And he'll always think of me as the guy who fucked him, the Canadian and all that. Who cares?"

◆ THE FIRING OF Peter Bavasi, inevitable as it may have been, did not happen spontaneously. Instead, it was a product of the meeting of minds, Paul Beeston's and Pat Gillick's, two very different people, with different backgrounds, different personalities, who would forge a strong personal and professional bond based initially on a common challenge: they both had to deal with this strange man, and they both had come to the conclusion that it was time to take action. It wasn't really a conspiracy. There weren't midnight meetings to plot strategy, there was no elaborate game plan to engineer Bavasi's demise. But they did talk, often, and they did decide in the fall of 1981 that they had only two options: to find employment elsewhere, or to work together to take Bavasi out. Individually, playing a game of he-goes-or-I-go wasn't necessarily an option. Beeston was still regarded as basically an accountant, and accountants, whatever their merits, are easily replaceable. Gillick had seen enough working for the New York and Atlanta organizations to understand that no baseball job is sacred, especially with a team that had yet to win more games in a season than it lost, and that had just experienced its worst-ever season at the box office. The Jays could let Beeston go, and the outside world would hardly notice. They could let Gillick resign and frame it for the consumer as part of a much-needed restructuring, an attempt to put a better product on the field. Bavasi's departure would be more difficult to explain, since in so many ways he was still Mr. Blue Jay and Mr. Toronto Baseball, the man who introduced the city to the game. And so for Beeston and Gillick to mount an outright challenge was a calculated risk—the calculation being that the owners understood enough to know just how destructive Bavasi had been and understood the value of the other two to the organization. They could attempt a power play, but they had to be prepared to take another job.

It was Beeston who set in motion the events that led to Bavasi's downfall. Since the time in 1978 when he had actually accepted a job with Labatt, Beeston's relationship with his boss had deteriorated. The beginning of the end, Bavasi claims, was Beeston's first taste of public notoriety, when he was quoted in the press explaining how the books of a sports franchise can be manipulated to tell two different stories. Given the tense, volatile relationship between owners and players, it certainly added fuel to the fire, to the point that it was still being brought up during the strike of 1994–95.

Beeston doesn't deny having said it, but maintains that in truth, it was Bavasi's fault.

"He was the cause of my famous quote that you could take a $4-million profit and turn it into a $2-million loss," Beeston says. "He told everybody that we made $4 million. I said I can make a case that we lost $2 million and get every national accounting firm to agree to it. This was one of those ones where he was bragging, and there was no reason to brag. We had a tremendous year that first year. It's laughing at people. We're a bad team and we're making all this money. Plus we're in the sports industry where your success is measured in wins and losses and championships, not in dollars and cents."

Really the Beeston–Bavasi dispute was a long-term problem that had simply taken time to come to a head. There remained dissension within the ranks, and some members of the board were also beginning to not-so-quietly question Bavasi's management style. Beeston caught flak from both ends. "What he never understood," Beeston says of Bavasi, "was that I used to protect him from the directors and protect him from the staff. I was the buffer above and below for him. He never will acknowledge it. He will never, ever understand. It would have come from above or below. That was part of my last line to him."

The precise nature of the final confrontation between the two remains unclear. Bavasi refuses to acknowledge that anything out of the ordinary took place. "There was no defining moment. Paul may be able to describe for you a certain flashpoint, because frankly he was up there from the beginning and this has been his only job. My life has taken a number of interesting turns since, all—as far as I'm concerned—wildly successful, financially and from a cultural standpoint. Whatever problems existed or successes existed back in 1976 through 1981, I don't recall as well. But if you're in the same place on the same path in the same thing, your memories are probably more vivid. So Paul's may be. If there was a flashpoint, I don't recall it. But I do know that I was difficult."

Beeston says that something happened, something only he and Bavasi know for sure, and that for him, it was the final straw. He found and accepted a new job, at the high-powered Toronto law firm McMillan Binch, where he served as business manager, a non-lawyer principal of the firm and, according to Beeston, a partner in everything but name. (Bavasi refers to the job, derisively, as "an office manager with a more glorious title.") When Beeston quit, Bavasi phoned Hardy to pass on the news. He told Hardy that he already had someone in mind for the post, someone from another organization in baseball who would perform Beeston's duties and take on additional responsibilities as well.

Hardy was suspicious. He told Bavasi to wait, that he wanted to talk to Beeston himself and find out why he was leaving. It wasn't out of any sense that Beeston was irreplaceable—in fact, Hardy had become convinced after five years in the business that with the help of baseball men like LaMacchia and Mattick, he and Peter Widdrington could run the club by themselves if they had to. But Hardy had also come to distrust Bavasi and had come to distrust the ways of baseball in general. The handling of the Mattick firing, in particular, he had found distasteful. "By that time, I had lost confidence in Bavasi because I had found that he had really lied to me about Mattick," Hardy says.

Beeston went to see Hardy, who was staying, as was his custom when he visited Toronto, at the Royal York Hotel, and explained his decision to quit. He went through the same song and dance as he had back in 1978, when he'd agreed to leave the Blue Jays for Labatt: personal development, more time with the family, the need for change, etc. "I never went to anyone and said get rid of Pete," Beeston says. "I didn't have to. I have great confidence in myself. The confidence in myself in '81 was that when I was gone, he was gone. I knew. He didn't. So I didn't have to say anything. I'd be the sacrificial lamb."

"He was reluctant," Hardy says. "He was very reluctant. He said that he was unhappy, that he found it difficult, that it was no fun. Finally, after a lot of probing, I got him to tell the truth."

Given the opening, Beeston let loose, painting a picture of a tyrannical boss, a terrified, demoralized staff, and others on the verge of leaving. Among the latter, he told Hardy, was Pat Gillick, who would soon follow him out the door if Bavasi remained in place. "The killer," Hardy says, "was that he told me that Gillick shared the same view."

Later, Hardy met with Gillick and asked him if that were the case. His loyalty to Bavasi, a fellow baseball man and the man who had hired him, prevented him from coming out and saying it, though it was certainly implied. By then, Hardy understood that within the game, no one would ever criticize an employer or potential employer in public, for fear of future reprisals. Still, the full implications of what was about to take place began to settle in. Beeston was gone. He assumed Gillick was gone as well. For an organization at a critical point in its history, it would be a significant, destructive blow, though potentially how destructive it could have been became clear only in hindsight.

"I realized that either we could keep one and lose two, or keep two and lose one. What was in the best interests in the long term?" Hardy says. Widdrington was in China (he learned of the change by reading the *International Herald Tribune*), and Webster by then had long deferred to Hardy when it came to the business of the ball club. "I guess I made the decision that Bavasi had to go," Hardy says. He went to Webster, told him what he planned to do and received his blessing.

"If I had been chairman of the board, I would have said this guy did fine work. We're grateful he got us started. But now he's started causing problems," Bavasi says of his own firing. "He doesn't have enough to do. If we lose Gillick, he goes and takes the guts of the baseball operation. Beeston's important to us for other reasons. You can always hire an accountant, but he was a Canadian and he was the senior guy on staff, so he was important. My persistent behaviour in search of excellence for the club began to grate over time, and particularly so after everything was set. There was nothing I could noodle around with any more, so now I could start bothering people."

Bavasi's and Hardy's memories of their final meeting differ only slightly.

"I think it was in November sometime [it was November 22]," Bavasi says. "It might have been a Tuesday [it was a Sunday]. Peter Hardy, who was then the vice-chairman of the board and the Labatt liaison—he was like a father confessor and a mentor and a lovely man. He had the soul of the poet and he was the soul of the Blue Jays. Not the heart, but the soul. He came into my office in the old stadium. He just closed the door and he said, 'It's time for you to resign.' It's time for you to resign—six words. Well, okay. It's time for you to resign. Period. The door was closed. That was it. I wasn't surprised. I had been up there five-and-a-half years. I was worn out, emotionally. Frankly, I had done everything I felt that I needed to do to get the thing set up. Then it was just waiting, and I wasn't much for waiting."

"I said, the time has come," Hardy says. "You're disliked. The day for a change has arrived. You've got a choice. You can resign. Or you can be fired."

Bavasi chose the former, and predictably, he chose to do it in style, relishing the opportunity for one last public performance. A press conference was called for the next day, though no one in the city had an inkling as to what was going to be announced. Perhaps a big free agent signing. Perhaps a trade.

"He was even organized then," Beeston says. "We've still got his note of what he had to do. This guy was so organized that he had a list of things that he had to do on his last day." The night before, Bavasi met with Gillick to discuss the minute-by-minute plans for his leave-taking. Gillick noticed that Bavasi had scheduled his arrival at the press conference at the downtown Sheraton Hotel half an hour after his departure from Exhibition Stadium—at most a ten-minute drive. He would arrive fifteen minutes past the event's scheduled starting time. Why the delay? Gillick asked.

"It's like rock stars," Bavasi told him. "They always come on late. They always like to keep the crowd waiting."

Finally the moment arrived, and Bavasi stepped to the podium and announced that he was gone. "The thrill of building the Jays is over," he told the gathering. "The creative process is over for me. I need new challenges, new excitement." And however true that was, the real reason for his departure didn't come to light.

"The funny thing about Pete is that I think he convinced himself he resigned," Gillick says. "I think at the time he convinced himself that he was resigning. You know—the thrill is gone."

Bavasi was thirty-nine years old and he had been given the boot, though it was years before he would admit it, usually sticking to euphemisms such as "Sickness set in—they got sick of me and I got sick of them." But one who sensed the truth early on was Trent

Frayne, then writing for the *Toronto Sun,* who noticed that there wasn't a single member of the team's board of directors at Bavasi's farewell press conference—unusual for someone who was supposed to be leaving with regrets after successfully getting the team off the ground.

"I regret that I didn't forge certain personal relationships," Bavasi says of what went wrong at the end. "I should have. But I wasn't capable of it at the time because of my immaturity and this obsession with the detail of running the team. As foolish as this sounds, to have created personal relationships and spent time on a personal level would have somehow detracted from what my charge was. I did not consciously do that but that's apparently what happened, as I reflect back at the age of fifty-two. That must be what happened. I was too young at the time and too immature to really discharge my responsibilities well. I didn't coach and mentor like I do now. I'm fifty-two now—I was thirty-nine then. And I regret that. You're young, you're immature, you're headstrong, lots of energy. I regret that I didn't have the maturity in Toronto, because if I did I'd probably still be there."

By coincidence, there was a party being held that night at His Majesty's Feast, a restaurant then located in a hotel just off Highway 401 near Jane Street, where patrons could pretend they were dining in the time of King Henry VIII. It had been planned for a month and a half, a reunion for all those who had been fired from the organization or who had quit under the Bavasi regime, as well as those who remained in the front office.

"It was remarkable," Beeston says. "It was like this thing was divine will."

Chapter 11

BAVASI WAS A tough act to follow, but someone would have to do it. The Toronto Blue Jays had just fired their president, and they would need a new chief executive to take his place. Not another Peter Bavasi, if indeed another of those existed, but surely a veteran baseball man of some sort to oversee the operation, to keep a steady hand on the tiller, to protect the owners' investment and the owners' interests and to build a winning team.

Just as soon as he found out that Bavasi was gone, Herb Solway started making lists. Headhunting was his kind of job, and as someone who had been around the team from its pre-history on, who knew better what kind of person would be qualified for the job? Still, there was one possibility that didn't occur to him, one candidate close to home whom he never would have seriously considered.

"I was making suggestions until Peter Hardy told me he was taking it himself," Solway says. "I had not thought of that. I was submitting names and talking about people, then suddenly realized that there was another plan, and that Hardy was planning to do it himself. And Hardy did an outstanding job. Until you really know Hardy, he really surprises you. He has different qualities as a CEO than most people do. He understands an organization. He understands what everybody's role is. He understands that you've got to let people play their role, that you promote from within, you give people chances, and so on. He believes in that strongly."

"I appointed Peter. I asked him to do it," Peter Widdrington says. "And you're quite right, there were a lot of people surprised. I got a lot of criticism from a number of people that this was a dumb thing to do, because he didn't know anything about baseball, that he wouldn't be the guy, that he couldn't stand up to all of them. But he stepped in—and I knew how capable he was."

He was, in many ways, a dream boss, a vestige of a kind of old-style business world that is hard to imagine in the mean 1990s. Hardy is a quiet man, extremely shy. Grey-haired and bearded, he has a grandfatherly way about him, but any illusion of softness disappears very quickly in conversation. He is tough and to the point, sometimes brutally so, and he has little tolerance for balderdash. He is straight with people, and he likes people who are straight with him. Though very much of the brewing trade, Hardy gradually had become more comfortable with baseball, though not with the ethics of the baseball business. But that was beside the point. If he was going to run a baseball team, he would run it his way, the way the brewery had been run, in many ways the antithesis of what Bavasi and others of his background were doing in the sport. With Hardy's appointment, the great cultural conflict within the franchise ended. The Blue Jays would become a different organization than any other in the game. It would be costly, financially, and in the beginning there was no assurance that it would work as well as or better than the tried-and-true methods developed over the last century. But Hardy wouldn't have it any other way.

"We had two very able people in Gillick and Beeston," Hardy says of his decision to assume the presidency of the team. "I planned to act temporarily as CEO and then find someone to take over within six months. Howard Webster never seemed all that enthused about looking for somebody. Finally after six months we had a meeting, and he said, 'Why wouldn't you carry on with it?' Here he's asking the representative of his partner to become in effect the acting CEO. Before the first year was up, he said, 'Why don't you just carry on?'"

As vice-chairman of the board, Hardy had already brought some of the Labatt way of doing things to the very different environment of professional baseball. Most of it didn't show up at the major league level, where players, managers and coaches were generally treated well and paid well. Instead, Hardy concentrated his efforts in the minors. There, young men, away from home often for the first time, had to adapt to the pressures of the game and often had to adapt to a foreign culture. Coaches and managers operated with little security and few fringe benefits. At the end of each season, a bad record or a new cast at the top of the organization could result in instant firing.

"Why are baseball people so insecure?" Hardy once asked Al LaMacchia.

"Because no one has ever let them know they are appreciated for fear that if they did, they'd have to give them a five-dollar raise," he was told.

In the ideal world, the company looked after its people, even if there was no direct return involved, understanding the long-term benefits. (Which is not to suggest that Hardy couldn't act decisively, and perhaps a bit ruthlessly, if he felt the situation demanded it. The firing of Don McDougall is a case in point.) In baseball, only direct return mattered, and the people themselves, from the players on up, were expendable, filling a space in the system that could just as easily be filled by someone else. Hardy, on his own, decided that was unsatisfactory and decided to change it. He initiated programs within the Toronto Blue Jays' organization that were unheard of elsewhere in baseball. Minor league managers were given a mid-season vacation to spend with their families. Minor league coaches were extended medical and dental benefits for their families. Players in the minors were given access to a food program. In each town, it was arranged for a local restaurant to provide each player with one square meal a day—something that eighteen-year-olds don't necessarily provide for themselves, even if you give them an allowance. "The sensitivity there was that you were bringing kids in—and particularly the Latin kids who couldn't even order properly in the restaurants," Widdrington says.

"His influence I think was pretty big," Mattick says. "Especially in the minor leagues. He tried to make everything better for the minor league player, such as clubhouses and everything. And he installed a program to get better nutrition for the players, which is a big thing in the minor leagues. Of course they'd get meal money on the road, but at home they'd pay their own expenses. So he made me and others have a restaurant where these kids could go, and if they ordered a six-dollar meal, they'd pay three dollars and the club would pay half of it. At that time, I still think it was probably unknown in baseball that any organization would do that. And that was his idea. He made us carry it out. He was very concerned about where the kids lived in the cities where they played. I can remember one time he asked me if I had all the kids in the right spots. I said the general managers are taking care of that. He said, 'That isn't what I asked you. Do *you* have?' He was very concerned about it and he let us know about it. He had a big impact."

"It was an appeal to the managers that they were the surrogate parents of those kids in the game," Hardy says. "Our wish was for the managers to carry out the responsibility in such a way that they were a surrogate parent, and that in the event that they didn't make it in baseball, you'd send them back to their parents better kids than when they came. That was our responsibility."

At the beginning and end of each season, there would be an organizational dinner, where players could meet Hardy, be apprised of the team's financial position and what lay ahead. At the major league level, there was even an offer to be guided through the club's books, an offer that only a few players (Ernie Whitt and Buck Martinez being two of them) ever took up. "I wanted to eliminate the distrust that was there and build trust in the organization," Hardy says. "You treated people with dignity and honesty in your dealings with them."

Think ahead for a moment to the strike of 1994–95, to the atmosphere of complete antagonism, to the angry rhetoric flung back and forth between the owners and the players, and you realize immediately how far the Blue Jay way of doing business, as directed by Hardy, was from the baseball norm, then or now. Other organizations scoffed at what seemed like needless frills, needless expenses. But Hardy believed that in the long term, you reap what you sow, that if the organization was a very good, very secure place to work, the best people would want to work there, and they would thrive within that environment.

"He and I used to go down and visit the minor league teams," Widdrington recalls. "I remember once we landed in Florence, and instead of a limo they sent out some car from the funeral parlours. In talking to the players—I always had to bring Hardy in and beat him over the head: talk to these young kids, you are the chairman and the CEO. Hardy's very shy but he would [do it] and he'd do a good job. One of the things Hardy noticed was that the season was very very long for the managers and coaches. Very long. And they never got to see their family. Hardly ever. He put in some system which still exists today where the coaches and manager can get two or three days off a couple of times during the summer. And they go home and see their families. We put that in and as I recall we got criticized throughout the baseball world. They thought that was just about the dumbest thing that anybody had ever done. I don't think anybody does it today other than us. But it's gained us more positive goodwill from the guys."

Hardy would have an impact on all the important figures in the Blue Jay front office: Beeston, Gillick, LaMacchia and the rest. But he forged a particularly strong relationship with Bobby Mattick. "Peter was very, very good to Mattick," Widdrington says. "And Mattick also sees Peter as a guy of about his age—they have a lot in common." They also were very different, given that Mattick, with the many stops made during his career, was by definition a product of the baseball culture that Hardy found so repulsive. In all those other places, Mattick had sensed at some point that it was time to move along—sometimes it was his idea, sometimes the organization's. But in Toronto, he stayed put, as did virtually every other key member of the baseball side of the business. You can attribute some of that to Pat Gillick and the personal loyalties that he enjoyed. But give credit, too, to Hardy, for creating a non-traditional baseball environment in which baseball men could feel real security, perhaps for the first time in their working lives.

"Hardy brought stability," Gillick says. "We knew what to expect day in and day out. We go out and do our jobs without having to worry about Pete going off one way or the other. Peter Hardy has an extremely caring, passionate side for people. That was something that he instilled in the organization. He lifted that to a higher level than anywhere else in baseball."

"People from outside of our organization," Mattick says, "would have given their eye teeth just to come with us."

THE PIECES HAD begun to fall into place. The baseball men had been allowed to go about their business, acquiring talent, making deals, hiring the right field manager. The front office turmoil ended with Bavasi's departure, and the vastly different management style brought in by Peter Hardy attracted talented people and allowed them to do their best work. Most baseball franchises were increasing rapidly in value, so the need to make an operating profit year to year was relaxed, since the owners' equity was growing by the minute. There is a huge element of chance in operating any professional sports franchise, but on paper, the Toronto Blue Jays now had all the tools necessary to succeed on and off the field.

Success, that is, measured against any other major league base-ball team: draw a couple of million fans a year, contend for a championship every decade or so, and secure a spot in the local sporting scene, co-existing with football and hockey the way baseball co-existed with football and hockey in other multi-sport markets.

But what no one could have anticipated in the early 1980s was the social and economic factors particular to Toronto at the time that would allow baseball to become much more. Nowhere in North America was there such an opportunity, something that Bavasi had at least begun to understand before his ceremonious departure.

"You're planting a tree in an area of the richest, densest soil in the world," he says. "Because you are planting what would become the Toronto Blue Jays in the centre of banking, commerce, industry and media in Canada, at that time the second-ranking movie-going city in the world. The legitimate theatre gross on a per capita basis was higher than Broadway. The number of complimentary tickets given out for events was the lowest in North America. These were important signposts, that this was rich, dense, nitrogen-loaded soil. So you take baseball and you dump it right in there and you play to all of your constituents. Make sure it's styled properly. Make sure your operation is styled in a way that is attractive to all constituents—the corporate community, children, the family audience. We've got to price it right, we've got to style it right, we've got to look right, it's got to be the most public of public enterprises."

Do all that, and then catch the wave. In November 1983, the Toronto Argonauts of the Canadian Football League won the Grey Cup for the first time in thirty-one years, a watershed moment in the local history of sports, but not in the way anyone at the time would have expected. The Argos' long, hopeless quest, far from discouraging their fans, had come to be something of a rallying point and their tragic failures part of a myth to be embraced. Like the Chicago Cubs or the Boston Red Sox, the Argos' inability to win a championship was something that could be worn as a badge of honour—the best fans, after all, are those who stick around not only in good times, but especially in bad. To have been an Argonaut supporter and to have suffered through all the flawed saviours, the dashed expectations, through Leon McQuay's fumble in the 1971

Grey Cup game that cost the team victory, was the test of true infatuation.

In the first two years of the Blue Jays' existence, the Argos actually enjoyed two of their most successful seasons ever at the box office, drawing in the neighbourhood of 45,000 fans a game. But from then on it was a long, consistent decline. That Grey Cup game in 1983 was the moment the two franchises crossed, the Blue Jays on their way to becoming the city's premier sporting obsession, the Argos on their way to becoming an afterthought. It's interesting to speculate that the Argos might have been better off not winning, better off keeping that strange mystique alive. Other things contributed as well, especially a short-sighted CFL television policy that kept many games off the screen in Ontario, while more and more baseball games—and National Football League games—became available. But the main factors that led to the Argos' downfall, and especially led to the ascendance of baseball in Toronto, were really out of their and the Blue Jays' control.

In 1983, the Canadian economy was just beginning to emerge from a debilitating recession. The years that immediately followed were marked by a phase of conspicuous consumption. It was a time when growth seemed unlimited, when many found new wealth, when development raged out of control. The heroes of the time became stock promoters and real estate speculators. Housing prices skyrocketed, making paper millionaires of those who five years before had simply invested their savings in a place to live. People poured into Toronto, from poorer parts of Canada and from every corner of the world.

Baseball rode that economic tide for a whole host of reasons. The most obvious was that the team was finally emerging from the expansion doldrums. Here, at last, was a cast of young Blue Jay stars who might eventually be the equals of any in baseball. The marketing of the club had always been sound, lacking only the sex appeal of winning. That would come now, and adding to the hard core who had followed the team faithfully since its inception would come the natural bandwagon jumpers. The Argos' recent success aside, the city had hardly been overwhelmed by championships, having suffered through the Leafs' perpetual awfulness since their last Stanley Cup victory in 1967.

Add to that a socio-cultural fact of life in the new Toronto. There was a time when the city had been secure in itself, secure in its Protestant, Anglo-Saxon, Canadian virtues, secure in the fact that while it might not be as exciting as Manhattan or San Francisco or even Montreal, it was certainly a better place to live. Toronto the Good took on ironic meaning later, but then it had the ring of truth. Look at the continuing debates over dry neighbourhoods, look at the blue laws, which hung on long after they had been discarded by cities of equal size, look how long it took to get beer into the ball park: this was a backwater, but the residents of Upper Canada liked their capital that way.

In the early 1980s, pushed on by the likes of Paul Godfrey, whose own vulgarian sensibilities mirrored those of so many of the nouveau riche, being Toronto the Good was suddenly no longer good enough. Rather than defining itself in national terms—the metropolis of English Canada—the city's movers and shakers decided they needed recognition by the entire continent, if not by the entire planet. The phrase "world-class city" was trotted out again and again to explain away any development, any mega project. What had started with the CN Tower, a strange monument to nothing, started to encompass the entire civic culture. This was a happening place, a sophisticated place, an exciting place, if only someone would notice.

Sports always plays a part in civic identification, to a greater or lesser degree depending on the times. At its most organic, it represents the basic statement of heritage, cheering for your neighbours, your family, your friends: they are me, I am them, we live here, and here is better than where you are. Beginning in the late 1970s, that relationship began to become far more complicated, as the business of sport stripped away the last vestiges of that original connection. Players could move more freely from place to place, owners (like Harold Ballard) could invert the fantasy, turning it cynical. The money paid to athletes became a daily subject in the sports pages. The home team, at least in a city as big and desperate for acceptance as Toronto, began to represent something else, not life as it had always been, but life as it might be. It was a way of shedding the old insecurities, of leaving the old neighbourhood behind. In that context, having the Argos beat up on the Saskatchewan Roughriders, or even on their traditional rivals, the Hamilton Tiger-

Cats, didn't advance the cause one little bit. But if the Blue Jays could somehow hold their own with the mighty Yankees, if they could turn American eyes northward by beating the Boston Red Sox or the California Angels, it was like winning membership in an exclusive club.

One night, early in the history of the franchise, ABC's "Monday Night Baseball" made its first visit to Exhibition Stadium, with Howard Cosell at the mike. Alfredo Griffin played the game of his life in the field, Cosell couldn't say enough about him, and you could feel the city's chest puff up just a little bit. Never mind what a bunch of rubes the local television folks must have seemed, rushing to interview Cosell as though *he* were the story. It was one of the first of many such moments—up to and including Joe Carter's World Series-winning home run in 1993—that seemed like Sally Field saying, "You like me. You really like me."

Whether it was beer in the ball park, the advent of all-sports television, the building of a new, gaudy, one-of-a-kind, monstrously expensive stadium, they all played into the myth. Toronto was growing up, getting bigger, getting better, getting more like those other emerald cities. What it meant was that if you arrived in Toronto from Lethbridge, from Sri Lanka, from Hong Kong, from Poland, from Uganda, you learned how to ride the subways, you learned to wear a warm coat in winter, and you learned about the Toronto Blue Jays. And because of that, baseball in Toronto came to mean more than baseball anywhere else. The city that had allowed the old Maple Leafs to pack up and leave without regret turned the game into an obsession.

Four million fans in a season: the modern world defies that kind of consensus. There is no common religion, no common political movement, nothing that can put that many people from diverse backgrounds—economic, ethnic, gender, it crossed all the lines—in one place for any purpose. Baseball in Toronto would do that. Going to the game, watching the game, listening to the game would become an act of faith.

◆THE TEAM BOBBY COX took over in 1982 was the beginning of that, having all the raw materials, at least, of respectability for the first time in the history of the franchise. The infield featured John Mayberry at first base—with Willie Upshaw waiting in the wings. Damaso Garcia at second and Alfredo Griffin at short held their positions until Tony Fernandez pushed one of the middle infielders aside. At third an unlikely platoon combination—right-handed and left-handed players sharing a position—of Garth Iorg and Rance Mulliniks proved extremely effective. In the outfield, George Bell, after spending a season on the big league roster as a Rule Five draftee, went to Syracuse for a year of seasoning. But Jesse Barfield would play a full season in right, joining Moseby and veteran Barry Bonnell. Behind the plate, Whitt platooned with the veteran Buck Martinez, a good defensive catcher and a stabilizing factor with the young pitching staff. Stieb and Clancy anchored the rotation, joined by Luis Leal and Jim Gott. For a closer in the bullpen, Cox had at his disposal both Dale Murray and Joey McLaughlin, acquired from the Braves before the 1980 season. In the split year of 1981, McLaughlin had ten saves, a 2.85 ERA, and a decent strikeout-to-walk ratio, though shoulder problems cut short his season in 1982.

The 1982 Jays finished just six games under .500 and technically moved out of the American League East basement for the first time in their history, finishing in a tie for sixth with the Cleveland Indians, seventeen games back of the division-winning Milwaukee Brewers. They weren't officially eliminated from the pennant race until September 14, the best ever for a full, 162-game schedule. Attendance, while not yet back to pre-strike levels at 1,275,978, was still up considerably from 1981.

Then, in 1983, what had only been hinted at the year before came to pass: the full blossoming of the Toronto Blue Jays. Here was evidence of good decisions made, of savvy deals and draft picks, of players picked from the scrap heap who actually had something left, of the right kind of leadership on and off the field. Upshaw, the former Rule Five draftee, becoming the first Jay to drive in one hundred runs. Three starters—Clancy, Stieb and Leal—posted winning records while a fourth, crusty veteran Doyle Alexander, rescued after being released by New York, rebounded from losing his first eight decisions of the year to win six for Toronto. Lloyd Moseby, the former top draft pick, finally showed his potential, hitting .315 with eighteen homers and eighty-one RBIs. Jesse Barfield hit a team high of twenty-seven home runs. And Cox platooned his players masterfully, turning two average third basemen, two average catchers and two average designated hitters into combinations that would rival the best in baseball.

The season began, as it hadn't begun since 1977, with a victory on Opening Day. The Jays went on to lose six of their first eleven, then, trailing Cleveland 7–5 entering the bottom of the ninth, won the game on two two-run homers from Cliff Johnson and Moseby. That victory proved to be an omen: the club won twenty-two of its next thirty-five games, went a franchise record 18–9 in the month of May, and moved into first place. Three Jays were named American League players of the week in succession: Luis Leal, Moseby and Dave Stieb. At the All-Star break, the Jays held a one-game lead atop the American League East, and Stieb was chosen to start the big game at Comiskey Park. They were the story of baseball, and all those big-name American television commentators joined in the chorus: this was one great organization, this was the team of the future, and perhaps even the team of today. Toronto ate it up, ate up all the attention, the acknowledgement from the south, ate up this attractive, young, exciting, winning baseball club.

Then, during one memorable terrible trip to Baltimore, came a game that all Blue Jay fans who were around at the time have permanently etched in their memories—aside from the original Opening Day in the snow, the first universally remembered moment in franchise history. It was August 24. The night before, the Jays had hammered the Orioles 9–3, closing in on first place. Heading into the bottom of the ninth inning, they again seemed on the verge of victory. Jim Clancy, in search of his fourteenth win of the season, had been brilliant, throwing a three-hitter, while the team had provided him with a 3–1 lead. But he faltered slightly—with two out, there were Orioles on first and second. Catcher Joe Nolan, a lefty, was due up, and playing the percentages, Cox brought Dave Geisel, another left-hander, in to face him. Baltimore manager Joe Altobelli countered with pinch-hitter Benny Ayala. It was a gutsy move on his part, since he'd already used his other catcher, Rick Dempsey. If the game went into extra innings, there appeared to be no obvious candidate to play behind the plate.

Ayala hit a bouncing single off Geisel to score one run. The next batter, Al Bumbry, then hit a ground ball to the left side, which should have been a relatively simple play for shortstop Alfredo Griffin. Or at least it would have been if third baseman Garth Iorg, trying to make the play, hadn't tipped the ball past him. The tying run scored, and the game went into extra innings.

No problem. The Jays had won twelve extra-inning games in a row at that point, dating back to the same date a year before. Baltimore sent reliever Tim Stoddard to the mound in the tenth, along with battery-mate Lenn Sakata, the Orioles' second baseman, who hadn't caught in a game since Little League (and who had made two errors at second the night before, earning a chorus of boos from the fans at Memorial Stadium). He wasn't the only Oriole playing way out of position. John Lowenstein, an outfielder, was at second in Sakata's place, and Gary Roenicke, who'd never played third in the majors, was at the hot corner. It figured that any ball in play would be an adventure, though that became a moot point when Jays' designated hitter Cliff Johnson promptly homered off Stoddard his twentieth of the year—and the Jays led 4–3.

What followed may have been the most bizarre sequence in Blue Jay history. Tippy Martinez came in to pitch for the Orioles, and three successive Blue Jays reached first base: Barry Bonnell, Dave Collins and Willie Upshaw. Three successive Blue Jays, emboldened by the thought of running with a non-catcher in the game and a non-infielder at second, were then picked off by Martinez. (Since Martinez kept throwing the ball to first baseman Eddie Murray, Baltimore pitching coach Ray Miller joked afterwards. "He was the only guy out there he recognized.") It was a balk move, Bobby Cox complained, and Upshaw in any case appeared to be safe. No matter. The O's were out of a terrible jam. They came to bat in the bottom of the inning, facing Joey McLaughlin, Toronto's flawed closer. Eddie Murray walked. He went to second on a ground out. John Shelby was intentionally walked with one out, to set up the double play. Pitcher Randy Moffitt came in to face Gary Roenicke and struck him out. Then Sakata came to the plate. It wasn't a great pitch, but it wasn't that bad, Moffitt said later. A slider that didn't really hang, but didn't really break, either. Sakata, no power hitter, caught it just right, and the ball hooked over the left-field fence. A three-run homer. A 6–4 Orioles victory.

Team president Peter Bavasi unveils the Blue Jays logo, 1976.

Metro Chairman Paul Godfrey and Ontario Premier Bill Davis turning sod for the Exhibition Stadium renovation, 1974.

Tibor Kolley/ *The Globe and Mail*

The first Opening Day, April 7, 1977. Snow didn't flatter Exhibition Stadium.

Tibor Kolley/ *The Globe and Mail*

Among the frost-bitten fans, Baseball Commissioner Bowie Kuhn (foreground), Paul Godfrey (behind Kuhn), and leaning forward near the far end of row one, Don McDougall.

Tibor Kolley/*The Globe and Mail*

Pat Gillick in 1976. He'd spend almost the entire first year somewhere other than Toronto, scouting talent.

Paul Beeston and the ever-present cigar. From a Welland-born accountant to the man who could have been Commissioner of Baseball.

John McNeill / *The Globe and Mail*

Roy Hartsfield demonstrates the fine art of sliding at the first spring training—Dunedin, Florida, 1977.

Dennis Robinson / *The Globe and Mail*

The skipper dispenses locker room wisdom to Ernie Whitt, Dave McKay and the rest.

James Lewcun / The Globe and Mail

Peter Bavasi: without his hiring in 1976, the Blue Jays might never have taken flight; without his firing in 1981, they might never have become a successful team.

A manager for the future: Bobby Cox signs on in 1981.

Gillick with Dave Stieb: the pitcher was the Blue Jays first homegrown star, though his temperament often got in the way of his talent.

The first heartbreak: about to lose a third straight game to the Tigers at Exhibition Stadium, part of the final week collapse in 1984.

The Blue Jays win the mini-pennant—Doyle Alexander celebrates his AL East clinching win over the Yankees on October 6, 1985.

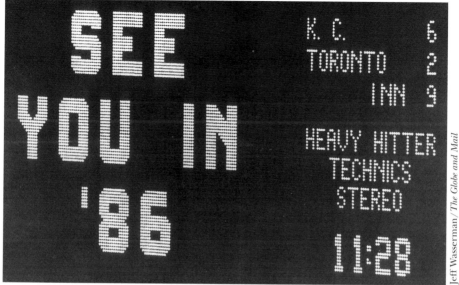

Jeff Wasserman / The Globe and Mail

The second heartbreak: Oct. 16, 1985. Jim Sundberg's wind-blown triple destroyed World Series dreams in the ALCS against Kansas City.

Thomas Szlukovenyi / The Globe and Mail

Jimy Williams was the logical choice to take over when Bobby Cox left unexpectedly after the 1985 season, but his tenure as manager would be the most difficult in franchise history.

Barrie Davis / The Globe and Mail

In Tom Henke, the Jays finally found their closer—here with Jesse Barfield whose home run swing and rifle arm made him a fan favourite.

Thomas Szlukovenyi / The Globe and Mail

Kelly Gruber, perhaps the best pure athlete ever to wear the Toronto uniform. Never would a local superstar fall so far, so fast.

Randy Velocci / The Globe and Mail

The best of friends: although it wasn't his idea, Pat Gillick was all smiles announcing that Cito Gaston would return to manage the Jays for the 1992 season.

Randy Velocci / The Globe and Mail

Although Jack Morris failed to produce in the 1992 playoffs, his tenacity and 21 wins during the regular season were keys to the first championship.

Randy Velocci/*The Globe and Mail*

The Home Opener, April 10, 1992: Devon White and Joe Carter, acquired in two of Toronto's most significant trades, would be key members of the first championship team.

Robbie Alomar and Juan Guzman celebrate winning the ALCS over Oakland in 1992. Alomar, the best player ever to wear the Blue Jays' uniform, was the series MVP.

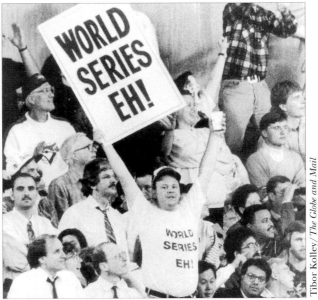

The World Series finally comes to a part of the world that isn't the United States of America. Unthinkable, eh?

Pat Gillick at his farewell press conference after 19 years with the Jays.

The next night, Dave Stieb threw nine shutout innings, and Bonnell homered in the top of the tenth to give Toronto a 1–0 lead, only to lose on a two-run double off Roy Lee Jackson in the bottom of the tenth. The night after that, in Detroit, it was a tenth-inning Alan Trammell home run off starter Jim Gott that ended matters. Those three games, three heart-breaking extra-inning losses, marked the turning point in the season and exposed the team's fatal flaw—its bullpen. The Jays dropped four of five games, falling five back of the Orioles on August 30. By Labour Day, the notion of challenging for the pennant was pretty much a pipe-dream. The Jays finished 89–73, in fourth place, nine games behind the eventual World Series-champion Orioles.

But in the process, Toronto had experienced its first real taste of pennant fever, its first real opportunity to win a championship in a big-time, big-league sport since the Leafs' last Stanley Cup in 1967. That summer, baseball for the first time became Toronto's own, as those who had perhaps caught a game or two during previous sea-sons were suddenly glued to their televisions or radios, or were snapping up some of the nearly two million seats sold at Exhibition Stadium. (Television ratings for the team soared. By mid-season, the Jays were routinely attracting more than a million viewers a game.) Scoreboard watching, magic numbers, it all became part of the casual fan's vocabulary, and the notion of a Toronto team, a Canadian team, actually appearing in the World Series—something expansion fans can't even dream about—suddenly seemed entirely possible. So did the possibility that it would be the Jays—not the Montreal Expos, the "team of the 1980s," who had flopped badly even as the Jays had prospered—who would get there first.

At the end of 1983, Canada's sports writers and broadcasters were polled, as they always are, to name the country's team of the year. The Argonauts would have seemed an obvious choice—after all, it's not every year a team ends a thirty-one-year championship drought.

But the winners, by a score of seventy-six to sixty-eight, were the Toronto Blue Jays, the vote making plain what would soon become obvious. The torch had been passed.

Chapter 12

THERE HAD BEEN a second part to Paul Godfrey's master plan to remake Toronto (just as he, with the help of plastic surgeons, would remake himself). The baseball team, thanks in large part to the hard work and deep pockets of others, had become a reality in 1976, and for that the people were eternally grateful. But the abomination down at the Exhibition grounds that housed them, the stadium that had been thrown together to secure the team, would never suffice in the long run. In the early days, when baseball was still a novelty, they could pretend that it was just different than those other parks—different than the modern stadiums in Cincinnati and Pittsburgh, different than the historic parks in Boston and Chicago, different than Dodger Stadium. Not worse, just different; homely on the outside, but like Jarry Park, a cosy little place to watch a new team take its first steps.

They could say that, but it was a lie, one that became obvious the first time a patron sat down the right-field line and suffered permanent spinal damage trying to twist and watch the play; the first time, on a day when the "good seats" were filled, a fan was forced into the far end of the bleachers and sat a mile behind the centre-field wall; the first time, in April or September, a cold harsh wind blew off Lake Ontario, the frigid effect transferred directly from the aluminum seats. The first time sitting through one of those interminable rain delays—why call a rain-out when you can start the game at 10:15 P.M. and still keep the box office receipts?

There were, of course, a few—a very few—dissenting opinions. "I loved that ball park," Bobby Cox says of Exhibition Stadium. "I'd take that park over any park I played in. I liked it that much. It just felt like a baseball park to me. It was right on the water. It was open. The wind would blow different ways every night. And the carpet was fast as shit. It was a park I liked to manage in, because I knew the park. We took advantage of that park more than any other club. We never bunted much because we had so many left-handed hitters we could always hit the hole. We had left-handed hitters hit pop-ups over the fence. We played a different game than other teams that came in there. And the fans were right there to watch it, on top of it. You walked right from the dugout into the clubhouse. Two steps, you're in it. It was just a perfect little ball park. I hate domes. I can't stand them."

Cox may have been dead wrong about Exhibition Stadium, but he was dead right about domes. Though an enclosed stadium seemed like the obvious solution in Toronto, the truth was that watching baseball or playing baseball under a roof wasn't a great experience either. The game was in fact best suited to more intimate confines and to being played on natural grass rather than artificial turf. But merely building a new conventional baseball stadium didn't jibe with the grandiose vision of Godfrey and other like-minded civic boosters. They wanted something monumental, something that—like the CN Tower—would make people stand up and take notice. Bigger was better, gaudier was better. The Toronto stadium movement, which actually predated the baseball team and was born of a time before franchises routinely held politicians for ransom in search of new facilities, took on a life of its own.

The first rumblings about a Toronto dome began not long after the world's first, the Houston Astrodome, opened for business in 1965. Jim Service, the mayor of North York when Godfrey was first elected to council, went on the record in 1969 with a plan to have such a stadium built in what was then a sleepy borough of Metropolitan Toronto. A public opinion poll at the time showed that only 21 percent of the population was in favour of the idea. But, still, Godfrey ran with it, even as he was busying himself with bringing a baseball team to Toronto.

It would be a long time coming. Legend has it that it was the Grey Cup game in 1982, held at Exhibition Stadium, that finally provided the necessary political will. From his covered seats in the north grandstand, Ontario premier Bill Davis watched as the game was played in a downpour and watched as the fans rushed for cover. That convinced him. By 1983, he was on the record as saying that a dome was "inevitable," though certainly not the kind of dome that eventually was built. Davis proposed a $150-million basic model and hoped that the three levels of government would kick in to pay for it. The federal government wasn't interested, though, and so an alternative financing scheme would also have to be part of the package.

In June of 1983, Davis appointed his old friend Hugh Macaulay, the former chairman of Ontario Hydro, to head a commission that would recommend a site for the new stadium. Eight months later, Macaulay reported back that the best place to build would be next to the Downsview Airport in North York. It was at the geographic centre of the city, and it was easily accessible via Highway 401 and public transit. But the politicians balked. The federal government, which controlled the airport, didn't want a stadium there, and Toronto mayor Art Eggleton, desperate for a stadium within his city's limits, lobbied to build at the CNE, to try to revitalize the site.

Then private enterprise rode to the rescue and settled the issue. The real estate arm of Canadian National, which controlled the former railway yard lands between Front Street and Lakeshore Boulevard in downtown Toronto, had been lobbying the local governments without success for permission to undertake a massive development of the property. Here was its opportunity. It offered up land near the base of the CN Tower where the stadium could be built, right in the core of the city. And in return, it could use the stadium as a hub for future development, which of course would now be quickly approved.

In January 1985, in one of his last acts as premier, Davis announced that the stadium would be built on the railway lands. Soon afterwards, Toronto City Council approved the plan, along with another for development of the railway lands by CN.

The only remaining question was a significant one—financing. In August 1983, a feasibility study had been released, which read in part: "Our analysis indicates that private financing is not a viable method for the domed stadium. The main reason for this is that projected net operating revenues are insufficient to generate positive cash flows (after debt service)." That was true and would eventually prove to be truer than anyone could have imagined at the time. But it was also the case that government wasn't going to be able to build the dome alone. It required a novel scheme, a combination of private investment and public underwriting, of shared profit and shared risk.

It was Trevor Eyton, the chief executive officer of Brascan, who finally came forward with a proposal to form a private consortium that would invest in the dome in return for promotional or concession exclusivity in the facility. Twenty-five companies would kick in $5 million each. And in an attempt to generate more revenues, the project would become more diversified, more grandiose. Instead of the simple, bare-bones stadium that Davis had envisioned, it would grow to include restaurants, a $6-million health club and a hotel. A project once budgeted at $150 million would wind up costing more than four times that. (And despite the promises of shared responsibility, it was the province that wound up being taken to the cleaners. While the consortium members would participate in any profits, they were protected against any losses. Unable to climb out from under the massive financing costs, the province wound up writing off $300 million before eventually selling the dome to private interests.)

The possibility was also raised that the stadium could somehow be built with a retractable roof, something that had never been attempted before. Certainly that's what the fans would prefer—sitting in the open on sunny days, when a dome can feel particularly gloomy, but otherwise shielded from the elements. In theory, having a roof that opened might allow for natural grass, which the ball players would prefer to artificial turf. "The retractable roof is a technology that is on our doorstep," Godfrey said, not that anyone really took him seriously. But what better way to make the world notice than to build something that didn't exist in the United States, in Europe, in Japan?

There remained the natural uncertainty inherent in any political decision-making process, the possibility that at some level of government, or after a government changed following an election, the plan could get scuttled. The Blue Jays' ownership knew that, but they also knew that they needed a new stadium if they were to ever make money on an operating basis in the future, especially given the way baseball salaries seemed to be spiralling ever higher. And so behind the scenes, even as the plans for a dome went ahead, they pursued the possibility of a privately financed stadium. It wouldn't be a domed stadium or a multi-purpose stadium, since as the feasibility study had indicated, those couldn't pay for themselves and they weren't particularly suited to baseball. The Jays' project instead would be a baseball-only facility modelled on Royals Stadium (now called Ewing M. Kauffman Stadium) in Kansas City, regarded then and now as the model modern ball park. (It should be noted that it was built long before new old-style stadiums like Camden Yards came into vogue.) It was intimate but large enough, with about forty thousand seats, all angled to view the centre of the diamond. No obstructions, no bad sight lines, with the possibility of private boxes, in-stadium restaurants and some of the other amenities that teams were turning to in order to increase their revenues.

The Blue Jays loved the idea of controlling their own facility and thereby controlling their own revenues. Buying land and building from scratch wasn't financially viable in the midst of a real estate boom, but in 1984, a deal was proposed that made perfect sense. A developer and the Ontario Jockey Club, which ran Woodbine race-track, approached the Blue Jays about building on property next to the track in the northwest corner of Metropolitan Toronto. Although far from the city's core, a stadium there would be easily accessible from the city's main artery, Highway 401, without the traffic snarl that fouled up the roads around the CNE whenever a game was beginning or ending. As the city extended north and west, and with the enormous growth along the north shore of Lake Ontario, more people would find it easier to reach than a stadium built downtown.

It was also a sweetheart of a deal. The track would provide the land, in return for the parking revenues and any spin-off benefits from being located beside the stadium. The developer would build the place as part of a larger development in the area, which would include an enormous shopping centre. (Baseball would then become the magnet to attract consumers to the other businesses, which would pay handsome rents to be part of it.) And the Jays would get themselves a lovely little baseball park, free and clear, to do with what they'd like. Call it Labatt Stadium, call it Howard Webster Stadium, call it Blue Jay Field. Run your own concessions, build your own private boxes, stage the odd non-baseball event—a concert or a religious revival—and keep the money. It made too much sense.

Unfortunately, it came along just a little bit too late. Before any-thing more than a bare-bones plan had been worked out, the down-town dome project became a certainty. "It would have been nice to pursue that," Beeston says. "But as fast as it gained momentum, it quickly had its legs cut out from under it. The government and the brewery were very closely tied. We were at least told that this thing would be a good thing to have. Our point was, we don't want to play in a dome—build us a retractable roof. So they built us a retractable roof."

There's no doubt that the construction of SkyDome, especially because it coincided with the team's best years on the field, was a huge bonus for the Blue Jays. The stadium opened midway through the 1989 season, as the Jays were recovering from a terrible start and heading for a division title and a spot in the post-season. The ten thousand extra seats and all the extra corporate boxes would come in mighty handy during the glory years, when the team became the first to draw four million spectators, when every game was a sell-out. On balance, even with the convoluted mess that is the SkyDome consortium, the Jays probably made more money in the Dome than they would have in their own park. And the novelty of the place, with the first retractable lid in the world, was in itself a draw—at least until that newness wore off. But still, it's tempting to think of what might have been.

AND THEN THERE was beer, which in a direct and indirect way, also helped push Blue Jay attendance skyward. Back on that snowy day in 1977 when the Blue Jays first took the field, the fans had chanted "We want beer," knowing very well that no one was really listening. This was Ontario, after all, the land of midnight last call and "Ladies and Escorts" entrances, where liquor was sold at government stores in which stern-faced men brought the product from backroom shelves, quickly wrapped it in brown paper, and then handed it over to consumers who were meant to feel a degree of shame. The notion of sitting out of doors at a sporting event and quaffing a beer ran against the grain. They might do that in the United States, they might do that in Quebec. But in the early years of baseball in Toronto the Good, neither the team nor the provincial government was interested in pushing the level of tolerance. As Larry Grossman, the minister of consumer and commercial relations in 1977, put it: "I don't want somebody puking on my kid."

Peter Bavasi, a man who rarely tippled and who had a squeamish attitude towards drinking in general, shared that line of thinking. He had been the one, after all, to forbid his employees from having a beer over lunch, lest their breath offend a client later in the day. And so despite the fact that he worked, in part, for a brewery, putting beer in the ball park wasn't one of his top priorities.

Post-Bavasi, though, that changed. The demand for beer was still there, and the laws of the land were slowly being relaxed. Closing hours had been pushed back to 1:00 A.M. Liquor stores were being converted into self-serve outlets, where patrons could actually see the shiny bottle before they made their purchase. The capital of English, Protestant Canada was becoming ever more outward-looking, ever more drawn to the south, where you could drink a beer while you were driving, with a handgun sitting on the passenger seat. To have a dry ball park started to seem like a sign of rubedom, and that would never do.

In addition, beer would make the team more money, and beer was one of the owners' core businesses. With Bavasi gone, Labatt began lobbying the provincial government, never going public, never making demands, but gradually breaking down resistance. Premier William Davis wasn't one to act rashly, or to act at all unless he thought it wouldn't alter the political balance that had kept his party in power in Ontario seemingly from the dawn of history. By 1982, the time must have seemed just about right: beer at the stadium wouldn't cause temperance crusaders to crash the doors of Queen's Park, and it wouldn't cost him votes in the heartland. Maybe it would actually win him a few.

"Baseball and beer went together," Beeston says. "And we were the only stadium in baseball that didn't serve beer. Obviously Ontario had a lot to do with it, because those were the rules. We never really pushed it. Then we started pushing in 1980–81–82, basically in conjunction with when Peter left. Because Peter wasn't a big drinker. Peter wasn't going to upset the apple cart, and in some respects that's understandable. Here would have been an American coming in here and saying, 'Here's what you have to do.' It's much easier for me to do. Because I'm Canadian, so I can talk about it: 'This is stupid, we're in the dark ages not selling beer at the ball park.' Part of the point of selling beer was that we could control it a lot better, which proved to be true, because it took away the mickeys. We used to have bins after every game of the mickeys and twenty-sixers and everything. We had fights and guys getting drunk. As soon as beer became available, once the novelty wore off—we used to sell two beers per person—we're down to half a beer per person now."

The long-awaited announcement came on July 7, 1982, at the Ontario Legislature. Dr. Robert Elgie, the minister of consumer and commercial relations, announced that beer would be sold on a trial basis at Exhibition Stadium, Hamilton's Ivor Wynne Stadium and Ottawa's Lansdowne Park during professional sporting events. If, by the end of 1983, the suds had turned fans into an ugly, rowdy lot, the sales would cease. But if the greater availability of beer didn't lead to further societal deterioration, it would continue forever. Interestingly, beer was not approved for indoor facilities, including Maple Leaf Gardens. The explanation was a strange one. Dr. Elgie said that because the arenas housed many different age groups (more than baseball?) and many different sports, including the violent boxing and wrestling, selling beer there wouldn't be appropriate.

Paul Godfrey said of the decision, which would receive quick approval from Metro Council: "It's the right move to make with the hot weather."

On July 30, 1982, Godfrey sold the first ceremonial beer to William Turner, a fan from London, Ontario, who just happened to head the line. Finally, more than five years after the franchise began, Torontonians would be able to enjoy the full baseball experience.

THE 1984 SEASON began with enormous optimism, based on the fact that the Blue Jays had made their first real run at a pennant in 1983 and on the possibilities of their young talent maturing. Dennis Lamp arrived, along with Bryan Clark, the two pegged to finally shore up the bullpen. Joey McLaughlin was finally released in May. "I tried to slit my throat with the razor," he joked, "but I missed...high and outside, I guess." The starting pitching, with Stieb, Clancy, Leal and a rejuvenated Doyle Alexander (he would finish the year 17–6 with a 3.13 ERA) was solid, and the offence, led by Dave Collins, a threat at the plate and on the basepaths, while not quite up to the standards of the season before, was still dangerous.

The Detroit Tigers, though, made everyone else's aspirations moot, starting the season at a phenomenal 35–5 and leading the American League East from wire to wire. For the first half of the season, the Jays hung tough, winning fifty games and closing to within three-and-a-half on June 6. Entering September they were still in the race, trailing by nine-and-a-half. But the magic that had allowed them to win nineteen consecutive one-run games early in the year vanished, and late-inning blown leads again became the norm, as both Lamp and Clark were major disappointments. The club had one last chance to catch Detroit in mid-September, but in two series with the Tigers, they ended by losing five of six, including a humiliating three-game sweep at Exhibition Stadium, where the cumulative score was 24–10.

The Tigers went on to win the American League pennant and the World Series, while the Blue Jays, who finished second in the division with eighty-nine wins—the same record as in 1983—returned to the search for that elusive closer.

Off the field, things had never looked better. For the first time, the Jays had topped the two-million mark in attendance, drawing 2,110,009 to Exhibition Stadium, making the club one of the top attractions in all of baseball. But still, the team wouldn't make much money, if any, on an operating basis. The Jays had broken even in 1982, thanks to the $700,000 the team received from the Boston Celtics in return for allowing Danny Ainge out of his baseball contract to play basketball. In 1983, attendance increased dramatically, but again the club budgeted for a loss. Despite drawing nearly 200,000 more fans in 1984, Beeston said that the club would again be $100,000 in either the black or the red. With a payroll of $8 million, gross revenues in the neighbourhood of $20 million and a depressed Canadian dollar, the Blue Jays managed to achieve what had become their corporate goal since the day of Bavasi's departure: put a good product on the field, spend what you have to, responsibly, and don't plan on losing money.

But now it was time to win something. All along, the baseball side of the organization had stressed developing their own talent and plucking young prospects from other teams. The big-money free agent route was the other way to go, but some of the big spenders in the sport—the Yankees and Angels first among them—had already proven that that was no sure thing. Going into 1985, though, the Jays seemed just a player away from contending. They might have won it in 1983 with a decent closer in the bullpen. They might have made a real run at the Tigers in 1984, with a decent closer. In 1985, the nucleus of the team would be that much better. The offence, the defence, the starting pitching, it all looked solid. It was time to finally go out and get that last piece of the puzzle.

In the end, it wasn't a free agent, but a trade, that would bring the Jays their messiah—the biggest trade in the franchise's history to that point. In 1984, Bill Caudill had enjoyed an enormously successful season with the Oakland Athletics, saving thirty-six and winning nine. To get him, the Jays would have to surrender a couple of valuable players: Alfredo Griffin, the shortstop who had been the lone bright light during dark times past, and Dave Collins, the versatile outfielder who had ignited the Jays' offence with his hitting and base-running and who had been named the Jays' player of the year in 1984. But both also seemed expendable, what with Tony Fernandez sure to demand a place among the starting nine, and with Jesse Barfield earning an everyday place in the outfield. In February, the Jays brought Caudill to town to announce that they had signed him to a five-year, $7-million deal, a huge commitment from an organization that would become known for its reluctance to extend contracts beyond three years. Caudill, the fans were told, was a personality, a practical joker, a free spirit who would liven up the clubhouse while turning late-inning leads into automatic victories.

"I'm not Superman," Caudill said. "I'm not going to be able to do it every time." Only in retrospect would the truth of that be evident.

There were other changes as well, as the Jays went to spring training, where they rolled to their best Grapefruit League record ever, 19–9. Gary Lavelle, a reliable left-handed reliever, was acquired from the San Francisco Giants in return for Jim Gott, who had never quite managed to establish himself either as a member of the starting rotation or as a reliever. Veteran Roy Lee Jackson and Bryan Clark were released during the spring. Jimmy Key, who had made the jump all the way from Double A the year before, became a starter. The biggest question mark was at designated hitter, after Cliff Johnson left as a free agent, signing with the Texas Rangers. The Jays got a pitcher from the Rangers' organization as compensation, a big, wild, hard-throwing right-hander from Missouri named Tom Henke. But with Caudill in the fold, he was sent to Triple A Syracuse to begin the season. Kelly Gruber, who some felt was ready to snatch third base away from the Iorg–Mulliniks platoon, showed himself to be not quite ready.

Two young players did stick on the Jays' twenty-five-man roster. Manny Lee and Lou Thornton were Rule Five picks from the Astros and Mets respectively, a shortstop and outfielder still too raw for the major leagues. But if Toronto wanted to keep them, they'd have to stay with the team all year, unless the Jays could work out some kind of deal with the other organizations. Since teams were starting to tire of having Pat Gillick snatch their best young prospects out from under their noses, that hardly seemed likely. Keeping them was a calculated risk, especially on a team that figured to be a contender. Those two roster spots could have been filled by veteran talent that might come in handy during the drive for a pennant.

The season did not begin auspiciously. Dave Stieb, as usual suffering from a lack of run support, lost 2–1 to Kansas City on Opening Day. Through the first fourteen games, the Jays were a .500 team. But then they ran off six wins in a row and found themselves in first place in the American League East for the first time since July of 1983. Key, who took Luis Leal's spot in the rotation (Leal would be demoted in July, never to return) became the first left-handed Toronto starter to win a game in five years. By the end of May, the team was cruising, 30–15, four games in the lead.

As is the case with all championship teams, some big things went right for 1985 Blue Jays. George Bell, who made all the highlight reels with his kung fu kick charge of the mound against Bruce Kison of the Boston Red Sox that June, emerged as one of the most potent offensive players in the American League. During one memorable late-season series in Chicago, he became just the seventh player to reach the centre-field bleachers in the old Comiskey Park and hit two other home runs off the left-field roof. The club's burgeoning talent was reflected in the fact that come July, four Jays were selected for the All-Star Game—Dave Stieb, Jimmy Key, Damaso Garcia and Ernie Whitt, with Bobby Cox along as a coach. But it was little things as well, moves and players who would be almost immediately forgotten once the season was done. Journeyman pitcher Tom Filer was called up from the minors and went 7–0. Still suffering from a lack of production in the designated hitter slot, Gillick traded Len Matuszek to the Los Angeles Dodgers for Al Oliver, who was then playing out the string of a distinguished career.

The greatest blessing, though, came in the form of a big, hard-throwing, near-sighted, raccoon-hunting country boy, a figure right out of the baseball cliché Hall of Fame.

"We thought we could win in '85," Cox says. "It was a big deal going out and getting Caudill. Even though he didn't do well, it still meant a lot to the team. Now in spring training we think we're going to win for sure, because now we've got a closer, and we've got Lavelle as well. Well, Caudill didn't do shit, really. But it was enough just having him there just making our players realize we could win. And then Henke came on in the middle of that season. Ball players are smart. They know what's going on too."

In 51.1 innings at Syracuse, Tom Henke had given up just thirteen hits, had an ERA of 0.88 and had eighteen saves. He arrived in Toronto on July 28, an object of much curiosity and perhaps the solution to the team's continuing bullpen problems, given Caudill's failings. By the end of the season, Henke had thirteen saves and had established himself as an intimidating, nearly-unhittable closer, that one element the team had always lacked.

In August, the Blue Jays played well, running up a 17–10 mark and sweating out a one-day players' strike. But their division lead, which started the month at eight-and-a-half games, shrunk to four by the time the teams turned for home on September 1. The New York Yankees were closing fast. August also marked the effective end of Caudill's Toronto career. On August 12, he blew a save against the Texas Rangers and admitted he just didn't have it any more. "I've reached the bottom of the barrel," Caudill said. "I'm playing for a tremendous team and I'm having a mediocre year. I'm embarrassed. I'm an embarrassment to myself."

Heading into the stretch, Gillick made the first of what would become a long series of moves to put the finishing touches on his team for the pennant race and beyond. Cliff Johnson had in some ways been more trouble than he was worth, outspoken, critical, a problem in the clubhouse, the target of some of Cox's most memorable outbursts. But when he left as a free agent after the 1984 season, he was also the best and most consistent designated hitter the team had ever had. On August 29, the organization decided that Johnson was worth tolerating, at least for another month or two, and so he was acquired from Texas. He returned to a hero's welcome, greeted by reporters at the airport as though he were the second coming of Babe Ruth. Though it would become part of the mythology of the first playoff season that Johnson's return was a key, the truth was that he hit .274—with precisely one extra-base hit, a home run.

On September 12, the Jays headed for Yankee Stadium and what would be the most significant series of the year, and the most significant to that point in franchise history: four games against the Yankees, with just a two-and-a-half-game lead atop the division. The confidence level in New York was high. There was a sense that the Jays wouldn't be able to handle the spotlight, that they would crumble under pressure. Street vendors sold Subway Series T-shirts, anticipating an October match-up of the Yankees and the Mets. Never had the crowd in the Bronx seemed quite so ugly: they booed "O Canada," though singer Mary O'Dowd did the anthem more harm than any heckler could. And anyone wearing Jays' paraphernalia in the crowd had to feel they were taking their life in their hands. After the Yankees won the opener 7–5, coming back from a 4–1 deficit in part because of two errors by Tony Fernandez, all those predictions of a collapse seemed to be coming true.

But that was as close as the Yankees would come. Toronto won the next three in a row, the great coming of age, the first real indication that the team was more than a frail front-runner. It was New York that fell apart afterwards, losing eight straight. The division title seemed secure with a four-and-a-half-game lead. By September 28, the lead was up to six. Then came a brief panic: three consecutive losses to Detroit, and the lead was down to two.

Appropriately, it was the Yankees who closed out the regular season at Exhibition Stadium, arriving on October 4 three games down, knowing that if they could sweep, the division would end in a tie, forcing a one-game playoff. With a record crowd of more than 47,000 watching, the Jays took a 3–2 lead into the ninth inning of game one and, with Henke on the mound, seemed sure to clinch. But light-hitting Butch Wynegar homered to tie the game, and then

Moseby dropped a routine fly, allowing the eventual winning run to score. The entire city of Toronto swallowed hard.

The game that produced the most famous image in Blue Jay history before 1992—Doyle Alexander pitching, George Bell catching that final fly and dropping to his knees—was actually rather routine: a 5–1 win in the season's penultimate game, with Alexander dominant, throwing a five-hitter. "Doyle got into a groove there where he was the best pitcher in baseball for a while," Cox says. "Doyle was the type of guy that doesn't really trust a lot of other people. He'd rather do it himself than trust somebody to do it for him. He's just made up that way. A very independent-type guy."

What a moment it was. Winning the first time, like so many other first-time thrills, can never be matched. "That was as good a year as you'll ever have in baseball," Cox says. "Especially when you have a young team that's never been there. That's when it's really fun. The first time is the most fun. It's the most exciting. I'll never forget that." Only losing the last, meaningless game kept the Jays from winning one hundred. Through two world championships, it would remain the franchise's best regular-season record.

◆ TO THE PLAYOFFS. There had been other comings-out, of course, the first game in 1977, appearances on "Monday Night Baseball" or the NBC "Game of the Week," chances for our great neighbours to the south to acknowledge (briefly) our existence. This was the big one, though, for even those who didn't care much about baseball tuned in for the playoffs and the World Series. And no Canadian team had ever made it to The Show. The Expos' one playoff appearance, in the strike-split season of 1981, had ended a Rick Monday home run short of the final championship showdown. If Toronto were to get there first, if Toronto, after all those years of chasing Montreal's coat-tails, would become the first foreign side to challenge for supremacy of America's National Pastime...then all that civic insecurity, all that boosterism, all that Paul Godfreyism would finally find closure. The city would be on the map.

And there was absolutely no reason, aside from inexperience, to think that the team wouldn't get there. Toronto and the St. Louis Cardinals were the two best teams in baseball over the regular season.

The Kansas City Royals, who would meet the Jays in the American League Championship Series, had just scraped into the playoffs with a late-season rush. Matched up position by position, pitcher by pitcher, the Jays seemed their equal or better.

The two managers, Cox for the Blue Jays and Dick Howser for Kansas City, took a fundamentally different approach to the series as far as their starting pitching was concerned, and their choices in the end were as big a factor as any in the outcome. Howser decided he could make the best use of his young staff by sticking with five starters in the playoffs: Charlie Leibrandt, Bud Black, Bret Saberhagen (the eventual Cy Young winner), Danny Jackson and Mark Gubicza. That meant that even his best pitcher wouldn't start more than twice, but it also gave him a tremendous amount of flexibility in the bullpen—which, aside from closer Dan Quisenberry, was the Royals' one real weak point.

Cox faced a very different situation. He had one clear ace—Dave Stieb—on his staff. He had two other reliable starters in Doyle Alexander and lefty Jimmy Key. Jim Clancy, his fourth starter, had been on and off the disabled list all season. And so Cox decided to shorten his rotation to three. Clancy would go to the pen, and if the series went the limit, Stieb would be available to start three times.

The series opened on October 8, with Exhibition Stadium gussied up in red, white and blue bunting, with a rickety, temporary press box erected down the left-field line to accommodate the overflow of reporters. Though it might seem strange to anyone who lived through later Toronto playoffs, any fan who wanted to could have walked up to the box office and bought a ticket right up until game time. It wouldn't be a good ticket—one in the far reaches of the north grandstand—and not a cheap ticket, not cheap like the four dollars those seats would normally command. Attendance was an issue: for the first game of the first major league playoff in Toronto history, there were 39,115 people in the stands. The crowds actually dwindled after that.

Those who came out for game one, and game two the following day, soon got over any jitters about whether their young team would shrink from the spotlight. Stieb, who was already being touted by some as the best pitcher in the American League, used his fearsome slider to shut out the Royals for eight innings, not allowing a runner past second base. The Jays were up 6–0 after four innings and sauntered to a 6–1 victory and a 1–0 lead in the series. Game two was very different, an offensive shoot-out that went to extra innings. And this time, it was the Royals who seemed to have a case of the post-season shakes. They had gone up 3–0 early against Jimmy Key, fallen behind 4–3, and then tied the game in the top of the ninth on a pinch-hit home run by light-hitting Pat Sheridan off the usually untouchable Henke. Then, in the top of the tenth, Kansas City took the lead, as Frank White singled in a run.

With Quisenberry on the mound to close it out in the bottom of the tenth, Tony Fernandez grounded to shortstop Onix Concepcion, who had come into the game as a defensive replacement. Concepcion double-pumped his throw, and Fernandez was safe at first. He moved to second on a ground out and then scored the tying run on Lloyd Moseby's single to right. Knowing that Moseby was a threat to run, Quisenberry tried to hold him close to the bag. But when first baseman Steve Balboni couldn't handle a throw, Moseby trotted into scoring position.

That left Howser with a decision to make. Left-handed designated hitter Al Oliver was coming to bat against the right-handed Quisenberry, with a base open. He could walk Oliver and pitch to the ever-dangerous George Bell. Or he could pitch to Oliver. Howser chose Oliver, who slapped a ground-ball single through the infield. The Toronto Blue Jays had a 2–0 lead in the American League Championship Series heading for Kansas City. The Royals were on the ropes after their tenth straight post-season defeat, dating back to 1980. "It's a depressing loss, a tough loss," George Brett said. "You don't see anybody drinking champagne and celebrating, do you?"

On the night of the off-day, between games two and three, a very confident Toronto brain trust went out for a night on the town, for what should have been a happy occasion. "It was funny," Pat Gillick remembers. "It was a little bit disappointing. I could never put my finger on it. We were in Kansas City after we had won the two games here. I'll never forget. Paul and Kay [Beeston] and Doris and I and Bob went to dinner. Bobby acted strange. It was really kind of a strange dinner. He was always a pretty intense guy. But we were up two games to nothing and we hadn't lost three games in a row all year. It was like something was really on his mind."

The Blue Jays would look back on game three as one they could have—and should have—won. Instead, Kansas City triumphed 6–5, led by Brett, who went 4–4 with two home runs, a double and a single, and who scored four runs, including the eventual game winner, driven in by a Balboni bloop single. Toronto partisans, though, would look back on one great play and two terrible calls. With Damaso Garcia on third and the Jays leading 1–0, Brett brilliantly snared a hard-hit ball by Moseby that looked like a sure double and from foul territory easily threw out Garcia at the plate. The other lowlights went to the umpires: Moseby called out on a pick-off at first when it appeared he was safe, Bell thrown out trying to steal second in the eighth inning, when he was certainly safe. "We were real aggressive that whole series, taking the extra base," Cox remembers. "It seemed like every time we did it, the umpire called us out. I watched tape after tape after tape. I was pissed about it. I was yelling at Bobby Brown, the league president, that you've got to do something about it. A couple of those go our way and we win pretty easy. It's no contest."

The fourth game would have enormous significance. Win, and go up 3–1, with two of the last three games at home. Lose, and it's a brand new series, now the best two out of three. Dave Stieb, starting for the Blue Jays on three days' rest, was nearly as good as he had been in game one, giving up just two hits over six-and-two-thirds innings. He was in trouble in the sixth, when the Royals scored their only run, walking Lonnie Smith, giving up a single to Willie Wilson, and then walking the red-hot Brett to load the bases. Hal McRae walked to bring in a run, but then Stieb escaped when Pat Sheridan popped up, and Frank White hit into an inning-ending double play.

But the Jays couldn't do anything with Charlie Leibrandt, who carried a 1–0 lead into the ninth inning. Time for another final at-bat comeback, time for more Al Oliver heroics. Damaso Garcia, a free swinger who rarely walked, opened the inning by walking on four pitches. Moseby followed with a double to right, and the game was tied. Howser then went to his bullpen, bringing in Quisenberry to minimize the damage. With a 2–2 count, George Bell singled, moving Moseby to third with none out. Bobby Cox then pinch-hit the left-handed Oliver for right-handed Cliff Johnson as designated hitter, and Oliver came through once again, hitting a 2–0 change up for a two-run double.

Tom Henke, who had come in for Stieb in the seventh, had a shaky bottom of the ninth, walking two and giving up a warning-track flyball before inducing an infield pop-up from Jamie Quirk to end the game. The Toronto Blue Jays were one win away from the World Series. It felt great. It felt like it was in the bag. "It was a great feeling," Cito Gaston says. "I never felt that way again until we won it."

Game five, October 13, Toronto's first chance to wrap it up. But it wouldn't happen against Danny Jackson. The Royals' fifth starting pitcher, coming off a 14–12 regular season, shut out the Jays on eight hits. "He doesn't even have any idea of where he throws the ball," Damaso Garcia said afterwards. "He's not the kind of pitcher who spots the ball or moves the ball around well. He just throws." Throwing was enough, though the Blue Jays did come close a couple of times. In the sixth, Garth Iorg singled and Ernie Whitt doubled, putting runners on second and third with none out. But Toronto couldn't push a run across. An inning later they loaded the bases, but Whitt grounded out to end the inning. Afterwards, George Bell told the press that the umpires were biased against Toronto because they didn't want a Canadian team in the World Series. For the Jays, that was still one win away, heading home.

Game six was a close, tense affair, a 2–2 tie through four innings. Brett homered in the fifth off Doyle Alexander to put the Royals ahead, and they added two more in the sixth. Toronto's bats had gone cold. They picked up a run in the sixth, but after that, reliever Bud Black (the game two starter) and Quisenberry shut them out through the final three. The Toronto Blue Jays were one win away from the World Series. But now so were the Kansas City Royals. In the Jays' dressing room, as that realization settled in, you could feel it slipping away.

October 16, 1985. A game full of opportunities taken and lost, of plays that affected the outcome, of decisions made, good and bad. But ask anyone now about the seventh game of the 1985 American League Championship Series, and the same things come immediately to mind. The pitcher. The hitter. The hit.

Cox says that he never wavered in his decision to bring back Stieb for game seven, again on three days' rest, rather than Jim Clancy, and the organizational hierarchy backed him in that choice. "I think that was the guy you wanted going," Cox said. "He didn't have bad stuff that day, but he wasn't on top of his game either. Clancy came in in relief. When he did come in he threw good. He hadn't pitched in a while."

The game drew the smallest crowd of the series, 32,084, which suggests that Toronto fans had already given up. But there were only 4,500 at Maple Leaf Gardens that night to watch the Leafs play the Washington Capitals, and so maybe it was the weather, maybe it was the stadium, maybe it was the ticket prices that kept them home. Kansas City was up 2–0 after four, Pat Sheridan scoring both runs, the second on a solo home run. Toronto closed to 2–1 in the fifth, when Garcia singled, then scored on Willie Upshaw's two-out double. Kansas City starter Bret Saberhagen had been forced to leave the game after just three innings, when a liner off Upshaw's bat bruised his hand. Charlie Leibrandt entered the game as his replacement.

The part everyone remembers occurred in the top of the sixth. Stieb, tiring, found his control deserting him. He loaded the bases with two walks and a hit batter, and then Jim Sundberg stepped to the plate to deliver the Toronto equivalent of Rick Monday's home run. "That little fucking pop-up," Cox calls it. "I thought it was an out. If it is we're still in the game then. We've got a chance of winning it. But that was Exhibition Stadium." It looked entirely harmless. Jesse Barfield, in right, drifted back, then farther back, then to the warning track. When the ball finally fell to earth, it landed on top of the temporary outfield fencing that separated the ball park from the empty expanses of the football turf. It bounced in, so it was a triple, and not a grand slam home run. A small mercy that. Three runs scored. The game was over then and everyone knew it, though they played all nine in any case. The final score was 6–2, and the Royals became only the fifth team in baseball history to that point to go down 3–1 in a series and come back to win. Stieb, who wanted it perhaps more than anyone, whose competitive fires burned so brightly that it made him a distinctly unpleasant human being, found a quiet corner of the clubhouse where no one could disturb him, and he stayed there a long, long time.

Toronto over the years had gained a reputation as a very forgiving sports town. The Maple Leafs, through their years in the wilderness, sold out virtually every night, and the Argonauts thrived through more than thirty years between Grey Cup victories. It has been suggested that the enormous success of the Blue Jays has something to do with that, that Torontonians will buy tickets in large numbers for anything, so long as they think it's first class.

But the reaction after the loss in game seven would suggest otherwise—the disappointing attendance, the tendency to blame the players for what had happened. "They Blew It," read the headline in the *Globe and Mail* the next day. It was sports editor Paul Palango's personal reaction to all of the "We Did It" headlines that had followed the division title, a way of reasserting journalistic distance. But for a large part of the population, that was also an accurate reflection of sentiments. When you consider that most teams, during their first trip to the playoffs (or during their first trip in a very long time, like the Cleveland Indians in 1995), are given the benefit of the doubt and are cheered no matter what the outcome, that kind of reaction in Toronto, the capital of politeness, suggested that maybe this town was a tougher sell than its reputation would suggest.

Within the organization, no one was paying much attention to the public's reaction, though. They were too busy trying to get over their own disappointment. Kansas City's win in the World Series only underscored the point: this Toronto team was one that could have won it all. And the veteran baseball men in the group knew how rarely those kinds of opportunities came along. Ask them in Boston. Ask them in Chicago.

"I think I suffered more at the end of that season than I ever have," Cito Gaston says. "I just kind of went down to the basement by myself and thought about it. That one hurt. It hurt a lot."

But once the pall lifted, and it was time to take stock, there was still the realization that, by and large, this was a young team, that its key components might still be getting better, that there was no reason the Blue Jays wouldn't be back in the post-season in 1986. With Bobby Cox at the helm, with the ownership willing to do what was necessary to win, they would get over the disappointment and be a better team for it. What manager wouldn't want to be in a situation like that?

"Those were four of the best years I ever spent in baseball," Cox says. "I loved it. I loved it there."

Chapter 13

BOBBY COX COULD have managed the Blue Jays forever, he could have been to Toronto what Walter Alston was to the Los Angeles Dodgers, skipper for life. No one questioned his abilities. No one really blamed him for the loss to the Royals. No one would be better able to lead the franchise to a championship, and beyond. The Beeston–Gillick brain trust had mapped it out perfectly. They had built a winning team, they had found and hired the man to manage that team, and they had won a title, falling just short of a league championship. Surely that would come, surely a World Series would come. Despite all the uncertainty inherent in professional sport, Beeston, Gillick and the rest had made it look like you could script success.

What they didn't know, though, was that the third musketeer had other plans. The rumour that Cox might be headed back to the Atlanta Braves had first begun circulating back in August, when the Jays were on a road trip in Chicago. It was met with blanket denials from all parties. On October 1, an Atlanta newspaper reported that Cox, who had been fired by Ted Turner as the field manager of the Braves in 1981, was Turner's first choice to become the team's general manager and manager in 1986. Again came the denials. "I haven't heard anything about it," Cox said. "I'm happy where I am…. I don't know what the guy wrote, but it seems like they've had everybody in that job." That part was true: virtually every big name in baseball, from Tommy Lasorda to Pete Rose, had been rumoured to be in line for the post. But sources confirmed that Cox was at least on the list, that the salary for the position would be in the range of $500,000, that it would include a multi-year deal (whereas the Jays made it a policy to offer managers just one-year contracts, in the manner of the Dodgers). As well, there was the fact that Cox still lived near Atlanta, in Marietta, Georgia, during the off-season. Going there would be going home. But there was a big difference between Turner wanting to hire Cox and Cox actually having been approached by Turner. Since Cox remained under contract to the Blue Jays until the end of the season, the latter would be considered tampering.

The issue naturally surfaced again on October 7, the day after the end of the regular season, with the Jays preparing for their first playoff appearance. Cox was asked if he planned to be back with the Blue Jays in 1986. "Yessir," he answered. Pat Gillick was also asked if he thought Cox was coming back. "Yup," he replied. The "yup" appears to have been sincere. Gillick, Beeston and the rest of the Toronto brass say that they ended the season with no reason to believe that Cox was leaving—despite the rumours. "Coxie was my friend," Beeston says. "Why wouldn't he tell me if that was the case? Why wouldn't he tell Pat?"

About the veracity of that "yessir," the jury is still out. It is indeed hard to believe that it was only after Toronto was eliminated by the Royals that Cox talked to Turner, considered his options, packed his bags and left. Still, the fact is that in the meantime, Turner had gone out and hired a field manager, Phil Regan. That position, and not being a front office man, was the job Cox seemed most suited for, and in the normal course of events, a general manager would be hired first and then allowed to hire his own field manager. So if it was a conspiracy on Turner and Cox's part, it was one that wasn't particularly well executed.

Today, Cox sticks by his story. "That was the hardest thing I ever did in my life, having to leave there. But I did it because it was a chance to work in [my] own home. I went in and talked to [Beeston and Gillick] after the season. They said Ted Turner had called and asked for permission to talk to me about managing the Braves. So I talked to him. It's pretty hard to turn down a five-year contract in your home town where you're working fifteen minutes away from your family. I didn't expect myself to go. The farthest thing from my mind was leaving there. I felt bad about it. You think about loyalty and that. And I was always one that preached loyalty. But when that came open and Ted wanted me there, it was hard to say no. I've never really gotten over it myself, because I loved those guys. If you had to work for anybody, you'd want to work for them."

"Those guys" haven't really got over it, either.

"It was very disappointing," Beeston says. "I will never know and they will deny it, but there was no question in my mind that they tampered, which really pissed me off. Because they didn't tamper after the season, they tampered during the season and during the playoffs. I knew that Cox was going, in retrospect, the day that he left here, which would be one or two days after the season. I looked and there was nothing in his office. Everything was gone. He was shipping things you wouldn't normally ship if [you were] going to stay. But I never thought of it at the time. But then I found out about two days later. By the time we went to St. Louis for the World Series, he had accepted the job. There was no back and forth. He wasn't going as a manager, he was going as a general manager. You couldn't really hold it against him. I never have been bitter with Atlanta over that, but I have been sincerely bitter about the fact that I will never believe that they didn't fucking tamper with him."

"It was a decision largely made as a family," Al LaMacchia says. "His wife was a girl from north Georgia. She wanted to move back. Her children loved Georgia. When you're in a second marriage like Bobby was—I said, 'Bobby, you have to keep her happy.' He felt bad about it. I know it upset a lot of people here."

◆ THE OBVIOUS CHOICE as Cox's successor was Jimy Williams. The Toronto Blue Jays, who prided themselves on loyalty and continuity and promoting from within, found a manager where managers are supposed to develop, in the third-base coach's box. When Cox left, deserting a young, talented team that had been within a few inches of the World Series and still had room to improve, there was no point in shaking things up, in deviating from the program. The program had worked, splendidly, and if Cox wasn't willing to continue, then the next best thing would be his right-hand man. "I said Jimy, absolutely, should be manager of the ball club, period," Cox says of his recommendation. "There was no doubt about that." Williams was popular with the players, known for his sense of humour. He had been successful as a manager in the minor leagues before coming to Toronto to work under Bobby Mattick in 1980. He was immersed in the team's own peculiar culture, and he was a comfortable fit. The Jays never looked anywhere else.

"He was A, a good person; B, a good teacher; C, he got along with the players; D, he had a good command of the job; E, he had previous managing experience in the minor leagues," Beeston says, listing the qualities that resulted in Williams's hiring. "He was maybe the best third-base coach in the game and he earned a chance. And he wanted it. Plus there was no one else on the team at that point. Cito wasn't ready, because he was never a manager in the minor leagues."

"We thought that he knew the personnel on the team and knew the team as well as Bob did," Gillick says. "So we thought it would be a normal transition for Jimy, a third-base coach, to come on over. At the time I didn't think it would be as difficult as it turned out to be. In hindsight, I think it's a pretty difficult situation to change roles."

Williams was from California, born on a ranch outside the town of Arroyo Grande, halfway between Los Angeles and San Francisco, not far from the Hearst Castle at San Simeon. His father raised beef cattle, and Williams and his six siblings grew up in an atmosphere of hard work and few frills. "We had three square meals a day, but I don't think it was that easy," he said. "I don't think we had a lot of things some other people had. But when you're a child, I don't think you really notice that. You just notice what you have and you don't worry about it." Williams himself was quiet, studious, popular in school and extremely serious about sports. At Arroyo Grande High School, he played basketball, ran cross-country, while playing for three different baseball teams at once. He also lost the second "m" in his first name—as a prank, he signed himself "Jimy" on a test one day. The spelling stuck.

When Williams was eighteen years old, his father died, and his high school baseball coach, Gene "Peewee" Fraser, took on an even more central role in his life. Already close, they became like father and son. "He was an all-around American boy," Gene's widow, Eleanor Fraser, remembers of Williams. "Jimy used to even work out on Sundays. My husband would get up with him and they'd go hit some balls. His sisters and my daughter would chase them. That was a weekly occurrence. People around town would kid our daughter about her 'brother.' They were that close.

"Baseball is his life," Mrs. Fraser says, but to that end there was one problem. By most objective standards, Williams was too small to be a big league shortstop: five feet, eleven inches, but just 140 pounds. "I was minute," Williams said. No one scouted him or attempted to sign him out of high school, so he enrolled in Fresno State College on a baseball scholarship, planning to study agribusiness and animal science and then return to the ranch. But still, he refused to give up on the idea of playing as a pro. During the summer, he travelled to Sturgis, South Dakota, and he played in the Basin League, where college players competed to showcase their talents and pick up some meal money. Jim Palmer, Jim Lonborg, Carl Morton and Don Sutton all played against him there.

Williams did well enough to attract the attention of Bobby Doerr, then scouting for the Boston Red Sox, who saw him playing for the semi-pro Alaska Goldpanners in the 1964 National Baseball Congress tournament in Wichita, Kansas. "He could play the heck of shortstop," Doerr said. "And he was a determined type of kid, so he would have improved his hitting. When you see a kid with a make-up like that, it really impresses you. They don't shy away from failure. They just battle it out." Doerr signed Williams, and he was assigned to Waterloo, Iowa, of the Midwest League.

The St. Louis Cardinals drafted Williams out of the Red Sox system in 1966 and, under league rules, were forced to keep him on their major league roster for the entire season or else offer him back to Boston. Williams appeared in only thirteen games, hitting .273 and knocking in one run. The next year, he started at Double A, moved to Triple A, and then spent the month of September with the Cards, recording two more major league at-bats, and no hits, in what would be his final appearance as a player in the majors. After another season in the minors, the Expos selected Williams in the 1968 expansion draft—which ought to have been his best opportunity to finally make the big leagues. But that winter, those hopes effectively vanished. "I picked up a Styrofoam cup and I just tried to throw it," Williams says. "There was no weight resistance. Something just happened. A freakish thing. I didn't think anything of it and then there was a sharp pain that went through [my shoulder]. It was close to spring training, and I hadn't worked out, throwing-wise. I was in St. Louis and I was going back to California for a few weeks to work out before I left for spring training. When I went home it still bothered me. It just kept right on bothering me."

Williams had torn the rotator cuff in his right shoulder, his throwing shoulder. It was misdiagnosed as tendinitis, and he was advised to play through it. He played for what was then the Expos' Triple A farm team in Vancouver, but finally he gave in to the pain and underwent surgery. There were two more seasons in the minors after that, but Williams was never again an effective player. He was twenty-eight years old when he quit the game, seemingly for good. He returned to St. Louis, lived with friends there, worked for the Ford Motor Co. for a short time and then bought part ownership in a 7 Eleven convenience store. "You work to live or you live to work," Williams remembers of the time. "And I was living to work."

In 1973, the California Angels rescued Williams, offering him the job of managing their Midwest League team in Davenport, Iowa. He jumped at the chance and proved to be more of a natural managing than he had ever been playing. He moved through the organization from class A to Triple A, where he won the Pacific Coast League championship with Salt Lake City in 1979. The next year, the Blue Jays hired him to work as third-base coach under Bobby Mattick. "When I managed in the minors, I never felt like I really had to manage in the big leagues to satisfy my goals," he said in 1986. "After getting there, I just said, hey, if you get to manage you get to manage; if you don't, you don't."

The truth was, though, that Williams wanted the opportunity badly—perhaps too badly, in retrospect. An injury had cost him any chance at a major league playing career. Nothing was going to cost him his chance at being a major league manager. Even before his inaugural season began, Williams was a changed man. The easy, friendly, funny guy turned tense, suspicious and driven. There is a big difference between being a coach and being a manager—the same one found in any organization between middle managers and the boss. A coach can, and should, play both sides of the fence. He can be the players' friend, the players' confidant, even as he is carrying out the manager's wishes. There is no pressure from the media, no sense that the responsibility of every win or loss is his alone. He can be a coach and still be himself, still live his life as it has always been lived. To manage, though, means stepping into the spotlight, taking charge, making the decisions, handling the personnel, in an environment in which every move, every action, is scrutinized. In his heart, Jimy Williams wanted that job. But perhaps also in his heart, he wasn't sure that he was up to it. And so, sitting beside the pool at his house one afternoon that winter, at a time when his dream was coming true, when he shouldn't have had a care in the world, Williams was instead wound as tightly as the guts of a golf ball.

"Who knows what a Jimy Williams is?" he said. "There are no statistics to show what Jimy Williams did in the big leagues because he didn't do shit in the big leagues. So the only way for me to show that I deserve an opportunity is, provided they are capable of winning, that I keep them from losing."

ENTERING 1986 WITH essentially the same team that had finished 1985 meant they had to at least duplicate what Cox had achieved, though real success could only be a berth in the World Series. On paper, the talent was in place to do just that, what with a strong starting rotation, a dominant closer in Tom Henke, a great offensive team that played above-average defence. But the hangover lingered throughout the organization. The effect of Jim Sundberg's windblown triple was still being felt by every player in the clubhouse.

There was also something else that hadn't reared its head during the Cox years: open player dissent. During spring training, Doyle Alexander, one of the heroes of 1985, announced that because of contract squabbles with the organization, he wanted to be traded. And Damaso Garcia, one of the offensive catalysts of the team, grumbled about being dropped from the lead-off spot to ninth in the order, allowing Lloyd Moseby to bat first. It wasn't Williams's decision alone—with the Blue Jays, major changes were almost always the product of a consensus among the manager, Gillick, Beeston, Mattick and LaMacchia—but it was Williams who had to implement it. The rationale was straightforward. Garcia almost never walked and so didn't meet the criteria of the classic lead-off man, who should have a high on-base percentage. But because of the way it was handled, Garcia felt humiliated—after all, the team had won a division and nearly gone to the World Series with him batting first. A rift developed between player and manager that never completely healed, and Garcia was never as effective again. In many ways, it mirrored the events to come two years later, the events that eventually cost Williams his job.

From opening day, the Jays stumbled, with Dave Stieb, Jimmy Key and Dennis Lamp all struggling badly in the season's early days. Garcia was back hitting lead-off after twenty-seven games, but that wasn't nearly enough to right him or to right the team. On May 14, at the end of a particularly disheartening west coast road trip, the players returned to the clubhouse after a game in Oakland to find a uniform and cap smouldering on the floor of the washroom. Through the charred polyester you could still make out the number seven—Garcia's number. In an act of frustration, he had sprinkled rubbing alcohol on the uniform and set it alight. The fans, though, interpreted the act differently, as one of disrespect towards the team and, by extension, towards the city. Garcia, never a great communicator, couldn't convince them differently, and so when he came home, the booing began. And there were other incidents that found their way into the newspapers, screaming matches with Ernie Whitt and Jesse Barfield, a two-round fist fight at the batting cage with Cliff Johnson. One of the most valuable and popular players of 1985 had become a pariah in 1986.

Through all the turmoil, and through the very bad play early in the season, Williams didn't seem to know how to react. The transition from coach to manager wasn't coming easily. Where Cox would have closed the doors, busted up a few lockers, and made his point known in no uncertain terms, Williams stewed quietly. It wasn't until May 21 that he finally exploded, but by then the Jays were stumbling along, three games under .500, and out of contention.

In the first week of July, Alexander and his similarly disenchanted pal, Jim Acker, were shipped to the Atlanta Braves for starter Joe Johnson and a hard-throwing but raw young right-hander named Duane Ward. After the All-Star break, when they were in fifth place, ten-and-a-half games out, the Jays began to play better. They moved to within three-and-a-half games of the division-leading Boston Red Sox by August 29. On September 5, turning for home, they had won ten of eleven games and were four-and-a-half back of the Sox in second place, the only team with a chance to catch Boston. But instead of making it a real pennant race, the Blue Jays folded, losing five in a row. On September 28, at Fenway Park, the Red Sox were in a position to clinch with a win. Williams decided to give Ward his first major league start, a move that didn't sit well with several members of the team, including catcher Ernie Whitt, because it smacked too much of concession. Ward crumbled, the Sox won 12–3, and the Blue Jays were finished. They lost seven of their last nine games, including both ends of a double header to Milwaukee, which closed the season at Exhibition Stadium. That left the Jays with a record of 86–76, in fourth place in the American League East. The team that had been so close to the World Series a year before had taken a colossal step backwards.

Still, Pat Gillick said he was "real happy" with Williams, and the manager's contract was renewed for the 1987 season. In the off-season, it became clear just how much of a good company man the skipper was. A clause in Dennis Lamp's contract guaranteed his full 1987 salary—$600,000—if he made at least forty appearances during the 1986 season. He had gone to the mound fifty-three times in 1985 but was ineffective the next year and found himself confined to the bench for long stretches—including one period of twenty-six days in which he wasn't called upon to throw a single pitch. Lamp figured that this was no coincidence, especially since he claimed that Gillick and Beeston had come to him in mid-season and offered him $25,000 to waive the appearance clause in his contract. When he refused, and then finished the year four appearances short, which allowed the Jays to buy him out for $100,000, Lamp filed a grievance against the team. And he might have won it if not for the fact that Williams convinced the arbitrator that it was solely his decision to sit Lamp down, and that he'd done it not for contractual reasons, but because he'd lost confidence in the reliever. Lamp lost his case, and Williams might have rightly figured that the organization owed him one.

◆THE 1987 SEASON belonged to George Bell on the field, just as the 1988 season would belong to Bell off the field. He was another Al LaMacchia discovery, a former prospect in the Phillies' system who had been hurt while playing in the Eastern League in 1980 and then headed straight back to the Dominican Republic. LaMacchia had seen him the year before and had been impressed. When he wasn't protected by Philadelphia and seemed to have disappeared off the face of the earth, there were only two possibilities: "I said he's either hurt real bad or they're trying to hide him," says LaMacchia.

LaMacchia asked Epy Guerrero, the Jays' man in the Caribbean, to find out what Bell was up to. Guerrero reported back that Bell had been working out with a Dominican team during the day and that he appeared to be physically fit. That news was enough to put LaMacchia on a plane bound for the islands. "The coach, without realizing what was going on, let George play the next morning," LaMacchia says. "He wasn't given strict orders not to play him. He played and I saw he was sound and I phoned Pat and said, 'He's sound, you've got to take him.'"

The Jays selected Bell in the Rule Five draft, which meant that he had to spend the entire 1981 season on Toronto's major league roster or be returned to the Phillies. (Gillick's other Rule Five catches: Willie Upshaw, Kelly Gruber, Manny Lee, Jim Acker and Jim Gott.) At first, Philadelphia tried to play it cool. "A guy from the Phillies called me and said, 'You took a cripple,'" LaMacchia says. "I said to him, 'I thought that was George Bell I saw playing the other morning over in the Dominican Republic.' Philadelphia was upset after that. They fired the guy that let him play that day—not knowing that I was there specifically to see George Bell."

It didn't take Bell long to assert his unique personality: a proud, sensitive man, a man not entirely comfortable in English or outside Dominican culture, a macho man, a man with a thin skin and a short fuse. When he arrived with the big league team, he lacked no confidence in his own abilities. Bell was there and Bell thought he belonged there. Unfortunately for him, the manager of the day, Bobby Mattick, didn't quite agree. "The first year I was managing we drafted him," Mattick says. "I didn't play him as much as he thought he should be played. We had a couple of go-rounds. I don't think he's too fond of me. But he's a gamer. He's a great competitor. He had a lot of ability. And he had a good heart, in the respect that he'd go out and give you a good day's work."

Bell got into sixty games, but the next year he was sent to Syracuse, where he spent all of 1982 and most of 1983. But by 1984, he was a regular in the Toronto outfield and immediately showed himself to be comfortable at the plate, hitting twenty-six home runs and driving in eighty-seven. "George Bell was probably the best natural hitter out of all of them," Cito Gaston says, taking in all the batters during his tenure as hitting coach and then manager. When you consider the group, including the top three batters in the American League in 1993, that is no small compliment. Defensively, though, Bell was another story. An adequate outfielder in his early years, he eventually came to be thought of as a defensive liability—and that prompted one of the worst organizational decisions in the history of the franchise.

To get Bell the hitter, a manager would have to put up with Bell the fielder, and especially with Bell the clubhouse agitator. Part of the problem was with the press, and a big part of that was language: Bell would say things without completely understanding the implications, then he'd react angrily when he thought he'd been taken out of context. He'd react again as his angry reactions made print. Reporters would sometimes circle his locker as though circling a caged animal, poking at it with a stick to get a rise. Off the field, on the road sitting in a hotel bar, it was an entirely different story. There, Bell could reveal a sweet side, a funny side; there, he'd seem more man-child than anything else. But with the television lights on, with the microphones pointed his way, the dynamic changed. When cornered, Bell would spout off—once suggesting that fans who booed him could "kiss my purple butt"—and the cycle would begin again.

The other place Bell often found himself in trouble was with his teammates. A constant needler, he was especially tough on younger Latin players, firing off criticism that he thought was funny, but that to others seemed simply dumb or cruel. With George Bell on your team, you knew there would be hard feelings sooner or later, and sooner or later he'd test the manager's authority.

"George Bell was not part of the Latin group. He was not part of the black group. He was not part of the white group. He was with all of them or by himself—it made no difference," Paul Beeston says. "He said exactly what he thought to [anyone]. His biggest fights were with the other Latins. But it didn't stop him from taking on Gruber, and it didn't stop him from taking on Moseby or Barfield. He would laugh at those guys reading the Bible, yell, 'Ah, that's horseshit,' and yet he was very religious himself. The man was a man of contradictions."

"George had no tact in him," Gaston says. "That's another language thing. He didn't speak the language well enough to do it.

Even if he did, with some of the Latin kids, he did it the wrong way. But his heart was in the right place."

Imagine that kind of complex, difficult personality type, imagine Jimy Williams's personality type, and consider that the longer Williams managed, the more strict his regimen became. This was a team that seemed to be underachieving, this was a manager who seemed to be getting more and more tense, more and more hung up on every tiny aggravation. Eventually, something was going to give.

THE PRE-SEASON CONSENSUS in 1987 was that it would be the Yankees and Blue Jays battling for the division title, and that's just how it was heading into June. The longest winning streak in Blue Jay history, eleven games—six over Baltimore, three over New York and two over Seattle—vaulted Toronto into the division lead, but that was soon followed by an eight-game losing streak that left the Jays a full five games behind the Yankees. Blowing hot and cold became a trademark of the team, and its final cold streak became its epitaph.

Bell was the first Blue Jay voted by the fans to start the All-Star Game, a triumph of talent over bad public relations. On August 9, in the middle of what was developing into a three-way pennant race, with Detroit added to the mix, Gillick moved to strengthen the starting pitching, adding ancient knuckleball pitcher Phil Niekro from Cleveland. He didn't win a game in a Blue Jay uniform and was released August 31 when Toronto picked up Mike Flanagan from Baltimore, a move that proved somewhat more significant.

Entering September, the Yankees had fallen out of the race, and it was Toronto and the surprising Tigers battling for supremacy in the American League East. With seventeen games left, the two teams—the two best teams in baseball—were deadlocked at 88–57. It came down to the final ten games of the season, when Toronto and Detroit faced each other seven times, beginning with four games at Exhibition Stadium. The Jays began the stretch with a record of 93–59, the Tigers 92–59. The stage was set for the greatest series of highs and lows in the history of the Blue Jay franchise and ultimately for one of the worst late-season collapses in the history of major league baseball.

Toronto won the first three games at home, two of them with dramatic late-inning rallies, but along the way paid a terrible price. In the first game, the Tigers' Bill Madlock, attempting to break up a double play, threw what looked like a cross-body block at Toronto shortstop Tony Fernandez, then in the midst of a career year at the plate and in the field. Depending on your allegiances, Madlock's assault was either a good, hard, aggressive slide or a dirty, deliberate attempt to injure. Fernandez flew high into the air and landed with the point of his right elbow striking a small strip of wood that separated the artificial turf from the dirt sliding area. He screamed in pain, clutched his arm and, as he was being helped off the field, doubled over in agony at the third-base line. The diagnosis: a fracture of a small bone at the tip of the elbow. The consequence: the end of Fernandez's season. Manny Lee became the starting shortstop.

Leading the division by three-and-a-half games now with just seven left, Toronto lost an opportunity to all but put the Tigers away when they dropped a 3–2, extra-innings decision at Exhibition Stadium. The star for Detroit was former Blue Jay Doyle Alexander, undefeated in a Tiger uniform, who pitched ten-and-two-thirds innings, giving up only a single unearned run.

The Jays then welcomed Milwaukee for three games, while the Tigers headed for Baltimore for four. Detroit would split. Toronto would be swept, losing Ernie Whitt along the way; he suffered cracked ribs colliding with Paul Molitor at second base, attempting to break up a double play. Heading to Detroit at one game up with three to play, Toronto was without two of its best offensive players and, in Whitt, one of the team's leaders. They were also without the hot bat of George Bell, who for the first and only time that season was mired in a terrible slump.

The key moments of those three games at Tiger Stadium are remembered by every Toronto partisan, even as they've tried to forget. In game one, Lee hit a three-run homer off Alexander, but still the Tigers persevered to win 4–3, tying the division with two games left. In game two, Flanagan pitched brilliantly through eleven innings. But in the twelfth, Williams turned the game over to Jeff Musselman, who loaded the bases with one out. He was replaced by Mark Eichhorn, with his submarine delivery, there to coax an inning-ending double-play grounder from Detroit shortstop Alan Trammell. He did just that. Trammell sent a sharply hit grounder right at the drawn-in Lee, who could have at least had the force at home. But the ball shot between his legs, allowing the winning run to score. With one game left, Detroit now held the lead by one. The best the Jays could hope for was a tie and a one-game playoff.

The finale: Jimmy Key was brilliant, throwing a complete game three-hitter. But the Jays couldn't score. And in the second inning, Detroit's Larry Herndon launched what looked like a routine fly to left, but it just kept going and going, finally sailing over the short fence and into the first row of seats. Maybe Bell could have played it. Maybe not. No matter. The season was over. The Blue Jays had won ninety-six games, the second-best record in major league baseball. They had put together what may still have been the best line-up, all around, in franchise history. They had enjoyed the greatest single offensive performance in franchise history: Bell's .308, forty-seven HR, 134 RBIs. They had seen Jimmy Key win seventeen, Jim Clancy win fifteen and Dave Stieb bounce back from the frustrations of the previous year to win thirteen. They had seen all three outfielders hit more than twenty home runs, and they had seen the emergence of Fred McGriff, who hit another twenty.

And they once again found themselves on the outside looking in when the playoffs began.

Chapter 14

D URING THE FINAL months of 1987, the men who ran the Toronto Blue Jays tried to fix something that wasn't really broken. On the field, they had exactly the team they wanted, the players they had developed or acquired. It was still young, remarkably talented, an offensive machine backed by a fine pitching staff. But for the unfortunate events of the last week of the 1987 season, they might well have been World Series champions. And then everything would have been different.

But the collapse of 1987, on the heels of the disappointing 1986 season, suggested that there was a pattern developing, that despite its on-paper strength, this team in its current configuration just didn't have the stuff to win. Normally, that's a situation in which managers find their jobs in peril. But Jimy Williams still enjoyed the full support of the Toronto hierarchy. The change would have to come in the field and in the clubhouse, something to alter the chemistry of the team, to allow a new face or two to crack the starting line-up. A fine adjustment—nothing drastic—designed to finally make the Blue Jays a champion.

In some ways it was an obvious choice. George Bell, the American League's most valuable player in 1987, was the greatest offensive force in baseball. But defensively, in left field, he had fallen from just above average to just below average. And two of Toronto's best young prospects—Syl Campusano, a "phenom" from the Dominican Republic, and Rob Ducey, a homegrown product of Cambridge, Ontario—were outfielders apparently on the brink of making it in the major leagues. At the same time, the Jays didn't have an obvious everyday designated hitter on their roster. There was a big kid named Cecil Fielder who seemed to have some raw potential, but making him a designated hitter so early in his career could only harm him down the road.

Logic dictated a shuffled line-up: Campusano (or Ducey) in centre field, moving Lloyd Moseby—who was prone to defensive lapses—to left; Bell to designated hitter. The team would still have the benefit of his power, and he'd come to understand that becoming a full-time hitter could only save his knees and lengthen his career.

"We wanted to be a defence-oriented club and George definitely didn't fit into that," Pat Gillick says. "The best place to kind of hide George was DH. But George thought that being a DH was just for old people, that he'd only be half a player, and he also realized that his value on the market would go down if he was only a DH. George has a lot of pride. I don't agree with George all the time. He liked to win, he liked to play. The only thing about George was that he wanted to win in his style, and that style didn't always coincide with the manager or the management. He doesn't like to take orders. George was a bit of a one-way street."

A meeting was called for mid-January, in Dallas, where Bell and his agents, the Hendricks brothers, Randy and David, would sit down with Gillick, Beeston, Williams and Al LaMacchia, in theory to discuss Bell's contract. (Bell had threatened to leave as a free agent after the 1988 season if he wasn't given a long-term deal.) In fact, the real agenda was to convince Bell that a change of position was for his own good. It did not go well. Gillick suggested the move to designated hitter. Williams made certain that Bell understood this was a permanent, not part-time shift.

Bell responded with the usual expletives and later told the press: "There's no way Jimy Williams can make me a DH, no matter what." The gauntlet had been thrown down. The battle of wills had begun.

And in the process, the brain trust had walked into exactly the type of situation they had so scrupulously avoided in the past. They had pitted their best player against their manager in a struggle that would surely produce negative fallout in the clubhouse. They couldn't give in to Bell, because that would undermine Williams's authority. But could they really afford to play chicken with someone so proud, so stubborn, and so valuable to the team on the field? "If we can work this thing out with George, I think we can be better off," Gillick said at the time. "It's a rocky situation, which could become a distraction."

That wasn't the half of it. Bell didn't report to spring training until the latest day possible, firing off messages from the Dominican Republic in the meantime to show that he meant business. "I don't really care about Jimy because he shows me he's got no respect for the players," he said two days before landing in Dunedin. "If you don't have respect for the players, they're not going to play for you." When he and Williams finally met on March 2, things didn't get any better. "After the kind of season I had last year, to come to spring training and have no job it's kind of hard....I don't think I'm hurt. I've been in more pain, mental and physical, and survived. I think I could play real good in left field. I've been doing that all my life and I'm only twenty-eight years old.... After ten years as a designated hitter, I could be 250 pounds. As a DH, all you do is sit and eat sunflower seeds." And more. "We came fourteen games out of first place [in 1986] because he messed around with the line-up and took [Garcia] out of the lead-off spot."

For an exhibition game at Grant Field on March 17, Bell's name was pencilled in as designated hitter. He lounged in the left-field bullpen until it was his turn to bat—something a player can get away with during the relaxed days of the spring. What he couldn't get away with was not bothering to come to the plate when his name was announced, which is exactly what Bell chose to do. Williams stormed out of the dugout, beckoned down the line, got no response, and finally sent Willie Upshaw to the plate in Bell's place. Then he marched Bell into the clubhouse, where the two exchanged views until the fourth inning. The result: one day's suspension and a $500 fine, the most Williams could levy without risking the ire of the players' association. "We just basically chatted for a while. Then I told him he had kind of backed me into a corner and didn't leave me any alternative. I'm the manager," Williams said. "I'm the manager. I'm going to get my way."

"Jimy was a very intense individual," Al LaMacchia says. "He felt [he was] the number one guy now, he became intense. He just took everything to heart. He wanted to run a stern ship. He was always on edge all the time. I think the downfall of Jimy Williams was George Bell. And I don't think it was totally Jimy Williams's idea. The approach we took was a little bit off. I felt that George would never accept it, which he never did. I was almost like a father figure to him. He immediately asked me what I thought. And my answer was that this will help you play longer because of your knees. Being so intense like Jimy was, when this incident happened he got more intense—almost paranoid, worrying about the way that people were looking at him and people were talking about him. George was going to make every attempt to get him out of there. That made him more on edge."

"That's not the way you handle George," Cito Gaston says. "It caused big problems on this team. Because players are still friends. You give me one bad apple on a team, he can mess up the whole team. Not that George was a bad apple. But what was being done to George certainly wasn't what he wanted to have done to him. What you do is you take him to the side and talk to him about it and then try and show him that this might be the way to go, because it's going to help the club. The front office has got to come forward and say it's not going to hold it against you at contract time. The thing that I remember George getting caught up about was the press making such a big deal about him and Moseby and Jesse being the three best outfielders in baseball. Now he's not one of them. I think that hurt him more than anything. I think that bugged him more than anything. Because he really loved that and he loved people saying that. And he lived up to it. And now to make him a DH and not a part of it—that really hurt him."

He wasn't the only one who was hurt. Moseby didn't like the idea of leaving centre any more than Bell liked the idea of leaving left. It was the marquee defensive position on the team, and for a rookie to be lifted from there was insulting. He didn't play out his discontent with the press or publicly with Williams. But if Bell needed any encouragement in his battle with management, if he needed someone to stoke the anger, he could find him just a few lockers away.

"In the situation with George Bell, we didn't give Jimy the support that we should have," Gillick says. "We handled the situation poorly. I think Jimy wanted to take a firmer hand with George and probably we kind of followed the procedure dictated to us by the union. Jimy's idea was that if the guy won't DH, we'll suspend the guy. And usually the procedure that you're supposed to go through is that before you suspend a guy you say this is what you did, we'll give you a warning. And if the guy does it again, you say, 'Well, okay, you did it again, we'll fine you five hundred bucks and the next time we'll suspend you.' That's the way that the Player Relations Committee tells us that we're supposed to do it. Well, Jimy wanted to jump right ahead to the suspension. We sort of said no. Looking back on it, we should have taken our lumps and said, 'George, you're suspended.' We didn't show the rest of the club that we were backing him."

By Opening Day, the situation, outwardly, had calmed somewhat. Bell would indeed start the year at designated hitter, and in several other ways it was a significantly different team that would take the field to begin the 1988 season. Gone were former stalwarts Garth Iorg and Willie Upshaw, the former released, the latter sold to the Cleveland Indians. First base would now be shared by platooning power hitters, Fred McGriff and Cecil Fielder. Kelly Gruber would take Iorg's place platooning with Rance Mulliniks at third. Nelson Liriano would be the starting second baseman. And behind the plate, platooning with Ernie Whitt, would be a young catcher who had surprised many by making the team: Pat Borders. The potential of that young talent, and the promise of the season before, made the Blue Jays all but consensus pre-season picks to win the American League East.

The opener was scheduled for April 4, at Royals Stadium in Kansas City, perhaps the most memorable kick-off to a year since Doug Ault's big day way back in 1977. George Bell, the reluctant DH, took out his frustrations by hitting three home runs, as the Jays won 5–3. That caused a lot of people to jump to conclusions, to claim that this was proof Bell had buckled down, accepted his new assignment and would be a productive member of the team. But George would have none of that. Instead, he talked about the reception that awaited him back in Toronto, about how he was now publicly branded a malcontent, about how the fans wouldn't love him the way they had. "Fifty-five percent of the people in Toronto are against me," he said. "I'm going to be booed in Toronto. I'm the bad guy."

What isn't so well remembered about the spring of 1988 was that the great experiment, the move that dominated spring training and that was supposed to vault the Blue Jays ahead of the pack, proved to be a bust before the month of April was up. On April 17, to be precise, Bell was back in left field, and Syl Campusano, who had won the starting job in Florida, was on the bench, having started the season hitting .115.

Bell had won, though he battled with Williams off and on throughout the season. But somewhere along the line, the team, the franchise, had lost. There were other factors, of course. Jimmy Key was on the disabled list early in the season, after having a bone chip removed from his elbow. Others did not play up to par (though Dave Stieb was revitalized and McGriff established himself as the everyday first baseman). The team crawled along, under .500 and essentially out of contention for most of the season. Damage had been done.

On July 26, the Williams–Bell feud flared into the open again, as Bell committed his thirteenth error of the season, and his seventh in nine games. Williams pulled him from the game in the sixth inning, they indulged in a screaming match, and the manager indicated that he'd reached a breaking point. "He will play when I want him to play and I don't know when that's going to be," Williams told reporters. "All I did was ask him when he was going to hit a cut-off man. See, it's okay when a guy gets a hit and drives in a run and you go and pat him on the back. But they can't handle constructive criticism. When you make two million a year, you think you're bigger than the team."

Bell would sit for three games, but then he'd be back in left field, where by the first week in August he had set a team record for errors. Now some of the heat turned on Gillick. He was Stand Pat, the guy who wouldn't or couldn't make a deal to improve the club. All summer long, the team played mediocre baseball, and the discontent grew. The Blue Jays were eliminated on September 25, losing to Cleveland, after having never really been in the race. Only a misleading sprint to the finish—they went 22–7 in September and October, and won their last six in a row—allowed them to finish at 87–75, two games behind the division champion Boston Red Sox, tied for third place.

Bell finished with twenty-four home runs and ninety-seven RBIs—not MVP numbers, but still, through the turmoil, he had remained a productive offensive player. But this was a sick, unhappy team, loaded with malcontents and whiners, lacking in character, run by a man who had clearly lost the respect of those who played for him.

And so something had to give, though it wouldn't give immediately. After a heated debate at the post-season organizational meetings, Gillick managed to convince the group that Jimy Williams deserved one more chance. "I think now that at the end of '88 we should have made a change," Gillick says. "It was at my insistence that we give Jimy another shot. That's why he came back in '89. I really thought we didn't support him as strongly as we should have. I blamed us for not giving him the support. We shared the responsibility, so I thought he deserved another opportunity."

IT IS EASY, at first, to underestimate Paul Beeston. The cigar, the ruddy cheeks, the big booming laugh. The fact that he never wears socks, at least as long as the climate allows. The fun accountant. The life of the party—as long as the party doesn't extend too late into the evening. People like Paul Beeston. They like him immediately. Before they know it, he'll be asking them questions about their life, about what they do for a living, and somewhere will crop up some kind of shared experience. It isn't Dale Carnegie stuff. What Beeston brings to the table, along with an exceptionally quick mind, is pure natural charm. Those who have had to sit across from him during difficult negotiations all put it the same way: you can be tooth-and-nail one minute, cursing each other, not giving an inch; then afterwards, out for a beer and a good time, with no hard feelings. For an executive, particularly a baseball executive, and particularly a baseball executive given the strained labour–management relations during the 1980s and 1990s, the ability to fend off grudges was a valuable one indeed. But there is more to the package than that—which is why Beeston could at the same time be considered for the post of baseball commissioner and yet maintain a strong friendship with National Hockey League Players' Association head Bob Goodenow, a tough union man. Beneath the happy-go-lucky exterior is a bright, confident, independent thinker.

Beeston grew up in Welland, Ontario, on the Niagara Peninsula, where his father was a popular high school teacher. He was no jock, though he participated in the usual collection of recreational sports. A fan, though, he was, a fan with the ability to soak up information.

He entered the University of Western Ontario, where as an undergraduate he studied economics and political science and generally had a good time, with no real idea of what he wanted to do with his life. There Beeston picked up the cigar affectation from his roommates, and there he started to let his hair grow long. In 1968, he graduated with a B.A. "I was never an A student but I was never a D student. Just a good solid C." At that point, he made the kind of calculated, practical decision that would seem to run counter to the carefree-guy exterior. Beeston decided to become an accountant. It was stable. It would provide a decent income. It would be a natural stepping-off point for any business venture he might want to pursue in the future. "All I knew was that when I got my CA, I'd be twenty-four years old and my life would be ahead of me."

Not that the leopard had completely changed its spots. Joining a firm that later became Coopers & Lybrand, Beeston kept the hair, kept the cigar, didn't adopt traditional foot covering, and continued to let his natural charm shine through—it wasn't the kind of image you'd expect from someone poring over the books. He quickly came to understand that his personality, rather than putting clients off, was an asset. "When I'd go out and do an audit, it was fun. You'd disarm people by making it so that it was a nice experience to have the auditor come in." He soon gained the reputation as a rainmaker—someone who brought clients into the firm—and was considered a rising star. By 1976, there was the promise of a partnership.

Of course, 1976 turned out to be a very eventful year. One of Beeston's London friends was an orthopaedic surgeon named Dr. Peter Fowler. One of Fowler's neighbours was the president of Labatt Brewing, Don McDougall. The brewery was at that point on the verge of purchasing the San Francisco Giants and moving them to Toronto. They would need someone on the ground quickly, a numbers guy with some sense of the game of baseball. McDougall asked Fowler if he knew of a likely candidate, and Fowler immediately came up with a name. "I used to be pretty good at trivia," Beeston once said of their original meeting. "McDougall didn't know anything about baseball. So he figured hey, this is impressive. Because I know all this stuff, I know about Babe Ruth, I know about Lou Gehrig, I know about the Georgia Peach. It didn't matter what it was. All that stuff impressed him, plus I had my CA."

McDougall says that wasn't the case at all, that he was just looking for a competent accountant and that Beeston certainly fit the bill. And the truth is that Beeston was hesitant at first. He had a secure, comfortable career ahead of him in London, while the notion of hooking up with a new sport in a new town seemed to carry some degree of risk. But then again, how many times in life are you given the opportunity to participate in the birth of a professional baseball team? There would always be audits that needed doing, always accountancy firms that needed help. This one wouldn't come along again. Beeston jumped.

Though he was the first employee hired (once the Toronto Giants had expired, and Toronto's American League team was secure), he was very much a background player in the franchise's early years. With Peter Bavasi at the helm and Gillick emerging as the team's baseball brain, there wasn't a lot of reason for anyone outside the office to pay attention to the man who kept the books. Years later, long after he'd been fired, Bavasi still talked about him in those terms—though it's true he also had something of an axe to grind. "I don't really remember a whole lot about him," Bavasi would say. "I've been away for so long. He was the accountant. He seemed like a friendly enough fellow."

But during those early years, while he was protecting Bavasi from above and below, Beeston was also coming to understand the business of baseball. There his personality helped him, just as it had in being the happy auditor. Those born of the game generally don't tend to warm up to those who are not of baseball. The implication is that you can't really understand baseball if you haven't played it, if you haven't devoted your life to it. The fraternity is cliquish and exclusive: no room for those who might have merely been fans. But Beeston, because he was likable, because he deferred in baseball matters, because he was always willing to listen to a story and pick up a cheque, slowly but surely managed to break through that barrier. The baseball people—even the old, difficult, cranky baseball people, like Bobby Mattick—started to like the guy and started to share their knowledge with him. Beeston listened, he absorbed the information, he forged relationships, all of which came in handy in the years ahead.

"Beeston is a fellow who's very, very shrewd," Peter Widdrington says. "Very observant. Very good at reading the political landscape. And he's very quick to assess the lay of the land. I don't mean that in a detrimental sense. And as he went along, he learned. He learned from a number of sources. He learned from Hardy. Once he started to deal more with some of the other baseball ownership, he developed quite rapidly. He runs an organization quite well. He's well organized himself. He's got a fairly good financial background, which is helpful. He wasn't hired as a hotshot. He's made his way up through the organization and he's made the best of his opportunities."

The most important relationship Beeston forged within the organization was with Pat Gillick. In so many ways, they were opposites. Beeston was the extrovert, Gillick the introvert. Gillick was the baseball man who didn't like the business side of the job, Beeston the number cruncher with a growing passion for the game. When they conspired together to end Bavasi's reign, it was a matter of common cause, of a common desire to get out from under their despotic boss. But what grew out of that confrontation was something more: an understanding that, together, they could run a baseball team. Neither one wanted to be the other, neither one coveted the other's turf. Though it was Beeston who finally emerged as president, he's also the one who once said, "We're all basically support staff for Pat Gillick," and meant it. They disagreed, but rarely fought. Their methods were different, but complementary, the basis of a true symbiotic relationship. With Gillick to protect him on the baseball side, to deal with a side of the business that couldn't be expressed on a spread sheet, Beeston was allowed to develop into something that had never really been seen before: a Canadian chief executive officer of a major league baseball team, versed in the business, versed in the sport, comfortable haggling with agents, dealing with his corporate masters, negotiating his way through the sport's internal politics. He could sit in the bullpen during spring training, swapping tales with the leather-skinned, tobacco-chewing, baseball lifers with complete credibility and comfort. That same ease he could bring to the board room.

"I can't imagine anybody who saw the way Paul would develop," Herb Solway says. "They might have thought he would be a good CFO, but who in their right mind would have thought he would be the chief executive officer? Let me tell you something. I give Pete Hardy a lot of credit for Beeston. He really saw the potential in Beeston more than anyone else. The growth in Beeston has been enormous. And I would have had great doubts Beeston was tough enough for that job. And I would have expressed those doubts if I was asked—at any time until shortly before he got the job. And believe me, he's plenty tough. But he grew into it. He's done a terrific job. Outstanding."

Until 1989, Gillick and Beeston existed as equals, vice-presidents of a company without a president, one given complete control over that which had to do with baseball, the other given complete control of everything else. Then Beeston was named president. It became his job to deal with whoever was heading Labatt at the time, keeping him apprised of what was happening with the baseball team, helping him to understand where the money was going. It was another role in which he excelled. But within the team hierarchy, the essential relationship remained intact. The Toronto Blue Jays were run in tandem by two independent but co-dependent partners. It would take more than a shuffling of titles to change that.

BY THE TIME spring training began in 1989, it seemed the turmoil of the year before had been forgotten. To a man, the Toronto Blue Jay players talked about a new attitude, a new atmosphere, as they assembled in Dunedin. And the embattled manager, welcoming his troops to the first day of workouts, could feel it too. For Jimy Williams, the words rolled off his tongue like poetry, intimating that perhaps the worst was over. "It's something that's just there," he said. "It's like the air. You can feel it, but you can't hold onto it. It's like electricity. You can't see it, but you know it's there when the light goes on. Because of a year ago, I feel the difference this year. But I don't really want to dwell too much on last year."

Through the spring, nothing could shake the bliss. There were very few roster changes for the upcoming season, which eased competitive tensions, and for a change there was no Blue Jay with hurt feelings after a tough contract negotiation or an ugly session of arbitration. Even George Bell, the bad boy of the year before, seemed a changed man or at least a man less willing to voice his discontent. During the off-season, Williams had assured both Bell and Moseby that their positions in the outfield were safe. Then, from Bell's agent came the word that this year, his client would be more than happy to appear as designated hitter from time to time. Not every game, certainly. Not every other game or even every third game. But once in a while would be just fine with him. It would have been fine in 1988 as well, if they just hadn't backed him into a corner.

As spring training neared its conclusion, Pat Gillick confidently predicted that his club would win the American League East for the first time since 1985. "I think our players are a little more mature than they were," he said. "I think they have a feeling that they let things slip through their hands last year and they want to show everyone that they have the best team."

Shortstop Tony Fernandez echoed those sentiments. "I think in the last two or three years, this is the first time this ball club has been close as we are right now. It reminded me a lot of 1985. It seemed like everybody was trying to do the little things to help the team win. I've got a feeling that we've got that back. I'll always remember 1985 because of the way we played. Nobody had a great year, but we played together. This year everyone has to forget about himself and think as a team. We certainly have the talent. We must play as a team and not worry about our stats."

The happy, unselfish, pull-together Toronto Blue Jays embarked on the 1989 season in Kansas City, beating the Royals 4–3 behind the pitching of Jimmy Key. But this was no good omen. It wouldn't be long before all the fine sentiments of the spring began to ring hollow. The Jays were off to a terrible start.

On April 30, Gillick finally pulled the trigger on a deal—his first in 607 days—swapping Jesse Barfield to the New York Yankees for Al Leiter. Barfield's production had fallen off for the past two seasons, and the Jays seemed to have young talent ready to step in the outfield, led by Rob Ducey. In Leiter, they got a young, talented, hard-throwing left-hander who was prone to wildness. Little did anyone know at the time just how long it would take Leiter to become a regular, productive member of the Toronto pitching staff.

After thirty games, Toronto was 10–20, six-and-a-half games out of first. It was the first week in May. The press and the fans were beginning to smell blood, beginning to sense that the Blue Jays would be forced to do what they'd never done before: fire a manager in mid-season. Beeston was asked, but Beeston wouldn't talk about it—at least not directly. "We came out of spring training thinking that we had the horses," he said, which was hardly a ringing endorsement of the man charged with turning that horseflesh into a contender.

The final straw was a desultory three-game series in Minnesota, which the Twins swept, winning the finale 13–1 on a Sunday afternoon. Gillick later said that they'd actually decided to fire Williams on the Saturday—after a 10–8 loss—but didn't want to do the deed on the road. He says now that he and Beeston came to the same conclusion independently, but that hardly required an act of telepathy. Toronto was 12–24. They had lost fifteen of their past nineteen games. They were in danger of falling out of the American League East race before the first of June. "Coming home on that trip I figured we've got to have a meeting tomorrow," Cito Gaston says. "I didn't think Jimy was going to get fired. I thought Pat would call us in and ask us what was going on."

There remained a counter-argument—the very same argument that had held sway within the organization during tough times past. Showing a manager the door during the season rarely works miracles. In nine cases out of ten, it's the talent that's the problem. It either wasn't there in the first place or it was seriously over-estimated by those who put it in place. The one case in ten occurs when a manager is so despised, is so little respected, that a team quits on him. They lie down, knowing that if a shakedown is coming, it's more likely to involve one head man than twenty-five players. When that's the case, putting a new face at the helm can have a dramatic effect. The same players who have been going through the motions suddenly play with intensity. Sometimes it takes a tough guy to instil discipline in the clubhouse. Sometimes it takes a nice guy, to relax the players, to make them forget about internal politics and get back to the game. Gillick and Beeston were hoping, rather than betting, that the change they envisioned would serve to jump-start their team before it was too late.

On Monday, May 15, Beeston and Gillick drove to Mississauga, where like many of the temporary Canadians in the Blue Jay organization, Williams lived in a rented townhouse. Williams greeted them at the door; they came in and sat down. It was eleven in the morning.

"Jimy," Gillick said. "Beest has something to tell you."

And so it was left to Beeston to tell him that he was being fired.

"It was tough," Beeston says. "There's no right time to fire anyone. But you owe people the courtesy of doing it right."

It was much tougher for Jimy Williams. To this day, despite resuming his career as Cox's third-base coach in Atlanta and going to three World Series in five years with the Braves—finally winning in 1995—Williams still refuses to discuss anything about Toronto, the good times or the bad. After Atlanta's championship, there was talk that he might be in line for the job managing the expansion Tampa Bay Devilrays, which would seem to suit his talents as an instructor and his personality far better than the Toronto job did. Older, wiser, aware of what went wrong, he might still be a good major league manager for someone and put his Blue Jay experiences behind him.

But for now, his bitterness towards the organization lingers long after the day he last took off the uniform.

Chapter 15

PAUL BEESTON AND Pat Gillick just kept right on driving. Not far away in the same suburban neighbourhood where they'd just gone to fire Jimy Williams, lived Clarence (Cito) Gaston, the Jays' longtime hitting coach. When the cryptic call came, he was working with his wife, Denise, in the garden, trying to forget about a disastrous road trip that had just ended with the team dropping three straight in Minnesota. "Pat and Paul are coming out to see me," Gaston said to his wife after taking the call. "What do you think it's about?"

He honestly didn't know, though any time the boss comes to visit unexpectedly it's like a policeman showing up at the door: you don't anticipate good news. "I didn't even think about me being fired," Gaston says. "I figured I was doing a good job. I had a lot of confidence in myself." But neither, in his wildest dreams, did he think that the president and vice-president of the Toronto Blue Jays were coming to his house to offer him the job of field manager. It was not a position to which he aspired, and even if he had, he had been with the Blue Jays long enough to know how the organization did business. No Toronto manager had ever been fired in the middle of a season. And though things were going very badly, though there was enormous pressure on the team to win, Gaston couldn't imagine circumstances under which Williams would simply be let go.

Once Beeston and Gillick arrived, it didn't take long for exactly that message to be delivered. "They got out of the car, sat at the table and said they'd just fired Jimy. I was shocked. This organization doesn't operate that way. They take care of their people." Then came the second shock: they offered Gaston the job, at least on a temporary basis. "I named off the other coaches, Al Widmar, John Sullivan—and Bob Bailor. I said, 'I'm happy with what I'm doing.' Beeston said, 'You're it. We want you to do it for a while.' I said, 'Just don't take too long.' I asked them how long and they said a week, maybe two. I said well, just don't take too long."

When the Jays held a press conference the next day to announce that Gaston would take over until a permanent replacement for Williams could be named, Gillick was asked if Gaston was a candidate for the job. "No, he's not," Gillick said, unequivocally, and at that point it was true. Even before the final decision was made to fire Williams, Gillick and Beeston had started thinking about a possible replacement, someone who might undo the damage done, and who, rather than being just an interim replacement, would be able to lead the team beyond the 1989 season. Their first choice—and especially, Gillick's first choice—was Lou Piniella, then a special adviser and TV broadcaster with the New York Yankees, working out the final year of a contract that had seen him both as general manager and field manager. Piniella had the right combination of youth, intelligence, strategic smarts and toughness. He would be exactly the type of guy necessary to win back the players' respect, to knock some of the malcontents back into line, and to at least allow the team to play up to its potential. It was early still, but even if the 1989 season was lost, the Jays would be in a position to contend the following spring.

But there were complications. Piniella was still under contract to the Yankees. And though it is considered proper baseball etiquette to step aside and allow an employee to take a better job with a different organization, Yankee owner George Steinbrenner didn't play by those rules. This was his chance to run his former employee, Gillick, through the wringer. If Toronto wanted Piniella badly enough, they were going to have to pay for him. "I remember saying to Steinbrenner, you couldn't do a deal with us even if we offered you Key and [Todd] Stottlemyre," Beeston says. "And George said, 'Pitching's not our problem.' He had no intention of letting Lou come here." Still, the Jays went ahead and interviewed Piniella, as well as Terry Bevington, then the first-base coach of the Chicago White Sox and regarded as one of baseball's bright young things, and Bob Bailor, the original Jay, then manager of the Triple A Syracuse Chiefs. (They also made overtures towards Bud Harrelson, but he declined, choosing instead to stay with the New York Mets.) It was Piniella who said, "Why are you interviewing me when you've already got the right guy? It's Cito."

Right or not, he was certainly a very different guy from his predecessor. Both Beeston and Peter Hardy had been adamant that whoever succeeded Williams ought to be his polar opposite as a personality, so that the players would respond. That was Gaston, outwardly calm, so relaxed he appeared passive, not afraid to lose the job because he didn't really want the job in the first place, not inclined to heavy discipline because he still remembered what it was like to be a player and because he understood how a player would want to be treated. He had never managed at any level of baseball, content instead to stick with teaching what he knew, the art of hitting. The intricate game strategies that the fan thinks are the core of managing, those he'd never really had to deal with. But building up a relationship with a group of young men from diverse backgrounds, earning their trust and their respect, making them want to go out and do what they were capable of doing on the field: that for Gaston came naturally.

"When I was a kid there were three things I wanted to do," Gaston says. "I've done two of them. I always wanted to be a major league player. I wanted to drive one of those big trailer trucks. And I wanted to sing. Well, I can't sing. My dad was a truck driver, so I learned how to drive one of those trucks. So you get two of three things—it's not bad in life. And now I have two other things, but I never asked for that."

Once again, there was an Al LaMacchia connection. As a scout for the then Milwaukee Braves, it was LaMacchia who visited the Gaston home in San Antonio, Texas, and signed Gaston in 1964. "He was a laid-back individual," LaMacchia says. "You had to start conversations with Cito and keep them going—yes sir, no sir [was his only response]. He was well brought up by his mother—a very religious individual and a good mother.... You could never see any emotion out of [Cito]." Gaston spent most of nine seasons in the minors before finally getting his break, when he was the thirtieth and final selection of the San Diego Padres in the 1969 expansion draft. A year later, he had the best season of his career, hitting .318, driving in ninety-three runs and representing the Padres in the All-Star Game. Gaston's production flattened out after that, and he became expendable in San Diego. In 1974, he was traded back to the Braves, where he roomed with home-run king Hank Aaron, the beginning of a relationship that later became important to Gaston's career. He saw very limited action in Atlanta—in his best year there, he hit .291 in 1976, but appeared in only sixty-nine games. In 1978, he was sold by the Braves to the Pirates and then was released at the end of the season. LaMacchia called and asked him whether he might like a shot at making the Blue Jays in the spring of 1979. Gaston declined. "At the time, Bavasi was here and I said no," he says. "The dad I got along fine with. But Peter I had experience with out in San Diego, so I said no. Peter to me was a guy who wanted to be like his dad. I think Peter's problem was that he tried to live up to his dad, but his dad had more class than he did, as far as I'm concerned. I don't care if he knows that I said that. Because Peter didn't know how to treat people and Buzzie does. Buzzie is a decent guy."

Instead, Gaston accepted a non-roster invitation to make the Braves. He hit .360 that spring, but still Atlanta cut him loose before the season began. "I could still play when I got let go. The funny thing about it, the guy who let me go was Bobby Cox." He and Cox went back a long time. They had won a Texas League title together in Austin and had played winter ball together in Venezuela. When Cox cut him, Gaston kept his feelings to himself. "I didn't say anything," he says. "I just said okay and left. Sometimes you're better off doing that. If I'd voiced my opinion or come on like I was upset, maybe he would have understood or maybe he wouldn't. Maybe he wouldn't have asked me to come into the major league camp. Maybe he wouldn't have asked me to be one of his coaches. Sometimes you're better off just walking away." Despite the offer of a job as a part-time scout, that's exactly what Gaston did—walk away. Convinced that he could still play, he headed for the new Inter-American League, a professional loop with teams in the countries associated with winter baseball. Gaston was in Santo Domingo when the league folded in June. With few options, he headed for Leon in the Mexican League, traditionally the final stop for old ball players who refuse to give up on a dream. For one season, it was fine. "Then I woke up one morning in a hotel room in Mexico—I wish I could remember the name of the town—and the bathroom was bigger than the bedroom. That's when I said you know you've hit rock bottom."

That would be it for baseball. Gaston and his first wife, Lena, planned to open a child-care centre. There were four years of deferred payments left from his last major league playing contract to help ease him through the transition. But then Hank Aaron called. By then Aaron had moved into the Atlanta front office, and he was offering his old friend a job as a minor league hitting instructor. "He called me three times and asked me if I'd come and work with him. I liked the way he put that but I refused him two times. I just didn't want to be back in baseball. I think I left baseball and I found out that no one really gave a shit about you. Even close friends, when times are bad, no one really did anything. I'm not a person that feels sorry for myself, so I got over that. But I thought some people didn't treat me properly as a player, and I thought that I should play a lot more than I did play, but because of dislikes and likes I didn't play. But I don't hold a grudge against people. It just takes me a while to get over things."

By the third call from Aaron, Gaston had got over things enough to accept the job. Cox invited him to major league spring training, and Gaston spent most of the strike-shortened 1981 season working with young players in the Florida Instructional League. Cox was fired by Atlanta that year and hired by the Blue Jays. One of the first calls he made was to the man he wanted as his new hitting coach—the first full-time hitting coach in the history of the Toronto organization. "He asked me to come up for an interview, and all we did was have breakfast. I didn't know much about the Blue Jays, but once I got into it I realized that this was an organization that really cared about people. They just blew me away with how much they cared about the players on and off the field."

And so less than two years after giving up on baseball, Gaston found himself part of a major league coaching staff with a young team on the rise. During the last years of his playing career, he'd had plenty of time to sit in the dugout and watch the game go by, to think about hitting, to think about strategy, to think about how a team ought to be handled. He began working with younger players, learning how to teach. "When I came in, a lot of old guys didn't want to help young guys because they were going to take their job. I wasn't going to do that." Cox would be an influence, but by nature they were very different personalities. "Bobby's a little bit more of a red ass than I am. When he played, he'd take a ball in the head if he could get an out. As a manager, he used to take [bats] and beat them up, throwing stuff. I don't think the players have ever seen me tear up the clubhouse. Where I get criticized a lot is that I don't go off like that. But Preston Gomez, who was my second big league manager, he always said that when people do that they're just making excuses. That's always stuck with me. You see guys throwing helmets and you see guys beating bats. It's because they have failed. Instead of taking it sitting down and trying to figure out why they failed, they want to show people their frustration."

Gomez, fair but strict, became Gaston's role model. Legendary hitting guru Charlie Lau was another one—he could maintain an air of authority, but still be one of the boys. There would never be a wall between Gaston and his players—not as a coach, where it's relatively simple to maintain normal relationships, and not as a manager, where that becomes much more difficult. His authority would have to come from a source other than the symbolic separation of boss and worker. "There's guys that I play golf with, I have meals with them, I go to parties with them. I'm that way because I've seen it go so far the other way when I was playing. Managers didn't even speak to you when you didn't get a hit for a couple of days. It's not like you're not trying. That's when you really need to talk to people, when they really need some encouragement.

"I've seen guys become managers that were coaches go completely the other way." In Jimy Williams, he had seen one of those up close.

Those experiences, those influences, and his natural, easy-going temperament, combined to make Gaston a very different kind of manager from his predecessor. In later years, in good times and bad, he would frustrate those looking for flashes of emotion, looking for virtuoso turns of baseball science, looking for someone willing to dress down his players in public when they failed, to play head games through the press. They would always be disappointed in Gaston. The talk shows would always be filled with second-guessers. And he, in his heart of hearts, would wonder sometimes if race played a part in the criticism. It wasn't that, at least not overtly, but it was a basic misunderstanding of the man and his motivation.

Plenty of the men who run baseball teams are called "players' managers," but few, in fact, seem to understand what it is like to be a modern major league ball player. Gaston's memories were fresh

enough, his experience recent enough, that he wasn't simply drawing on some nostalgic vision of players who would fall into line the
first time an imperious manager raised his voice. He would treat
them as he had wanted to be treated—like a man, not a boy, like
someone who could be responsible for his actions on the field and
his behaviour away from the field. The rules of Jimy Williams's
regime, the obsession with appearance and detail and form, immediately fell by the wayside. Gaston could do what Williams couldn't—
ignore small failings, small breaches of decorum. He could turn his
head and walk away. His players would come to know that he would
never criticize them publicly, that when the reporters piled into his
office after a game, he would explain away every mistake as though
it were an understandable part of the game. If there was something
to be said, it would be said behind closed doors. There wouldn't be
eruptions of the kind Cox became famous for. There wouldn't be
screaming sessions, confrontations in front of the entire team,
attempts to humiliate. Players with personal problems would find a
good listener, available to them in a way that Cox hadn't been, that
Williams couldn't be. And in those dark moments early in 1989,
they would find someone content simply to let them go out and
play, to let them enjoy what is still, at bottom, a game. They understood, Gaston believed, the implications of their terrible start. They
could look at the standings and know the challenge before them.
No need to hit them over the head with it. As interim manager, the
best thing he could do would be to create an atmosphere free of the
tension and dread that had preceded it. Let them play. Treat them
with respect. Don't get in the way. Don't impose your own style on
their style. Laissez-faire management, but with a set of underlying
principles. If you trust them, they'll come to trust you.

It doesn't have the sound-bite possibilities of one of those Vince
Lombardi aphorisms. It doesn't demonstrate its own genius, the
way a Tony LaRussa game plan might. It doesn't make anyone think
of the master manipulator, the Mike Keenan, playing with his athletes' emotions, making them hate him to make them better. Being
a nice guy, being a decent guy, trusting that big league athletes have
the ability to play like big league athletes: as a credo, it would be a
hard sell to the cynical press and the paying public.

But in the clubhouse of the Toronto Blue Jays in the spring of

1989, it was exactly the tonic required, and the team responded immediately, winning six of their first nine games under Gaston. Piniella wasn't going to be available. Bailor was deemed to be not quite ready for prime time. And Bevington, a disciplinarian, seemed just a little too much like Williams. (At least he did to Beeston and to Hardy. "I liked Bevington," Gillick says, pointedly.) It was becoming more likely by the day that, at least for the duration of the 1989 season, Cito Gaston would remain the manager of the Toronto Blue Jays.

"The players wanted me to stay on," Gaston says. "They came to me—Gruber was one of them, a few other guys—after we were starting to win a little bit. They said, 'Why don't you stay on?' The reason I took it was because of that and because Sparky Anderson said, 'Hey, take the job. If they offer it to you, take it.'... It came down to where we were winning and I hadn't heard anything from Pat or Paul. I said to my wife, 'You know, I think they're going to ask me to take this job. What do you think?' She said, 'Do what you want to do.'"

The Jays were in Cleveland, in the process of being swept by the Indians, when it became clear to Gaston that the job offer was imminent. "I remember sitting down in the lobby of the hotel there late at night by myself just wondering if I was going to take it or not."

The job was offered. Gaston accepted the assignment. But in at least one not so small corner of the organization, there remained reservations.

"Paul liked Cito," Gillick says. "But I don't know that anybody else at that time knew what Cito's style was. Cito was hard working and we knew he had good communication with the players. I thought we were back in the same situation with Williams. Here's a guy who's on the coaching staff who's going to be manager. We just got out of that situation. There was some reluctance on my part to say that was the way to go."

◆ FOR MOST OF the rest of the 1989 season, observers of the Toronto Blue Jays struggled to define the Gaston style. He was without an obvious schtick, without (his critics still maintain) a consistent method, a consistent game strategy. Undemonstrative, a bit uncomfortable with the press, he would never be the one to articulate it.

But the fact was that it worked. Not magic, maybe, but certainly something undefinable that changed a team of under-achieving, malcontent losers into the very picture of harmony and success. By the season's end, George Bell was even the designated hitter, and he was doing so without complaint. If Gaston could be criticized for being unable to carry out what armchair managers felt was elemental strategy, he also had to be given credit for the ability to work small miracles with human beings.

He was confirmed as manager for the remainder of the season on the last day of May, having put together an 8–7 mark as the interim boss. At that point, the Jays found themselves at 21–30 for the season, their worst record entering June since the disastrous season of 1981. But still, while not many may have felt a pennant was a real possibility, it could have been worse. No one else in the American League East that season seemed particularly interested in winning the division. The surprising Baltimore Orioles were in first after finishing as the worst team in the American League in 1988. They seemed to be doing it with mirrors, playing good, inspired, fundamental baseball under manager Frank Robinson. But they certainly weren't running away, and neither did any other club seem poised to do so. The Jays were awful, they trailed the pack, but mathematically they weren't out of it.

If you looked hard enough, there were bright spots: the play of Kelly Gruber, both offensively and defensively, laying claim to being the best third baseman in the league; surprising rookie Junior Felix, who was given an outfield job when Jesse Barfield was traded to the Yankees for pitcher Al Leiter and who brought with him a combination of speed and power the Jays had never really had before; Duane Ward, after a terrible start in which at one point he was the loser of record in four consecutive games, earning a share of the closer's role with Tom Henke; Fred McGriff, enhancing his credentials as the best young power hitter in the game, on his way to an American League home-run title.

THERE WAS ALSO the stadium. After construction delays and mounting public horror at the escalating cost, SkyDome opened for baseball business on June 4. It was a radically different place than Exhibition Stadium, obviously, but it was also different than any other park in the majors, including the other domes. The fast-food concessions, the giant screen in centre field, the hotel rooms looking down on the field, the Hard Rock Café in right field, the restaurants in centre: it seemed often like a shopping mall with a baseball game going on, incidentally, at its heart. There were no nods to baseball tradition, much less to Toronto baseball tradition. Instead, the architectural conceit seemed to be that this was the future, this was what sports stadia could become—places where the sport itself was just part of the attraction. And then there was the roof, which had its roots with Paul Godfrey and Bill Davis and a bit of bad weather and which had evolved into the most expensive gizmo in history. The fact was that aside from April and October, Toronto baseball weather wasn't all that bad, and besides, those who would push the buttons to open the dome began by taking an extremely conservative approach—this was a closed stadium that occasionally was opened, not vice versa. Still, it drew the requisite oohs and aahs, and it focused attention on the city just as had been intended: say SkyDome, and the public thinks Toronto just as they think New York when they hear Yankee Stadium. It also changed the economics of baseball in Toronto. Even though they didn't move into the Dome until June, the Jays drew more than three million fans for the first time in 1989. Because of the consortium arrangement, which split off much of the ancillary revenue, it wasn't the kind of financial bonanza some teams benefited from when they moved into a new building. But for a club that operated essentially on a break-even basis, those extra tickets sold represented extra dollars that could be spent on salaries in the future, a factor that soon became enormously significant in the team's success.

The irony of it all—which would be lost on Torontonians until after the bliss of consecutive World Series championships had ebbed, and the string of perpetual sell-outs came to a close—was that SkyDome also represented the end of the line. Even before the first pitch was thrown, other cities with stadiums to build were moving in other directions, both financially and aesthetically. Baltimore, Cleveland and Texas reacted against all that poured concrete, all that cookie-cutter sameness of the playing field, by building new-old ball parks that drew as their inspiration not SkyDome, but Wrigley Field and Fenway Park, even the long-gone Polo Grounds. Where domes were seen as necessary—generally in cities that played host to NFL football, where games might be played in December and January—the builders opted for more conventional, less costly designs. The Georgia Dome in Atlanta, the domed stadium in St. Petersburg, Florida, and one built much later in St. Louis, had all the revenue-generating potential (enhanced concessions, an enormous number of private boxes, club seating, etc.) but didn't bother with a $250-million retractable roof. And so what its architectural inventors had hoped would be the new prototype, to be exported worldwide, became instead one of a kind, a monument to their vision, as well as a monument to a kind of public spending on professional sport that seems unimaginable in the Ontario of the 1990s.

IN FOURTH PLACE at the All-Star break following a sparkling month of June, the Blue Jays came together during the summer months, finally looking like the team that left spring training the favourite to win the division. One deal provided a key ingredient. On August 1, Pat Gillick traded pitcher Jeff Musselman and a minor leaguer to the New York Mets in exchange for outfielder Mookie Wilson. One of the stars of the World Series winners in 1986, Wilson was on his last legs as a major leaguer, hitting just .205 at the time of the trade, and a defensive liability in the outfield. But he would provide a spark in Toronto that wasn't completely reflected in the statistics. Wilson brought speed and hustle and the kind of positive emotion that the team so often had seemed to lack.

By August 7, the Jays were within two games of Baltimore, and it looked like the over-achieving Orioles would fold. But instead, while Toronto was enjoying its best month in franchise history—20–9—the Orioles held tough. It wasn't until August 30 that the Blue Jays moved into a tie with Baltimore for first place in the American League East—but for a few meaningless days in April, the first time they'd been on top since October 2, 1987, near the end of a great collapse against Detroit. On September 1, the lead was theirs alone, not to be relinquished, but with Baltimore hanging on tenaciously, never more than two-and-a-half games back. For a team that had finished 54–107 in 1988 as the Orioles had, to be in a pennant race at all a year later was no small achievement.

The mini-pennant came down to a weekend series at SkyDome, with the Blue Jays leading by a game. If they won two of three, they'd win the division. Win one, and there would be a Monday playoff game in Baltimore. Get swept—and given the 1987 horror show, no one considered that out of the question—and it would be Baltimore advancing to the post-season. Not this time, though. Toronto won the first two to end the suspense and to put the capper on a remarkable comeback. It didn't matter that they finished the year with a record of 89–73—a far cry from the ninety-six-win season in 1987 that still wasn't good enough, or the ninety-nine wins in 1985. The American League East had been a pitifully weak division, and with the powerful Oakland Athletics waiting for whichever team captured the turtle derby, there figured to be an early exit from the playoffs.

But for Toronto, so much of that was beside the point. What was important was that a team that hadn't shown a great deal of character in the past, a team that had been racked by turmoil a year earlier and that seemed to have quit on its manager in the early days of the 1989 season, had come together behind Gaston, put itself back in the race, and then prevailed in the stretch drive against an equally determined opponent. The Blue Jays that season weren't a great team. They still made all kinds of mental mistakes. Lloyd Moseby was no lead-off man, though Gaston, loyal to the end, would keep him there. The pitching staff was flawed. All the more reason that, if you could ever claim a moral victory in the win-or-else world of professional sport, this was it.

By winning the division, the team also secured Gaston's immediate future as its manager. There had been talk during the fall that Gaston might still return to the role of batting coach in 1990, with Piniella or someone else taking over as manager. In September, with Beeston, Widdrington and Hardy especially vocal in his support, the decision was made to give the new man another season at the helm. "We made up our minds we wanted him back during the last week of the season," Gillick says. "We told him the day after we clinched the division and gave him a week to think about it." Think about it he did; in some ways, Gaston remained a touch hesitant, despite his success. "Cito was reluctant," Beeston says. "All of that stuff is true. He had a good job. He liked being the hitting instructor. He didn't like the limelight. He's grown to like it. But Cito was about teaching hitting and then going home. He had his family, he was happy living here. He figured he had more longevity with the organization as a hitting instructor than as a manager because he could see what was happening with these guys."

After thinking about it for a few days, Gaston accepted the offer. Though it didn't factor into his reasoning at the time, he had a larger obligation to do so. It was noted far and wide in 1989 that this was the first time a black manager had won a pennant in major league baseball, which said absolutely nothing about black managers and everything about the sport's backward attitude towards race, embodied in the colour bar and the post-Jackie Robinson absence of blacks and Hispanics in front-office and managerial positions. Gaston certainly understood what the breakthrough meant but refused to take the opportunity to make the obvious point—just as he had refused to speak out the night he managed against Frank Robinson for the first time, which was also the first time in baseball history two black managers had sat in opposing dugouts. His apparent lack of emotion, his unwillingness to make even the most basic political statement, was frustrating to watch— but again, as with his managerial style, that's the measure of the man. Today, Gaston acknowledges that perhaps he underplayed the event. "I never thought about it," he says. "The only thing I was thinking about was going in there and beating Oakland. And they beat the shit out of us. Now I think about it more than I did then. I think about what it means. And I was happy for Frank Robinson that year—and he got manager of the year that year. There's two black guys that managed to do something that certainly would have changed baseball in certain ways. Hopefully. And it did, because some guys got some jobs. I wasn't even thinking about that. But now I can see how important it was and how important it is."

The 1989 American League championship series would offer no surprises. A great team went in against a good team that was emotionally spent from digging itself out after a terrible start and then playing out a tough, month-long pennant race. The great team won. Decisively.

"In all honesty, we had a good team that year, but our team wasn't even close to their team," Gaston says. "Our guys were burned out. They were burned out to get there. They were beat. They were as tired as I was. We were just completely exhausted. We just spent everything we could to get there, and there wasn't much left. You didn't know you were going to get beat, because in baseball you never know you're going to get beat, but...." The unspoken words, left unspoken because the mythology of professional sport requires that it be left unsaid: the Blue Jays, after what they'd gone through in the past four seasons, were just happy to be there.

They played that way. Game one, a 7–3 Oakland victory. Toronto blew two early leads. Dave Stewart, the epitome of a big game pitcher, prevailed over Dave Stieb, whose reputation, based largely on that Jim Sundberg flyball, was just the opposite. Game two, a 6–3 Oakland victory. Rickey Henderson, the greatest lead-off man and the greatest base stealer in baseball history, took control of the game in a way that only he can, going two for two, stealing four bases, humiliating Toronto catcher Ernie Whitt (though stolen bases are as much the responsibility of the man on the mound), offering a great big, cocky, in-your-face to the Jays and their fans. Arrogant? Sure. But if you're that good, you can get away with it. Game three seemed to be going the same way, with Oakland up 3–0 early, until the Jays caught up with Storm Davis. A 7–3 Toronto victory seemed less like a turning point than a brief pause before the inevitable. Toronto didn't quit, though. In game four, Henderson hit two home runs, and Jose Canseco hit the longest shot yet hit in SkyDome, reaching the seats in the fifth deck in left field. Oakland pulled out to a 5–2 lead but the Jays scrapped back, finally losing 6–5, to sit one game away from elimination.

That one game proved notable not so much for the outcome—a 4–3 Oakland victory—but for the events of the final inning, which for the first time revealed a side of Cito Gaston few had ever seen. With Oakland leading 4–1 in the ninth, George Bell homered, leading off against Stewart to narrow the score to 4–2. Oakland manager Tony LaRussa then walked to the mound. Cerebral (he has a law degree), a bit smug, secure in his intelligence and unafraid to talk about it, LaRussa had come to be regarded as the model of a modern baseball manager. He was new school, a bit of a technocrat, someone who relied not on accepted wisdom but on the science of the game. If there was a right strategic move to be made, LaRussa had already thought of it. Sports writers, intimidated themselves, let the world know that this was one bright fellow.

It didn't take a genius to make the right move that day. In came Dennis Eckersley, the best closer in baseball, to lock up the victory. But as Eckersley got set to pitch, Gaston called time, walked onto the field, and asked the home plate umpire to check the pitcher for a foreign object. The Jays had come to believe during the series that Eckersley was using something to scuff the ball, changing the surface texture, making it move unpredictably—and all but unhittably—like a spit ball. There was talk that an emery board had fallen out of Eckersley's uniform in the visitors' clubhouse laundry, and that Whitt had seen him putting something down his collar during a previous appearance. Now was the time for a little psychological warfare, since the Jays had nothing to lose. Gaston demanded the search, umpire Rick Reed found nothing, and the entire Oakland dugout—especially LaRussa and Tony Phillips—erupted. Eckersley told Gaston that he could "go fuck himself," others screamed insults, some perhaps with a racial tinge. Gaston became so incensed that he stood and challenged his tormentors to come out and fight.

"Gamesmanship bothers me more than anything that happens out there," LaRussa said after the game. "I don't appreciate it. It gave me a little problem because, to me, the guy who managed their club is one of the finest men in the American League and he's a very talented baseball man."

Eckersley seemed shaken by the brouhaha. The next batter, Tony Fernandez, singled, stole second, went to third on Whitt's ground out, and then scored on Gruber's sacrifice fly. The Jays had pulled to within a run. Then Junior Felix struck out to end the game and the series. "We were beaten by a better team," Gruber said in the losers' clubhouse. "We hate to admit that. I think we have just as much ability. We just didn't play as well as they did."

Six years later, the wounds from that final-inning incident still hadn't healed, at least as far as Cito Gaston was concerned. "To have somebody cheat on you in that manner—that's what I remember about that series," he says. "I remember Tony Phillips yelling at me, and telling them, both of them, 'Well, get your ass across the line.' I challenged both of them. If you've got something to say to me, come across the line. Tony apologized to me later—actually sent his apology. Well, he can kiss my ass, because I'm not the one who was cheating.

"I think the way LaRussa took it—you know, we're going on, so don't try to start nothing—that's not what it's about. Because my job is to make sure that you're not cheating us. If I don't say something, who's going to say something? I know it's the last game and they've got us beat. If I'd have known that he was doing that earlier, I would have said something. I remember that more than anything."

If anything, Gaston's outburst had confirmed the wisdom of the decision to bring him back as manager. The front office hierarchy already knew they had someone who could bring calm to the clubhouse, who could get along with his players, who could motivate them. Now they also knew that they had someone who, when the occasion demanded, showed the kind of emotion that would make a team really respect him. It would be interesting to see what he could do with these players who held so much promise, but who had never been quite good enough. A new decade, a new stadium, a new attitude.

"It'll be nice to start the season off fresh," Gaston said, looking forward to the 1990 season. "We're going to work on fundamentals in spring training as much as possible. We can get better in that area. I think we've got a good enough club to go all the way."

Chapter 16

I N RETROSPECT, THEY seem like lost years, sandwiched between the Toronto Blue Jays' team of the 1980s, which would never be quite good enough, and the back-to-back world champions. Certainly they were in a transitional period, when the team on the field could have gone either way, when crucial deals and decisions were made. But they were also good years in the history of professional baseball in Toronto. A successful, well-run franchise proved itself to be the most successful and best-run in the game, pushing its value to unprecedented heights. In 1991, their second full season in SkyDome, the Jays became the first professional sports franchise of any sort to draw four million fans in a single season. When they entered the league in 1977, a million was the benchmark of success, two million outrageous. As the years passed, only the Los Angeles Dodgers crossed the three-million barrier. And so four million over an eighty-one-game home season in a fifty-thousand-seat stadium was truly remarkable, a sign of just how completely the Blue Jays had taken command of the local psyche and, to some degree, of how accepting, how forgiving, the Toronto sports consumer remained. Because even as the Jays were scaling the heights as far as attendance was concerned, they were giving every indication that the championship so long awaited simply wasn't in the cards.

In the spring of 1990, the baseball owners locked out the players, hoping to force a collective bargaining agreement more to their liking. (By then it had become as traditional as Opening Day in Cincinnati: the end of a contract meant some kind of dispute between the owners and players that might or might not lead to a work stoppage that might or might not threaten to cut into the season.) While certainly not the equal of the war-within-the-game that would abort the 1994 season, it was a bitter dispute that wiped out the first month of spring training.

Now there are those who might wonder, with no small justification, just why it takes baseball players a month and a half to prepare for the season in any case, whether the whole thing is just an excuse to shorten the winter for those in the game—including the journalists who cover it. Still, there was considerable debate about who would be most affected by the shortened spring, pitchers or hitters, about whether there would be more early-season injuries from lack of preparation. As a concession to those possibilities, teams were allowed to open the season with two extra bodies on their roster.

Some things, though, the lockout didn't change. When camp opened in Dunedin on March 20, George Bell wasn't there, setting the stage for his usual dramatic, late arrival. And as had been the case virtually every year since 1983, the Blue Jays were picked by many to win at least the American League East. Even a 4–10 Grapefruit League record—the worst of any major league team—failed to dissuade their supporters, nor did the realization that this was the youngest roster in the majors.

The Jays had a strong starting rotation anchored by Dave Stieb, Todd Stottlemyre and John Cerutti, with Jimmy Key returning from shoulder surgery. Tom Henke was there to anchor a talented bullpen that included David Wells, Jim Acker and Duane Ward. The outfield was strong with Bell in left, Mookie Wilson in centre, and some combination of Junior Felix and Glenallen Hill in right, and the infield, with young players Kelly Gruber, Fred McGriff and Tony Fernandez all still to peak, had as much potential as any in the majors. With Ernie Whitt's departure to Atlanta, it was left to Pat Borders, who had developed faster and farther than most would have imagined, and Greg Myers to handle matters behind the plate.

The designated hitter would be John Olerud, twenty-one years old, just the sixteenth player since the amateur draft began in 1965 to make his professional debut in the major leagues. He was a different personality type from the usual professional athlete, laconic in the extreme, shy to the point of being withdrawn. Early in 1989, while attending Washington State University, Olerud had collapsed after suffering a brain haemorrhage and later underwent surgery for the removal of an aneurism. But despite that life-threatening situation, he came back to finish the college season and then appeared in six late-season games with the Blue Jays. Even from that limited exposure, it was clear that Olerud possessed something close to the perfect swing. But he didn't have a natural defensive position aside from first base, then occupied by McGriff. Turning a player that young and that inexperienced into a full-time designated hitter carried considerable risk as far as his big league development was concerned. But the organization's—and especially Gillick's—commitment to Olerud was such that there was no thought of his playing anywhere but with Toronto.

Looking back, it's easy to say that the youth and experience of the 1990 Blue Jays never really gelled, that some players just weren't ready and others were just starting to prove that they never would be. At the time, though, it was like one long tease, where it appeared that the club was ready to break out and dominate what was a very weak division.

It never happened. Three times during the year, the Jays were as much as eleven games over .500. They led the division several times, but never by more than two games. At the end of August, they went into a terrible, pre-stretch-drive swoon, losing eight out of ten games.

Just a week before that collapse—when the Jays were still tied with the Red Sox in first—George Bell, sidelined with eye problems, provided the press with one of his habitual outbursts, reacting out of frustration, saying all the wrong things and burning bridges in the clubhouse. The other players didn't believe his eye problems were real, he said, the rookies weren't listening to the coaches and were making too many mistakes. Junior Felix, whose lack of a baseball brain would forever get in the way of his considerable athletic abilities, was probably the target of the last bit, but it didn't really matter. There was crazy old George, going off again just when the team needed it least, with Gaston—predictably—refusing to scold him publicly. "George says what he wants to. I don't have to have a muzzle around here on this club," Gaston said. "We have a lot of talent here but we've got some young guys and some old guys making mistakes. I'm not going to name names. I don't talk about my players in that sense." That Bell's own competitive desires fuelled his frustration, Gaston understood, but to the public that didn't really matter. He had been labelled long before not just as a bad left fielder, but as a bad left fielder with a bad attitude.

There was other, off-the-field news as well. On August 19, a little more than two months after his eightieth birthday, Howard Webster died. He had suffered a series of strokes and for the past several years had been effectively confined to his home, overseeing the family trust, but uninvolved in the day-to-day running of his business interests, including the baseball team. With Webster's death, the original ownership triumvirate, which had proved so successful, came to an end. By the terms of the agreement between Webster, Labatt and the Bank of Commerce, if Webster's estate decided to sell his 45 percent interest in the team, it would first have to be offered to the other partners. Since the bank, by law, could hold no more than its current 10 percent, that meant Labatt would have the opportunity to purchase a controlling interest in the franchise for the first time. The deal was completed on November 1, 1991, with John Labatt Ltd. buying the Webster share for $67.5 million. "By any of a half dozen measurements," Labatt's president and CEO Sidney Oland said, "it's the best franchise in baseball."

◆ TURNING FOR HOME at the end of August 1990, the Jays were just three games over .500 and six games behind Boston, the farthest they'd been out of first all season. Had they been chasing a better team, Toronto's chances might have been safely written off then and there, but the Red Sox were just a step beyond mediocre, so it couldn't be that simple, and the Toronto fans wouldn't that easily be let off the hook.

Still, even in those relatively dark times, they could enjoy a bit of history. On September 2, Dave Stieb—author of a hugely successful autobiography entitled *Tomorrow I'll Be Perfect*, the title often to be taken ironically, given his history of near-misses—finally threw his first no-hitter, as well as the first no-hitter in the history of the Blue Jay franchise, beating the Cleveland Indians 3–0 at cavernous Municipal Stadium. Stieb said afterwards that he didn't have his best stuff that day, that his 122 pitches—74 of them strikes—weren't the overwhelming blend of power and finesse on which he'd built his reputation.

There was a time when Stieb's slider broke as though it were dropping off a table. He couldn't do that consistently in 1990, but he did have a greater understanding of the pitching arts, and—just as importantly—the breaks went his way. Twice in 1988, in back-to-back starts, Stieb had been just one strike away from a no-hitter, only to have a higher power intervene. A routine ground ball hit a clump of dirt and skipped over Manny Lee's head. A bloop single dropped just beyond the glove of Fred McGriff. In 1989 against the Yankees, he came within an out of a perfect game, before Roberto Kelly's double continued the curse. It was surely some kind of cosmic payback for all those times Stieb reacted to a bad fielding play behind him by staring down his teammates, for all those games when he claimed it was "bleeders" and "chinkers"—and not legitimate hits—that beat him, for all the times when he sat at his locker and spit venom at reporters, after good performances or bad. How he atoned for those sins and was finally allowed his moment of perfection is anyone's guess.

Boston couldn't run away, and the Blue Jays couldn't catch them, even after Gillick pulled off a late-season trade, acquiring left-hander Bud Black from the Cleveland Indians on September 18. He arrived too late to be eligible for the post-season, had the Jays been able to qualify, and didn't really make much of an impact during his brief time in a Toronto uniform. But that deal foreshadowed other, more successful stretch-drive additions to come in future years.

One Blue Jay did pull his weight during the most important days of the long season. Kelly Gruber may have been the best athlete ever to wear a Toronto uniform, even if he wasn't the brightest guy in the world. (His teammates nicknamed him "Foggy," because at times he didn't seem to be fully engaged with the cosmos.) But at the plate or in the field, Gruber had no peer in 1990. That, and the fact that he was blond and handsome and projected a kind of aw-shucks country-boy vulnerability, made him not just the Jays' best player or their most popular player in 1990, but arguably the most popular athlete in Toronto. He finished the season hitting .274, with 31 home runs and 118 RBIs, the unanimous choice of local baseball writers as the Jays' player of the year and fourth in voting for the American League's most valuable player. But it was more than numbers. Few if any Blue Jays before him possessed the combination of skill and sex appeal or had the potential to cross over and become a pure celebrity beyond the hard-core baseball audience. By the end of the 1990 season, Kelly Gruber was on the verge of becoming a superstar on a team that was just about to reach new peaks of popularity. It was all there in front of him.

Diamond Dreams

◆THE DÉNOUEMENT FOR the 1990 Jays came on the final two nights of the season, with the Blue Jays playing at Baltimore's Memorial Stadium. They lost the first game 6–3, knowing that a Boston win over the Chicago White Sox the same night could eliminate them. The battle of the Sox went into extra innings, leaving the Blue Jay players to await their fate while watching television in the dreary visitors' clubhouse. (At least, most of the Jays were there. Others— including shortstop Tony Fernandez—were more interested in getting on the first bus back to the team hotel and complained when it was delayed as their teammates watched the game.) A large group of Toronto reporters watched the players watching the game, waiting to write an obituary for the Blue Jays' season. Ninety minutes after the Orioles had beaten Toronto, Ron Karkovice drove in the winning run for Chicago in the thirteenth inning, and the Jays lived to play another day. Those who had been watching so intently, George Bell foremost among them, finally changed out of their uniforms and headed for the bus, trying their best to act as though it was simply baseball business as usual.

The next night, October 3, brought another, equally dramatic, equally strange scene. The Jays knew that if they beat Baltimore and Chicago again beat Boston, they would finish tied for the division lead, with a one-game playoff to determine the mini-pennant the next day at SkyDome. Stieb, pitching for Toronto, gave up two runs in a little more than seven innings and, true to form, glared at Mookie Wilson, who got a late jump on a couple of line drives that it appeared could have been caught. At the end of eight innings, the game was tied 2–2. Meanwhile in Boston, the Red Sox had taken the lead, the action being relayed to Baltimore by way of the giant screen in centre field. The press box got the news first: the potential tying Chicago run was in scoring position. Then a line drive was hit into right field at Fenway Park, Tom Brunansky giving chase, finally disappearing out of sight and off the television screen. As the same image was replayed in the stadium between the top and bottom of the ninth inning, the Toronto players climbed out of their dugout to watch.

Suddenly Brunansky popped up, glove held aloft, the ball there, the game over, the division won. The Jays retreated down the steps. Tom Henke came out for the bottom of the ninth and threw the biggest, fattest, batting-practice fastball he could manage, right down the middle of the plate, begging Mickey Tettleton to do the deed. He obliged, knocking it out of the park, and it was time for the Blue Jays to pack for the long winter to come.

"I'll go home thinking that we were the best team in the division," said McGriff, who had been all but invisible during September and October. Just as they might have been the better team in 1987. And 1986. Just as they ought to have beaten the Royals in the playoffs of 1985. But losing when you should win can become a habit, the trait of a franchise—look no further than the Montreal Expos of the 1980s. The Blue Jays had come to look more and more like the Blow Jays, a team destined to never be quite good enough, to never really live up to its considerable potential.

Gillick understood that as well as anyone. The plan, begun in 1977, modified after the 1985 American League Championship Series, the team built largely through the Blue Jays' own farm system, had proven itself not quite good enough. And so even old Stand Pat knew that he could stand pat no longer. It was time for dramatic change, for an alteration of the grand design. The baseball winter meetings, held that year in Rosemont, Illinois, a suburb of Chicago, would be the scene for the two biggest deals in the history of the franchise, trades that would change the chemistry of the team on the field and in the clubhouse.

On December 2 came part one: Junior Felix and reserve infielder Luis Sojo were sent to California in return for centre fielder Devon White and relief pitcher Willie Fraser. In retrospect, it looks like a steal, even though Fraser turned out to be a useless throw-in. The Jays got a great defensive player, one of the real keys to Toronto's World Series championships, in return for two players who would never really amount to much. But at the point in his career at which he was traded, White seemed very much a risk. He had hit just .217 with the Angels in 1990, striking out 116 times in 125 games, and at one point during the season was actually demoted to Triple A Edmonton.

White's problems weren't based on any lack of ability, though. He lacked confidence, largely because of a series of run-ins with hard-nosed California manager and former Blue Jay Doug Rader (coincidentally, the same manager who while working in Texas could never find the key to unlocking Tom Henke's potential before the reliever was claimed by Toronto). Rader insisted that White, with his natural speed, ought to be a lead-off hitter, which by definition meant that he'd have to be less free-swinging, sacrificing power but cutting down on the strikeouts.

"I talked to Devo when they got him and asked him why he didn't like hitting lead-off," Gaston says. "He told us and he made some sense. This guy's first year he hit twenty-five home runs, and then they wanted him to go out and be a Punch-and-Judy hitter. I told him lead-off is only the first time up. You go up there and swing like you're a third-place hitter. Be yourself."

Cito Gaston would be criticized for many things as manager of the Toronto Blue Jays, even as his teams were winning championships. But there was no denying what may have been his single greatest accomplishment—rebuilding Devon White's confidence, creating a situation in which he felt comfortable and wanted, and then reaping the benefits of employing the best defensive centre fielder in baseball. White would never be a classic lead-off hitter, but his speed at the top of the line-up would nonetheless create problems for the opposition, as would his legitimate home-run power.

His greatest contribution came in the field. With White in centre, every pitcher was that much better and could throw strikes with that much more confidence. With White in centre, whoever was playing beside him in the outfield looked that much more competent, knowing that balls hit to the gap would be run down with his graceful, apparently effortless stride. Never before in franchise history had there been such defensive support.

Two days later came part two, a true blockbuster: the exchange of four legitimate all-stars—in fact, four players who would all be selected for the 1991 All-Star Game. Gillick had been negotiating with San Diego vice-president Joe McIlvaine about a straight one-for-one swap: Fred McGriff to the Padres in exchange for Joe Carter. It was a deal that made sense for both teams. The Padres were losing first baseman Jack Clark and so were in the market for a new one. The Blue Jays, having finally tired of George Bell, were planning on losing him to free agency. They also had made a big commitment to Olerud, whose only natural position was at first. Carter would play better left field than Bell and provide the same kind of run production. The trade was made.

But then, just to see if there was more room to manoeuvre, Gillick upped the ante: if we add Tony Fernandez, will you talk Roberto Alomar? It was a long shot. Gillick figured that since Alomar's father, Sandy Sr., was employed by San Diego as a coach, there wasn't much chance of prying the son out of the organization. But the Padres, knowing that shortstop Gary Templeton was just about finished, were in the market for a replacement. They had Bip Roberts and Joey Cora, who could both fill in for Alomar at second base. And McIlvaine, who was new to the job, didn't have a huge commitment to either Alomar or his father. In fact, for much of the previous season, both Alomars had been feuding with San Diego manager Greg Riddoch.

Whatever qualms Gillick might have felt about giving up Fernandez—a product of the Toronto system, a fine defensive shortstop with superior offensive skills, though a strange, moody young man whose head wasn't always in the game—disappeared when he thought about Alomar's potential. Here was the total package, a young player who was already just a notch below Ryne Sandberg in any consideration of the best second basemen in the game.

Sometimes trades are incredibly complicated, requiring weeks of delicate negotiation. And sometimes, even the biggest deals just fall into place. "It's all new to all of us," Jimmy Key said when he heard about the trade. "This is a team that hasn't made a whole lot of changes over the years but obviously they feel it is time to shake things up.... Everybody to a man knew we weren't good enough to win a World Series. With the changes we might be capable of anything."

There were other additions that winter as well: free agent reliever Ken Dayley from the St. Louis Cardinals, who was pencilled in as a left-handed set-up man; veteran Pat Tabler, a right-handed designated hitter and pinch-hitter. Manny Lee would take over from Fernandez at short, with hot prospect Eddie Zosky waiting in the wings. Any remaining thoughts of using Olerud in left field vanished when first base came open. Gaston said he'd want Carter playing right field beside Devo. And in left? Mookie or Mark Whiten, or Rob Ducey or another of the kids.

And no George Bell. It wasn't just his temperamental nature. Bell had been breaking down physically, had never had surgery on his injured throwing shoulder, as was supposed to have happened after the 1989 season. (Still, 1990 was hardly a washout. Despite his eye problems, Bell hit twenty-one homers and drove in eighty-six runs.) The Jays had made a token one-year offer at his 1990 salary level, but even that was withdrawn after the trade with San Diego was consummated. A day later, Bell's Blue Jay career officially came to an end, when the thirty-one-year-old signed a three-year, $9.3-million contract with the Chicago Cubs—a National League team, meaning that he'd have to play the field every day.

It was a sad, bitter parting for the only Blue Jay to have been named American League MVP, for Gillick's greatest steal in the Rule Five draft, for one of the most complex, misunderstood personalities to ever appear on the Toronto sports scene. Bell was hurt by the rejection. His tremendous pride was wounded. And so naturally, he left only after delivering one last shot. "That deal was just personal," Bell said. "Pat Gillick didn't want certain players. He probably wanted me to play in Japan or Mexico.... Pat Gillick ruined the chemistry when he brought Jimy Williams to manage. We were building a good team with Bobby Cox as manager. They treated me bad the last two months after the season. They really should have treated me better than they did."

MUCH IS MADE in the popular sporting press of intangibles: team chemistry, winning attitude or its converse, individuals with character who are good in the clubhouse and valuable in the dugout versus those of a more rancorous nature. Much of that is bunk. Usually, it can be said with some certainty that a more talented group of athletes will have the better of a less talented group of athletes, at least over the long haul. But as is the case in any workplace, emotion and desire do play a part. A hated boss, a boss who doesn't win respect, won't extract the maximum effort from his workers. If you're feuding with the guy next to you on the assembly line—or with the guy next to you in the dressing room—it might well interfere with your commitment to the task at hand. And some people are more goal oriented than others, are more able to think collectively rather than selfishly, to sacrifice their own needs for the good of all.

The Toronto Blue Jays of the late 1980s and 1990 seemed to lack nothing in the way of talent. But year after year, they were beaten by one team or another and were left to say—as Fred McGriff had said—that they knew they were really better. The trades made during the 1990–91 off-season, while they certainly added to the overall talent level (especially with the addition of Devon White), were also designed as an attitude adjustment. None of the three key newcomers had ever won anything in professional baseball. All had played for bad teams, in bad situations—hopeless, in the case of Joe Carter's tenure with the then-horrible Cleveland Indians. Here was their chance to come to a first-class organization with a winning record, a player-friendly manager and a team that was in contention virtually every season.

What they could bring to the mix was a kind of unjaded enthusiasm, a genuine thrill at having the opportunity to win that the old Jays seemed to lack. Add Alomar, White, Carter. Subtract Fernandez, Bell and McGriff: entering spring training in 1991, everyone was talking New Jays. They were picked to win at least a division once again, but this time it was because they were supposed to be different.

◆ SOME THINGS, THOUGH, hadn't changed. Cito Gaston, unbending in his loyalty to veterans, insisted all through the Grapefruit League season that Mookie Wilson would be his starting left fielder, despite ample evidence that he'd lost it, both offensively and defensively. And sure enough, on Opening Day Wilson was there, beside White and Carter, backing an infield of Olerud, Alomar, Lee and Gruber. (By season's end, Wilson was on the bench, Carter was in left, and Candy Maldonado, acquired in a trade with Milwaukee, had established himself in right.)

Pitching was the key to the team's success in 1991, all the more remarkable considering that the Jays' dominant short reliever was felled early by injury, and the greatest starter in Toronto history, coming off the best season of his career, was effectively finished before the end of May. In both cases, though, that bad fortune led to good fortune, as others rose to the occasion. After Tom Henke pulled a groin muscle on April 12, Duane Ward was once again forced temporarily into the full-time closer's job, handling it extremely well. His elevation meant that someone would have to step into the role of right-handed set-up man: enter Mike Timlin, a hard-throwing rookie who seemed born for the task.

On May 22 in Oakland, after a harmless-looking collision with a base runner, Dave Stieb went on the disabled list with a sore shoulder. A few days later, with the team in Baltimore, he experienced shooting pains from his back down his legs. A little less than a year after his no-hitter, his major league career had effectively come to an end, though no one knew it at the time. Stieb himself said that he'd be back soon enough, without surgery, ready to finish the season with Toronto, and for a time the team's medical staff seemed to agree with that assessment. But the pain never disappeared, and the back didn't heal on its own. Even after off-season surgery, the old Dave Stieb would never return.

The Jays' first response was the elevation of Juan Guzman, a pitcher acquired from the Los Angeles Dodgers in 1987 in exchange for second baseman Mike Sharperson. No one paid much attention to that deal—Guzman at the time was just another hard-throwing kid with control problems, whose minor league numbers hardly indicated a sure-fire big league career. He'd spent the entire 1990 season at Double A Knoxville, leading the league in strikeouts, and then, in two months with Syracuse in 1991, he had gone 4–5 with a 4.03 ERA before being called up. His first starts as a Blue Jay didn't inspire much confidence, but eventually he found his form, found his confidence and set a franchise record by winning ten in a row.

In June, though, Pat Gillick didn't know that was going to happen. He knew his team was in first place, but without Stieb and Henke it seemed vulnerable to one of the other teams in the division, none of which had yet hit their stride. If all those off-season moves were going to pay off, if a team built to win a pennant was going to have that chance, he'd have to find another reliable starter, and fast. The year before, Gillick had moved late in adding Bud Black. This time he moved early, sending promising young outfielders Glenallen Hill and Mark Whiten to Cleveland in exchange for knuckleballer Tom Candiotti and reserve outfielder Turner

Ward. "I'm not happy with the deal," Gillick admitted at the time. "In the long run it does not make a lot of sense. I think it's overpay. But you've got to deal with the present and for us we've got to do that with some pitching. This is purely a move with 1991 in mind."

Toronto had employed only one other true knuckleballer in its history, Phil Niekro, who had a brief tenure with the team in 1987. Because the pitch is so difficult to learn and it tends to be something pitchers turn to to save careers that otherwise seemed doomed to failure, Candiotti was a rarity—a young pitcher, in his prime, who had mastered the art. With the Indians, he had been a consistent winner on a consistently awful team, and so, like the other emigrés from bad situations—Alomar, Carter and White—he could be counted on in his desire to win. "I've had a big smile on my face all day because I'm getting out of Cleveland and going to a team that is really committed to winning," Candiotti said the day the trade was announced.

THE BLUE JAYS sat in first place at the All-Star break, five-and-a-half games up, the first time they had led the division at the season's mid-point since the glories of 1985. They had done it despite the injuries, not just to Stieb and Henke, but to Gruber and Rance Mulliniks as well, and despite the fact that Gruber's replacement, Ed Sprague, had reminded no one of Brooks Robinson during his time at third base. There was no sense of manifest destiny, even though the American League East was once again the weakest division in baseball, because of all those heartbreaks of the past. But still, as Toronto prepared to host its first All-Star Game, much of the old civic pride that the team had engendered almost from its arrival again came to the surface. This was one of those showcase moments, when the continent turned its attention to Toronto, and Toronto couldn't have enjoyed it more. Here was the miraculous stadium with its miraculous moving roof, something they didn't have in New York or Los Angeles or anywhere else. Here were Carter and Alomar and Key in the American League line-up, stars of a team that never seemed to get quite enough notice, quite enough respect. Until the day the Blue Jays reached a World Series, this was the greatest opportunity for self-affirmation their fans would experience.

By the end of the season, it would seem like a cakewalk, the first time during their years of contention the Blue Jays would win or lose the division without real pain. (Though their manager couldn't say the same. Gaston suffered with debilitating back problems much of the season and was forced out of the dugout for thirty-three games, with Gene Tenace temporarily taking charge.) Toronto could thank their division mates for the easy ride. On July 20, the Jays held a comfortable seven-game lead over the Tigers, eight games over the Yankees, nine games over the Red Sox. They then proceeded to lose eight out of ten games. At the end of the slump, they led Detroit by six, New York by eight, Boston by nine.

The Red Sox crept back into the race in September, closing to within two games with nine games left to play. Visions of 1990. But this time, thanks to a pitching staff that compiled a league best 3.50 ERA, thanks to the improved defence that had a lot to do with that statistic—and little thanks to an offence ranked eleventh in the American League—the Jays cruised home. There were a few signs of trouble, especially when both Candiotti and Timlin struggled during the final days of the season. No collapse occurred, though, and no unbeatable team emerged from the American League West to stand in the way of a first trip to the series. With that kind of pitching staff and with the Minnesota Twins emerging as the first post-season opposition, it looked very much like the breakthrough was at hand.

The division clincher came with all the necessary symbolism. On October 2, in the bottom of the ninth, with the California Angels leading by a run, Devon White came to bat against one of the game's best closers, Bryan Harvey. White singled, bringing Alomar to the plate. He grounded to second baseman Kevin Flora, a double-play ball but for the fact that White had gained an exceptional jump on his way to second. Flora was left with the choice of an easy play at first for one out or a difficult play at second to nail the lead runner, with just the outside possibility of a double play. He chose the latter and threw the ball away. As it scooted into left field, White turned on the jets and came all the way around to score the tying run. Alomar moved to second. Joe Carter stepped in to take his turn at bat.

In the great code of how to play the game, you don't try to steal third base when you're the potential winning run, already in scoring position, with nobody out. In the Roberto Alomar version, though, you take third any time they give it to you, any time an otherwise risky move seems just too easy to pass up. He swiped the base, trotted home on Carter's single, and the celebration began. That was the night the Toronto Blue Jays became the first team in the history of professional sport to draw four million fans in a single season, finishing at 4,001,526. Just try to find someone in Toronto who at that moment didn't have at least a passing interest. Just try to find a team and a game, anywhere at any time, that crossed so many demographic lines.

◇ON THEIR TWO previous ventures into the baseball post-season, the Blue Jays had been considered underdogs, the first time slight underdogs, the second time prohibitive. Entering the American League Championship Series against the Minnesota Twins in 1991, they were clear favourites, nowhere more so than in the eyes of those fans whose hearts had been broken so many times before. During the regular season, the Jays had beaten the Twins handily. On paper, they matched up well in virtually every position. As well, there remained the great bottom line, their pitching staff—during the regular season, Minnesota batters had hit just .218 against Toronto. Everyone knows that pitching wins championships.

Because that truism is to some degree actually true, the decision as to who would start Game One for the Jays was of paramount importance. The starter of the first game would set the tone for the series and in theory would be able to come back for games four and seven if necessary. For Toronto, the clear choice was between the knuckleballer Candiotti, who had faded a bit at the end of the season, and the rookie Guzman, who had been all but unhittable down the stretch.

In many organizations, that call would be the manager's and the manager's alone. In Toronto, it required a meeting of the entire baseball hierarchy and some kind of consensus. Cito Gaston would get the credit or the blame later on and would have the pleasure or pain of explaining his rationale to the press and public. But his vote would be only one and not necessarily one of those that eventually came down on the side of Tom Candiotti starting Game One.

In fact, in the aftermath of the disasters that followed, there wasn't any individual who would stand up and take responsibility for the decision. Gillick makes it clear that he thinks it was Gaston's idea. "Cito has always thought knuckleball guys have an opportunity to screw up the hitters," Gillick says. "He wanted to start with a guy who might throw the hitters off balance and screw up their timing. To be frank with you, I said, 'It makes some sense to me. If that's the way you feel, go ahead with it.' I was very open as to what our thinking was."

Gaston says it was an organizational decision—not his decision—but he also goes out of his way to lay blame at Candiotti's feet. "Candiotti was, to me, very disappointing," he says. "I think he was the most disappointing pitcher I ever had here. We put him out there to throw knuckleballs and he threw curve balls. He went against everything we tried to establish. Because believe me, if you face a knuckleball pitcher, the next day you're not swinging too well. Because it throws you off. We could have come back with Guzman, who stuck it up their butts the whole time. But we were trying to make it even easier for the other guys."

The buck may keep passing on that one for as long as anyone cares to remember the 1991 ALCS. The fact is that Candiotti came out in Game One at the always noisy Hubert H. Humphrey Metrodome and looked to all the world like a knuckleball pitcher afraid to throw his knuckleball. There's a reason pitchers develop a gimmick pitch—their basic repertoire of curves and fastballs and sliders isn't good enough to get anyone out. And so when Candiotti started throwing mid-speed heaters and big slow curves to the Minnesota hitters, they couldn't have been more pleased. He was gone after two-and-two-thirds, having already given up five runs, and though the Jays' hitters took a real run at the Twins' starter Jack Morris, it wasn't enough to overcome that early deficit.

Final score: 5–4 Minnesota. Still, all wasn't lost, and when the Jays bounced back to take Game Two 5–2, behind the pitching of Guzman, Ward and Henke, the series again seemed theirs for the taking. Back to the friendly confines of SkyDome with that one necessary road win already under their belts. There were even those who thought the Jays might not have to make a return trip to

Minnesota. But few of the Toronto fans were anticipating a Minnesota sweep.

There had been crushing, dispiriting losses before in franchise history, the seventh game in 1985, the collapse of 1987. But for sheer all-out, gut-wrenching despair, no low point was lower than the fold-up of 1991.

You could make excuses. You could point out that in pivotal Game Three, the Jays were leading 2–0 and looking confident, that in the fourth and fifth innings, they had runners at second and third with just one out and couldn't score either time. A run or two there and the Twins might have packed it in, and history might have been different. Or if only Joe Carter hadn't twisted his ankle when he ran into the fence trying to chase down a line drive that became a triple. He didn't play the field after that, and wasn't the same hitter for the rest of the series. Or maybe if in that same game, tied 2–2 in the top of the tenth, Gaston had called on Ward, rather than sticking with Timlin, who served up the game-winning homer to Mike Pagliarulo.

But none of that would fully explain why the Jays crumbled in Game Four, Morris having by far the better of Todd Stottlemyre, or why in Game Five they would lead 5–2, then allow the Twins to come back and tie the game in the sixth, before finally losing 8–5, with Ward and David Wells failing in relief. Gaston, in a rare show of emotion, had managed to get himself thrown out in the third inning, something the fifty thousand faithful might have tried if they'd known what was coming.

There is no uglier word in the sports vernacular than "choke" because it implies a whole series of ignoble traits, foremost among them the inability to produce when it counts the most. It had been whispered back in 1985, spoken quietly in 1987. Now, even the faithful were in full voice: this was one that should have been won and wasn't. No excuses. No alibis. And it had never felt worse.

Naturally, the blame fell first on Gaston. He had made obvious mistakes in the playoff, refusing to pinch-hit for the likes of Manny Lee, making the wrong moves too often with his pitchers. And for some within the organization, having Gaston as a scapegoat was just fine. There had always been an element within the club, Gillick being the prime mover, that didn't have an enormous amount of faith in Gaston's abilities. He had been a consolation choice, after all, when Gillick's man Lou Piniella was unavailable, when his second man Terry Bevington was judged to be too hard-nosed in the wake of Jimy Williams. After leading the team to the division title in 1989, Gaston certainly couldn't be replaced. (It can only be assumed that there was sensitivity as well within the organization as to their handling of one of only two black managers in the game at the time.) Beeston was tremendously loyal to Gaston. So was Peter Widdrington. But after the disaster of 1991, there was for the first time serious, open debate within the organization as to whether it was time to make a change.

The Gaston backers carried the day, and on October 24, the manager was rehired for the 1992 season. "The one thing we had some concern about, and it was put to rest this week, was the physical thing," Gillick said, denying that he had any qualms about Gaston other than his bad back. "We've been assured that, through therapy or through surgical intervention, Cito's going to be fine." Gillick allowed himself only the mildest, gentlest criticism of the skipper: "We think sometimes he's a little too loyal to his players. Sometimes you have to look at a player as a player instead of a human being."

Gaston himself would have none of that. In the past, he had remained relatively stoic when his managerial abilities were questioned. But the criticism hurt nonetheless, and he came to wonder whether perhaps some of it had to do with the colour of his skin. Not overt racism, perhaps, but a more subtle bias that might cause people to question him in a different way than they'd question a Sparky Anderson or a Billy Martin. The chip was there, and when the questions came, when they came even on the day the team was giving him a new contract and a vote of confidence, Gaston bristled.

"We might have been outplayed," Gaston said, "but we weren't outmanaged."

OBVIOUSLY, THE NEW faces brought on board in the winter of 1990 were not enough. And so Gillick set off once again to find the missing ingredient. The Jays, with their record attendance, had money to spend and had the appeal of a club on the verge of a championship.

Big-time free agents, the kind who in the past had been loath to cross the border, fearing high taxes and cold weather and all of that "foreign" stuff, now might find Toronto an appealing place to set up shop. "I thought going into the [1992] season that we probably needed another couple of veteran guys to get us over the hump and another pitcher," Gillick says. "There was certainly a lot of uncertainty about whether Stieb could come back and pitch."

One of the veteran guys available might have seemed like an obvious fit. The Jays still weren't getting much production out of their designated hitters, a lament that went back many years. Mulliniks was near the end of the line, Tabler couldn't fill the role every day. They had been desperate enough in 1991 to bring in Dave Parker for the stretch drive, hoping that he might have something left. So why not Dave Winfield? The veteran outfielder was already a favourite of Toronto fans, especially after the way he'd handled the famous seagull-killing incident of 1983, when an errant warm-up toss (or perhaps not so errant) ended the life of one of the resident gulls at Exhibition Stadium. Winfield was very briefly charged with cruelty to animals, took the whole thing as a joke instead of an insult and showed himself to be a bit brighter than the average ball player in the process. Though he was now forty years old, he was coming off another productive season, having hit twenty-eight home runs and driven in eighty-six for the California Angels. Compared with the Jays' DH numbers in 1991— .252, 5 HR, 56 RBIs—Winfield would obviously represent a great leap forward. Only one problem, though. Winfield insisted that he still wanted to be an everyday outfielder, something the Jays couldn't offer him, with Carter, White and now Maldonado comfortably established. "We're not interested in him unless Dave changes his position about playing on defence," Gillick said the day Gaston was rehired. "We don't think that in this particular park on this particular team he could be a defensive player."

The first priority, then, was a starting pitcher, someone with both the arm and the grit to win the big game. Stieb had undergone back surgery on December 3, and although his doctors said he could be ready for spring training, it was no sure thing. Candiotti had left for the Los Angeles Dodgers as a free agent, though after his non-performance in the playoffs, that hardly seemed a significant loss.

There were two prime candidates for the job, and two prime bidders for their services. The bidders were the Blue Jays and their division rivals, the Boston Red Sox. One of the candidates was left-hander Frank Viola. And the other was the hero of the just-completed World Series, Jack Morris, who had exercised an option in his contract that made him an unrestricted free agent at the end of the 1991 season. Of course, that just happened to be the greatest moment of his career, surpassing even his heroics with the 1984 World Champion Detroit Tigers. After finishing off the Jays, Morris was unbeatable in the World Series against Atlanta, including a ten-inning shutout in Game Seven that has gone down as one of the gutsiest performances ever by a pitcher in a must-win game. That kind of character, that kind of desire, that kind of will to win was exactly what the Blue Jays still seemed to lack, and so Morris became their primary target. "Everybody knew that Jack was sort of an obstinate, cantankerous kind of guy but also a terrific competitor who liked to win," Gillick says. "We just kept talking."

At the winter meetings in Miami Beach, negotiations continued with Morris's agent, Dick Moss. Afterwards, it was Beeston who came in to close the deal. He had developed a relationship with Moss as well as one with Morris, and as had been the Jays' practice, the guy most likely to get the deal done, whether it was Beeston, Gillick or Assistant General Manager Gord Ash, took over the negotiations.

Gillick headed off to the Virgin Islands on vacation. He had continued to talk to Winfield's agent, Jeff Klein, and it seemed that Winfield might have softened his insistence on playing the outfield. But as Gillick departed Toronto, nothing appeared imminent.

The Morris deal, announced on December 18, was significant: three years, two of them guaranteed for a total of $10.85 million. Morris became the fourth $5-million player in baseball history, and the first $5-million Toronto Blue Jay. Everything about him suggested that even at age thirty-six he was worth every penny of it. After the signing, Beeston and Morris, as both were wont to do, celebrated well into the early hours of the next morning. Meanwhile, Gillick was relaxing, but was never far from a phone. One of the calls he took was from Klein, informing him that his client had decided he wanted to be a Blue Jay. Just before returning home,

Gillick phoned Beeston with the news, which the president received without enthusiasm, since the Morris signing had already taken the Jays a million dollars over the payroll agreed to by Labatt. "I didn't know we were even interested in this guy," Beeston says. "I told Pat, 'I know where he ain't playing. He ain't playing here.'"

After that conversation, Gillick made one more call before getting on his plane. It was to Klein. "I told him, 'I'm going to be in the air, but I think you should talk to Paul. He really wants to talk to you. You'd better call him right away.'"

"The phone rings in my office," Beeston remembers. "The guy says, 'Hello, this is Jeff Klein, Dave Winfield's agent. Pat Gillick says you want to talk to me.'" Several expletives and five hours later, Beeston and Klein had struck a deal: one year, $2.3 million.

"They've acquired a versatile guy who can do a lot of things," Winfield said when he was introduced to the Toronto press, with typical modesty. "Cito knows I'm going to contribute. He's got another asset when you're talking about personality and that kind of stuff in the clubhouse."

Even Bo didn't know Bo like Winfield knew Winfield.

Chapter 17

CHAMPIONSHIP SEASONS BEGIN just like other seasons. The players gather in February, take a long, languid stretch in the Florida or Arizona sunshine, and pronounce themselves ready for a fine campaign to come. The manager, surveying his charges as they go through their paces, says that he sees the making of something special, veterans in their prime, past failures who will bounce back, kids who will move to the fore, all the ingredients that might be whipped into a winning unit. The general manager, a little more wary, adds it all up and says there might be moves to come, that the team that will take the field Opening Day might still contain a few surprises. And none of it seems too urgent, at least in the early days. Part of the purpose of spring training, after all, is the building of faith, the fostering of hope, the reassurance of the ticket buyer that this year might well be the one.

In 1992, the Toronto Blue Jays arrived in Dunedin as they had arrived in other years since the mid-1980s, as a team many people felt was due to win. The addition of Jack Morris and Dave Winfield seemed to provide the necessary character and grit that the club had so noticeably lacked in bowing out of the 1991 American League Championship Series. Those past disasters added a bit of tension to the proceedings, since the win-or-else imperative had never seemed so strong. Nowhere was it felt more directly than in the manager's office. The great Cito Gaston debate was one that would never really be resolved, not among the fans, not within the organization, not even after he'd won back-to-back World Series, though it at least stayed dormant through the celebratory parade. Entering 1992, discontent with the manager was growing in intensity, to the point where three weeks before the season began, Gillick was asked whether his manager was on the hot seat. "I would say no," he said, none too convincingly. "Here's the whole thing. You get a feeling when the players have lost respect for the manager and when the manager has a hard time communicating. There's no indication of that at all with Cito so, no, he's not on the hot seat, not at all."

For his part, the manager thought the question shouldn't be whether his job was on the line, but why his employers hadn't offered him more security than a one-year contract. Gaston's bad back had been repaired by surgery a month before. His replacement when he was forced into traction during the 1991 season, Gene Tenace, had become his bench coach, someone to sit in the dugout and collaborate on strategy. "There's a guy over there [Jim Leyland], he's got the same record that I've got and he's got a five-year contract," Gaston said before a Grapefruit League game against Leyland's Pittsburgh Pirates. "Nobody's been trying to fire him." It is no small irony that four years and two championships later, during a spring game against those same Pirates, managed by the same Jim Leyland, Gaston was still saying much the same thing.

Two things were givens throughout Gaston's term as manager of the Blue Jays: no matter what he did, an element of the public didn't respect his abilities, and no matter what he did, Gaston reacted to that element with a chip on his shoulder, with a sense that he had been unfairly denied the kind of status, recognition and security afforded the likes of Leyland and Tony LaRussa.

Before they had any impact on the field, the Blue Jays' off-season player acquisitions had a dramatic impact on the economics of the ball club. Since the move to SkyDome, the club had been making by far the biggest profits in its history. The year before, en route to the division title, the Jays made $17.5 million for their owners. The year before that, the disappointing 1990 season, the profit had been $14 million. In 1989, with the terrible start, the mid-season move to the Dome, and finally an exciting pennant race culminating in a division crown, the Blue Jays made $10 million—though that figure was reduced to $4 million after the team paid its share of the damages resulting from the major league players' successful collusion lawsuit.

Staying in contention year after year, but never winning at all, has ironically always been the road to the biggest, most consistent profits in any professional sport. A championship—or the moves necessary to win a championship—is invariably what sends a team's payroll skyward. But sometimes, in some places, you have to win, and you have to spend to win. Before the 1992 season, the Jays, who had traditionally been small players in the free agent market, jumped in with both feet. Their payroll, which had finished at about $30 million in 1991, jumped all the way to $45 million. At the same time, having already crossed the four-million barrier in attendance and loath to raise ticket prices, there weren't many ways to increase revenues to offset the increased payroll. Even if they sold out every game in 1992, the team would be able to increase its overall attendance by only 74, 000.

A decision had been made. All those near misses, which Toronto fans had tolerated so well, would eventually take their toll. SkyDome's novelty would wear off. The public's interests could shift. If they remained the same old Blue Jays, good but never good enough to win it all, the team might eventually be faced with the same situation as the Montreal Expos, whose loyal patrons could tolerate only so many heartbreaks. In Toronto, no one was going to go broke upping the payroll by $15 million, of course. Labatt had enjoyed the years of profit (not to mention its ever increasing equity, thanks to the skyrocketing franchise value), and even if a World Series team couldn't significantly increase the turnstile count, it wouldn't hurt subsidiaries like TV Labatt and TSN, which were by and large Blue Jay-driven. It wouldn't hurt beer sales either. Paul Beeston would always maintain that success for the franchise wasn't measured by the bottom line, but by wins and losses, and that philosophy was consistent over the years. Still, the truth is that it wasn't until 1992 that the bottom line became entirely secondary to winning a championship.

◆ THE JAYS OPENED the season at Tiger Stadium on the sunny afternoon of April 6. All the omens were right that day at the corner of Michigan and Trumbull. Dave Winfield drove in the first run of the season. John Olerud hit a home run. And Jack Morris, making his thirteenth Opening Day start in a row, showed Blue Jay fans something they had never really seen before. There had been great pitchers who wore a Toronto uniform, courageous pitchers as well. But Morris's tenacity and his sense of occasion were something beyond the norm. This was a new team, the spring after his greatest personal triumph, in the park where he first became a star. Baseball doesn't operate on pure adrenaline, pure emotion, the way football often does. But Morris at his best played the game like a linebacker, like someone whose will was at least as important as his arm. Through eight innings, he dominated the Tigers, shutting them out, holding them to three hits (two of which didn't leave the infield) as the Jays built a comfortable 4–0 lead. But the measure of the man came in the bottom of the ninth.

The lead-off hitter for Detroit, former Jay Cecil Fielder, stroked a solo home run. For most major league starting pitchers, that would signal the end. No possibility of a shutout. No runners on base to count against your ERA. A reliable closer in the pen, who with the lead cut to three could now claim a save. Everybody gets to pad their stats, everybody's happy. So give the manager the look that says "I want out of here right now."

Except that Jack Morris doesn't have that look in his repertoire. "If I get to the ninth, then there's only one job to do and that's finish the ball game," he said that day. "If you're going to bail, bail in the fifth. [Minnesota manager] Tom Kelly understood that. [Detroit manager] Sparky Anderson understood that. When I'm out there, unless there's something wrong with me or I'm dead tired, I'm not going to take myself out."

He wasn't going to take himself out, and Gaston wasn't going to take him out. The next batter, Mickey Tettleton, tapped back to the mound. One out. By that point—in fact, for most of the previous three innings—Morris had nothing left but his fastball. Gaston finally decided to at least visit the mound, then retreated to the dugout. Rob Deer, who had looked at third strikes the first three times he faced Morris, followed with a homer to make it 4–2. But the die was cast. Morris was going to finish, he was going to get those final two outs. It took 144 pitches, and it was worth a whole lot more than one win in a 162-game schedule.

Much is made in professional sport of character in the clubhouse, of the intangible contributions that certain players are supposed to make beyond their value in the field of play. Really, there's nothing mystical about it—just the same kind of group dynamics that make a person a positive influence in any workplace. Someone who has been around, who has experiences to share, who has the type of personality that makes others want to listen, can be invaluable. With Winfield, with Morris, as well as with the less recognized

Candy Maldonado, the Blue Jays acquired three players who each found a constituency.

"There were guys that Winfield took and did a good job with as far as making them good players," Gaston says. "Joe's one of them. Devo's one of them. He tried to do it with [Derek] Bell but he wasn't listening. And then Jack took some of the pitchers under his wing. Stottlemyre certainly admired Jack and so did Jimmy Key. And then Candy took the Latin guys. He talked to them and showed them how to win. These guys were buffers for me in a lot of ways. They did their job."

The tone of the new leadership was set on May 7, at the Kingdome in Seattle. The Blue Jays had jumped out to the best start in their history, going 12–3 over the first fifteen games of the season, with Roberto Alomar leading the offensive charge. Teams that win championships, though, have a knack not just for front running, not just for winning the games they're expected to, but for manufacturing victories at times when it would be easy enough to accept a loss and get even another day. This was one of those nights, as the Jays entered the ninth trailing 7–3. They began to rally and were down 7–4 with the bases loaded and two out when Winfield stepped to the plate against the Mariners' reliever, Mike Schooler. He fell behind in the count 0–2 and then had the composure to take two balls. On his next pitch, Schooler hung a slider over the middle of the plate, and Winfield lined it over the left-field fence to win the game. It was his sixth home run of the young season, and the four RBIs brought his total to twenty. "I'm just trying to be myself," he said. "I'm trying to bring my skills to a very talented team, a team that's been close. There's a lot of excitement and underlying hope on this team, a hope that we can do it."

The Jays led their division from the beginning, but the surprising Baltimore Orioles hung close for most of May and June. On June 26, Toronto was tied with Oakland for the best record in the majors, but Baltimore was only a game back. Jack Morris's record was 9–3. Juan Guzman, experiencing no sophomore jinx, was 10–1. Though Jimmy Key's record was only 4–6, his earned run average sat at just 3.05. Dave Stieb was still struggling to regain his old form, and Todd Stottlemyre continued to find it difficult to harness his considerable talents in a way that would make him a consistent major league pitcher. The Jays had the arms and they had the offence—though Kelly Gruber was again injured, this time with a sore shoulder. They looked like the total package. On July 4, after eighty games, they were 49–31, the best record ever for a Blue Jay team at that point in the season. (Both the 1984 and 1985 teams had been 48–32.) The lead over the Orioles had stretched to three games, the largest since April 25.

By now it was Gruber's knee that was bothering him, but the team was now used to operating without him. Never had a Blue Jay club seemed so confident, so much like it simply expected to win. Joe Carter, Roberto Alomar and Juan Guzman went to the All-Star Game, a dress rehearsal, it seemed, for the exposure they'd be sure to receive during the playoffs in the fall.

◆ NOT LONG AFTER that, on July 22, a column appeared in the *Globe and Mail* under the byline of Marty York that would signal the beginning of the end of Kelly Gruber's major league career. Always controversial, always a thorn in the team's side, York traded in rumours and agents acting as spin doctors, and unnamed sources, which meant that while he was refreshingly irreverent towards the beloved home team, he also tended towards black and white stories that didn't reflect the usually-grey truth. But every once in a while he would come across something that no other reporter had, and it would turn out to be dead-on accurate.

Such was the case with the famous Kelly Gruber water-skiing incident. At the same time as Gruber was supposed to be rehabilitating his injured knee, he was spotted by several people at the Muskoka Sands resort in northern Ontario water-skiing, playing tennis and running well without any kind of noticeable limp, York reported. That led naturally to a discussion of Gruber's reputation among his teammates as a malingerer and the revelation that behind his back, they referred to him as "Mrs. Gruber," presumably as a slight to his masculinity. Tests done on Gruber's knee had shown no ligament or cartilage damage, but still he'd insisted it was too sore to play on. And yet, despite the ritual denials that followed, here was clear evidence that a guy being paid a major league salary was obviously dogging it. The booing, which had begun at SkyDome before the water-skiing report, intensified thereafter, and the man who had once been the city's most popular athlete was reduced to a whipping boy. Of course the manager didn't say much about it for public consumption—that was the Blue Jay way. But privately, Cito Gaston had long ago made the decision that Gruber lacked character.

"He didn't want to play," Gaston says. "He probably had as much talent as anyone who ever played here. He just didn't care to play. Gruber should go back and look at all the times he was hurt and why he was hurt and some of it was a bunch of crap. What I tried to do was play it off to the side because I didn't want it to affect the rest of the guys. And I got away with it for a few years. Then the last year he was here, the players were sick of him. Because we needed this guy. And he did go out there and play in the end and help us win. He could have made it a lot easier for all of us that year if he'd played all year. He made it tough for us to win in 1992 because of a lack of playing. I think the players got turned off."

◆IT CAN BE argued that August was the month in which the Toronto Blue Jays proved they could win a World Series, even as they were losing game after game. After coasting through the first half of the season, clearly the superior team in their division, the Jays saw Juan Guzman go on the disabled list with a bad shoulder and the rest of their starting pitchers go south, with the exception of Jack Morris. Acquired for what he could do in the post-season, Morris proved his mettle by giving the Jays a quality start every five days when no one else seemed capable of providing even a middling five or six innings, winning five games during the month. Inevitably, the division lead shrunk, and the ghosts of Blue Jay failures past suddenly began to linger in the dark corners of SkyDome. By August 25, having lost six of the last seven, Toronto sat only two games ahead of the Orioles, with the real stretch drive still to come and without the pitching, apparently, to get the job done.

Two days later, Pat Gillick completed the deal of his life. With every team in a pennant race looking for pitching, he managed to liberate David Cone from the New York Mets for a decent but unspectacular minor league outfielder named Ryan Thompson and a utility infielder, Jeff Kent, who might someday develop into a

low-end major league regular. There were a hundred guys like Kent
and Thompson in and around the American and National Leagues.
And there were three, maybe four pitchers in all of baseball with
Cone's credentials. Sure, the Mets were dismantling the World
Series' team of the mid-1980s and were trying to lessen the cost of
salaries; sure, Cone would become a free agent at the end of the
season in any case. But of all Gillick's late-season acquisitions, Cone
was the one who most suggested his mastery of the business. Other
teams could have traded for him, should have traded for him. But it
was Gillick who landed him, giving up next to nothing in return.

The impact on the field was immediate: a great starting pitcher
dropped into the middle of Toronto's starting rotation. But the
impact off the field shouldn't be underestimated. Baseball players
by and large understand the business of the game. They know that
not every franchise tries to win every year, that under the sport's
current economics, many franchises begin a season with no real
chance to compete unless everything falls their way. By acquiring
Cone, Gillick sent a message to his players. Already they had one of
the highest payrolls in the majors, but they were willing to spend
more if it was necessary to get to a championship. Already they had
what appeared to be a pitching staff capable of winning the
American League East, but the Jays' management and ownership
clearly aspired to something greater. "All I can say is, wow," Pat
Borders said the day the deal was consummated.

"It's a good day for us," Cito Gaston confirmed.

"What it tells me is that this organization is trying to win this
thing this year," Morris said.

"I think he's the starter we need to win the division," Gillick
added. "I think what people have been doing a little too much is
thinking we've locked this division up and what we're worried about
is the playoffs. I think people have been worrying about the playoffs
and the World Series but they're putting the cart before the horse."

Cone would pitch very well down the stretch—very well, but not
spectacularly, compiling a record of 4–3 with a 2.55 ERA. But
there's no doubt that his acquisition did provide a confidence boost
for the team just at the time when, in other years, they might have
been ready to fold. Like the Rickey Henderson deal a year later, the
case can be made that the Blue Jays could have gone on and

achieved what they did without Cone on the staff. But the only certainty is that with him, they would win it all.

◆LOST TO A degree in the August slump, in Cone's arrival, in the turn for home on September 1, was the end of Dave Stieb's career as a Toronto Blue Jay. In so many ways, he was the epitome of what the franchise had been all about: a young player whose potential they spotted when others might have passed him by. A product of their system who jumped quickly to the major leagues in the team's darkest years, because there wasn't anyone else. A huge talent, but a flawed talent, despite finally nailing down that no-hitter. Dave Stieb would never win twenty games, though several years it looked as if he might. He would never pitch a team to a championship. Though he had as much pitching ability as any of his contemporaries, he also lacked something, the quality Jack Morris possessed in abundance, the ability to lead and lift a team on his own. You can't do that when you turn and glare at the players behind you if they make an error.

Stieb made his last start for Toronto on August 8, lasting just three innings before elbow tendinitis forced him out of the game. It was merely the latest physical breakdown to mar his final two seasons with the club. On September 23, he acknowledged that he was finished for the season and probably forever as a Blue Jay. "I've accepted that," he said. "It looks like I'll watch the playoffs from the sidelines again." The Jays held an option to buy out the remaining year of his contract at the end of the season for a million dollars, and though no one was saying anything for the record, it looked certain that that was what they would do. Stieb, though, still held out some faint hope that he might be back. "In their mind I'm not sound. All that talk about loyalty—I hope some of it still stands. I realize they've paid me a lot of money and I haven't given them a lot the last two years. But [the injuries] have been out of my control. There are twenty-seven other teams out there. I will pursue that avenue if they aren't interested."

There is something perfectly Stiebian (that is, ironic, pathetic, and somehow just) in the fact that four days later, Morris became the first Toronto pitcher to win twenty games in a season, the benchmark for excellence among starters. It had taken several tries and was accomplished only after Morris came back to pitch following a two-hour rain delay at Yankee Stadium, with the Jays leading 9–0 but the game not yet official. Morris and Stieb didn't like each other, largely because at various times when he was pitching against Toronto, Morris suggested that Stieb lacked courage, that he'd bail out after five innings with a win rather than pitch on, that he'd blame others rather than himself when things went wrong. Of course Morris had his own flaws—a personality that could be cantankerous in the extreme. But though he probably had less natural ability than Stieb, his character led him to be just a little bit better when it counted, rather than not quite good enough.

By the time the Jays had righted themselves in September, only the surprising Milwaukee Brewers remained to challenge them for the division title, the Orioles having closed to within a half game before falling to a season-ending slump. From August 29, the Brewers won twenty-two of twenty-nine games, so that entering the final week of the season, they trailed Toronto by only two. Of course, that could only provoke unpleasant memories of collapses past, but with this group that wasn't about to happen. There was an edge, a tension around the team, a fear of losing, but also a fear of a different sort. "I think that everybody in Toronto feels like their jobs are on the line, including our manager," David Cone told a reporter, the kind of observation only a newcomer playing out the final days of his contract could make. But it was true—if they didn't win in 1992, with this team, with this payroll, something would have to give. As far as the division was concerned, though, despite the Brewers' brave run, it was never really an issue.

The celebration was delayed once, when the Jays beat the Tigers 8–7 and then had to sit and wait as Milwaukee finally triumphed over Oakland, pushing over the winning run in the eleventh inning against Dennis Eckersley. That left Toronto needing just one more win or one Milwaukee loss. Juan Guzman responded by throwing a one-hitter through eight innings, and though Tom Henke made things interesting, loading the bases and walking in a run in the ninth, the Jays prevailed for a 3–1 victory, which led to an appropriately muted celebration for a team that had walked around all year wearing T-shirts emblazoned with the slogan "3-for-3" under their uniforms: division–pennant–series. This time, no moral victories, no excuses. Their final record was 96–66, the final attendance 4,028,318, another record. But success would be measured only by who won the last game of the year.

THE OAKLAND ATHLETICS were at the end of their run as a great American League power when they met Toronto in the 1992 American League Championship Series. The team built by Sandy Alderson and managed by Tony LaRussa had been a truly wondrous baseball machine at its best, with the speed of Rickey Henderson, the power of the Bash Brothers, the starting pitching of Dave Stewart, the peerless relief work of Dennis Eckersley. But it's also true that that great collection of talent, backed by LaRussa's managerial acumen (just ask him) had won precisely one World Series. There were those who thought they had a shot to beat Toronto, especially given the Blue Jays' series of shameful post-seasons past. But still, these A's didn't have the look of a winner the way they did back in 1989.

As well, Toronto had Morris, the man who had almost single-handedly pitched Minnesota to the World Series the year before. No Tom Candiotti nonsense this time around. A three-man rotation, with Morris, David Cone and Juan Guzman, as fine a trio as any major league team could muster. Put that together with the Ward Henke combination in the bullpen, and the advantage was clearly Toronto's.

Morris's performance in Game One at SkyDome established a shocking pattern. He faced Stewart, who had never lost in league championship series play, and they duelled into the ninth. But with the game tied 3–3 and his bullpen warmed and ready, Gaston decided to do the same thing he'd done back on Opening Day in Detroit—let Morris go until he had nothing left to give. Harold Baines homered. The Athletics won. And those who doubted the manager's abilities (few at that point were doubting Morris's abilities) had one more piece of evidence to make their case.

The Jays bounced back in Game Two, with Cone beating Mike Moore 3–1, a game best remembered for a play that wasn't made.

On an Oakland double steal, the ball skipped past Borders for a wild pitch. But with Alfredo Griffin hollering at him to let it roll, Borders watched the ball tumble into the Toronto dugout, rather than attempting to field it. Even though he had crossed the plate, Willie Wilson was sent back to third base, since the ball was dead the minute it left the field of play. He never did come around, and the run not scored proved crucial to the outcome.

Game Three, the first at the Oakland Alameda County Coliseum, was a messy affair. But this time, Toronto's bats—and Oakland's three errors—were the difference. In the second inning, Winfield reached base on an error, took third on a wild pitch and then scored on Candy Maldonado's single to make it 1–0. Alomar homered. Maldonado homered. Manny Lee hit a crucial triple. The Blue Jays won 7–5, recapturing the home field advantage and moving to within two victories of the World Series.

All of which made Game Four the pivotal moment in the series and arguably one of the pivotal moments in the entire history of the Toronto franchise. The difference between a 2–2 tie, reducing the series to a best of three, and a 3–1 Toronto lead, with two games left at SkyDome, was enormous. And for a team that had never won a playoff series, that desperately needed to get over the hump, this would be the game that finally showed a killer instinct, an ability to play with confidence rather than falling into self-doubt the minute things got tough. The game looked early on like an Oakland rout, as Morris once again couldn't do the job, while the A's starter Bob Welch cruised into the eighth inning with a 6–1 lead. But the Jays started to chip away, scoring three runs and forcing LaRussa to bring in Eckersley an inning earlier than normal. The Jays hit two run-scoring singles, but he closed the inning with a flourish, striking out Ed Sprague, pumping his fist in the air, and firing a few obscenities in the direction of the Toronto dugout, suggesting just where the boys in blue might put that little white ball. The bad blood from the 1989 ALCS was still there.

That left the best closer in the game three outs away, with a two-run lead, an automatic if there ever was one. But in the ninth, Devon White led off with a sinking line drive to left, which Rickey Henderson misplayed into a three-base hit. That brought Alomar to the plate. He would have a sensational series for Toronto, eventually being named MVP for a brilliant display of hitting, base running and defence. But really, the playoff, the post-season and his entire tenure in Toronto was encapsulated in this one moment—first working Eckersley to a full count, and then lining a ball over the right field fence to tie the game. Alomar raised his arms the moment he hit it—an uncharacteristic bit of styling, but also the perfect counterpoint to Eckersley's gesture the inning before—and then slowly began his home run trot. "That was best game I ever played in my whole life in baseball," Alomar said later. Right there, in an instant, the Toronto Blue Jays shed the Blow Jays image. They wouldn't win it until the eleventh, when Pat Borders's sacrifice fly brought home Derek Bell with the go-ahead run. But by battling back and finally chasing Eckersley, the Jays had erased the Oakland mystique, conquered their own tendency to choke, proved to themselves that this team was different than the rest.

The full celebration of that fact would have to be postponed until the clubs returned to Toronto. Dave Stewart, once again demonstrating his big game grit, dominated the Jays in Game Five as the A's won 6–2. His opposite number, David Cone, pitched poorly on three days' rest, and, perhaps a little too relaxed with a 3–1 series lead, his teammates made three errors behind him. But any doubts vanished immediately in Game Six. Rickey Henderson dropped a harmless flyball from Devon White, the first Blue Jay hitter of the day, Carter homered one out later to make it 2–0, Guzman pitched exceptionally well, and the celebration began early. Toronto cruised to the pennant with a 9–2 victory, and the same fans who a year earlier had experienced humiliation at the hands of the Minnesota Twins, who must have wondered whether their heroes would ever find their way to the World Series, were left to gloat, to sing "Na, na, na, hey, hey" at the hated A's, to chant "We want Eck." They stood and cheered through the top of the ninth, knowing for the first time that Toronto—and Canada—was going to the Show.

"Everybody says that we choke in the end, and we didn't," said Alomar. "So now the monkey, we can take it off our back."

In the locker room afterwards, even as the players were acknowledging that there was one step left to climb, it was hard to contain the joy. Some of the younger players—Derek Bell foremost among them—found it particularly difficult. Dave Stieb had a reputation among some of his teammates for being aloof, arrogant, apart from the rest—though given the fact that in 1992 he'd battled injuries all year long, understood that his career might be grinding to an end, and probably didn't feel as much a part of the team as he might have, that was at least understandable. And now, noticing that Stieb had left the clubhouse, the rabble-rousers took it upon themselves to drain beer after beer into his locker. For everything he'd meant to the team over the years, Stieb certainly deserved better.

"There were pictures of my kids in there," Stieb said. "That made it worse. But I know who did it. They said I left right away, but it was forty minutes, and the thing is I was upstairs congratulating Paul Beeston and Pat Gillick. It's not like I left the building."

Derek Bell had come to Toronto as a blue-chip major league prospect, a shoo-in for a starting spot in the Blue Jays' outfield for years to come, the natural heir to Candy Maldonado in 1993. But his part in that little incident, combined with others that suggested a terminal case of immaturity, caused Gillick, Gaston and the rest to sour on Bell and to eventually give up and trade him away before the 1993 season began. "He was a young kid," Gaston says, "who just didn't know what he wanted."

◆ THE ATLANTA BRAVES brought their own subtext to the fall classic. Here was a franchise that had rebuilt from the depths with a fine farm system, with a fine manager in Bobby Cox, and with plenty of owner Ted Turner's money. Turner, the broadcast baron who invented CNN, was a very different kind of proprietor than the one the fans in Toronto had become accustomed to. So hands-on was he that at one point during his tenure, he actually saw fit to suit up and take over the team in the dugout. But by 1992, the more manic edge of Turner's energy was focused elsewhere—on establishing his own Olympics, the Goodwill Games, on his relationship with the actress Jane Fonda, on various broadcasting projects. He had left the team to Cox and general manager John Schuerholz and they had built a powerhouse, which had slipped into the series with a dramatic, seventh-game, bottom-of-the-ninth victory over the Pittsburgh Pirates.

If anything, Atlanta was even more starved for a championship of any kind than Toronto. The Braves hadn't won anything since moving to Georgia from Milwaukee in 1966, and no other professional sports team that called the city home had ever won a title. They were due at least as much as Toronto was due. They had been upset the year before by the Twins in seven games, even though man for man, they appeared to have the better talent. The experience of that loss, the experience of beating the Pirates, surely would harden them for the battle ahead. Their starting pitching was at least the equal of Toronto's, their position players very closely matched. A lot of people would tell you that in Cox, they had the better manager. And standing there in the third-base coach's box they had Jimy Williams, who still wasn't willing to forgive and forget. He wanted it, Cox wanted it, Turner wanted it, the players wanted it. Just the way Toronto wanted it.

The Braves would also become players in a proxy war, with the National Pastime up for grabs, trying to keep the foreign interlopers from claiming the World Series the way Paul Henderson and the plucky lads fought off the Russians in 1972. Of course, that was a crock—there weren't any Canadians playing for either side, and Toronto if anything craved acceptance as a quasi-American city, rather than hoping to seize something by force from its friendly neighbours to the south (despite the fact that Atlanta had beaten Toronto out for the right to host the 1996 Olympic Games). But for the television broadcasters, who'd be struggling for ratings with a Canadian team in the big show, it would at least provide a storyline—a storyline that for one memorable night almost managed to spin itself into a B-grade international incident.

Heading into the series, the Blue Jays' brain trust once again met to discuss the pitching assignments for the series, but this time came away with a different answer. They had won the ALCS with a three-man rotation, but only Juan Guzman had seemed really comfortable coming back and pitching on three days' rest. So they would add Jimmy Key to the mix, a lefty, a finesse pitcher, who figured to be particularly effective against Atlanta's largely left-handed line-up. Also, in the National League park, with no designated hitter, Gaston had to find a way to get Dave Winfield's bat into the line-up. Winfield would play in right field. Against left-handers, Joe Carter would move to first and John Olerud would sit. Against right-handers, Candy Maldonado would move to the bench. The Braves would counter with their big three—Tom Glavine, John Smoltz and Steve Avery—the best rotation by far in the National League.

In Game One at Atlanta's Fulton County Stadium, Canadian fans for the first time were treated to all the pomp and circumstance, to the playing of "O Canada," to a World Series game that actually involved another part of the world. And then the Jays were treated to some tremendous pitching. Glavine, the Cy Young award winner, hadn't pitched well against the Pirates. But opening against Toronto, he gave up just four hits, allowed just one run on Carter's fourth-inning homer and faced just thirty batters, three over the minimum. For the Jays, Morris repeated his pattern from the ALCS, not pitching all that badly, but being prone to mistakes at the worst possible time. In the sixth inning, with the game scoreless, he threw a batting-practice fastball to Atlanta catcher Damon Berryhill, who hit it out for a three-run homer. The man the Jays had signed to take them to the promised land, the pitcher who was supposed to save his best for October, was winless in the post-season.

In many ways, the most remarkable thing about the flag incident that preceded Game Two of the series was not just that it happened, but how few people noticed that it had happened. If the Marine colour guard were oblivious to the fact that they were flying the Canadian flag upside down—that would be with the stem of the maple leaf pointing up—they were joined by thousands of others in the stadium who didn't catch on to what was happening. Canadians, however, did take offence, albeit in a quiet, self-conscious Canadian way. They'd have their say back in Toronto.

The game itself is best remembered for a terrible call at home in the fourth inning, when Roberto Alomar was clearly safe attempting to score on a wild pitch, and umpire Mike Reilly called him out. It is remembered because Cone, returning to face the National League opposition he had so dominated in the past, was mediocre, giving up four runs on five hits over four innings. It is remembered for a notable managerial decision by Cito Gaston, the kind for which he is routinely roasted. In the top of the ninth, with the Jays trailing by one, one out, and Derek Bell on first, he sent right-handed Ed Sprague in to pinch-hit for Duane Ward, rather than the left-handed Rance Mulliniks. "It was Sprague all the way," Gaston said, explaining his decision afterwards. It is remembered for exposing the Braves Achilles' heel—short relief—when Sprague lined Jeff Reardon's first pitch fastball out of the park, for the runs which eventually won the game, 5–4, Tom Henke settled matters in the ninth, as Terry Pendleton popped up to Kelly Gruber to end the game, and after catching the ball Gruber offered his own version of the "tomahawk chop," the mock-Indian gesture and chant by which the Braves' fans saluted their team and offended aboriginal people everywhere. The series was tied 1–1 heading across the great unguarded border for the first time, and here were the Toronto Blue Jays, confident enough for a little "in your face."

It is a testament to the civil temperament of Canadians that before Game Three, with the upside-down flag still foremost in everyone's minds, vendors selling inverted Stars and Stripes outside SkyDome all but went broke. The Marines, who had screwed up in the first place, asked for a chance to make good. Their colour guard marched proudly into the stadium, to a warm round of applause, and all was forgiven. (One hates to think what might have happened if it had been the other way around, if Old Glory had been desecrated on Canadian soil. The image of a smoking crater comes to mind.)

But that was hardly the highlight of the night. In the fourth inning, the fans were treated to one of the greatest plays in the long history of the World Series, followed by one of the worst calls by an umpire, which negated another great play. It made for a memorable moment. With runners on first and second and nobody out, David Justice, the graceful and powerful Atlanta outfielder, launched a line drive off Juan Guzman to straightaway centre field. Off the bat, heading for the deepest part of the park, it seemed at very least like a two-run double. But Devon White thought otherwise. Alone among the great centre fielders in the game, White had the ability to seemingly cruise to a ball, never desperate, never running too hard, yet always arriving in time to make the catch. He could also turn away from a ball, head straight to the fence, then turn and pick up its flight. With the crack of the bat, he headed for centre, turning only at the last minute to find the ball. Then he leapt, making a remarkable catch just as his body slammed into the padded wall.

"Yeah, I've made a couple," White said. "But this is a World Series, so it's going to be in the top catches I've made. But I get more pumped up when I go up over the fence and bring one back. But this one is definitely up there. It was in the ball park and I knew I had a good shot at it as long as it wasn't high up off the wall."

Far away in the infield, the Braves' base runners—Terry Pendleton at first, Deion Sanders at second—had already made up their mind that the ball would fall in. At least Pendleton had. Making the kind of base-running error that you're supposed to get out of your system in Little League, Pendleton actually passed Sanders, who was returning to second to tag up, just in case. That meant Pendleton was out automatically, the second out of the inning after Justice. The throw came in to John Olerud at first base, and he touched the bag—though it turned out he didn't need to, since Pendleton was out already. Olerud in turn fired the ball across the infield to Gruber, who ran after Sanders, now stranded between second and third. Gruber dove to make the tag, and television replays showed clearly that he'd caught Sanders on the heel, which should have completed the triple play. But second-base umpire Bob Davidson—completely in tune with his crew's horrible performance throughout the series—missed the tag and called Sanders safe at second. Guzman struck out the next batter, Lonnie Smith, to make it a moot point, other than the fact that the world was denied the second triple play in World Series history.

The Jays rallied to win in the final two innings. In the eighth, Gruber, the water-skiing pariah, in an 0–23 drought, the longest in post-season history, hit the biggest home run of his career to tie the game and temporarily reclaim the undying love of the people of Toronto. Then in the bottom of the ninth, the Braves' bullpen problems again cost them a game. Avery had pitched well through eight innings of a 2–2 tie but gave up a lead-off single to Alomar to open the bottom of the ninth. Cox called for hard-throwing Mark Wohlers. Alomar immediately stole second, putting the winning run in scoring position but also allowing the Braves to walk Joe Carter intentionally, setting up the double play. Winfield, who all year had impressed with his power, flashed a bit of finesse, laying down a perfect sacrifice bunt to advance the runners. With Sprague pinch-hitting, Mike Stanton came in to issue the intentional walk and load the bases. That set up the showdown—Reardon versus Candy Maldonado, with the infield drawn in to cut down the lead runner at the plate. Maldonado slapped a soft liner just into the outfield, and the game was over, 3–2 Toronto, and a 2–1 Toronto lead in the series.

There was plenty of poetic justice in the fact that Jimmy Key was given the start for Toronto in Game Four and that he responded to the assignment with the kind of masterful control pitching that had been his trademark. Key, who had been plagued by injuries off and on during his career, was a product of the Jays' own system; he was the first and only great lefty the system had produced and a solid citizen in the clubhouse. That this would be his last start for the team, that he would leave as a free agent during the off-season (the result, for the most part, of the Jays' policy of refusing to guarantee contracts for more than three years) wasn't something either side had wanted. But this World Series start was something Key very much deserved.

He would claim the victory after pitching seven brilliant innings and then surviving a bit of a scare in the eighth, thanks to his mates in the bullpen. After Otis Nixon, the lead-off hitter in the game, had reached base (and was then picked off), Key retired twenty of the next twenty-one batters in succession. Meanwhile, the Jays pecked away at a nearly equally brilliant Tom Glavine, Borders homering in the third for a 1–0 lead, White driving in Gruber for a 2–0 lead in the seventh.

Ron Gant led off the Atlanta eighth with a double. Then Brian Hunter beat out a bunt, sending Gant to third. Damon Berryhill came up bunting as well, but popped up for an out. The next hitter, Mark Lemke, lined a ball off Key's glove that Gruber fielded, throwing out the runner at second. Still, Gant came across the plate, narrowing the score to 2–1. Gaston walked to the mound and took the ball from Key, who left to a standing ovation. Duane Ward came in and struck out Nixon, who reached first when the ball skipped past Borders. He then coaxed Jeff Blauser into grounding out for the de facto fourth out, and the inning finally ended. Tom Henke pitched the ninth: three hitters, eleven pitches, three outs. The Toronto Blue Jays were one win away from the World Series.

And who better to put it away than Morris, who could make up for all his playoff failures with one last stellar performance in front of the home fans? The anticipation that night at SkyDome was unlike anything Toronto had experienced before, not seventh-game tension, but something sweeter, more secure, the possibility of winning a championship, but knowing at least that it wouldn't be lost this time out.

The feeling didn't last long. In the fifth inning, with Atlanta at bat, the game tied 2–2 and two out, Nixon singled. He stole second when Morris and catcher Pat Borders botched a pitch-out, the ball sailing all the way to the backstop. Deion Sanders followed with a single, scoring Nixon. Then Terry Pendleton doubled, putting runners at second and third. With Todd Stottlemyre and David Wells ready to go in the bullpen, Gaston decided once again to stick with his starter. He had Morris walk David Justice intentionally—Justice had homered earlier in the game—and then pitch to Lonnie Smith. Smith took a ball, fouled off two pitches, and then hit a grand slam home run over the right field fence, all but locking up a 7–2 Braves' victory that would send the series back to Atlanta. Once again, Morris just didn't have it, though the notion that he lost it only in the post-season really wasn't entirely accurate (his World Series line: ten innings, ten runs on thirteen hits). All year, he had given up runs—his ERA was 4.04 in winning twenty-one games during the regular season—but he had enjoyed tremendous run support and had a knack for getting outs when he needed them most. In the playoffs, the big pitches became big mistakes, and the fans were uncharacteristically unforgiving. They booed vociferously when Gaston finally came out to lift Morris, booing the pitcher, booing the manager, booing even though their heroes would still lead the World Series three games to two. "The booing could have been more for me than Jack. But people forget real quick," Gaston said. "Without Jack we would not be here. He deserved a chance to work his way out of it. It just didn't work out. I feel bad for him. He made a few pitches he'd like to have back."

Back to Atlanta for the most important baseball game in Canadian history, one that, by the time it was done, would outstrip the snowbound Opening Day in 1977 and would forever erase the sad memories of 1985 and beyond. David Cone started for the Blue Jays, his last appearance before free agency, and so if winning a

World Series wasn't motivation enough, there was the good old bottom line. Steve Avery, the left-hander, countered for the Braves. In both bullpens, only the Game Five starters, Key and Avery, and the projected Game Seven starters, Juan Guzman and John Smoltz, were unavailable for service.

Toronto took the lead in their first at-bat, in a style that was very much the measure of the 1992 team. Devon White singled, stole second, advanced to third on Roberto Alomar's ground-out to the right side, and then scored on Joe Carter's line drive, which glanced off David Justice's glove for a two-base error. Deion Sanders tied it in the third—and anyone who has ever doubted Sanders's prowess as a baseball player, which sometimes tends to pale beside his football exploits, ought to go back and look at the 1992 Series to understand what might have been if he'd devoted his energies full-time to the game. He doubled off the glove of Joe Carter, who was playing first in the National League park, stole third, and then scored on Terry Pendleton's sacrifice fly. Homering in the top of the fourth, Candy Maldonado put the Jays back in the lead, 2–1. The inning might have produced more, but Borders—in the midst of his MVP series—was thrown out attempting to score from second on White's single.

In the bottom of the inning, Alomar made a defensive play that will live forever in the highlight reels: diving right to snare a ball hit by Jeff Blauser, rising to his knees, and then in one motion standing and throwing to first, to nail the runner by half a step. Defence up the middle: during the years the Jays employed Alomar and White at second and in centre, no one had it better. In the final game of 1992, they also had fine starting pitching: Cone survived six innings, surrendering one run on four hits, perhaps the best and certainly the most significant performance of his short, two part, Blue Jay career.

Still, it's the events of the late innings that everyone remembers: a series of moves and counter-moves, of near misses and lucky breaks and bad decisions that added up to a championship. Consider the seventh inning. With two out and Todd Stottlemyre pitching in relief, Nixon singled. That brought the red-hot Sanders to the plate. Hoping to negate Sanders from the left side and hoping even more to slow down Nixon on the base paths (holding and throwing out runners would never be a strong suit of even the best Blue Jay teams), Gaston called for the lefty David Wells, a free spirit, a rough-and-tumble personality, who had often clashed with his manager in the past. That left Cox to make a decision: go with the hot hitter or play the percentages? He decided to play it conventionally, bringing in the right-handed Ron Gant to face Wells. But that match-up proved secondary to what was going on on the base paths: Wells held Nixon close, and then when he tried to steal, Borders threw him out at second to end the inning.

Entering the bottom of the eighth, Toronto held a one-run lead, with Duane Ward and Tom Henke ready to close out, as they had so often before. First it was Ward's turn, and Gaston's turn to get away with one of those non-moves for which he is famous. Here it was in the late innings, the World Series on the line, and Winfield was still playing right field, where he hadn't played all year, though all baseball logic would have suggested a defensive replacement. And there was Winfield, running down a Ron Gant ball in the gap, making a spectacular catch and saving extra bases.

The Braves' brain trust had its own decisions to make, and anyone looking for a sign of things to come could have watched Joe Carter double down the left field line in the top of the ninth (he'd be stranded at second) and wonder why Atlanta wasn't guarding the lines late in the game, the way most teams do. The answer: because Jimy Williams, whose duties with the team included positioning the infielders, didn't believe in guarding the lines, convinced that there was more chance of a single through the hole than a ball scooting down the line, which is true. But a ball through the hole gets you one base. The alternative is a bit more serious.

Tom Henke's pitching line in the series entering Game Six: two innings, no hits, no runs, two saves. And so Toronto's chances of wrapping up its first World Series looked pretty darned good with three outs to go. But Atlanta already had one miracle comeback under its belt, the two-out, bottom-of-the-ninth rally in Game Seven of the National League Championship Series in which they beat the Pittsburgh Pirates, so they knew it could be done. Jeff Blauser led off with a single, slapping a ball between third and short, with Gruber guarding the line. Damon Berryhill followed with a sacrifice bunt. Lonnie Smith, the hero of Game Five, walked on a full count. That brought up pinch-hitter Francisco Cabrera, who had driven in that series-winning run against the Pirates. He lined the ball hard to left, where Candy Maldonado took two steps in and then came to a terrible realization: the ball was hit a lot harder than he thought and was about to sail over his head, where it would score the tying run, the winning run, and send the series to Game Seven. He was left to do the only thing he could—jump. He just managed to snare the ball in the webbing of his glove.

Two out. One out away from the championship. Otis Nixon was coming to bat. Alomar and Carter walked to the mound and offered Henke a bit of advice: bust this guy inside, and you'll get him. Don't throw him anything out over the plate. The first pitch was an inside fastball: Nixon swung and missed. The second pitch was another fastball, inside, over the corner: Nixon took it for strike two. "I thought we were going to win it right there," Pat Gillick says. "We were one strike away." For reasons difficult to explain, Henke's third pitch was a forkball, right over the middle of the plate. Nixon hit a blooper into left that dropped in front of Maldonado. Candy came up throwing, with Blauser just rounding third, but he wasn't close, firing the ball into the screen behind home plate. The game was tied. "I'm usually pretty calm at a game but when they tied the game at that point, at that point where I was so sure we'd won, I was a little squeamish," Gillick says. Ron Gant flied out to White to end the inning.

In extra innings, it is a manager's game. Nothing across in the top of the tenth. Gaston leaves Henke in for a rare second inning of work, then, with two out in the bottom of the inning, brings in Jimmy Key to face the left-handed Sid Bream. The strategy works. In the bottom of the eleventh, Cox chooses to stick with Charlie Leibrandt, who had pitched the tenth. With one out, he hits Devon White in the thigh. Alomar follows with a single to centre, putting runners at first and second. Carter flies out harmlessly to centre for the second out of the inning. Winfield—who might well have been lifted earlier for a defensive replacement—steps to the plate. He has had an awful series, nearly as awful as his one other appearance in the series, in 1981: this time just one RBI, and one extra-base hit. Again, Williams chooses not to guard the lines. And Cito Gaston has a premonition. They happen every once in a while: one suggested the car accident earlier in the season that almost cost third-base coach Rich Hacker his life. This time the vision is of a ball hit over third base. Gaston leans over and says to Tenace: "It's going down the line." On a 3–2 pitch, Winfield hits a grounder directly at the spot where the third baseman stands when he guards the lines. Instead, it skips past Pendleton for a double. Two runs score. Four–two Toronto.

It is still Jimmy Key on the mound in the bottom of the eleventh, as the Blue Jays try to finally close it out. Blauser leads off with a single. Berryhill hits a double-play grounder to shortstop, but Alfredo Griffin boots it, and both runners are safe. Pinch-hitter Rafael Belliard does exactly what's asked of him, dropping down a perfect sacrifice bunt, and there are runners at second and third with one out. Brian Hunter grounds to first for the second out, scoring Blauser, and moving Berryhill to third. And up comes Otis Nixon.

"One thing about Jimmy Key is he's always been honest," Gaston says. "I like that. When you go out there, be honest with me. He told me he hadn't had good luck with this guy." Gaston was left with no alternative but to go to the bullpen. His choice: Mike Timlin, best known for coughing up the Mike Pagliarulo homer a year earlier in the American League Championship Series. All around the baseball world, people are shaking their heads. "I'm a manager who doesn't forget what guys do for me," Gaston says of his unwavering loyalty principle. "And maybe that will be my downfall someday." Someday, but not in the sixth game of the 1992 World Series. After fouling off the first pitch, Nixon tries to bunt for a base hit down the first base line. "I don't know if Cox really wanted to see a bunt right there," Gaston says. The ball doesn't go far enough to get past Timlin, who scoops it up and throws to Carter, who has scrambled back to the bag.

Game over. Series won. In the east, it was ten minutes before one in the morning.

Across Canada, those who had stayed up late, who had suffered through the late-inning tensions, who had fretted through this postseason, who knew the playoff disappointments past, who remembered the heartbreak of 1987, who could trace the arc of Jim Sundberg's flyball, who had once believed in Joey McLaughlin and

Danny Ainge and Roy Lee Jackson and Lloyd Moseby and Jesse Barfield and Jim Clancy and Luis Leal and Rick Bosetti and Cliff Johnson and Jeff Musselman and Rob Ducey and Sylvestre Campusano, who had felt the cold wind off Lake Ontario at Exhibition Stadium, who had thrilled at the news that big league baseball was finally coming to their home town, who remembered, vaguely, that other stadium down by the lake, who first loved the game through the old Maple Leafs, knew this was their moment.

Perhaps there had been a couple of bigger sporting signposts in the history of the nation: Paul Henderson's goal, certainly, and that night in 1988 when a Canadian was crowned fastest man in the world (though that thrill, of course, was fleeting). But like those spots of time, the Blue Jays' victory was a rare opportunity to stand and shout, to tell the world who you were and where you came from, to claim a victory as your own in the face of the great colossus to the south. This imported game, with its deep historical roots, with an audience that now crossed so many barriers, had delivered in a way that nothing else could.

And as strange as it might seem, those for whom it should have been sweetest of all might have felt it less than the rest.

"When we won those two World Series, you can't appreciate how isolated we were from the feeling that was going on in the city and the province and the country," Paul Beeston says. "You're coming in here, which is a fortress. You're parking, you're taking buses to tarmacs, you're taking one plane and getting on another one. They take you right to the hotel. You don't get a feeling for that stuff. You don't know what's happening."

What was happening was a city in celebration of itself, a country in celebration of itself.

Chapter 18

A ND SO THE only thing to do was win another one. To say that
would be easier said than done grossly understates the case.
Since the beginning of the free agency era in baseball, which created market forces and player movement that those dynasties of the
past didn't have to contend with, only one team had managed to
repeat as World Series champion—the New York Yankees of 1976
and 1977. The game, or at least the business of the game, had
changed in such a way that it had become nearly impossible to hold
a great team together for any length of time without spending an
inordinant amount of money. At the same time, the competition
could improve itself rapidly, rather than having to rely simply on its
existing roster and farm system.

Both forces factored into the Jays' thinking after the 1992 championship. There was a sense, at least on the part of Pat Gillick, that
the status quo probably wouldn't be enough in 1993. Simply keeping the same team intact for another year would create an
unhealthy complacency and wouldn't take into account what the
Yankees or Orioles or Tigers or Brewers might do to close the gap.
And several key players would inevitably exercise their option and
leave. That was a given since for any free agent being part of a
championship team often represents the greatest opportunity of a
career to cash in. Several key members of the 1992 Blue Jays had
that chance: Joe Carter, David Cone, Jimmy Key, Tom Henke, Dave
Winfield, Candy Maldonado. Even though the Jays had made
money in 1992 (thanks, Beeston said, to the $2 million generated
by the playoff run), they were already carrying a payroll in the
neighbourhood of $48 million. And so some of the beloved would
have to go, some of them would have to be replaced.

In the minds of the Toronto public, Winfield meant more than
all the rest. Already a favourite when he had come to town as a visiting attraction, Winfield had during his single season with the team
managed to become the most popular player on a very popular
team. It had to do with his great season, with the part that great season played in a championship. It had to do with the hit that won it

all. It had to do with his plea for more noise in SkyDome, which was answered so heartily. It especially had to do with Winfield's own well-developed instinct for public relations. Unlike most ball play-ers—unlike most professional athletes—Winfield understood the whole equation, understood that image plus performance equalled wealth. Always available for interviews, always ready to say the right thing, articulately, at the right time, he maintained very high media visibility and used that platform to sell himself. If anyone doubted his importance to the Jays finally coming together and winning a championship, they needed only to listen to Winfield for a while, and he'd get the message across.

Because of all that, Winfield and his agent, Jeff Klein, figured they had the Blue Jays' management at their mercy. How could they possibly not sign a local icon without turning their precious public against them? And so the ante was raised, the years in the contract were raised. Winfield, closing in on forty, without a defensive posi-tion, played it as though he were invaluable and in his prime. And the Blue Jays' brass didn't much like that.

Baseball's annual winter meetings, so eventful for Toronto the previous two years, would be held in Louisville. The first order of business for Gillick, even as Winfield postured, would be bringing Joe Carter back into the fold. This was Carter's one career opportu-nity to come up with the kind of contract that provides lifetime financial security. He was as reliable as any offensive player, driving in a hundred or more runs a year with good teams and bad. As well, there was at least one club that wanted him as much as or more than the Blue Jays did—the Kansas City Royals. Carter was from Kansas City and lived there in the off-season. In fact, he was so com-mitted to his family life that the people in the Blue Jays' organiza-tion rarely spoke to him, never mind seeing him, between the last day of the season and the first day of spring training. It figured that if the offers were equal, Carter would choose Kansas City, to be close to hearth and home. The offers weren't equal: the Jays offered $25 million over four years, but in accordance with club policy, only three years were guaranteed. The Royals offered the same money, but with all four years locked in.

In the end...well, Carter said it was God who made the decision, who suggested to his subconscious that Toronto was the place he ought to be. On December 7, he signed with the Blue Jays. From that moment on, there was a surprising amount of coming and going for a team that had just won a championship. The same day that Carter signed, Beeston and Gillick called Winfield's bluff, acquiring free agent Paul Molitor to be the team's full-time designated hitter. They hadn't really planned it that way. Returning from Kansas City, where they had met with Carter and his agent, Beeston and Gillick had to change planes in Chicago. They had tentatively scheduled a get-together with Molitor, who had become a free agent, and his agent, Ron Simon, but it was a terrible rainy night, and there was some question whether it was worth bothering with the drive from O'Hare airport. Molitor had spent his entire career with the Milwaukee Brewers and many viewed him as the heart and soul of that franchise. He might be playing the field now, but surely when push came to shove, Milwaukee owner Bud Selig would pay up, and Molitor would finish his career where it began.

The Toronto contingent decided in the end to go ahead despite their doubts, a decision that proved to be one of those fortuitous twists of fate. The meeting stretched into dinner, which in turn stretched over four hours, and at the end of it both Gillick and Beeston were convinced not just that Molitor was ready to leave Milwaukee, but that he could replace Winfield in more ways than just at the plate. Not only was he articulate and intelligent, he was ready to relocate his wife and daughter, full-time, to the city of whatever club that signed him. (No Blue Jay had made Toronto his permanent winter home since Rick Bosetti from 1978 to 1981). Whatever public relations fallout would come from Winfield's departure, Molitor surely would be able to handle it. He'd provide some different offensive options, more speed and the ability to bat at the top of the order. And he was motivated: Milwaukee, the stereotypical small-market franchise, had become a dead end. Only an incredible combination of luck and timing would allow the team to compete for a championship. Molitor didn't have the time to wait. He wanted very much to win and figured that in Toronto, he would be given that opportunity. And so Molitor became a Blue Jay, agreeing to a $13-million contract for three years with an option. No one was more surprised at the news than Dave Winfield and his agent.

A day later, the transformation of the team continued. The Blue

Jays traded Kelly Gruber, out of favour with everyone in the organization and due to earn $4 million in 1993, to the California Angels in return for Luis Sojo, the utility infielder who had already had one stint with the club. Gruber's departure created a hole at third base (only the converted catcher and World Series hero Ed Sprague seemed a possibility to step in), and Sojo hardly seemed like fair value, but the Blue Jays had become convinced that Gruber would never again be what he once was.

The pitching staff was bolstered with the addition of Danny Cox, still battling back from ligament replacement surgery (the so-called Tommy John operation) in 1989. With Henke's imminent departure and Ward taking on the closer's role, Cox was pencilled in as a set-up man or perhaps even as the fifth starter. There were also a couple of holes in the starting rotation: Cone seemed set to sign elsewhere, and the team had been unable to work out a deal with Key, who was still holding out for a guaranteed fourth year. The Jays decided to move in a different direction, signing free agent Dave Stewart to a two-year, $8.5-million contract. Stewart the team knew well, from the no-hitter he had pitched against them in 1990, and from his gutsy winning performances for Oakland in the 1989 and 1992 American League Championship Series. (The day Stewart signed, the Jays simultaneously withdrew their offer to Key, who received the news by fax while on a Caribbean cruise.) "He's a big game pitcher," Gaston said of Stewart. "Go back as recently as the playoffs against us this year. When they needed a win, he got it for them. When he gets the lead he won't give it up."

As new faces were arriving, familiar faces were departing. Cone went first, signing a three-year, $18-million contract with Kansas City, a contract remarkable for the fact that the first $9 million was paid up front as a signing bonus (Cone, a smart fellow and a union activist, anticipated, correctly, that there was a labour shutdown on the horizon and wanted his money in the bank when it happened). The Jays, Cone said, were never even in the running to sign him. He leaned towards Kansas City because it was his home town. Then Candy Maldonado signed a two-year, $3.5-million deal with the Chicago Cubs. Though he was a personal favourite of Gaston's, Maldonado became expendable because of an organizational decision to give Derek Bell a starting spot in the outfield.

On December 15, Tom Henke—who had received a token offer of a one-year deal from Toronto—instead opted for a two-year, $8-million contract with Texas, the team with which he'd started his major league career. There was talk that he might be finally starting to lose his overpowering fastball, relying more and more on the forkball and becoming less and less effective in the process. But Henke had convinced his new employers that that wasn't the case.

Finally, two days later, Winfield signed with the Minnesota Twins, returning to his home town. As a final gesture, he called his own farewell press conference in Toronto, just to bid adieu to his loyal fans and to turn up the heat on the Blue Jays' front office. The Toronto sports scene had never before—and likely would never again—experience anyone quite like him.

◆AND SO IT would be a very different Blue Jays team in 1993 from the one that had just won the franchise's first World Series. But Gillick and others in the front office had come to think that that wasn't such a bad thing. Ward and Bell both looked ready to step up, as did Todd Stottlemyre. Stewart had the same kind of character that had made Jack Morris such a valuable addition the year before. Jimmy Key would be the toughest of the free agents to replace. But, still, a starting rotation of Morris (who figured to bounce back from his post-season disappointment), Guzman, Stewart, Stottlemyre, with Cox or some promising kid in the fifth spot, would be competitive with anyone else in the division, especially given the strength of the bullpen. Molitor, a class act, had been stuck for years with a hopeless franchise. Surely he'd rise to the occasion. Heading into spring training, shortstop was a question mark, since Manny Lee was also a free agent, as was third base. Still, changing the mix a little bit, shaking up the personalities, would help the Blue Jays stay hungry, would help them maintain an edge.

Spring training was unusually placid, the tension of years past replaced by the quiet confidence of a team coming off its greatest triumph. For the first time since he'd taken the job, there were no serious questions about Gaston's continued tenure as manager. The only really distressing news was that Stewart had suffered a tear in his throwing elbow and would begin the season on the disabled list.

Gaston anointed Morris his Opening Day starter, continuing a long tradition for the pitcher and showing faith that he was indeed ready to return to form. The fifth spot in the rotation remained open for most of the month of March, though a young product of the Jays' system, Pat Hentgen, seemed to have the inside track. David Wells was ruled out as a candidate for the job from the beginning, and since he'd made it known he didn't like pitching out of the bullpen—and he had some very public run-ins with Gaston—it was fair to assume that his future with the franchise was in question.

There was one other developing story during the spring. Derek Bell, handed a starting outfield job on a World Series championship team, didn't seem to really want to claim it. He went about his business with an attitude that suggested overconfidence and immaturity. Gaston watched and waited and grew more and more frustrated at Bell's mental errors. The final straw may have been watching Bell doubled off second base on a routine pop-up to the third baseman during a Grapefruit League game. Though no one doubted Bell's talent and his physical ability to succeed in the major leagues, the team had run out of patience. On March 30, he was traded to the San Diego Padres for Darrin Jackson, who brought with him a reputation as a very good defensive outfielder with decent pop in his bat—in 1992, he'd hit seventeen home runs and driven in seventy runs. Still, Jackson was twenty-nine to Bell's twenty-four, and in making the deal, the Jays were giving up on one of the best outfield prospects they had ever developed. "I don't know if Bell played himself off the team," Gillick said. "But we don't feel he showed the dedication we'd like."

"I have no regrets," Bell said when informed of the deal. "Why would I have any regrets?"

The same day, the Blue Jays released David Wells. Both Ken Dayley and Al Leiter looked ready to finally make a contribution at the big league level (Dayley had been plagued by vertigo since being acquired as a free agent before the 1992 season, and Leiter had suffered through a host of maladies, most notably blister problems on his throwing hand, since being acquired from the Yankees in a 1989 trade for Jesse Barfield). As well, both Leiter and Hentgen were out of options, meaning that they couldn't be returned to the minor leagues without clearing waivers and where both would likely be lost to the team. But Wells's departure wasn't just the result of a numbers game. His non-conformist nature just didn't fit with the program. In the past, the Jays had tolerated talented "characters" like George Bell, Cliff Johnson and Dave Stieb, despite the problems they might cause in the clubhouse. But a championship had finally been won with what was by and large a group of happy campers. That seemed the best formula for a repeat.

FOR THE OWNERS of the Blue Jays, spring brought confirmation of what they already knew to be true. The magazine *Financial World,* in its annual evaluation of professional franchises, rated the Toronto baseball club as the third most valuable in all of professional sport, trailing only the Dallas Cowboys and New York Yankees, and tied with the Los Angeles Lakers with an estimated value of $155 million. It was an astounding figure given that the team had only cost $7 million seventeen years before, and given the fact that Toronto was not New York or Los Angeles and didn't have the America's Team veneer that had made the Cowboys so successful. Despite the World Series, the Jays still weren't really marketable south of the border. Their licensed goods, with a design that still had a distinctly 1970s aesthetic, weren't particularly fashionable. The franchise's value instead was based on the fact that the team had caught the fancy of a very large percentage of a relatively large market and had developed a strong following throughout English Canada. Because of that, it had a lucrative local television contract and sold more seats than anyone else in the game. Still, even the most optimistic forecasters back in 1976 couldn't have imagined that the Blue Jays would someday stand behind only the mighty Yankees as the most valuable franchise in all of professional baseball.

The Blue Jays opened the defence of their World Series title in Seattle, getting clobbered 8–1 by the Mariners and seeing a Jack Morris who looked very much like the guy who couldn't win during the playoffs. Bad starting pitching was the rule during the first two months of the season. This Blue Jay team could score plenty of runs, easily the most potent offensive machine in franchise history. But both Morris and Stewart, when the latter returned from injury, looked like they might well be at the end of the line, not unlikely since they were thirty-eight and thirty-six years old respectively. Juan Guzman began slowly, Todd Stottlemyre was the same old frustrating Todd Stottlemyre. Hentgen looked good in the fifth spot, but who knew how long that would last? Unknown pitchers their first time through the league sometimes experience success only until opposing batters learn their patterns and begin to exploit their weaknesses.

Despite the off-season shakeup, the team seemed to be suffering from a post-series hangover, playing just .500 ball through the first thirty-four games of the season. Gillick tinkered with the line-up, releasing Dayley (who never fully recovered from his balance problems), demoting first baseman Domingo Martinez, a promising hitter who would never displace John Olerud, and picking up a young outfielder named Willie Canate, who would be used largely as a defensive replacement. The biggest change, though, was forced upon him. The veteran Dick Schofield, who had won the starting shortstop's job in spring, broke his arm on May 13. As replacements, the Jays had only Alfredo Griffin and rookie Domingo Cedeno, both of whom would be just barely adequate, which wasn't good enough for a team hoping to win another championship.

On June 10, Gillick made what would be his most significant deal of the year, acquiring Tony Fernandez from the New York Mets in exchange for Darrin Jackson. Jackson had never really found his form in Toronto, hitting just .216. With Toronto's already potent offensive line-up, it would be easier to sacrifice some offensive potential in the outfield—giving the job to journeyman Darnell Coles or Canate—in order to shore up the infield defence, knowing that Fernandez could also contribute more at the plate than either Schofield or his replacements. It was also, of course, a homecoming of sorts. Since being dealt away from Toronto in the trade that brought Roberto Alomar and Joe Carter to town, Fernandez had embarked on a difficult, frustrating journey. That first spring with the San Diego Padres, he told reporters that God would avenge in rather direct fashion the way he had been treated in Toronto. (Fernandez's religious beliefs went beyond those of even the most fervent born-again Christians. He could often be found after games sitting almost inside his locker, with his face buried in the Bible. But his faith seemed to bring him very little comfort or joy.) He made the National League All-Star team, but eventually was caught up in the San Diego fire sale of big salaries and dealt away to the Mets. Fernandez wasn't a New York kind of guy. The aggressive, often hostile sports press in the city drove him to distraction. At the same time, age and injuries seemed to have robbed him of his brilliant natural gifts as a fielder. Coming back to Toronto, then, back to the organization that had scouted him, signed him, groomed him for the major leagues and employed him for more than a thousand major league games, was a second chance, one that Fernandez seemed to relish. The brooding, miserable loner who had left was replaced, at least temporarily, by someone who was genuinely glad to be there.

AS THE FIRST half of the 1993 season drew to a close, the Blue Jays led the American League East, though not comfortably, and more because the opposition seemed doomed to mediocrity than as a tribute to their own excellence. A 13–3 streak immediately after the Fernandez trade, which made it seem the Jays might run away with the division, was followed by a string in which the team lost ten of eleven games leading up to the All-Star break.

As the manager of the defending American League Champions, it was Cito Gaston's privilege to guide the American League team in the All-Star Game, which would be played at the beautiful new Camden Yards ball park in Baltimore. In true Gaston fashion, he used the opportunity not to make a point about race and baseball—he was the first black man to manage an All-Star team—but to make a point to his players that they already understood very well. In the Gaston world view, loyalty was all. Having played in the major leagues and having fresh memories of being treated badly, of being betrayed by those who had managed him, Gaston believed that the first rule of running a successful ball club was to back your players no matter what. When there was a choice to be made—your guy or somebody else—the choice was obvious. And so after Alomar, Carter and Olerud were voted to the team by the fans, Gaston exercised the All-Star manager's prerogative and brought Devon White, Duane Ward, Pat Hentgen and Paul Molitor along with him. Following the predictable criticism that arose from the decision, his players acquitted themselves well. Alomar became the first Blue Jay to homer in the All-Star Game, White drove in the go-ahead run, Carter went 1–3. But it was the finish of the game that enraged the home fans in Baltimore. With the American League leading 9–3 in the ninth, the Orioles' fine pitcher Mark Mussina still hadn't made an appearance. Gaston chose Ward to finish the game, which prompted Mussina to begin warming up on his own in the bullpen, showing up the manager and sending the fans into a frenzy. They never forgave Gaston in Baltimore, and in his heart of hearts, Gaston never forgave Mussina. "By standing up [to warm up], he showed me he's a person with little class," Gaston said at the time. "Screw him. I just won't take him next year."

Beginning the second half of the season, the Blue Jays' record was 49–40, the best in the American League despite the pre-All-Star swoon. "We've got too good a team to go the way we're going," said Morris, whose 5–10 record was certainly part of the problem. "I don't believe that this can continue. If it does, there's a whole lot of us who'll have reason to accept blame. We're too good to be doing what we're doing now." They would finish with a July record of 12–14, in what would be their only losing month of the season, with the starting pitchers going a woeful 4–12.

The blame would not fall on the hitters, in any case. The top of the Toronto order, dubbed WAMCO—White, Alomar, Molitor, Carter, Olerud—had become nearly a modern-day Murderer's Row, with not just power, but speed, bat control and the ability to score all kinds of runs in all kinds of different ways. Surprisingly, it was Olerud who led the charge. From the day he arrived in Toronto, fresh out of college, the talk had been that he possessed something close to the perfect swing, a clean, consistent stroke and a great hitter's eye. It was an article of faith within the organization that Olerud would take those skills and become a dominant major league hitter. His first three big league seasons didn't really support that faith—his pattern seemed to be an average in the mid to upper .200s, sixty or seventy runs batted in, fifteen, maybe twenty home runs someday, which was just barely adequate for someone playing first base, a position most teams reserve for a power hitter. Still he was young, and the front office, especially Gillick, who had put so much into Olerud's signing and who had developed a close relationship with his family, was willing to be patient.

Not even Olerud's greatest admirers could have predicted the events of 1993. With a new confidence, surrounded by other great hitters, fully adjusted to the major leagues, a year more mature: whatever the reason, John Olerud became the best hitter in baseball. Hitting .400 for an entire season, as had last been accomplished by Ted Williams in 1941, had become the sport's impossible dream, as unapproachable as Joe DiMaggio's fifty-six-game hitting streak, less likely than hitting sixty-one home runs. Perhaps it was better pitching, more fresh arms, that made it next to impossible. But part of the challenge, as well, would be the constant, intense media pressure that would follow any hitter who seriously gave chase to the mark. In that respect, the 1990s were far different from the 1940s, when Williams was at his peak. Every stop along the way, every road trip, every new city, there would be a horde waiting with notepads and tape recorders and cameras, asking the same questions about dealing with the pressure. George Brett, the last man to seriously make a run at .400, had faced the barrage and handled it reasonably well. But Brett wasn't a painfully shy, introverted kid who had never really known the spotlight's glare before.

It's hard to remember exactly when the Olerud talk got serious: June probably, before the All-Star break, and certainly through July, the month he might have been expected to fold, but didn't. On August 1, his average stood at precisely .400, and there still seemed the possibility that he would make it. But at least one member of the Blue Jay organization believes that the burden of expectations finally affected Olerud, that while he remained as externally calm and unemotional as ever, in the end he just couldn't handle the attention. "John might not ever admit this," Cito Gaston says. "Knowing John, I think that John could have hit .400. I just think that John was hounded so much by the media that he backed off. Because he's not that kind of person. And I'm not sure that that hasn't ruined him to this day."

◆ TWENTY TIMES, THE Blue Jays would fall into a tie for the division lead, but they would never relinquish it. The pitching problems continued all season, most notably the decline of Morris. Every starter with the exception of Juan Guzman and Pat Hentgen spent time on the disabled list. Still, with Hentgen's breakout season, which showed no signs of turning sour, and with Dave Stewart slowly rounding into form, Toronto, with its magnificent bullpen, seemed to have enough pitching to win at least the division. That wasn't the organizational goal, though—this was another year to pull out the stops in an attempt to win a second World Series. And since money was no obstacle, there was the opportunity for Gillick to make one more late-season move. For a time, it looked as if the Jays might land Seattle left-hander Randy Johnson, one of the hardest throwers in baseball and, with Toronto's erratic starting pitching, just the ticket to nail down another championship.

But instead, Gillick went in another direction, making a move that seemed almost excessive, given the Jays' offensive output. On July 31, the team traded pitching prospect Steve Karsay, the highest-rated starter in Toronto's minor league system, to the Oakland Athletics in exchange for Rickey Henderson. He had been the Jays' chief antagonist in the 1989 ALCS and had had his moments in the 1992 series—at least before kicking off the deciding game by dropping a routine flyball. Though he might not have been quite the freewheeling base stealer of the past, he would provide Toronto with an everyday left fielder and the first pure lead-off man in franchise history, someone with a high on-base percentage who could make things happen once he reached first.

As to Henderson's real impact on the 1993 team, there remains considerable debate. His numbers for the final month of the regular season were just about the same as Darrin Jackson's, who had been labelled a complete flop during his tenure with the team. Defensively, Henderson was just average. And aside from his long-time friendship with Dave Stewart, there was little sense that he was a noticeable factor in the clubhouse. Still, there are those who will crunch Henderson's numbers and prove that he was a far better lead-off man than Devon White, that his batting average alone didn't tell the tale. Beeston, Gillick and Gaston say much the same thing about Henderson's tenure: maybe they could have won a World Series without him, but we'll never know.

On September 9, the Yankees moved into a first-place tie with the

Blue Jays. But from that point on, Toronto was untouchable, winning sixteen of the next eighteen games to capture the division. Along the way, after Morris was pulled from his start against Detroit on September 15, it was confirmed that the pitcher had suffered a partial tear of the medial collateral ligament in his right elbow, that his season was over, and that the Blue Jays would in all likelihood not pick up his option for 1994, instead buying out the final year of his contract for a flat $1 million.

Unlike Henderson's, Morris's contribution to the championship years was obvious beyond discussion. In 1992, he had not only won twenty-one games, but had been the only starting pitcher to hold the line in August, when the team might otherwise have collapsed. By the time the post-season rolled around, he simply had nothing left, and the winter off wasn't enough to heal an arm that had apparently just used up its lifetime allotment of pitches. Morris also brought to the team a genuine tenacity, an unwillingness to give in. In other years, the club's personality had lent itself to those late-season collapses. But with Morris in the clubhouse, that wasn't going to happen.

The Blue Jays clinched the division crown relatively early, on September 27, a cold, rainy night at Milwaukee's County Stadium, with hardly anyone in the stands. A double play in the bottom of the ninth sealed a 2–0 victory and set off a rather muted celebration, although for one member of the team, it was particularly sweet. Winning pennants of any kind wasn't old hat for Paul Molitor. Doing it in the city where he had spent all the seasons of his major league career made it that much more special. "I think the guys played so hard that year for Molitor," Gaston says. "I think everybody wanted to see him win it."

There would be one final bit of regular-season dramatics. Playing the Baltimore Orioles in the final game of the season, the Blue Jays had the opportunity to do something that hadn't happened in a hundred years: produce the top three hitters in the league. Olerud, though he'd fallen off in the chase for .400, would easily win the American League batting title, hitting .363. Molitor was firmly ensconced in second at .332. That left Roberto Alomar in a neck-and-neck battle with Cleveland's Kenny Lofton for third spot.

During the game, John Brioux, the Jays' travelling secretary, monitored the Cleveland game and phoned down to the dugout reporting on Lofton's at-bats. Each time Lofton got a hit, Alomar responded with a hit. After reaching base in his first two appearances, Gaston removed him from the game, leaving his average at .326 to Lofton's .325.

A SIGNIFICANT BODY of baseball opinion suggested that the Blue Jays would match up badly against the Chicago White Sox, their opponents in the American League Championship Series. Certainly, the Sox seemed to have the advantage in starting pitching, with staff ace Jack McDowell, winner of the American League Cy Young Award, hard-throwing Alex Fernandez, rising young star Jason Bere, and the finesse left-hander Wilson Alvarez, the kind of pitcher who had typically given the Blue Jays fits. Chicago could also score runs, thanks in large part to the bat of Frank Thomas, the big, intimidating first baseman who had established himself as one of the game's premier power hitters.

But despite all of the on-paper questions—Toronto hitting versus Chicago pitching, and so on—the series in many ways would come down to a couple of intangibles, baseball truths that were all but impossible to uncover from reading box scores.

Dave Stewart, whatever his regular season record, was unbeatable in Championship Series play.

Jack McDowell, whatever his regular season record, could not beat the Blue Jays in a game that counted.

In Game One, played at Chicago's New Comiskey Park, Juan Guzman had a jittery outing for Toronto, walking eight White Sox in six innings, throwing an ALCS record three wild pitches and hitting one batter. But timely outs, or a lack of timely Chicago hitting, resulted in eleven stranded base runners, and by the time he left after six innings, Guzman and the Jays had a 5–3 lead. That immediately became 7–3, with all seven runs charged to McDowell, who surrendered thirteen hits in fewer than seven innings of work. There were some scary moments in the bottom of the ninth, when Duane Ward walked the first two Chicago hitters. Then he settled matters, dramatically, by striking out the side.

In Game Two, it was time for the Stewart end of the playoff equation. After a bout of wildness, including three walks in the first inning, he cruised through the first five, allowing just two hits. Then in the bottom of the sixth came what might well have been the defining moment of the series. Frank Thomas led off with a single. Robin Ventura followed with a single, sending Thomas to second. Ellis Burks walked to load the bases. "The go-ahead run is on first," Gaston recalls. "And I'm thinking, 'Man, Dave, I've seen you do this before and get out of it. Can you pull it off one more time?'" The next hitter, Dan Pasqua, in the line-up at first because Thomas had been relegated to designated hitter because of a sore elbow on his throwing arm, popped up to shallow centre. No runs scored. Lance Johnson worked to a 1–2 count and then popped up. No runs scored. Pinch-hitter Warren Newson took Stewart to a 3–0 count, then grounded back to the mound, where Stewart snared the ball, trotted to first for the final out, then jumped in the air to celebrate. Toronto won the game 3–1 to lead the series 2–0. In the history of League Championship Series play, no team had ever lost the first two games at home and then come back to win the pennant.

Game Three returned the series to SkyDome, where fan confidence was understandably running very high, and a sweep seemed a real possibility. But Hentgen, a nineteen-game winner during the regular season (a total second in team history only to Morris's twenty-one the year before), was hit hard by the Sox, giving up six runs in fewer than four innings. Meanwhile, Alvarez went the distance for Chicago, giving up just one run on seven hits and claiming a 6–1 victory. Along the way, he became the first pitcher in seventeen post-season games to hold Pat Borders without a hit, leaving the Jays' catcher and 1992 World Series MVP just one hit shy of Hank Bauer's major league record.

Still facing the prospect of losing a short series, the White Sox showed real fortitude in Game Four. They pulled out to an early 2–0 lead, when centre fielder Lance Johnson—who hadn't hit a home run in 699 at-bats—lit up Toronto starter Todd Stottlemyre. The Jays came back to lead 3–2, chasing Chicago starter Jason Bere. Then came the nightmare sixth inning, which left Toronto fans to wonder once again about their manager's acumen. Stottlemyre had pitched well until giving up a game-tying home run to Frank Thomas to lead off the inning. With two out, he walked Ellis Burks and Bo Jackson, and everyone in the building felt it was time to get him out of there. Everyone but Gaston, who didn't even have a pitcher warming in the bullpen, having decided that Stottlemyre could work himself out of the two-out jam. He was wrong. The light-hitting Johnson just missed a second homer, instead tripling off the centre field wall, and two runs scored. The game finished at 7–4 for the White Sox. Chicago had won two in a row at SkyDome, evening the series at two, reclaiming the home field advantage. The momentum, surely, had shifted their way. And their staff ace was scheduled to take the mound for Game Five.

That would be their staff ace, Jack McDowell, forever helpless when facing the Jays. This time, he lasted just two-and-a-third innings before Chicago manager Gene Lamont lost his patience and gave him the hook. For Toronto, Juan Guzman pitched brilliantly, allowing just one hit—an Ellis Burks home run—in seven innings, striking out six. Coming into the game with a 5–1 lead, Ward closed, but not without incident. Tim Raines led off with a single, Joey Cora and Thomas struck out, and then Robin Ventura hit a two-run homer to make it 5–3. Ward hit the next batter, Ellis Burks, bringing the tying run to the plate in the form of Bo Jackson, the multi-sport superstar who had made a dramatic comeback to baseball after undergoing hip replacement surgery. Jackson had been having an awful series at the plate—0–9 with five strikeouts to that point. With a 1–1 count, Ward served him a fastball, right down the middle of the plate, which he just missed, fouling the ball. He swung through the next pitch, striking out to end the game.

Which brought things back to Stewart, who once again did all that was asked of him. He had spent the day before, an off-day that fell on Thanksgiving Monday, serving turkey dinner to the home-less at a Toronto shelter, an act for which he shunned publicity. That was typical of Stewart, whose intensity on the mound played in sharp contrast to his gentle off-field demeanour, his soft, high-pitched voice, his intelligence and his social conscience. The next day, the fierce competitor with the famous "death stare" returned. In seven-and-a-third innings, he allowed just four Chicago hits, then handed things off to Ward in the eighth with a 3–2 lead—one of those rare moments when Gaston broke his own rule about saving his closer for a single inning's work when his team had the lead. Ward struck out the final two batters in the eighth, then watched as Devon White homered for one run, and Paul Molitor tripled in two more, ending the suspense. Ward did allow a solo home run by Warren Newson in the bottom of the ninth, but the celebration on the South Side that night took place in the visitors' clubhouse: a second straight American League Championship, a second straight trip to The Show. Though there might have been some debate— Paul Molitor's .391 average and five runs batted in would have been enough most years—really, no one but Stewart could have claimed the award as the series' most valuable player.

PROFESSIONAL SPORT WORKS best with a storyline, with some kind of subtext to give meaning to what are, after all, simple exercises in play. And if there isn't one, a legitimate one, somebody will surely invent it. That's why there are sports writers, that's why there are television pre-game shows and there is endless between-play blather. Somebody's got to explain to the poor, simple consumer exactly what's going on.

In that sense, it was fortuitous that the Philadelphia Phillies, and not the Atlanta Braves, would serve as the Blue Jays' World Series foils. No one had expected it to happen. The Braves, having added Greg Maddux to their already formidable pitching rotation, were odds-on favourites to win the National League and, if they had won the pennant, would have been the bettors' choice to conquer the defending champions. The Phillies, a rag-tag group by contrast, had an agreeably scruffy veneer, thanks to the portly, unkempt, outspoken first baseman John Kruk, and to centre fielder Lenny Dykstra—nicknamed Nails—the undisputed leader of the team, famous in sporting circles for a record use of the word "fuck" in his as-told-to autobiography.

Real baseball, though, is not rotisserie league, and sometimes strange things happen. Strange things like the Phillies beating the Braves, like the curse of Bobby Cox and Jimy Williams and Ted Turner and Jane Fonda still holding strong. Once upon a time, the Blue Jays had been regarded as the epitome of big-game choke artists. Now that title belonged to the team from Georgia, who would be left to watch the second cross-border World Series on television.

The Blue Jays provided a nice contrast to the Phillies' cartoon cast. Their reputation, especially outside of Canada, was as a bland, business-like bunch, a rich organization with fat-cat owners and a state-of-the-art stadium that did everything by the book. No question who the sentimental favourites in the series would be, what with a bunch of guys who looked as if they could play for a slo-pitch team taking on a side with such a corporate veneer. The workers versus the bosses. The lunch buckets versus the briefcases. Except, in this case, even the exploited labourers make millions of dollars.

The series opener at SkyDome began with the usual fanfare and was in some ways a microcosm of the entire Blue Jay season. Guzman started and, as in the first game of the ALCS, had difficulty with his control. The Philadelphia hitters were known for their patience at the plate and worked Guzman for six walks to go with five hits in five innings. Three times the Phillies pulled ahead, three times the Blue Jays' offence roared back, battering Philadelphia starter Curt Schilling for sevens runs (six earned) in fewer than six innings. It was a sloppy game in which the Blue Jays made three errors, but in which, ironically, a defensive play would be the greatest highlight. Lenny Dykstra hit into right field a soft blooper that seemed certain to drop for a single. But then Roberto Alomar leapt, extended his body parallel to the artificial turf, and snagged the ball before it fell to earth. Even for the Toronto fans, who had become used to Alomar making seemingly impossible plays, it was something special. But in the end, it would be the overpowering Toronto offence that was the difference in the game. This time, Devon White was the hitting star, with a home run, three runs scored and two driven in. Al Leiter pitched two-and-two-thirds innings of sparkling relief to get the win and Duane Ward picked up the save as the Blue Jays won 8–5.

The return of Dave Stewart for Game Two inspired plenty of confidence among the faithful, but they were about to learn a painful lesson: the infallibility thing applied only to league championship series. Against the Phillies, Stewart pitched himself into trouble, as he had against Chicago in the second game of the ALCS. But this time, there would be no Houdini miracles. In the third inning, he walked Dykstra and Mariano Duncan, wild-pitched them to second and third, then gave up consecutive base hits to Kruk and Dave Hollins. An out later, Jim Eisenreich homered on an 0–2 pitch and it was 5–0 Philadelphia. The Jays pulled back to 5–3 on a Carter home run and an RBI double by Tony Fernandez. But reliever Tony Castillo gave up a home run to Dykstra in the seventh to make it 6–3 Phillies. Everything seemed in place for a routine finish when Philadelphia manager Jim Fregosi summoned closer Mitch Williams in the eighth. The former Chicago Cub, dubbed the Wild Thing because of his chronic control problems, had enjoyed a career year with the Phillies and was one of the major reasons they had won their division. But he did tend to make things interesting, because he had great difficulty holding base runners and because every once in a while, he just couldn't throw strikes. The Jays scored one on Williams in the eighth when Molitor doubled, stole third, and then scored on Olerud's sacrifice fly to make it 6–4. Alomar followed with a walk and then, taking advantage of Williams's weak move to first, stole second. But it turned out that the Phillies, in scouting Toronto, had picked up on one of Alomar's tendencies: after stealing second, he often attempted to steal third on the very next pitch. Alomar broke before Williams began his delivery and was easily thrown out at third to end the inning. Williams survived the bottom of the ninth, and the World Series was tied at one, heading for Veterans Stadium in Philadelphia.

By that point, a pattern had been established. This Series would be dominated not by starting pitchers, not by fine defence, but by offence, which both sides possessed in abundance. That factored into Gaston's thinking as the games moved to a National League park, where he would no longer have the luxury of employing a designated hitter. A year before, he had moved Joe Carter to first base, putting John Olerud on the bench, so that Dave Winfield's bat could remain in the line-up. This time the decision was a bit more complicated. The Jays' designated hitter, Paul Molitor, had once been a very good defensive player, though shoulder problems had seriously hampered his ability to throw. And Olerud was now the best hitter in the American League. Still, with left-hander Danny Jackson due up for the Phillies, Gaston chose to replace Olerud with Molitor at first base. Among Gaston-bashers, when one of his against-the-grain decisions doesn't work, it's because he's not smart enough, and when it does work, it's because he's lucky. He was lucky or prescient that night in Philadelphia: Molitor came within a double of hitting for the cycle, drove in three runs and scored three more, then began a key, inning-ending double play in the seventh, as the Jays won 10–3. Hentgen made up for his disastrous appearance against the White Sox by giving up five hits and a single run through six innings, with Danny Cox and Ward mopping up.

Now there was another decision for the manager to make.

PHILADELPHIA'S GAME FOUR starter would be Tommy Greene, a rightie, which meant that Olerud would surely have to return to the line-up. So what to do with Molitor? Earlier in his career, before his shoulder had become a problem, Molitor had played third base—the last time he'd actually fielded the position was during the 1991 All-Star Game. When Toronto earned a berth in the World Series, he was asked whether he'd be comfortable playing third for a game or two, if the situation arose. Molitor said he thought his shoulder could handle it (playing in the first and quite possibly last World Series of his career, Molitor would hardly have been expected to say anything different, though there was the question of whether he might hurt his team in the process) and relayed the same message to his manager. "I think [Gaston's] concerns about injury are maybe over-dramatized," Molitor said. He explained that he'd offered to play third during the meaningless games of the final weekend of the season, anticipating just such a situation, but Gaston had decided against it.

Even after Game Three, after Molitor had knocked in three runs, Gaston wouldn't give. "I think I'll stick by what I said earlier." Olerud would be back. Ed Sprague—at that point in his career a below-average fielder who was having a mediocre series at the plate—would remain at third, and Molitor would be available as a pinch-hitter. Though he said his mind was made up, Gaston did allow as how he'd think about it.

And so, of course, the next night, that impetuous, unpredictable Cito had Molitor pencilled in on his scorecard at third. Still, the events that followed made what appeared at the time to be a momentous decision seem rather insignificant. It wasn't just that Molitor enjoyed a relatively uneventful evening at the hot corner, but that Game Four turned out to be as bizarre and incident-laden as any in World Series history. To call it a classic would be misleading: this was four hours and fourteen minutes of sloppy, bad baseball, the longest game ever in the Fall Classic. The Phillies' fans, suffering through it all on a cold, wet night at Veterans Stadium, must have felt as though it went on even longer than that.

It began auspiciously for the visiting side, with Toronto scoring three runs in the top of the first off Tommy Greene. But with Todd Stottlemyre pitching for the Blue Jays, their supporters knew there were no sure things. He might be unhittable. He might be absolutely awful. He might be both during the course of an inning.

Before the game, Philadelphia mayor Ed Rendell had joked that even he could have hit the fastball that Frank Thomas had sent sailing out of SkyDome against Stottlemyre in the fourth game of the American League Championship Series. In his typically hot-headed fashion, Stottlemyre tried to get even for the remark on the day of the Jays' victory parade at SkyDome, telling the assembly, as well as a national television audience, that Rendell could kiss his butt.

That he waited until then to offer his witty rejoinder is a measure of just how badly Stottlemyre pitched during his lone World Series appearance. In the bottom of the first, the Phillies scored four runs to take the lead on just one hit, helped along by four walks, three of them consecutive. In the top of the second, Stottlemyre drew a walk of his own off Greene, only to be thrown out in humiliating fashion, trying to advance from first to third on a single. He knocked himself woozy with a head-first slide and opened an ugly gash on his chin. Stottlemyre did manage to pull himself together to pitch the bottom of the second, giving up two more runs on Lenny Dykstra's first of two homers before calling it an early evening.

There was more, much more to come. The Jays scored four in the third, chasing Greene, to take a 7–6 lead. But Al Leiter, summoned from the bullpen, couldn't come close to holding the advantage. The Phillies tied it in the fourth and then scored five in the fifth (Dykstra and Daulton homering), apparently putting the game away. It was during that inning that Gaston walked to the mound to take Leiter out, only to see the wrong pitcher trotting in from the bullpen. The dugout phones were malfunctioning, leaving the manager to manually signal which pitchers he wanted warming up. Gaston thought he was calling for the left-hander Tony Castillo. Instead, he got right-hander Mark Eichhorn—Castillo wasn't even throwing. After consultation with the umpires, Castillo was allowed to go into the game and warm up on the mound, Eichhorn was allowed to return to the pen, and walkie-talkies were located, so that proper communication might be resumed.

Obviously, Gaston wasn't seriously anticipating a comeback. In the top of the seventh, Toronto trailing 13–9, with the pitcher due to lead off, he sent Castillo to the plate rather than use up another arm in the bullpen. (Castillo struck out.) The Jays did nothing, while the Phillies scored another run in the bottom of the inning to make it a five-run lead with six outs to go. The series seemed certain to be tied 2–2.

In any game, or series of games, you can arbitrarily assign turning points, moments when it was all won or lost. And always, it's really more complicated than that. Undoubtedly what won the World Series was Joe Carter's career highlight in Game Six. But the top of the eighth inning in Game Four stands out the way beating Dennis Eckersley in the fourth game of the 1992 ALCS did as a sign of what was to come. Even in a long, strange game, when they could have comfortably surrendered, knowing they'd play again tomorrow, the Blue Jays fought back to win—aided and abetted, of course, by the man whose life and career would be altered irreparably by these few fall games, Mitch Williams.

Actually, it was reliever Larry Andersen who started the inning, departing with one run across thanks to Dave Hollins's error, leaving runners on second and third with one out. "Something is going to happen when Mitch is out there," Roberto Alomar says. "When he came in, we said we've got a chance, something is going to happen." What happened: a run-scoring single by Tony Fernandez (his fifth RBI of the game); a walk to Pat Borders; a strikeout of pinch-hitter Ed Sprague for the second out; a two-run single by Rickey Henderson; a two-run triple by Devon White. Six runs across. Fifteen–fourteen Toronto. Mike Timlin and Duane Ward finished without incident, and a close, tense series was suddenly on the brink of completion.

There would be one more echo of that 1992 ALCS. Just as Dave Stewart had bounced back to beat the Jays when Oakland seemed dead and buried, Curt Schilling came out for Game Five with a discredited, exhausted bullpen behind him and Juan Guzman throwing for the other side—and pitched a masterpiece. "I don't think we had any choice but for him to pitch nine," Kruk said. "I think our bullpen was pretty much depleted after last night. And if they weren't depleted, they were shellshocked." The Phillies scored their only runs in the first two innings. Dykstra walked to lead off the game, stole second, moved to third on an error, and scored on a ground-out. In the second inning, Darren Daulton led off with a double, then seemed destined to be stranded, as Kevin Stocker came to bat with two outs, with a base open and the pitcher due to hit behind him. But no intentional walk followed. "Normally in the National League, you really like to have the pitcher leading off the next inning," Gaston said afterwards, explaining his strategy. "The starter should be able to get the eighth hitter out in the early innings." The eighth hitter doubled Daulton home.

There was really only one Toronto rally of consequence. With runners on first and third and nobody out in the eighth (and no sign of the Wild Thing warming up in the bullpen), Henderson grounded back to the pitcher. Willie Canate, pinch-running at third for Pat Borders, wandered off the bag and was thrown out in a rundown, a cardinal base-running sin. That killed any real hint of a Blue Jay comeback. Schilling wrapped up a five-hit shutout—just the second time Toronto had failed to score in a game during the 1993 season—and somewhat unexpectedly, the travelling roadshow headed back to Toronto.

◆ OCTOBER 23, 1993. Even better than the first time. Better because it's at home. Better because you could be there, or you had been there, you knew the place even if you had never known that sound. Better, of course, because of how it ended, how it felt that night, the tension, the apprehension, the fear—the old fear, the Blow Jays fear, tougher to shake than anyone would have expected, softened by the confidence of having won it before. Dave Stewart would be the right guy to throw the clincher. And there was nothing overly intimidating about the Phillies' starter Terry Mulholland. It's the first inning, Devo walks, Molitor triples him in, Carter sacrifices Molitor home, Olerud doubles, Alomar singles for another run: WAMCO, the unstoppable, and the party begins.

The Phillies scratch back for one in the fourth, but in the bottom of the inning, the Jays get another. Alomar doubles, advances to third on a ground-out, then comes home on Sprague's sacrifice fly. One more in the fifth when Molitor homers. It's 5–1. The game's more than half finished. Stewart is cruising. The bullpen is rested and ready. The 1992 ALCS clincher all over again. Map out the parade route and man the barricades on Yonge Street!

Except that any really good story requires the conquering of adversity for the sake of dramatic tension. In the seventh, the Phillies chase Stewart, beat up on Danny Cox, take a whack at Al Leiter. Five runs on five hits and the visitors suddenly have the lead. History is not kind to teams that lead seven-game series 3–2, then lose Game Six. You can look it up.

Nothing more through eight-and-a-half. The Phillies prepare to close it out. Which means—well, every single soul in SkyDome knows what it means, every person watching at home across the country knows that Philadelphia manager Jim Fregosi has no real choice. You dance with the one that brung you, even when that date happens to be Mitch Williams, who has turned into a parody of himself during the series: the great, big, hard-throwing country boy who is a marvel when he gets it across the plate, only that isn't nearly often enough. They'd gambled on Williams after the Cubs gave up on him, they'd lived through all those anxious moments when he pitched the team to the brink of disaster, then came through just before falling. But that Mitch was different than this Mitch: a few miles an hour off the fastball because of a long season's wear and tear; only one pitch left that he could consistently throw for strikes, the hard-breaking slider. There was a sense now every time he walked to the mound that neither the manager nor the catcher nor the guy on the mound really knew for sure where the ball was going. Time, if you love the Phillies, to say a silent prayer to the deity of your choice.

Henderson leads off. Sure, you can make the statistical case, sure, you can argue that he was an essential part of a championship even if watching the game on the field didn't really bear that out. The bottom line is that Henderson was mostly ordinary during his Blue Jay tenure—Gillick even went so far as to admit the deal was a mistake—but in this one at-bat, perhaps he made up for everything. Thinking walk from the start. Stepping out and staring at Williams, to intimidate. Standing in an even more extreme crouch than usual, reducing his strike zone to nothing. Daring Williams to throw a strike through the eye of a needle, knowing he couldn't do it. Drawing the walk. The next hitter, Devon White, flies out, a fundamental mistake, since he doesn't advance the runner into scoring position in a one-run game. Molitor follows with a single, sending Henderson just as far as second.

Due up: Joe Carter. And on deck—not John Olerud, who'd been lifted for a pinch-runner earlier in the game, but Alfredo Griffin. It was conceivable, then, that Williams could walk Carter and still save the game. He could face Griffin, or more likely a pinch-hitter like Darnell Coles, get a double-play ground ball and be hailed as a hero. You couldn't walk Carter intentionally—having the go-ahead run at third with someone as wild as Williams on the mound would be courting disaster. But if someone was going to beat you, it probably shouldn't be the guy who knocks in a hundred runs or more each and every season.

"This is what baseball is about," Carter said afterwards. "I dreamt about this in the backyard as a kid."

The first pitch: a ball. The crowd—given its size, the confines and the situation, certainly the loudest in the history of Toronto—turns it up a notch, trying to scare Williams into a walk. The second pitch: ball two. Louder still. No matter what Williams offers here, hard to think that Carter will be swinging. The third pitch: a called strike. Now Carter again goes into hitting mode. Looking for a slider, since the fastballs aren't coming over the plate. Looking for something down low, where he likes it, something that he can pull. Looking a little too hard, it turns out. Williams throws one in the dirt, and Carter swings over it. Count even, but the advantage now goes to the pitcher. Carter can't afford to let anything borderline by. Williams gets the sign for the slider. The ball is near knee high, and breaks inside, right into Carter's power zone. "I was trying to pitch him away," Williams said later. "I made a mistake and he hit a mistake. You try to pitch to a hitter's weakness." Carter swings a power-hitter's swing, not trying to dink the ball over the infield for the single that would tie the game. Trying to hit it out.

He may have been the last one to know. It felt good off the bat, but was it far enough, was it high enough? Running down the first base line, Carter loses the ball in the lights. But the sound tells him—a sound heard only once before, thirty-three years ago, when Bill Mazeroski's home run won a World Series for the Pittsburgh Pirates.

In Toronto, it is 11:39 P.M.

Joe Carter, forever the man who hit it.

Mitch Williams, forever the man who gave it up. "I'm not going to commit suicide," he said. Neither would he pitch again for the Philadelphia Phillies. Death threats from the good fans of the City of Brotherly Love would follow him home to Texas. His major league career was effectively over.

The series' most valuable player, though, wouldn't be the one immortalized in every highlight. Paul Molitor had hit .500, scored a record seventeen post-season runs—ten in the World Series alone—had twelve hits, two home runs and eight RBIs. Of all the celebrants who sprayed champagne in the clubhouse and then returned to the field to accept the World Series trophy and salute their fans, no one enjoyed it more.

DESPITE FINISHING THE season with the largest payroll in the American League, $51,575,034, the first team ever to top $50 million, the Blue Jays broke even in 1993—thanks to playoff revenues, and not taking into account, of course, the monies earned by other Labatt offshoots like TSN and TV Labatt, which profited because of the enormous interest in the team.

But as Paul Beeston always liked to say, success was measured in games won, and not by the bottom line (at least that was a line he could still use in the salad days of 1993). A few weeks after the victory, the Jays' organization that had built that winner received an enormous compliment. For the first time in the history of its Sportsman of the Year award, the *Sporting News* split it between two worthies: Pat Gillick and Cito Gaston. It was an acknowledgement of Canada's team by the traditional bible of America's national pas-time—and an irony surely lost on the magazine's editors, given the fact that Gaston and Gillick were hardly joined at the hip.

Heading into 1994, there would be some minor cost-cutting. The nucleus of the team—White, Alomar, Molitor, Carter and Olerud—as well as Guzman, Hentgen, Ward, Stewart and the other stalwarts of the pitching staff, were already under contract. This time, rather than the kind of wholesale change that had followed the first championship, what followed would seem more like tinkering. The Jays declined to offer arbitration to Rickey Henderson, dumping his contract, and assumed that in any new deal, he'd want more money and more years than they were willing to offer. Gone, too, was Tony Fernandez, relieving the club of his $2.1-million salary. Again, the thinking was that though Fernandez wanted to return to Toronto, the one place where he seemed comfortable, and though he'd been a vital cog on a championship team, the Jays weren't willing to pay that kind of money or commit to more than a one- or two-year deal. They had a young shortstop named Alex Gonzalez, a minor league sensation, apparently just a year or two away from the majors. And so Toronto opted for a less costly fill-in—veteran Dick Schofield—who was re-signed to play the position until Gonzalez was ready. Of course, Jack Morris wouldn't be back either. His place in the rotation was tentatively awarded to Al Leiter, who in 1993 seemed to finally be overcoming the various physical problems that had made him a bust since his arrival in Toronto.

Merely fine adjustments for the best team in baseball. The 1994 Blue Jays, in theory, could be even greater. Guzman was still getting better. And Hentgen had just begun to come of age. And there was all that offence, plus the best closer in the game.

"We're going to keep winning," Gillick said. "I'm more excited about going for a third [championship] than I was going for a second."

Chapter 19

N o ONE COULD have imagined then what lay ahead. As Tom Cheek was hollering "Touch 'em all, Joe," as SkyDome was erupting, as an entire country leapt from its seat to cheer one of the great, defining moments in the history of Canadian sport, it was hard to understand that nothing could be taken for granted from that second on.

Duane Ward, the untouchable closer, had thrown his last effective pitch as a Toronto Blue Jay. Two years later, he was struggling to even stay in the game with another organization. Juan Guzman, the best young starting pitcher in the American League, would lose something—a mental something, not a physical something—and find his career in jeopardy as well. The next World Series would take place not in 1994, but in 1995, following a terrible, destructive strike that wiped out the end of the 1994 season and forever altered fans' attitudes towards their athlete-heroes. Pat Gillick, the Blue Jays' master builder, architect of the two championship teams, would take his (as it turned out, temporary) leave of baseball a few months later, an event Paul Beeston and the others in the organization had anticipated, but at the same time never really believed would happen. And perhaps most importantly, the one unquestionable key to the success of professional baseball in Toronto—the ownership of the franchise by John Labatt Ltd.—would draw to a close, as that historic Canadian company faced takeover and division.

Those forces, beyond their control, set the Blue Jays on a path they thought they'd never take—from first to worst: the shifting baseball business; the shifting business environment faced by their corporate masters; an injury to the worst possible player at the worst possible time.

Trace the baseball strike of 1994–95 to whichever point in history you choose, to the previous labour dispute or the one before that, to Andy Messersmith or Curt Flood, to the Black Sox scandal or the anti-trust exemption. To paint it as inevitable, to say that something had to give, though, is wrong. Something had to give only because the people who run baseball decided that something had to give, that it was worth the risk of alienating the fans and losing a World Series to win a Pyrrhic victory. They decided that history could be rewritten, that the genie could be stuffed back into the bottle if this time they played tough and stayed tough. On every other occasion when baseball management and players had come to blows, it was the players and their union who had reigned victorious. In the face of lost revenue, in the face of union leader Marvin Miller and his successor, Donald Fehr, the owners would wave the white flag, open the doors and continue to run largely profitable businesses in a limited free-market environment. It wasn't so bad operating a legal monopoly that could also claim to be America's pastime.

Still, there had always been a hawkish element within baseball that sought something more—a way to push down players' salaries, skyrocketing out of sight because other owners, richer owners or larger market owners, decided they could afford to pay those salaries and still make a buck. In denial of the fact that the players weren't just their labourers—they *were* the product—the hawks hoped to break the players' union the way the National Football League had all but destroyed the National Football League Players' Association. That football players, aside from the stars, are relatively anonymous on the field, that the strategy employed by the NFL—using replacement players—carried with it enormous risks, didn't seem to matter. The issue was control, control of the game, and especially control of the money in the game. That was what the hard core wanted back.

In the past, though, they had been a distinct minority. Moderates held sway, and the calming influence of a commissioner, with the power to act "in the best interests of baseball," had prevented the game from operating purely on the basis of owner greed. The death of Bart Giamatti, the ousting of Fay Vincent, the ascendance of hardliners—especially Chicago White Sox owner Jerry Reinsdorf—and the increasing revenue gap between have and have-not teams changed all that. Baseball was rapidly marching towards a war of its own creation, one that neither side could win. Those who favoured the status quo—the players, and the more successful, large-revenue franchises like the Blue Jays and the Atlanta Braves—would be drawn into the conflict whether they liked it or not. In the not too

distant past, Paul Beeston had been talked about as a possible commissioner, someone from the management side who was trusted by
the players, who ran a successful franchise, and who seemed to have
a vision of where the game ought to go. As the situation deteriorated in 1994, Beeston was still trying to play the diplomat, still trying to work out compromises. But much of the time he was left
watching the downward spiral, powerless to stop it, opposed to the
owners' strategy but (unlike Baltimore owner Peter Angelos) a good
company man willing to spout the party line in public.

And so even as the Blue Jays were celebrating their championship, the more aware members of the club, like union rep Paul
Molitor, knew that the season to come would be a tough one, not
so much on the field as at the negotiating table. They sensed that
this time, it could be different, not a nice tidy little strike or a one-
day lockout, but the war to end all wars. Other players, and the
fans, might have spent their time dreaming about the possibility of
a third straight championship. But the realists, the pessimists, wondered whether the inconceivable might happen, whether there
might not be a World Series to win.

OF MORE IMMEDIATE concern, however, was the health of Duane
Ward. At the close of the 1993 season, he was widely acknowledged
as the finest, most reliable closer in the game. What was not so
widely acknowledged, in the enthusiasm surrounding WAMCO and
the Jays' starters, was that Ward was the single most important element in the team's success. With him waiting in the bullpen, the
starters knew they could give their all for seven or eight innings and
then hand over the ball with confidence. With him waiting in the
bullpen, the hitters knew that if they could score enough runs to
take a lead into the late innings, that lead was secure, or that if they
managed to come from behind, that advantage wouldn't be handed
right back to the opposition.

Pitchers pitch better with that kind of security, hitters hit better,
players in the field are more alert defensively. And the other members of the bullpen, knowing their role, knowing that someone else
would take care of the real pressure situations, could relax and
develop their talents. At the same time, Ward made Cito Gaston a

much better manager—something Gaston would be the first to acknowledge. There's nothing more soul-destroying to a team, and more likely to call into question its leadership, than missed opportunities, blown leads. With Ward available, Gaston could make one move, game in and game out, and be nearly certain of the outcome.

No one saw it coming. There was the World Series, the euphoria, then there were the reports in January that all was not well, that Ward was experiencing soreness in his pitching shoulder of unknown cause. It was significant enough that the Jays considered making an offer to free agent pitcher Gregg Olson, just in case, but not serious enough that anyone questioned Ward's availability for the coming season.

The stories continued through spring training. On February 24, Dr. James Andrews, an orthopaedic surgeon famous for his work with professional athletes, was called in to look at Ward's shoulder, and an MRI examination was done. There was no sign of any damage. On March 12, Ward's bullpen mate, Danny Cox, had a cortisone shot in his sore shoulder, while Ward was doing some soft tossing. He was supposed to start throwing off the mound in two or three days, since no problem had been uncovered, but Gaston said that might be put off, perhaps for as long as a couple of weeks. "He's gotten a little bit better and Dr. Andrews said the last time he checked him he thinks he's gotten a little bit better, but they just think that he should probably be even better," Gaston said. "I guess you would say it's a setback."

Then Gaston uttered a prophetic phrase that echoed a year, even two years later: "Ward has been a very valuable person here all this time. People that don't know it, they will know it."

On March 15, Ward was given clearance to throw off the mound, after a bone scan failed to reveal any problems. Cox also seemed to be making progress. And Roberto Alomar, who had broken his leg playing winter ball in Puerto Rico, saw his first spring action. It looked like the defending world champions might yet round into form. As spring training approached its conclusion, Ward continued to improve. By April 6, he was throwing nearly as hard as ever, though he was deemed not quite ready to start the season in his familiar role. "I thought he had some good velocity but I don't think he had the control he would have liked to have had," Gaston said. "It was the best I've seen him throw [this spring]." Until Ward was ready, Todd Stottlemyre would temporarily leave the starting rotation to become the closer. "We're not going to put Ward out there in a pressure situation right away, anyway," Gaston said. Still, there would be no need for a rehabilitation stint in the minors. Soon enough, Ward would be ready to step right back into the major league line-up.

Two days later, those hopes were dashed. Ward had trouble working out the kinks in his arm as he prepared for a pitching session. "He had a little trouble getting loose and he decided just to go out and throw long tosses," Jays' trainer Tommy Craig explained. It was time to shut it down, to back off once again, to see if the arm would get better on its own. By April 20, Ward was throwing softly off the mound again, and the shoulder was feeling better. A visit to Dr. Frank Jobe, the California-based wizard who pioneered what came to be known as "Tommy John surgery," confirmed the diagnosis of tendinitis. There was nothing structurally wrong, no need to operate. A week later, Ward seemed ready to come off the disabled list for the first time in 1994. He was throwing to hitters in four-minute stints, getting his fastball up as high as eighty-seven miles an hour. "But if I need another day, I'll take another day," he said. "But it feels good right now. It's nice to wake up in the morning and not be sore."

There would be another setback in early May, another shutdown, followed by the slow process of building the arm up again. On June 21, Ward threw ten minutes of batting practice, pronounced himself 85 percent fit and said that he thought he'd be back pitching for real in a week. "I'm going to take this a day at a time because before I was too eager to put a timetable on it," Ward said. "I was letting it go a bit. I was throwing harder than I did last time."

Then, on July 6, came the last straw. Ward had been sent to the Jays' Florida farm team in Dunedin on a rehabilitation assignment, to prepare for his return to the major leagues. In his third outing, a game against the Vero Beach Dodgers, he gave up two runs on three hits in a single inning of work and decided that something wasn't right. "Enough's enough," Ward said. "I don't feel I quit. It was time to get something done."

It was widely suggested that the decision could have been made months earlier, that Ward had stubbornly held out against exploratory surgery, and that the team had been unwise to let him try to work things out on his own. But Ward defended his choice, saying that it was Dr. Andrews who had advised the cautious approach. And, to no one's surprise, Gaston backed him up. "It's *his* arm," the manager said.

The surgery took place on July 8. What had been diagnosed as mere tendinitis turned out to be a partially torn rotator cuff (the rotator cuff is made up of four muscles in the shoulder). Dr. Andrews "cleaned up" the joint and repaired the tear, which had probably occurred the year before. Ward wouldn't be able to throw at all for four months, but would be ready in theory for spring training and the regular season in 1995.

"Hopefully everything is going to be as good as new if not better than new," he said.

The problem is that the Toronto Blue Jays' organization believed that, not just about Ward but about the entire team. What happened to them in 1994 just seemed so inexplicable. The injuries, those were acts of God, and to be fair, Darren Hall, a thirty-year-old career minor leaguer, actually came on and did a reasonable job in Ward's place—though he certainly wasn't the same kind of intimidator on the mound. But they weren't the only reason the defending World Series champions, returning nearly intact but for a couple of promising kids inserted into the Opening Day line-up, didn't really contend after the last week of April. There seemed to be a post-series malaise, something that hadn't happened after 1992 perhaps because of the more dramatic changes made to the line-up. Leads were blown. Defensive plays weren't made. The rookies, Carlos Delgado and Alex Gonzalez, who looked so promising in spring (and in Delgado's case, who looked like the second coming of Babe Ruth in the early days of the season) proved to be not quite ready for prime time. And most puzzling, Juan Guzman, all but untouchable for most of the previous three years, had become an ordinary pitcher. He was 16–5, with a 2.64 ERA in 1992, 14–3, 3.99 in 1993. In 1994, his numbers were 12–11, 5.68, which couldn't be explained by any kind of physical malady.

As the Jays played out the string after the All-Star break, there were two ways the organization might have interpreted the results. They could consider it a fluke, an off-year, a few great players having less than great seasons, all magnified by Ward's absence. Or they could decide that this club was suddenly past it and begin the rebuilding process.

Perhaps if the season had played out to a 162-game conclusion, they would have chosen the latter course. Then the evidence might have seemed more conclusive, and then there would have been the normal opportunities in the off-season to deal, to sign free agents, to re-tool the club with the intention of contending again, if not in 1995, then in 1996 and beyond.

But they didn't do that. They looked at that 55–60 record, the first losing season for a Toronto Blue Jay team since 1982, and decided it was a fluke.

And then time stopped on the twelfth of August. Baseball shut down, and there were real consequences. On September 14, Bud Selig, who in the role of acting commissioner had come to symbolize everything that was wrong with the game, announced that the rest of the 1994 season and the World Series had been cancelled, the first time that had happened in ninety years. "There's an incredible amount of sadness," Selig said. "There is a failure of so much."

In so many ways, it was the perfect time for a man born to the game to make his exit, stage left.

PAUL BEESTON FIRST heard the news back in 1991. He was on the road, negotiating a new contract for Roberto Alomar with the second baseman's agent, Jaime Torres, when he was told over the phone that there was an interesting item in one of the Toronto newspapers. His partner, his confidant, his friend, Pat Gillick, had informed a reporter that he'd be retiring in three more years. Gillick hadn't told anyone else that, except perhaps his wife, Doris. But when Beeston returned to Toronto, Gillick confirmed that yes, those were his intentions—to walk off into the sunset, with nothing left to accomplish in baseball. The fact that his team would win two World Series those last two seasons, the fact that baseball then immediately descended into its darkest period in modern history, would make it that much easier.

"It became a self-fulfilling prophecy," Beeston says. "Because people kept saying, well three years has become two-and-a-half.

Two-and-a-half is now two. Now it's one-and-a-half. And I think at the end he was confused as to whether he wanted to retire or not retire."

Why did he want to leave? Gillick never really did answer the question, probably because he didn't know the answer himself. He was fifty-seven years old and had experienced a couple of health scares. But Mattick, LaMacchia, both of them old enough to be his father, were still there, living the baseball life and loving it. Gillick said that he'd become tired of following schedules, that he wanted freedom of movement. In some ways, he felt burned out, in need of a recharge. He said that he wanted to learn to fly an airplane, find time to finally take up the game of golf. He'd travel—he'd always travelled but now it would only be for fun. There was no other suitor, this wasn't a ploy to secure a higher-paying job with another organization. At the end of October 1994, the time had simply come. The duo who had built the franchise in the wake of Peter Bavasi's departure—which of course was also to some extent their doing—now became a solo act.

At least that was the party line. Beeston, though, and the rest of those who had worked with Gillick since the first days of the franchise had other thoughts in the back of their minds. They figured that he wasn't really going anywhere, or at least that he couldn't stay away. He'd be back, eventually, they'd create a job for him where he could do what he loved best—scouting—without the headaches of the other aspects of the general manager's portfolio.

And in the meantime, they put the longstanding succession plan into effect. True to their organizational philosophy, they would not go out and pluck the next Gillick from some other team. Instead, they would develop from within—or rather, they had been developing from within a candidate who would be fully prepared to step into the general manager's job once Gillick took his leave. Someone without the mystique, certainly. Someone who was far less of a traditional baseball man, more reflective of the game and the business of the 1990s. Someone without even the kind of baseball validation that seems to come automatically with being American. Few of the four million people who pushed through the turnstiles at SkyDome during the glory years would ever have heard of Gord Ash, unless they checked out the fine print of the team directory or closely followed contract negotiations through the papers. Had they taken the time to find out, they would have learned that he was one of their own.

"In retrospect, it sounds like a corny Hollywood movie," Ash says. "I'd always had an interest in baseball, and I can't pinpoint to you why. When I was a kid I played all the sports, hockey and football, but I had this attraction to baseball. I would go to Maple Leaf Stadium. My parents were sports minded. They took me to some games. We lived in the west end and could take the Bathurst street-car down to the park. The last year they were there, I worked selling tickets." From the Maple Leafs to the Blue Jays: in Ash, the circle was complete.

By the time the big leagues came to town, Ash was working, none too happily, in a bank. He had graduated from university hoping to go to teacher's college, but jobs were scarce in the profession unless you were willing to go far afield. "I was just scrambling for anything," he says, finally securing a training position with the Canadian Imperial Bank of Commerce.

A friend of his had taken a part-time job working in one of the Jays' ticket wickets at Exhibition Stadium, for the few extra bucks it provided. On Victoria Day in 1977, the team was expecting a crush of customers and was short enough bodies to man the windows. Ash's friend asked him if he'd like to help out for the day, a one-shot deal. "You go and they assign you some tickets for that game. You put your face in the window and sell away. And usually after an inning and a half, you close up, balance and go and watch the game." Ash enjoyed himself thoroughly and especially enjoyed being around baseball. "This is a passion with him," Beeston says. "He was a fan. Anyone who would be married, and working in a bank, and then start selling tickets part-time had to like the game." The one shot turned into a part-time job. By September, he was asking George Holm, the team's ticket manager, to keep him in mind if anything full-time came along. Holm called with some weekend work during the winter. "I didn't know until later that was his way to test how real your interest was," Ash recalls. By mid-January, Holm was convinced that Ash's heart was in it and offered him a full-time job.

"It was about 15 or 20 percent less than I was making at the bank, but at the time I didn't have any obligations. So it wasn't a money thing. I just absolutely hated what I was doing. Every day it was exactly the same. So I bailed out of that and started on the first of February 1978 in the ticket office. I worked in the mail-order area, processing mail orders. It didn't take long for the excitement to wear off, because aside from being in a sporting environment, it was essentially the bank all over again."

The next winter, the groundskeeper at Exhibition Stadium left, and the Blue Jays were looking for a replacement. "Now I had no experience. I had no idea," Ash says. But tired of the routine in the ticket office, he applied for the job and was hired. His responsibility, along with a two-man crew and a bunch of part-time kids, was to make sure the field was in shape for games. "I faked my way through that with common sense. If it didn't rain, it was a piece of cake. If it rained, you were in big trouble. I think during the 1979 year, it might have rained every day.

"What I really enjoyed was that every day was different. The guy driving the Zamboni would quit and you'd have to find somebody else. I didn't think it was heading anywhere necessarily other than that I enjoyed it."

Ash spent a year as groundskeeper, then moved into an office job as the team's assistant director of operations, a post he held for three years. By 1983, Gillick's assistant, Elliott Wahle, who handled some of the contract negotiation, had left his post, which hadn't been filled. Wahle, like Ash, wasn't a baseball guy, which gave Ash the idea that maybe he could handle the job. At the same time, the Jays' director of operations, Ken Erskine, resigned because of illness. Ash found himself at a crossroads. He could continue on the stadium operations side of the organization, or he could try to make the huge leap into the business of the sport itself. "I was a little more confident about my abilities. And now I was starting to think this can be a career. I hummed and hawed about it. Pat hummed and hawed about it. I think Paul probably hummed and hawed about whether it was the right thing."

Finally, a year after Ash first applied for Wahle's former job, Beeston decided that it was indeed the right thing, and Ash was named administrator of player personnel, a role that involved dealing with the Jays' minor league affiliates and negotiating minor league contracts, with very little contact with the major league club. "It was a lot like teaching babies to swim. They throw you in and you figure it out," says Ash.

"He was a student of the game," Beeston says. "He'd hang around and want to know what was happening, what trades were happening. I would do this and I would do that. That's great. When you don't have to make the decision anybody can do it. From Gordie's point of view it was very obvious very early on. He just kept on taking on more. He ran the draft the last six or seven years. He ran the organization meetings. Because Pat didn't like doing it."

Ash in many ways followed the same path as Beeston—a Canadian and a non-baseball man learning at the knee of the Blue Jays' wisemen. Al LaMacchia gave him important advice early—shut up and listen—and he took those words to heart. "He earned their respect by asking a lot of questions and more importantly listening to the answers," Beeston says. "He knows what he doesn't know, which is the key to anybody's job."

"I didn't really feel like I had an opinion to offer," Ash says. "I was just trying to soak up as much information as I could." It took three or four years before he became more confident, before he noticed that his private opinions were starting to match up pretty consistently with what Gillick, LaMacchia and Mattick were saying and doing. "At that point, I said to myself, this might not be so tough after all."

The tough part wasn't so much the baseball lore, the baseball science, but winning acceptance among the fraternity, and especially from Gillick himself. Ash accomplished it. "Gillick distanced himself from people," Herb Solway says. "He does his job, and Gillick is a bit suspicious of non-baseball people anyway. It's remarkable that Gordie Ash has got this relationship with him, coming from that background. It shows you really how much talent Gordie has. Gordie's terrific, a really first-class guy. You can imagine how long it must have taken him—a little Toronto guy who wasn't a baseball player. What could he know about baseball? I believe if you asked Gillick—if you gave him some truth serum—he would say that if you didn't grow up in baseball, you don't know it, you can't know it, and your opinion isn't worth anything."

"The thing about a non-player is that you've got to be a good listener and you've got to be able to decipher facts from fiction,"

Gillick says. "And if you're organized, you can do pluses and minuses and you have a pretty good read on your people and a little bit of an instinct about people, then I think you'll be fine. Gord's very intelligent. He knows what his strengths are and what his weaknesses are."

Eventually, the Ash–Gillick partnership came to resemble in some ways the working relationship Gillick had enjoyed for so many years with Beeston. In both cases, the two men complemented each other's skills and shored up each other's weaknesses. For all of Gillick's prodigious feats of memory, for all of his attention to detail, there were aspects of the job that he didn't particularly enjoy. He wasn't one to study the "blue book," the basic business rules of the game. "Gordie was into the detail part of it and he combines that with his passion for the game, and he listens to the people he should be listening to," Beeston says.

Ash also enjoyed the game of negotiation in a way that Gillick, who was always especially sensitive to the player's point of view, never did. "Gordie's tough and he's smart," Beeston says. "You go away on a trip and he's prepared. It's a different style going away to negotiate a contract with him and Pat. I used to get on an airplane with Pat and I'd have to pull out all this shit and start writing it down on cocktail napkins. Gord gives me everything, the history of the comparables, what we've been paying the person. And Gordie doesn't mind the tension of an argument. Gordie doesn't mind saying no. Pat had to always have somebody there who would say no. Because he would have given it to them. And he knew it. He knew it."

By the time of Gillick's departure, Gord Ash had found his comfort zone. Never a player on the field, he had become a player in the baseball board rooms, respected by other general managers, by agents, ready to step up, part of a wave of young executives whose primary baseball education had been in the business, not in the game on the diamond. Toronto baseball fans might not have paid much attention to Ash's ascent, but at least one other baseball organization did. When television executive Tom Werner bought the San Diego Padres, he phoned Beeston to inquire about potential general managers. Beeston suggested Ash, who was interviewed for the job and who in the end lost out, narrowly, to Joe McIlvaine. "They would have taken Gordie," Beeston says, "except that McIlvaine had the bigger reputation and they were trying to make a splash."

The Jays wouldn't have stood in his way if he'd had the chance to go, but they were relieved when he stuck around.

◆ THE BASEBALL STRIKE. Gillick's retirement. The collapse of the team on the field. But the biggest baseball story in Toronto didn't even make it to the sports pages until it was almost over. In any assessment of the Toronto Blue Jays, any attempt to explain the team's success, ownership always comes first. The Labatt/Howard Webster/Bank of Commerce partnership (and after Webster's death, Labatt essentially running the show on its own) meant more than any player, any executive, any strikeout or home run. They paid the bills and put enough money in the system to build a winner. They gave their baseball men autonomy, to the point that Beeston and Gillick could joke with each other that they might as well have owned the team. They created a synergy between television and sport and beer and a stadium that made for a secure, stable environment most other professional sports franchises in North America would envy. Toronto fans couldn't name the owner—no George Steinbrenner, no Marge Schott, just a big, beneficent corporate backer that also sold them their suds. Money, or at least the bottom line, was never part of water-cooler discussions about the home team. Only the winning and the losing. And from that atmosphere grew consumer confidence, and from consumer confidence grew record attendance, and from record attendance grew significant revenues that were ploughed back into the team to build a consistent winner and finally a champion. Take away the owners, take away their approach, and all of that could be called into question.

The first intimations that it wouldn't go on forever came in February 1993, between the two World Series, though Beeston was probably the only one in the Blue Jays organization to really pay attention. In a move that was front-page news across the country, Brascan, which had controlled John Labatt Ltd., sold the company for $993 million. The buyers were investment dealers, who in turn parcelled the stock off to pension funds and insurance companies. "The day that Brascan sold their interest, the company was in play," Beeston says. "There was no major shareholder." A year after the

STEPHEN BRUNT

sale, those who had bought in were beginning to have serious concerns about the direction of the company. The purchase of a Mexican brewery looked disastrous, largely because of the collapse of the peso. In the summer of 1994, Labatt was one of the bidders for Madison Square Garden, a move that didn't sit well with shareholders, who were already questioning the company's large entertainment and sports holdings, which included not just the Jays, but The Sports Network, and through TSN the Toronto Argonauts and a 41 percent share in SkyDome. Pressure began to mount to get back to the core business—beer—and to shed some of those other assets.

To that end, a plan was unveiled in the summer of 1994 to split off the sports and entertainment holdings and to offer 49 percent of them to the public. But largely because of the uncertainty generated by the baseball strike and the National Hockey League lockout, there was little interest. For fiscal 1994, the same sports and entertainment properties that had made a $3-million profit the year before were responsible for a $10-million loss.

At the same time, the takeover talk began. Attempts to take a "poison pill," which would have made a takeover more difficult and expensive, were voted down by the shareholders. Then the rumours began in earnest that someone was going to make a move on the company. "I think the only person [in the Blue Jay offices] that might have been totally aware of it was me, and I wasn't afraid of it," Beeston says. "I was too dumb, confident, naïve. We were insulated from Labatt. We've basically run autonomously from Labatt. Our pay scale isn't Labatt's but TSN's is. Our pension plan and benefit plan isn't Labatt's but TSN's is. The way that we do things here is not the same as Labatt. We've run this as a separate company. It was very successful. We've increased the value of the company. Good earnings. Great success on the field. Held up as a model for all kinds of sports franchises."

But what if a takeover specialist like Onex got hold of it, starting stripping Labatt of its assets and peddling them separately? What if someone bought the baseball team who wasn't like Peter Hardy or Sam Pollock, Sid Oland, Peter Widdrington or George Taylor, Labatt's head men who took Beeston's and Gillick's word for how things had to be? "There was a period there where I wondered what is going to happen," Beeston says. "I like my life. Now all of a sudden

Jerry Schwartz [of Onex] is going to own it or these Belgians are going to own it. Then you have to say to yourself, I hope that it just goes on the way it is but if it doesn't go on the way it is, I've had twenty great years. We've had a lot of fun, met a lot of interesting people. I hope they don't do anything to screw up what I thought was a pretty good organization with a huge and generous future ahead of it."

Onex made its run in the spring of 1995, with a $24-a-share, $2.3-billion offer. Labatt's management scrambled to find a second bidder, someone with more roots in the beer industry, and eventually came up with Interbrew SA, the Belgian brewing giant best known for its signature brand Stella Artois. The Belgians won the day with a bid of $28.50 a share, $2.7 billion, and in July 1995 officially took control of the Labatt assets. By law, they would have to divest themselves of TSN, which was eventually purchased by a group of its former executives. By choice, the brewer indicated that it would sell both the Argonauts and the Blue Jays, but that it was in no hurry to do so. The uncertainty of the baseball labour situation and the general uncertainty surrounding the Canadian Football League meant that neither franchise could be sold for its real value. The Belgian brewers applied to Major League Baseball for temporary permission to own the club—for six months, which expired on January 26, 1996. They were welcomed into the fraternity just so long as they were willing to keep Beeston at the helm. When the six months expired, they were given another six months.

But still, their intentions were unclear, and there was little sense that it would—or could—be business as usual for the most successful team in baseball. It was now off into the great unknown.

"The game itself is at a watershed," Beeston said. "The team is at a watershed. The ownership is at a watershed. We don't know who owns us, the industry's fucked up, and the team's in last place. It's a joy to be alive."

Chapter 20

I T WASN'T THEIR strike, after all. The old system under which the business of baseball was run had served the Toronto Blue Jays rather well. They had won a couple of championships and made a handsome profit in the good years, despite the fact they were taking in Canadian dollars and paying out American dollars. And so there was no conceivable reason for anyone associated with the franchise to be an agitator, to be willing to risk everything to break the players' union and rewrite the collective bargaining agreement in the owners' favour. If anything, they'd go to the wall in support of the status quo.

But at the same time, the Jays had earned a reputation as loyal team players within the baseball establishment. Paul Beeston had a decent working relationship with Bud Selig, the Milwaukee Brewers' owner, who was temporarily running the sport. He talked to Jerry Reinsdorf, the owner of the Chicago White Sox, widely regarded to be the one pulling Selig's strings and the real driving force behind the anti-union hawks. The Blue Jays' owners might dissent in private, around the meeting table, but in public they would line up with the other owners and back the majority's will.

Entering the spring of 1995, it became clear that the strike wasn't going to come to a negotiated conclusion, that this time both sides were holding firm, were willing to engage in a possibly sport-destroying game of chicken. Faced with that, the Blue Jays assessed their beliefs, assessed their responsibilities to the other owners, and tried to have it both ways. Perhaps it was a matter of principle, perhaps they sensed that their consumers weren't as rabidly anti-player/anti-union as many of the baseball fans in the United States, perhaps they understood that by demonizing the players, they would be degrading the very same product they would eventually have to sell. In any case, Beeston shrewdly staked out a morally defensible middle ground, where he could appear to be both a conscientious objector to the owners' tactics and a solid member of the baseball fraternity.

Reluctantly, the Jays recruited their own squad of "replacement players"—strikebreakers, really, pulled largely from the low-level, unaffiliated, minor leagues—and offered them the chance to pretend to be big leaguers for a few weeks. Every day, the pretend Jays would assemble at Dunedin Stadium, go through their paces and eventually play out a parody of the Grapefruit League season.

But Cito Gaston wouldn't be there. Like all major league managers, he was contractually obligated to head up whatever team the owners decided to field. The Blue Jays, though, understood a couple of things—that whenever the strike ended, there would be divisions within the clubhouse between the strikers and anyone who carried the taint of the strikebreaker, and that Gaston, as a former player and member of the union, would be made tremendously uncomfortable if he were forced to manage the replacements. (Whether they took into account Gaston's own politics, which tend towards the progressive, pro-labour end of the spectrum, is another matter.) The sensible solution, then, would be to let Bob Didier, the manager of their Triple A affiliate, the Syracuse Chiefs, handle the *faux* Blue Jays. Gaston could stay back at the Englebert Recreation Complex, the team's minor league facility across town, where he'd never have to cross paths with the strikebreakers and where he could spend his time productively assessing the organization's young talent.

External forces also helped form the Jays' strike philosophy. The New Democratic Party government then in power in Ontario had changed the province's labour laws, effectively banning the use of replacement workers. It was unclear whether that stipulation would apply to the Blue Jays, whether they were the same as any other Ontario-based company or whether, through their association with the U.S.-based American League, they might be somehow exempt. But it wasn't in the interests of the team or its ownership to challenge the law. They didn't want to showcase strikebreakers at SkyDome in any case, they didn't want to foist an inferior product on their consumers—especially considering that many of their consumers might be sympathetic to the players' association. Here was the perfect out. Without having to take a real stand, as Peter Angelos had in Baltimore (Angelos broke ranks with the other owners and simply refused to employ replacements), the Jays could get out of the whole mess by citing Canadian law. Sure, they'd field a replacement team—but it would have to play somewhere else, somewhere like Dunedin, where the mockery of the major leagues would be well hidden from Toronto ticket buyers.

It wouldn't ever come to that, though as the end of March approached, it certainly seemed that it would. Didier, a gung-ho sort, took to managing his "big league" team with a tremendous amount of enthusiasm. But even with free admission, few fans bothered to make the trip to Dunedin Stadium. The usual flock of Canadian snowbirds who came south for spring training stayed home. Talks between the owners and players were on and off, there were false hopes followed by crushing disappointments. What became clear was that there was no give from the players, and for the first time in their long history of labour disputes, no sign of the owners crumbling, aside from Angelos's actions. They had gone this far, they had killed a World Series. Clearly this was a battle they were willing to fight to the end. The strikebreakers would play. Sooner or later, the owners figured, the union would break, and the players would come crawling back. Sure, there would be lasting damage to the game and to the business, but the hawks, in their myopia, had decided it was worth it.

They had made one small miscalculation, though. Along the way, the owners had unilaterally decided to eliminate salary arbitration, the players' right to bargain individually with clubs, and the anti-collusion provisions of the collective bargaining agreement. That brought the National Labour Relations Board into the picture, acting on a complaint from the players that the owners weren't negotiating in good faith. After investigating, the NLRB agreed and went to court seeking an injunction that would reinstate the rules of the previous collective bargaining agreement. Don Fehr, the head of the players' association, said that if the court ruled in their favour, the players would return to work immediately and work under the old contract while a new one was being negotiated. (Like the Blue Jays, the players had thrived under the old status quo. The strike had been pre-emptive, based on the assumption that the owners were prepared to lock the players out in the spring to force their agenda through.)

On March 31, two days before the replacement season was to begin, U.S. District Court Judge Sonia Sotomayor granted the injunction, leaving the owners in an untenable position. The day before, they had voted 26–2 (with Baltimore and Toronto objecting, but Toronto also willing to abide by the vote) to begin the season with replacements. Now, with the real players coming back, they had only two choices: lock the players out, forgo the replacement player strategy, and continue to play the waiting game, risking further court sanctions; or open camp and try to put a good face on it without ever acknowledging defeat.

In this instance only, the saner heads prevailed. "The players are back, the game is back, and we are very happy about that," Selig announced following an owners' meeting at the Chicago O'Hare Hilton on April 2. The strike was over after 234 days. There would be a 1995 season, starting on April 26, with a regular season of 144 rather than 162 games. Nearly 800 of baseball's 1,069 players were unsigned because their contracts had expired during the stalemate. Another 200 players were free agents. There would be an enormous amount of work to be done in a little over three weeks, just to put teams together for Opening Day.

During that owners' meeting in Chicago, after it had been decided not to lock the players out, Beeston found himself in conversation with David Glass, an executive of the Kansas City Royals. The Royals were one of the self-described "small market" teams who had been bound and determined to radically alter the sport's economic structure with revenue sharing and a salary cap. Now, stuck with the old system, under which they claimed to be headed for financial ruin, they were going to dramatically make their point to the players and the fans—just as the Montreal Expos would a few days later.

"Any of our players are available," Glass told Beeston.

"Any of them?" Beeston asked, a bit incredulous. "Any of them including Cone?"

"Any of our players are available," Glass reiterated.

"And that," Beeston explains now, "is how it happened."

◆ENTERING THE ABBREVIATED spring training of 1995, the Toronto Blue Jays' brass had to make a fundamental decision about their club and make it very quickly, without definitive evidence one way or the other. Before the strike, the 1994 season had been a disaster. A World Series champion had become an also-ran, a loser, but there were extenuating circumstances: injuries, off-years by players who hadn't had off-years before, the post-championship hangover, the distraction of the labour dispute.

If the strike-shortened season had been a measure of the real Blue Jays, then it was time to rebuild, or at least to shake up the existing line-up. With all the free agents available, that would be a relatively simple matter. But if 1994 had been a fluke, an aberration, a down year for a team that still possessed the talent of a champion, then only minor tinkering was in order. Surely Juan Guzman would bounce back. Maybe Duane Ward would return, as the doctors said he could. Add a decent starting pitcher or two, and the offensive support would certainly be there, with White, Alomar, Carter, Molitor and Olerud.

Momentously, disastrously, Beeston, Ash and the rest opted to write off 1994 as just one of those years, to return in 1995 with the club essentially intact. The only major alterations would come in the pitching rotation. Todd Stottlemyre had filed for free agency, though his heart remained with the team, and he wanted very badly to return. The Jays had declined to offer Dave Stewart salary arbitration, figuring that at age thirty-seven he was too near the end of the line to justify a $4.2-million salary. They could re-sign Stottlemyre and still probably afford to dip into the free agent pool for another starter—one who interested them was Erik Hanson, the former Seattle Mariner, who would wind up showcasing his wares at the union's free agent camp in Homestead, Florida.

There was also the Cone possibility. Trading for Cone and absorbing his salary would preclude signing a first-rank free agent. But he was also a sure thing, one of the three or four best starters in the game, the 1994 American League Cy Young Award winner and, of course, he'd been a part of their own 1992 championship team. And if not Cone, there were other pitchers available by trade as small-market teams tried to unload salaries. The Expos had put Ken Hill on the block and were anxious to make a deal as quickly as possible.

For Gord Ash, this would be the first real test of his tenure as Gillick's replacement, an opportunity to pull off the kind of deal or signing that the fans would immediately recognize as the right one.

For quite a while, it looked as if his catch would be Hill, a very good starter without an outrageous contract. The Jays could absorb his salary and still have enough left to sign Stottlemyre or another free agent. But at the last minute, Montreal general manager Kevin Malone chose to look elsewhere, dealing Hill to the St. Louis Cardinals, leaving Ash frustrated and angry. Relations between Canada's two major league clubs had never been cordial, but it's unlikely they were ever chillier than at that moment.

Ash then turned his attention to Kansas City and Cone. In the end, the trade fell into place quite easily. The Jays gave up three minor leaguers, pitcher David Sinnes, infielder Chris Stynes and infielder Anthony Medrano. Of the three, only Stynes was regarded as a blue-chip prospect, though in the past under Gillick, the Jays had shown an uncanny ability to deal away promising young players who never really lived up to their reputations when they landed with another organization. For the Royals, the real impetus for the deal was Cone's salary—$5 million. Anything they received after shedding that chunk of payroll was a bonus. (They might have also had other reasons for being happy to see Cone go. Perhaps it was just a coincidence, but Cone was also a union activist and one of the main player spokesmen during the strike, while the Kansas City ownership was as hawkish as any.)

The trade was announced at a hastily called press conference in the media dining room at Dunedin Stadium. "It's a Pat Gillick special, five months early," Ash said, alluding to the late-season deals that had become a trademark of his predecessor. But in his look, in his manner, Ash was saying something else: I'm in charge; this is my work; this is a Gord Ash special. An ordinary guy from Toronto could do it just as well as the baseball guru whose job he'd taken.

The reaction among the baseball press and in the Blue Jays' clubhouse was immediate: with this one move, the club had instantly become a serious contender for a third straight World Series (keeping in mind that the 1994 Series had never happened). When Cone arrived the next day, Joe Carter made a huge show of dropping to his knees and bowing before him, shouting "The saviour, the saviour is here." That silliness aside, the trade was supposed to deliver a message to the players after the flop of 1994. The organization was still serious about winning; it would still spend the money and acquire the talent. Now it was up to them to respond.

For his part, Cone seemed delighted to be back with Toronto. "I can guarantee you the players are looking at the Blue Jays and Peter Angelos and the Orioles and saying, 'These are the people I want to play for,'" Cone said. "People who are willing to buck the system and stand up for what they believe in." And so perhaps there had been another side benefit from the Jays' qualified objector status during the strike (though that statement seemed ironic a few months later, when the club was desperately trying to sign free agents and finding no takers, despite their admirable labour-management stance).

With Cone and his salary on board, Todd Stottlemyre became an afterthought. "Todd's is a situation we're going to have to re-evaluate," Ash said, meaning that in effect, whatever offer had been on the table was now rescinded. The Jays had been trying to sign Stottlemyre to a long-term deal before the strike, and both sides seemed willing, simply dickering over the price. (The pitcher's agent was asking for $10 million over three years. The Jays offered $7.5 million.) Stottlemyre felt a tremendous loyalty to the organization, which had suffered through his ups and downs. He wanted very much to remain a Toronto Blue Jay.

In retrospect, Beeston feels that this was one instance where the team did wrong by one of its players. "The only two guys that I think we ever screwed here were Todd and George [Bell]," Beeston says. "And they're the two guys who were more loyal to the Blue Jay colours than any Dodger was loyal to the Dodger colours. We wanted to talk to Todd, but we got Cone and we couldn't afford him. We now know that Todd felt betrayed at the time and I now know...why Todd felt that way. And I apologized to him."

Looking at a payroll that now approached $44 million, Ash had only enough money left for a fifth starter, a veteran free agent, probably coming off a down year, who might still have a decent season left, and perhaps enough for a veteran outfielder. He settled on Danny Darwin, most recently with the Boston Red Sox, and Candy Maldonado, a Gaston favourite during his days with Toronto. It was all falling into place in that Blue Jay way: combine a rotation of Cone, Guzman, Hentgen, Leiter and Darwin with the offensive and defensive skills of the starting eight, and the club had the look of a contender.

In addition, the best closer in the game was back. On the same day the Blue Jays traded for Cone, Duane Ward appeared in camp. He said he expected he'd be ready for regular season, was throwing at 80 percent velocity, was experiencing no discomfort in his throwing shoulder. Pitching coach Galen Cisco tried to hold him back, to make him take it slow, but Ward was in a hurry to make up for lost time. "I keep telling him," Ward said, "that I've only got three weeks." Three weeks to Opening Day.

◆ BASEBALL, THE GAME, the business, the cultural institution, was mortally wounded by the strike of 1994–95. Neither the owners nor the players could have anticipated what they'd face when the major league teams headed north. Other strikes, other interruptions, even the one that led to a split season in 1981, had never really caused any permanent fallout. The fans returned like sheep, drawn by their own loyalties, drawn by their love of the sport. They could be abused, they could be treated like rubes, and still they'd line up to buy tickets.

No more. The empty seats during the opening week of the season, the hostility of some of the fans, and even worse, the absolute ennui of so many others, showed that this time, it had gone too far. People remembered the cancellation of a World Series, they remembered what had been taken away from them. And they weren't prepared to forgive and forget.

Toronto fans, though, were a slightly different breed. They hadn't found so much to hate about their owners or their players. There was still a lasting affection for the organization that had produced consecutive championships, and the disappointment of the 1994 season, perhaps because the campaign was left forever unfinished, never really sunk in. It was more as though this were a continuation of the great years, the winning years, as though that other stuff was just a bad dream. The home opener, which was also the season opener, didn't sell out weeks in advance, as had been the case in the past. In fact, the last ticket wasn't purchased until the game with the Oakland Athletics on April 26 was already two innings old. But in the overall baseball climate of the time, the relationship between the Blue Jays and their fans remained among the best in the game.

On Opening Day, that relationship would only be enhanced. With Cone pitching for Toronto, and Dave Stewart—who had decided to return to Oakland as a free agent—pitching for the A's, the Blue Jays coasted to a 13–1 win. The eleven runs Toronto scored in the second inning tied a team record for the most ever in a single frame. The next day, Pat Hentgen took to the mound, and again it was no contest. Ed Sprague knocked in five runs, including a grand slam, and the Jays triumphed 7–1. Two games into the season, Toronto sat atop the American League East by half a game, and all was right with the world.

Who knew then that it was the last time they would lead the division all season?

WHAT WENT WRONG in 1995 is impossible to explain by examining any particular game or series of games, any one injury, any one disappointing performance. In the seasons when they were successful, many things went right for the Blue Jays that might have gone the other way. And now it was time to even up.

It is possible to make the case that the troubles began and ended with Ward, who, despite his optimism in the spring, was never close to a real return to form. On May 11, he made his first appearance since the final game of the 1993 World Series, taking the mound at SkyDome in the eighth inning of a tie game against the New York Yankees. In two-thirds of an inning, Ward gave up three runs on two hits and seemed to have none of his former velocity. The next day, he was placed on the fifteen-day disabled list with a sore shoulder. After a rehabilitation stint at Syracuse, where he pitched six innings in six games, giving up fourteen hits, ten runs, and recording just four strikeouts, Ward took one last stab at the major leagues. He made three June appearances with the Blue Jays, surrendering runs every time, and then on June 23 was placed on the disabled list to stay, his big league career apparently over.

To compound Toronto's bullpen problems, Darren Hall, who had done a commendable job as Ward's replacement in 1994, spent most of the season disabled with elbow problems. He appeared in just seventeen games and recorded just three saves versus seventeen in 1994.

Without a legitimate closer, relievers like Tony Castillo, a reliable middle man, were forced out of their most effective roles. Starters, without the confidence to hand the ball over to the bullpen, pitched deeper into games, losing effectiveness themselves. And the entire team, which had cruised through the Henke–Ward years knowing that if they took a lead into the late innings, it was almost certainly safe, now knew that there were no sure things. Consider one of the season's most memorable low points, on June 4, when the Jays took an 8–0 lead over the Cleveland Indians at Jacobs Field with Cone pitching, and wound up losing 9–8, when Paul Sorrento homered off Hall with two out in the ninth.

The Jays were bad, and they were consistently bad. After going 3–2 in April, they were 11–16 in May, 9–16 in June, battled back for a respectable 15–14 in July, only to clearly give up in the second half of the season, with an 11–18 August and gutless 7–22 in September and October.

The last time they were at .500 was May 15, when their record was 9–9. The last time they were as high as second place was June 2. By the All-Star break, they were last in the division at 27–40. They would be in last place from September 10 on and finish 56–88, tied with the Minnesota Twins for the worst record in the majors, the worst winning percentage for the franchise since the dark days of 1979, the first back-to-back losing seasons for the Blue Jays since 1981–82.

The individual numbers were obviously just as discouraging. Juan Guzman continued his puzzling decline, twice spending time on the disabled list with mysterious soreness in his right shoulder and while active compiling a 4–14 record, with a 6.32 ERA. During one stretch, Guzman lost a franchise record nine games in a row. Hentgen was 10–14 with a 5.11 ERA and, while not missing a start all season, set his own unfortunate team marks, becoming the first Blue Jay pitcher to give up five home runs in a single game, against Cleveland May 26, the first to walk nine in a game, against Seattle on July 15, and tying a team record by giving up thirteen hits to the Angels on July 20. He also led the American League in runs allowed. Darwin was simply awful, compiling a 1–8 record with a 7.44 ERA before being released on July 18. The only real bright light in the rotation was Al Leiter, finally putting together a full season without injury and going 11–11 with a (in 1995 Blue Jay terms) sparkling 3.64 ERA.

With matters obviously hopeless by mid-season, the Blue Jays' front office did something that it had scarcely done before—not since 1982, the last year of the post-expansion doldrums. They gave up. Surrendered. Quit. Acknowledged to themselves, to their players, and to their fans that they weren't going to win anything in 1995. They weren't even going to come close. And so it was time to do what others had done in the past, to be for the first time on the opposite side of the fence. The Jays would deal to dump salary and to enhance their future. Someone else would trade for that one player—a Toronto player—who might help them win a pennant.

Anyone and everyone was on the block: Joe Carter, a consistent RBI producer, the World Series hero, but just a year away from retirement, he said; Roberto Alomar, among the best players in baseball, but a free agent at season's end; John Olerud, under-achieving for a second straight season, his big salary an impediment to moving him; Devon White, the nonpareil centre fielder, who would also be a free agent at year's end. The Blue Jays weren't winning with them, and with the $44-million payroll they represented, the organization might as well save some money and get something in return.

The only real bidding, though, was for Cone, the saviour of spring training, whose arrival was supposed to be the harbinger of another golden season. On July 28, Ash sent him to the New York Yankees in return for three pitching prospects: Marty Janzen, Jason Jarvis and Mike Gordon. Of the trio, Janzen was regarded as the closest to a sure thing, but he was still a year or two away from the big leagues. In effect, the Jays were telling their fans that it might well be 1997 before winning baseball returned to SkyDome.

It was hard for some to take. It was hard, also, for some of the players to take, especially Alomar, who sat out the day after the Cone trade and who expressed displeasure at not having been dealt away himself. Not much was made of it at the time—the Jays had bigger problems than a single pouting superstar. And in fact, before and after the deal, Alomar was one of the few Jays to enjoy a consistently fine season, both at the plate and in the field. But later, long after the season had concluded, Alomar's one-day sit-down, combined with the fact that he hadn't played the final weekend of the year because of a bad back—in the process protecting his .300 average—would be held against him by the fans, with the active encouragement of Toronto management. As unlikely as it might have seemed that any one player could be used as a scapegoat for all the bad times of 1994 and 1995—and as unlikely as it might seem that that player could be someone as popular and accomplished as Alomar—that's exactly what happened in the fall of 1995.

◆THE FANS HAD watched a terrible August, September and October; they'd watched their beloved team apparently quit. As the crowds dwindled at SkyDome, the stadium suddenly began to seem like a cold, empty place, and any sense of belonging, of being part of an event, part of a community, dissipated in the dead air. A new element crept into those water-cooler conversations about what was wrong with the Blue Jays: cynicism. For the first time, fans felt let down not just by the team, but by the organization. Here was a group of superstars, still raking in some of the highest salaries in the majors, and by all appearances they were simply going through the motions.

If you're operating a professional sports franchise, there's no worse message to send your supporters than that they're being played for suckers.

◆IT CAN HAPPEN in any long-term relationship. Lines of communication break down. Old assumptions no longer hold true. People change, their goals change, their ideas change. And sometimes, the other party is the last to notice.

For nineteen years, Paul Beeston and Pat Gillick had built a rock-solid personal and professional bond. Originally, it had developed out of mutual need—Beeston's of baseball expertise, Gillick's of a front office ally—and a mutual loathing of Peter Bavasi. They stood together to get Bavasi ousted and they stood together afterwards, building the franchise, staying out of each other's way, enjoying their autonomy, enjoying their success. Their few tiffs were trivial—a dispute over the signing of Dave Winfield, a dispute over a bottle of wine stashed in the office that wasn't supposed to be opened but was. Though very different personalities—Beeston outgoing, ebullient, immediately likeable; Gillick guarded, cryptic, calculating—they meshed brilliantly. Any attempt to explain the success of the Toronto baseball franchise has to take into account their personal chemistry.

But by the time Gillick retired in 1994, they clearly didn't know each other as well as they once did—or at least Beeston didn't know Gillick as well as he thought he did.

Beeston never really bought into the notion that Gillick could simply walk away from baseball. Almost from the beginning of his "retirement," he thought he sensed signs of restlessness, signs that Gillick would have to return to the game. "Everybody's got to work at retirement," Beeston says. "And he wanted it to come like *that*. I'm retired, this is it. And it doesn't work that way. Pat tried to take up golf. I think he's probably played his last game of golf. He went out five or six times. Never bought clubs. He never took up flying. But he did get recharged. You could see it coming. As we got into spring training [in 1995] he said, well I'll go to Arizona. Then down to Florida. He did his best to stay out of the picture, because it was very difficult for him. But he really couldn't."

Gillick describes his retirement in absolutely opposite terms.

"I was very happy doing what I was doing," he says. "I was very content. I certainly wasn't itching to get back. My wife sort of got on me a little bit from the standpoint that she thought it was too early for me to retire. That was one thing. But I felt very comfortable with it. I was fine. She sort of feels that you have to get up in the morning with a purpose, with some idea of what you want to do. I set my own schedule and my own agenda. Sometimes it was a busy day and sometimes it wasn't a busy day. And I quite enjoyed that."

Still, it's true that when Gillick came to spring training in 1995, ready to resume some kind of role with the club, there was a certain awkwardness about the situation. Gord Ash was the general manager now, and it was Gord Ash's team to run. Gillick, presumably, was available if things began to fall apart, but no one anticipated that happening. "I suppose you could say it was an option if Gordie failed and he wanted to do it," Beeston says. "But no one was cheering for Gordie to fail and no one was working to make sure he was unsuccessful."

It was left to Gillick to define his new role. Beeston had told him, "You've earned the right to have a year off. You come and go as you want to go and we'll use you if you want to do it." They might have sketched it out more clearly if the relationship had continued into 1996, but in the beginning, Gillick was simply paid a healthy salary to make himself available—and at the same time to keep out of Ash's way.

"Why wouldn't he do it?" Beeston says. "Good money. You set your own kind of life-style. You don't have the responsibility of talking to the press unless you want to talk to them. Your reputation is sterling and you've got everything the way you want it. He's doing his charitable work. He was doing his speaking. He could travel. To me it looked like he was enjoying himself, other than the fact that I knew that he was getting itchy."

The "itch" wasn't that worrisome, because in his heart of hearts, Beeston believed that Gillick would never—could never—leave Toronto and the Blue Jays. His opinion was backed by what he'd come to know of the man during their years together and by the fact that there had been many opportunities for him to leave, none of which Gillick had ever taken up. Most recently, it had been the two expansion teams, Arizona and Tampa Bay, looking for someone to build an organization from scratch and turning naturally to the person who had done it better than just about anyone else.

"He would phone me and tell me about the offers, and I'd say, 'Pat, this is what I think you should do. Here's what you should ask for,'" Beeston says. "'First of all, you don't need the money, so the most important thing is make sure you have the proper job description and know who you're reporting to. Those are the two things you've got to worry about. So if you want to work for Phoenix, if you want to work for Tampa Bay…'"

In the end, Gillick would let the suitors stroke his ego, he would enjoy his status as the most desirable free agent in baseball management, he'd enjoy the fact that every time he turned down a job, his value seemed to go up. Then he'd return to hearth and home.

And so Beeston didn't see it coming. Not even a little bit. Gillick says he certainly didn't plan it, wasn't even feeling antsy, was prepared to live the quiet life for the rest of his time on earth. "Frankly," he says, "it came as a shock to me too."

As to the actual train of events that led to Pat Gillick's departure from Toronto, both men's memories jibe just a little bit better. On Wednesday, October 18, Russell Smouse, a lawyer and the main adviser to Peter Angelos, owner of the Baltimore Orioles, put in a call to Beeston. They were looking for someone to head up their baseball operation, he said, and would like permission to talk to Gillick about the job.

Beeston told Smouse what he'd told all the others who'd phoned in the past with the same request: "He won't go." But Smouse was insistent that the message be passed along in any case, and asked Beeston to call Gillick as soon as possible. (The whole issue of "permission" was actually a moot point. Gillick had no contract with the Jays beyond a handshake, and in any case, it was a policy of the organization never to stand in the way of an employee who wanted to leave for any reason.)

Gillick was in Whitehorse, Yukon, at the time, making an appearance on behalf of the Special Olympics. "They want to talk to you in Baltimore," Beeston told him when he reached him on the phone. "It's a place you don't want to go. But if you believe this one...." Beeston then laid out everything Smouse had said, explained that he seemed like a decent, polite fellow, and suggested Gillick at least call him back. The part about Baltimore being a place Gillick wouldn't want to go, Beeston felt, was self-evident. Angelos, as he had shown by his actions during the strike, was an extremely strong-willed man who was used to getting his own way. What he wanted now was to win a World Series, immediately, which would make him a very difficult employer for any general manager.

After insisting he wasn't interested, Gillick finally acknowledged that it would be best if he at least returned Smouse's call. They chatted briefly the next day and agreed to have a more extensive conversation on Friday. It was then that Gillick, while maintaining that he wasn't interested in coming back to work for anyone, laid out some of his specific objections to moving to the Orioles. "I told him I was a little bit disappointed in the way things had been handled with Roland Hemond and Phil Regan [respectively, the outgoing general manager and field manager]. There had been stories leaked in the summertime that they were going to talk to Cleveland about Danny O'Dowd. I said I didn't really think that was the way to go about your business, that Roland Hemond might be maybe in some people's minds not the best general manager in the world, but he was a great human being. And I didn't think it was proper for them to do that."

Smouse said that the story had broken despite their best efforts to be discreet and that in fact both Hemond and Regan were being let go that day. He also told Gillick that the team planned to hire Davey Johnson, who had just been fired by the Cincinnati Reds, as the Orioles' new field manager. That struck Gillick as odd—normally, any incoming general manager would have been given the option of putting his man in that job. "I don't think that I'm particularly interested," Gillick said, once again.

But the Orioles were insistent. The club brass, including Angelos, would be travelling to Cleveland for the third game of the World Series, he told Gillick. Could they meet in person? "Well, if you come over and you're there, there's no reason I wouldn't talk to you," Gillick said. But on Tuesday morning, the day before Game Three, Smouse phoned Gillick at his Cleveland hotel to say that Angelos and company weren't coming after all. Could he instead fly to Baltimore on Wednesday or Thursday for a meeting?

Gillick said he wanted to think it over. He talked to his wife, Doris, who said she didn't think there was any harm in listening. And so he called Smouse back and told him he'd be in Baltimore Thursday morning, with the intention of flying back that night in time for Game Four. At that point, he also told Beeston what was going on.

Then Gillick got cold feet, which was what Beeston had counted on. The day he was to leave, he phoned Smouse in Baltimore to say he wasn't coming. "I'm really not fired up about this thing," he said. "I haven't got fired up like I really want to come over there. I'm wasting your time. Why not just go ahead and look to somebody else."

Beeston heard that Gillick hadn't gone to Baltimore and became convinced there was nothing to worry about. "First he's not interested, then he's interested, then he's not interested." It didn't sound as if this time would be any different than all the other overtures. After his little flirtation, Gillick would surely fall back into the warm embrace of the Blue Jay organization.

As for Gillick, he says he "completely forgot about it" after that last chat with Smouse and went on with his life.

He forgot about it until November 12, when with Ash and Bob Engle, the Jays' assistant general manager, Gillick travelled to Phoenix for the annual baseball general managers' meetings. While walking the grounds of the hotel, he ran into Davey Johnson, who had gone to the meetings because the Orioles still hadn't hired a general manager. Gillick and Johnson had played together in the minor leagues thirty years earlier and had maintained a friendly relationship. "Why don't you come back?" Johnson said, pitching the Orioles' job. Gillick, once again, said that he wasn't interested. But that night, returning to his room after dinner, there was a message on his voice mail—Johnson calling to say that he'd spoken to Smouse and Angelos and was wondering if he and Gillick might be able to sit down and talk at length.

The next day, they chatted for an hour and a half. Johnson extolled the virtues of the franchise and its owner, talked about what they might accomplish together. Gillick found himself starting to think seriously about the possibility once again. He asked for time to consider the offer, then went back to his room and phoned his wife. "If you have any thoughts about getting back in," she said, "you'd better do it before you're sixty."

Gillick called Johnson on Friday, November 17, and told him he was willing to listen to what Angelos had to say. A meeting was scheduled in Baltimore for the following Monday. And then Gillick called Beeston.

"He said that Davey Johnson had been kind of pushing him and pressuring him," Beeston remembers. "He and Davey Johnson were great friends. And he said he was going to Baltimore to be interviewed on the Monday. I thought, here we go again. I'll believe this when I see it. After that I never gave it too much thought. I figured once he meets Angelos, that will be the end of it."

In fact, meeting Angelos was the real beginning of it. "He really has a strong feeling for Baltimore, the city and the fans, and he really wants to win," Gillick says. "There are a lot of guys who you could go to work for in this day and age who just want to survive, or just want to get into baseball. But this guy wants to get in and he wants to win. He's a very competitive guy."

That competitive nature manifested itself in his pursuit of Gillick, the unattainable, the guy everyone wanted but couldn't have. Angelos, with his powers of persuasion and his chequebook, was going to get him, no matter what. He offered Gillick carte blanche, full authority to run the baseball operation, plenty of money to spend on free agents, and plenty of money in his own pocket. One last time, Gillick said, "Let me think it over." But this time it was different. "I called them on Wednesday and said if I can work out some deal that's satisfactory, I'll come over there."

Beeston was in New York, attending a meeting of baseball's audit and budget committee, when he was summoned out of the room to take an urgent phone call.

"It's Pat. We've got to talk. I went down there yesterday. I met with these guys. I think I'm going to take the job."

"Don't even think about it until you talk to me," Beeston said. "I'll be back tonight."

They talked the next day. "I gave him every reason in the world not to take the job—in my opinion. You don't want to go there, you don't want to work for this guy, you follow the stock market, you're big in Canadian stocks.... For some reason I still didn't think he'd go. I thought that my persuasive talents, such as they may be, would give him all the reasons not to go. Why would he want to get back into it? Why do you want to work for a guy that's going to make sure that you've got to win?

"I said to him, 'Just go write me a job description. Just tell me what you want to do.' That was the first thing I said to him. 'Just go write a job description.' The dough here was fine as far as I knew. It wasn't quite as good as it is in Baltimore, but it wasn't bad for not working—well, that's not fair, because he did work. It wasn't bad for not having the pressure and the responsibility. The team's going bad and he doesn't feel any pressure."

Beeston reluctantly gave his okay for Gordon Kirke, the Jays' lawyer, to work for Gillick, negotiating his deal. Friday and Saturday passed, with no further word. "I came into the offices Sunday and he was cleaning out his office. That's when I knew it was for real. I had tears in my eyes. It was very emotional. For him it wasn't very emotional. I don't know why. He's a very emotional person. But he was very unemotional. 'I've made up my mind, I'm going, thanks very much. Really enjoyed it.' I'm thinking, shit. The son of a bitch is actually leaving. All of a sudden it was for real. It hit me on the Sunday and for two or three days after."

A series of press conferences announced the move. Simultaneously, Gillick was introduced in Baltimore, while in Toronto Beeston announced that he had left. Gillick had always been the one to cry at the drop of a hat, Beeston the one to joke his way through any situation. This time it was Beeston crying in public. "It's going to be…different," was all he could say, before breaking down.

"It was very traumatic for me. I didn't think it was going to be. But it was a loss. I was very emotional. But by the time his press conference was over, I knew he wasn't dead. It wasn't like losing your brother who had died—it was like losing your brother who had taken up residence in another country."

The next day, Gillick returned to Toronto to bid the city farewell. (Though not in a permanent sense. His wife continued living in Toronto, and when he could, Gillick commuted back and forth. More than anyone else in the American baseball fraternity, Gillick had really taken to Canada and made it his home.) Beeston teased him about wearing a shirt and tie for the Baltimore press conference but reverting to his normal sweater when he came back to Toronto. "It's club policy," Gillick explained. "Then why," Beeston wondered, "would you ever work there?"

Just like old times. Except it could never be like old times again.

"I still don't understand it," Beeston says. "To this day I don't understand it. I know him better than anyone else and I suppose I don't know him. I've said that over the years—there's a part of him I don't know. And this just manifested itself. Everything I thought before about not really knowing him—I didn't. It was just so atypical of him. He's very organized. He's very emotional. He's very loyal. And then all of a sudden, he's gone."

◆ GILLICK'S FAREWELL WASN'T the only shock Beeston suffered during the fall, a time when it became clear there was little that could be taken for granted any more.

The sale of Labatt to Interbrew hadn't immediately influenced the way the baseball club did business. Beeston now reported to a representative of the Belgian brewery, based in New York, for whom he outlined the Blue Jays' finances and projections just as he had done in the past for whoever was running John Labatt Ltd. But the bottom line had changed rather dramatically. Attendance in 1995, for a seventy-two-game home schedule, fell to 2,826,483—an exceptional number considering the after-effects of the strike and how bad the team was. Those in the Jays' front office, though, understood that the salad days were over. No longer would they be able to count on automatic sell-outs, on drawing four million fans year after year. It was time to return to the reality faced by other major league franchises and to budget accordingly.

It would also be in everyone's interest to turn a profit or at least to break even. The team had lost millions of dollars in 1994 and 1995 (as much as $15 million in 1995 alone). It was assumed that Interbrew's ownership would only be temporary, that at some point it would sell all or part of the team, having no real interest in the baseball business. A franchise that proved it could make money, even in the uncertain economic climate of professional baseball, would be far more valuable than one that lost large amounts of money—even if it were successful on the field.

The Jays estimated that they could draw 2.6 million fans for eighty-one home dates in 1996—erring on the side of caution. With those revenues, with their existing television and radio contracts, and with a 73-cent Canadian dollar, that allowed them to spend $30 million in payroll and maintain the real possibility of making money. "It's got nothing to do with Interbrew," Beeston says. "Interbrew phoned and said, 'If you need more money, you can have more money.' I said, 'No, you're falling into the trap of new owners. We can weather the storm. We've won two of the last three World Series. We had a run at it. And we're trying to build back so that we can have another prolonged run at it.'"

Four key members of the Toronto Blue Jays had become free agents after the 1995 season: Paul Molitor, Devon White, Roberto Alomar and Al Leiter. The team would also, through trade or a free agent signing, have to come up with a new bullpen closer. And it would have to decide whether to exercise a contract option on Juan Guzman or let him walk away after two disappointing seasons in a row.

With big dollars already tied up in John Olerud and Joe Carter, Toronto clearly wasn't going to be able to re-sign everyone. And so based on the club's needs, and based on the realities of the market, it was time to set priorities. White would be number one. His defensive play in centre field had a trickle-down effect to the pitching staff. He made every pitcher better, every pitcher more confident to throw strikes, knowing that just about any ball hit to the outfield would likely be caught. There was also a sense that White would be motivated by something other than pure cash in deciding where he played in 1996. His career had been reborn in Toronto, and that was largely thanks to Gaston, who did an enormous amount to restore White's confidence. The Jays' thinking was that all things being equal—or even if Toronto's offer was a little bit less than what some other team might put on the table—White would return to security and to Cito.

"We wanted Devo," Beeston says. "There's no question we wanted Devo."

They didn't get Devo, who opted to sign with the Florida Marlins instead, largely because, he said, his father, who lived in Jamaica, couldn't handle the long plane flights to Toronto to visit him. "There's not enough of that in this world," Beeston says. "I'll take him at face value on that.... He went to a place where they play in the heat, they play in the rain. They're not a contending team. And they paid him more money than we offered him" ($9.9 million over three years, against the Jays' offer of $9 million).

No hard feelings, Beeston said when he phoned White after the signing was announced. "When you're sitting in the dugout and I'm sitting in Toronto and it says rain delay in Florida, I'll be laughing at you."

"The real reason I didn't sign with you," White shot back, "is because you don't wear any socks."

All very civilized, all very cordial. Thanks for the good times and so long.

The Jays would have loved to have kept Molitor, as much for his presence in the clubhouse as his presence on the field. But they didn't really have a job for him. After another fine season in the minors, it was time for Carlos Delgado to make the jump to the major leagues, permanently. His only real defensive position, though, was first base, occupied by John Olerud, who wasn't going anywhere. The Jays planned to rotate those two players and Joe Carter through the designated hitter's spot, which left Molitor the odd man out. He could come back to Toronto as a part-time player, earning part-time player money. Or he could go somewhere else and play every day, which would help him reach his three-thousandth career hit.

Molitor's decision was no surprise: signing with the Minnesota Twins, his home-town team, where he'd play every day in one position or another. Again, Toronto's attitude was warm and supportive. Thanks for the memories. Thanks for helping us with that championship. If you ever want a front office job after you've retired, give us a call.

Alomar's was a much more complicated situation. Throughout the 1994 and 1995 seasons, his agent, Jaime Torres, had been trying to press the Blue Jays into making a pre-emptive strike, to sign his client to a long-term contract before he became eligible for free agency. And all through that period, when asked about his intentions, Alomar said exactly the same thing: that he wanted to stay in Toronto, that he was comfortable there, and that he hoped a deal could be worked out. But if nothing came of the negotiations, he'd test the open market and sell his services to the highest bidder.

The Jays used the uncertainty of the baseball economy to keep Torres at bay. How could they commit to a huge, long-term deal, when they had no idea how the marketplace for players would be affected by the strike? Hearing that kind of talk for the better part of a year, Alomar decided that it was probably time to move on. He was also encouraged by the fact that Torres had told him that as one of baseball's very best young players, he would be entitled to one of the highest salaries, if not the highest, in the game—perhaps as much as $10 million a year.

Beeston and Ash sat down with Torres after the season at a Toronto restaurant called Splendido's. The team's opening offer: $15 million over three years, or much the same as Alomar had earned in his previous contract.

"The Toronto price," Torres announced, "is $25 million."

"Jaime, let me ask you a question," Beeston fired back at Torres. "Is the Toronto price a discount or a premium?" He never got an answer.

"I wasn't surprised it was $25 million," Beeston says. "I was surprised it wasn't $32 million. I was surprised it was only for three years. He never got it. But it came out subsequently that that's what he asked the Yankees for. Then he asked Baltimore for $23 million. It was coming down. In the end, Robbie got the job he could get that would meet his criteria of a team in contention in a good facility in front of a lot of people with the dollars."

The fact that the Jays didn't sign Alomar really isn't so surprising. With a $30-million payroll, they had decided that they simply couldn't afford him, even though with his age and his skills, he was one player who could conceivably be part of a Blue Jay championship team of the future. Still, it might be a bit tough to explain to the suddenly jaded Toronto baseball consumers why the best player to ever wear the uniform had been allowed to simply walk away, especially after all those years of sell-out crowds.

It's open to debate whether Gord Ash created the "Roberto Alomar has a bad attitude" line, or whether he simply exploited feelings that already existed, exacerbated by what appeared to be outrageous salary demands. Whatever the case, once the Jays realized for certain that they had no chance of signing Alomar, Ash encouraged the notion that it was a case of good riddance to bad rubbish. If Alomar was going to come back, he said, he'd have to demonstrate more leadership in the clubhouse. The spectre was raised of that one-day sit-down, and of that final weekend off, and by and large the public bought it. He'd already left, but still they ran him out of town on a rail. Give us scrappy young players who never say die, even if it means we don't win as many games. Don't give us...well, don't give us the best second baseman in baseball.

(For his part, Beeston played good cop to Ash's bad cop. "I like Robbie. I will continue to like Robbie," he says. "A guy's entitled to a bad day, a bad week, a bad month. Here's a guy for four-and-a-half years everybody says is the greatest. A great guy. Marches to his own drummer, does things his own way but everybody is happy. Now all of a sudden he has a bad period. Someone tries to shoot him with a gun. Now that will wake you up a little bit. Then Cone, then everything else. Why hold it against the guy? I never held it against him. I'll tell you, he's a helluva guy. Robbie's not a guy with a lot of close friends but Robbie's not a guy that ever bothered anybody. Who could say that Robbie Alomar ever bothered them?")

Lost in all the talk-show and newspaper vitriol was one small irony. If Alomar was really such cancer on the team, wasn't it curious that the fellow who ended up signing him knew him better than just about anyone in baseball outside of Toronto? Wasn't that Pat Gillick, sitting there, beaming, while Alomar inked his three-year, $18-million contract to play for the Orioles? It may have been a bargain-basement price, compared to what Torres had started out asking for, but it was still a lot of pay for someone who allegedly didn't come to play every day.

Alomar's defection left the Jays 0–3 in the free agent sweepstakes, but each situation carried with it extenuating circumstances. The fourth guy they wanted, they needed, and in his case, they had another card to play. Al Leiter owed them one. "We carried that son of a bitch," Beeston says. "Loyalty is too strong a word these days, but that's damn well what it was all about. He got a couple of World Series rings, a couple of World Series cheques. And he hardly ever pitched. He pitched one inning one year."

Leiter also fit with the new rebuilding program. He was relatively young, he was a lefty, he probably had four or five more good seasons in him. And his price tag would fall somewhere in the middle of the pack: affordable, useful, youthful. "We didn't really full court-press any of those guys other than Leiter," Beeston says.

They were told it would take $9.4 million over three years to bring him back to Toronto, more than Leiter would require to play in an American city, because he was suddenly concerned about Canadian taxes. The Jays offered $8.25 million. "Maybe we were oblivious to the Leiter situation," Beeston says. "Maybe everybody knew except us. It's kind of like somebody gets caught fooling around on their wife. The last person to know is the wife because no one will tell her." When Leiter signed with the Florida Marlins for $8.6 million, apparently his intended destination all along, the Blue Jays didn't even get a call back, asking them if they were willing to match the offer. That left Beeston particularly bitter. Always loath to criticize his players past or present, no matter what the circumstances, he could hardly contain his anger whenever Leiter's name came up.

"It changed my whole opinion of players," Beeston says. "Assholes you can deal with because you know what you're dealing with. But when you think you're dealing with a pretty good guy... I don't think he had any intention of coming back here—I don't care what he said. I don't think he ever intended to come back here. As soon as he had his free agency, he was gone. He was leaving here. He used everybody else, including us."

Beeston phoned the president of the Marlins the day the signing was announced and told him he hoped Leiter lost every game he pitched for his new team.

The search for a closer didn't go much better. There were only a handful of big-name relievers on the open market—Rick Aguilera, Randy Myers, Jeff Montgomery. Each talked to the Blue Jays. Each said they were interested. Each signed elsewhere. And each time, it seemed the Blue Jays were the last to know they were out of the running. (Would Pat Gillick have struck out like that? more than one fan was heard to wonder.)

Once upon a time, free agents had been hesitant to sign with Canadian teams. Ball players, not the most worldly individuals, got edgy about the prospect of living in a foreign country, dealing with foreign taxes, dealing with anything that was different. But through the years, the Blue Jays had managed to change that impression by running a first-class organization, looking after their players (and their other employees) so well that they would want to come to Toronto, and once they got there they would want to stay. It was a huge point of pride for Beeston, one that could be traced back to Peter Hardy and the old Labatt's credo.

Now, the franchise was being rejected left and right, and neither Ash nor Beeston seemed to know why. What about those nice things David Cone had said, about how the Jays' position during the strike made them the kind of team every player would want to join? What about the loyalty shown to players like White and Leiter, which wasn't being repaid in kind?

Ash did make some moves to shore up the roster. When Leiter went to Florida, the team decided to gamble on Guzman for another year, signing him for 1996 after imposing a 20 percent pay cut, the maximum allowed under the collective bargaining agreement. Otis Nixon, a free agent who'd played in 1995 with Texas, was signed to take White's place. He couldn't match up defensively—at age thirty-seven he was obviously a short-term solution—but he was certainly competent, and also he provided a real base-stealing threat and a lead-off man's on-base percentage. Erik Hanson, whom the Jays had talked to the previous spring, arrived to become the number one starter. He'd enjoyed a tremendous comeback season with the Boston Red Sox as they won the American League East in 1995. Now he was happy to be the number one man on a team that was clearly in transition.

Finding a closer required more creativity. Shut out of the free agents, Ash instead made a deal with Seattle, sending pitchers Paul Menhart and Edwin Hurtado to the Mariners in exchange for their set-up man, Bill Risley, a hard-thrower who seemed to have the right emotional make-up for the bullpen's marquee job. If he didn't pan out, they'd take a look at rookie Tim Crabtree, or perhaps even veteran Mike Timlin, who'd always had the stuff to close, if not the temperament.

Still, the incoming players had the look of a patchwork job, of second choices and long shots. Gone, perhaps forever, was the old aura of the master plan, that the Toronto Blue Jays were one step ahead of the opposition, rather than fighting to catch up. So much had slipped away in such a short time, there was the real feeling of watershed. The tumble to last place. The change of ownership. The departure of Gillick.

"I said to Peter Widdrington, it's unbelievable," Beeston says. "Maybe that's what hit me. That it was the end." And for a time, Beeston considered his own mortality. Maybe, with everything in flux, it was time for him to move on, as well. Walk away knowing what had been accomplished, escaping the uncertainties to follow. Get out while the getting was good, while his reputation was still intact, as Gillick had done. Find a new challenge, make a whole lot of money, and remember the Blue Jays as they were.

Beeston thought about it. Then he decided to stick around. "I'll tell you what," he says. "I don't want to leave chapter two in last place. It's not something I could walk away from right now. I could be fired. I could be asked to leave. Someone else could buy the club and come in here. There are all kinds of scenarios that could get me out of here. But it ain't going to be of my own volition."

DUNEDIN, MARCH 1996. The first page of chapter two. There is something about the early days in Florida, before the exhibition games have even begun, that offers a chance for renewal, which is surely why the ritual of spring training was born in the first place. All teams are equal. Everyone can win. Rich teams, poor teams, start out the same. Labour disputes, collective bargaining, how can you even consider it when the sky is blue and the grass is green and air is so damp, so tropical, so unlike the Canadian winter left behind? For the fans, even the fans at home, it's a time to dream about the best possibilities, to play out the combinations in your head, to think of what it feels like to sit in the stands on a hot July afternoon, with a beer and a hot dog and only a ball game on your mind.

Those reveries had taken on a bit more urgent tone over the past ten years as the Toronto Blue Jays prepared for the beginning of their seasons. Each move, each battle for a starting position, was imbued with extra meaning, because even the identity of the fourth outfielder or the back-up catcher might have some significance on the way to a championship.

This time, though, there was no overriding pressure, there were no all-consuming expectations, and the manager, especially, seemed to be thriving without that weight on his shoulders. There had been the usual talk over the winter, the usual phone-in show babble about how Cito Gaston wasn't the guy to head a young team that would be short on established talent, that would probably have to manufacture runs to be competitive, that would have to play a far more aggressive brand of baseball than was suggested by his laissez-faire approach during the championship years.

It's not that Gaston had stopped listening to his critics. It's not that it didn't still bother him. He continued to wonder why, given his team's success, he wasn't accorded the same respect as a Tony LaRussa or a Jim Leyland, and you'd have to think he'll wonder about that forever, because it doesn't seem to be in the cards. But his manner preparing for his sixth Opening Day at the helm suggested a man without a care in the world. He sat in the dugout beside one of the diamonds at the minor league complex, watching players take infield practice, cracking jokes with reporters, at peace with himself and with the task at hand.

Gord Ash seemed somewhat less content, which was understandable given the circumstances. He had also come under tremendous
scrutiny during the off-season. As free agents fled the franchise, as
the team's first, and second, and third choices to fill the closer's
role opted to go elsewhere, Ash had appeared to be as confused as
anyone as to why it was happening. He had assumed Pat Gillick's
mantle, but he hadn't yet assumed the aura of infallibility. It might
come, but the performance of this particular team would have
much to do with it. If they exceeded expectations, he—and certainly not Gaston—would get the bulk of the credit. And if they
failed miserably, some would point to Gaston, as usual. But others
would wonder if the talent just wasn't there, which is the general
manager's department. In this brave new world, faith was something you had to earn.

Still, even with the sense of one cycle ending, another beginning,
there was still much that was familiar in Dunedin and environs.
Bobby Mattick sat and chewed the fat and soaked up the sunshine,
looking like just another of the tanned pensioners who made
Florida their retirement home. Gillick passed through, but in his
new guise, that of the enemy, a role he seemed to relish. Joe Carter
rolled into camp and immediately held court, talking about himself
in the third person, hedging on his pledge to retire after 1996, wax-
ing enthusiastic about the team's young talent. John Olerud, now
the longest-serving Blue Jay, was handed the clean-up role. He was
working on his public persona, but still seemed nearly as shy as the
silent fellow who arrived straight from college, who had trouble
squeezing out a single sentence without extreme discomfort. Juan
Guzman pronounced himself healthy of mind and body. Erik
Hanson talked about leadership. And everywhere, there were kids,
kids who in the past would have been just getting a taste of the big
leagues before heading to the minor league camp. Kids who, in
1996, would make up the bulk of the starting roster.

Then there was Beeston. Sun visor. Big cigar. No socks. Fresh off
the plane from Toronto, his laugh filling the place, talking to Cito,
talking to Ash, drawing a crowd as he set out the new master plan,
sounding only optimistic notes, despite the overwhelming pes-
simism generated over the past twenty-four months. Everything
would be fine. The team would draw at least 35,000 fans a game—

no problem. If they could hang in the race until mid-season, the Interbrew folks would be willing to invest in one of those Pat Gillick specials, a Rickey Henderson, a Tom Candiotti, a David Cone. What hadn't changed, he wanted understood, was that everyone still had only one goal in mind.

"The odds are against us," Beeston said. "There's no question about that. But that doesn't mean we can't try to do it. There's a lot of guys here that you're asking to do things that they've done before. [Juan] Guzman has won a lot of games in a season before. Pat [Hentgen] has won a lot of games in a season before. [Erik] Hanson has won a lot of games in a season before. [John] Olerud has hit well. Joe [Carter] has hit well. Stranger things have happened. I'm going into the season expecting that we're going to win."

Meanwhile, Gaston sat back and enjoyed the show. He'd heard the sound of that voice for fourteen years. He'd enjoyed Beeston's enthusiasms. He'd prospered because of his loyalty and had survived in his managerial post largely because of his backing. As long as Beeston was still there, even if Belgians were writing the cheques, these were still the Toronto Blue Jays. Down, but temporarily. Different, certainly. But in spring, you can believe that anything is possible.

"Hey, it's not impossible," Cito Gaston said. "And I think it should be quite interesting."

Index